# ICT4D

Information and Communication Technology for Development

General Editor TIM UNWIN

**CAMBRIDGE**
UNIVERSITY PRESS

CAMBRIDGE UNIVERSITY PRESS
Cambridge, New York, Melbourne, Madrid, Cape Town, Singapore,
São Paulo, Delhi

Cambridge University Press
The Edinburgh Building, Cambridge CB2 8RU, UK

www.cambridge.org
Information on this title: www.cambridge.org/9780521712361

First published 2009

A catalogue record for this publication is available from the British Library

ISBN   978-0-521-71236-1 paperback

ACKNOWLEDGEMENTS
All ITU data, tables and figures are reproduced with the kind permission of ITU.

# Contents

# Preface and acknowledgements

Many people have contributed to the ideas and agendas contained within this book. I am especially grateful to colleagues with whom I have worked in the UK's Department for International Development, UNESCO and the World Economic Forum for their insights and inspiration. In particular, the following have had a major role in shaping my thoughts or in contributing specific advice on my own chapters: Carmela Abate, Mohamed Abida, Armelle Arrou, Boubakar Barry, Martin Bean, Lídia Brito, Greg Butler, David Campbell, Julie Clugage, David Crespo, Jean-Claude Dauphin, Bob Day, Geraldine de Bastion, Rutger Englehard, Julie Ferguson, Marije Geldof, Adrian Godfrey, Ed Holcroft, David Hollow, Dorothea Kleine, Bas Kotterink, Boying Lallana, Andrew Law, Liz Longworth, Sugata Mitra, Kate Lloyd Morgan, Brenda Musilli, Monika Muylkens, Helen Nicholson, Leonard Mware Oloo, Michael Pereira, Caroline Pontefract, Peter Rave, Sally Reynolds, Tony Roberts, Michelle Selinger, David Souter, Mike Trucano, Mathy Vanbuel, Dan Wagner, Myles Wickstead, Alex Wong, Meng Xingmin and Tae Yoo. I am also particularly grateful to colleagues at Cambridge University Press who have provided helpful editorial and production support, notably Fiona Kelly, Keith Lloyd, Sue Glover and Annette Stuart.

To make the text easier to read, the dates when web pages were originally read have been removed, except when these are of historical interest or they are no longer live. Otherwise, all web pages were checked for accuracy in February 2008.

Tim Unwin
Virginia Water
March 2008

# Acronyms and glossary

| | |
|---|---|
| ACDI/CIDA | Agence canadienne de développement international/ Canadian International Development Agency: the Canadian Government Department responsible for international development (http://www.acdi-cida.gc.ca). |
| ADSL | Asymmetric Digital Subscriber Line |
| APDIP | See UNDP-APDIP |
| Blog | An abbreviated form of 'weblog' (*q.v.*) |
| BPL | Broadband over Power Lines |
| BPR | Business Process Re-engineering |
| CD | Compact Disc: CDs were originally introduced in 1982 to store digital audio. A 12 cm CD contains about 80 minutes of audio. |
| CDMA | Code-Division Multiple Access |
| CD-ROM | Compact Disc Read-Only Memory: a compact disc that contains digital data of any kind and is accessible by a computer (12 cm in diameter). |
| CEPAL | Naciones Unidas Comisión Económica para América Latina y el Caribe (see also ECLAC) (http://www.eclac.cl) |
| CGAP | Consultative Group to Assist the Poor: a consortium of 33 public and private funding organisations working together to expand poor people's access to financial services (http://www.cgap.org). |
| CORBA | Common Object Request Broker Architecture |
| COTS | Commercial-Off-The-Shelf |
| COWs | Computers on Wheels |
| CPU | Central Processing Unit |
| DAC | Development Assistance Committee of the OECD (*q.v.*) |
| DCE | Distributed Computing Environment |
| DFID | Department for International Development: the UK Government Department responsible for international development (http://www.dfid.gov.uk). |
| DSC | Development Support Communication: a model, initially developed by Coldevin for the FAO (*q.v.*). |
| DSL | Digital Subscriber Line |

| | |
|---|---|
| DVD | Digital Video Disc (also known as Digital Versatile Disc): an optical disc storage format with a diameter of 12 cm used for high-quality video and sound. The DVD specification was finalised in 1996. |
| ECDL | European Computer Driving Licence (http://www.ecdl.com) |
| ECLAC | The UN's Economic Commission for Latin America and the Caribbean (see also CEPAL) (http://www.eclac.cl) |
| ECOSOC | United Nations Economic and Social Council (http://www.un.org/ecosoc) |
| ECPAT | End Child Prostitution, Child Pornography and Trafficking of Children for Sexual Purposes: ECPAT International is a network of organisations working to eliminate the sexual exploitation of children, and has Special Consultative status with ECOSOC (*q.v.*) (http://www.ecpat.net). |
| EFA | Education for All: six goals agreed by representatives from 160 countries at the World Education Forum held in Dakar in 2000. |
| EHR | Electronic Health Record |
| FAO | Food and Agriculture Organization of the United Nations (http://www.fao.org) |
| FidoNet | FidoNet (http://www.fidonet.org) consists of some 10,000 computer systems worldwide, forming a network that exchanges mail and files via modems using a proprietary protocol. |
| FOSS | Free and Open Source Software |
| GAID | Global Alliance for ICT and Development |
| GATS | General Agreement on Trade in Services |
| GDP | Gross Domestic Product: the total market value of all final goods and services produced in a country in a given year. |
| GEOSS | Global Earth Observation System of Systems (http://www.earthobservations.org/geoss.shtml) |
| GIS | Geographical Information System: a computer-based system to capture, store, retrieve, map and analyse spatially resolved data. It enables layers of information about a particular place to be displayed and related to one another. |
| GNI | Gross National Income: the total value of goods and services produced within a country, plus income received from other countries, minus payments made to other countries. |
| GSM | Global System for Mobile communication: the dominant 2G digital mobile phone standard for most of the world. |
| IANA | The Internet Assigned Numbers Authority: provides centralised coordinating functions for the global internet (http://www.iana.org). |
| ICANN | Internet Corporation for Assigned Names and Numbers: responsible for the global coordination of the internet's system of unique identifiers (http://www.icann.org). |

| | |
|---|---|
| ICDL | International Computer Driving Licence |
| IDRC | International Development Research Centre (http://www.idrc.ca) |
| IFC | International Finance Corporation |
| IICD | International Institute for Communication and Development (http://www.iicd.org) |
| ILO | International Labour Organization: the tripartite UN agency bringing together governments, employers and workers (http://www.ilo.org). |
| Internet | The global network of interconnected computer networks that is used to transmit data. It enables services such as the World Wide Web (see WWW), e-mail, VoIP (*q.v.*) and online chat to take place. |
| IP address | Internet Protocol address: the unique number that enables a device to be identified and to communicate with other devices in a computer network using the Internet Protocol standard. |
| iPods | Portable media players designed by Apple Computers. First produced in 2001, and initially intended as a device to play music, new versions were rapidly developed to play video. They can also serve as external data storage devices. |
| IPR | Intellectual Property Rights |
| ISDN | Integrated Services Digital Network |
| ISP | Internet Service Provider |
| ITSM | Information Technology Service Management |
| ITU | International Telecommunications Union: the international organisation within the UN system in which governments and the private sector coordinate global telecommunications networks and services (http://www.itu.int). |
| K-12 | 'K through 12': an abbreviation for 'kindergarten through 12th grade', which is the usual US expression for primary and secondary education; 12th grade is generally studied by 17- and 18-year-olds. |
| LAN | Local Area Network: a group of computers and ancillary devices that share a common communication line or wireless link, usually within an office or home environment. In contrast to Wide Area Networks (WANs) they serve a smaller geographical range, they have higher data rates, and they do not require the provision of telecommunication lines by an external supplier. |
| MDGs | Millennium Development Goals (http://www.un.org/millenniumgoals) |
| MPTC | Multi-Purpose Tele-Centre |
| MSP | Multi-Stakeholder Partnership – distinguished from PPP (*q.v.*) because MSPs include a diversity of partners other than just |

the private sector and the public sector, and thus also place emphasis on civil society and international organisations.

| | |
|---|---|
| MSPE | Multi-Stakeholder Partnership for Education |
| NEPAD | New Partnership for Africa's Development (http://www.nepad.org) |
| NGOs | Non-Governmental Organisations |
| OECD | Organisation for Economic Cooperation and Development (http://www.oecd.org): an international organisation helping governments tackle the economic, social and governance aspects of a globalised economy. |
| PC | Personal Computer: a computer designed for personal use, in contrast to a server (q.v.). |
| PDA | Personal Digital Assistant: a handheld digital device, usually with a touch-screen. Initially mainly intended as a personal organiser, PDAs are now being used for a wide range of functions including accessing the internet, sending and receiving e-mails, word processing, playing games and reading digital books. |
| PLC | Power Line Communication |
| PPI | Private Participation in Infrastructure. The World Bank Private Participation in Infrastructure Project database contains data on more than 3,800 projects in 150 low- and middle-income countries (http://ppi.worldbank.org). |
| PPP | Public–Private Partnership (see also MSP) |
| PRSP | Poverty Reduction Strategy Paper |
| RAM | Random Access Memory |
| RFID | Radio-frequency identification |
| RNFE | Rural Non-Farm Economy |
| RSS | Really Simple Syndication: Web feed formats used to publish frequently updated content. |
| SDC | Swiss Agency for Development Cooperation (http://www.sdc.admin.ch) |
| Server | A computer that provides services to other computers. |
| SME | Small- and Medium-sized Enterprise |
| SMS | Short Message Service: permits text message on GSM (q.v.) networks. |
| SOA | Service-Oriented Architecture |
| TFP | Total Factor Productivity: measures growth of output given constant levels of labour and capital input. |
| UN | United Nations (http://www.un.org) |
| UNCTAD | United Nations Conference on Trade and Development (http://www.unctad.org) |
| UN DESA | United Nations Department of Economic and Social Affairs (http://www.un.org/esa/desa) |

| | |
|---|---|
| UNDP | United Nations Development Programme (http://www.undp.org) |
| UNDP-APDIP | The United Nations Development Programme-Asia Pacific Development Information Programme (http://www.apdip.net) |
| UNECA | United Nations Economic Commission for Africa (http://www.uneca.org) |
| UNESCO | United Nations Educational, Scientific and Cultural Organization (http://www.unesco.org) |
| UNFPA | United Nations Population Fund (http://www.unfpa.org) |
| UNGIS | United Nations Group on the Information Society (http://www.ungis.org) |
| UNICEF | United Nations Children's Fund (formerly, United Nations International Children's Emergency Fund) (http://www.unicef.org) |
| UPE | Universal Primary Education |
| URI | Uniform Resource Identifier: a string of characters and/or numbers used to identify a resource, most often on the World Wide Web; often popularly referred to as a URL (q.v.). |
| URL | Uniform Resource Locator: popularly used as a synonym for a URI (q.v.), although more correctly it is a subset of URIs referring specifically to locators. |
| USAID | United States Agency for International Development (http://www.usaid.gov) |
| VoIP | Voice over Internet Protocol: the routeing of voice conversations using an IP network, usually the internet. |
| VPN | Virtual Private Network |
| VSAT | Very Small Aperture Terminal: a two-way satellite ground station with a dish antenna that is smaller than 3 metres. |
| Web | An abbreviated form for the World Wide Web or WWW (q.v.) |
| Weblog | A website, usually in the form of a diary or commentary, in which entries are given in reverse chronological order. Usually abbreviated to 'blog'. |
| WGIG | Working Group on Internet Governance (http://www.wgig.org) |
| WHO | World Health Organization (http://www.who.int) |
| Wi-Fi | Wireless Fidelity |
| Wiki | An interactive website that enables users to add and edit material. It is particularly useful for collaborative authoring. |
| WiMAX | Worldwide Interoperability for Microwave Access (see http://www.wimaxforum.org) |
| WIPO | World Intellectual Property Organization: a specialised agency of the UN dedicated to developing a balanced and |

|      | accessible international intellectual property system (http://www.wipo.int). |
|------|-----------------------------------------------------------------------|
| WSIS | World Summit on the Information Society (http//www.itu.int/wsis/index.html) |
| WWW  | World Wide Web (also abbreviated to the Web): a global information space containing text, images and multimedia, made accessible through uniform resource identifiers (URIs) (*q.v.*). It is made available through the internet (*q.v.*). |

*Mobile computing: computer on motorbike, Uganda, 2008 (source:* Tim Unwin).

# Contributors

**Michael L. Best** is assistant professor at the Sam Nunn School of International Affairs and the School of Interactive Computing at Georgia Institute of Technology. He is also a Fellow of the Berkman Center for Internet & Society at Harvard University. Professor Best is co-founder and Editor-in-Chief of *Information Technologies and International Development* published by the MIT Press.

**Martin Crow** is president of KampungCyber.com, an ICT consultancy based in Indonesia that specialises in e-government, public–private partnerships and community-level e-strategy development. He has directed research and coordinated technology projects in developing countries worldwide for clients including the World Bank, IADB, USAID, IDRC and others.

**Bob Day** has, since the 1980s, been using science, technology and ICTs to promote poverty eradication, while working for the Medical Research Council and the Council for Scientific and Industrial Research in South Africa. In 2003 he founded Non-Zero-Sum Development to pursue this passion in a more focused way. He works with leading development organisations on initiatives across Africa and in the Pacific region.

**Peter Greenwood** is a Director of the consultancy Non-Zero-Sum Development, based in Pretoria, South Africa, which is involved in initiatives related to the knowledge economy, the information society, science, technology and innovation, with a particular focus on the alleviation of poverty and promotion of socio-economic development in Africa and elsewhere.

**James Guida** is Director of the international ICT development firm Leading Associates and formerly the Resident General Manager of the Government of Indonesia's ISP. For the past ten years he has been engaged in e-government in developing countries and transition economies.

**Misha Kay** is the head of the World Health Organization's Global Observatory for e-Health. Prior to joining WHO he worked for the Open Society Institute, funded by George Soros, where he established the first consortium of academic institutions in the former Soviet Union and Central Europe to receive scholarly e-journals in science, technology, medicine and social sciences at low cost or free.

**Charles Kenny** is a senior infrastructure economist in the Sustainable Development Network of the World Bank, where he concentrates on issues connected to corruption and the political economy of reform. Prior to that, he worked in the Global Information and Communications Technology department of the World Bank and IFC.

**S. Yunkap Kwankam** is CEO of Global eHealth Consultants and Executive Director of the International Society for Telemedicine and eHealth. He was previously eHealth Coordinator at the World Health Organization in Geneva; Professor and Director of the Center for Health Technology at the University of Yaounde; and Chairman of the Technology Commission of the National Epidemiology Board of Cameroon.

**Ariel Pablos-Mendez** is Managing Director of the Rockefeller Foundation, and was previously Director of Knowledge Management and Sharing at the World Health Organization. He is a physician and epidemiologist, and is also an Associate Professor of Clinical Medicine and Public Health at Columbia University.

**Michelle Selinger** is Director of Education in the Asia Pacific region for Cisco's Internet Business Solutions Group. She has a background as a school teacher and an academic in technology and education. Until 2007 Michelle was the global education strategist for Cisco's Corporate Affairs advising on technology in education across the world focusing on developing countries.

**Tim Unwin** is UNESCO Chair in ICT4D and Professor of Geography at Royal Holloway, University of London. Between 2001 and 2004 he led the UK government's *Imfundo: Partnership for IT in Education* initiative. Between 2007 and 2008 he was Programme Director and then Senior Advisor to the World Economic Forum Global Education Initiative's *Partnerships for Education* programme with UNESCO, and he currently serves as Chair of the Commonwealth Scholarship Commission and as High Level Advisor to the Global Alliance for ICT and Development.

# 1 | Introduction

## Tim Unwin

[The] danger of an exclusively technical civilization, which is devoid of
the interconnection between theory and praxis, can be clearly grasped; it
is threatened by the splitting of its consciousness, and by the splitting of
human beings into two classes – the social engineers and the inmates of
closed institutions.

(Habermas, 1974, p. 282)

This book is about how information and communication technologies (ICTs)
can be used to help poor and marginalised people and communities make
a difference to their lives. Theoretical notions concerning 'development'
and 'empowerment', about 'poverty' and 'marginalisation', and about ideas
of 'difference' underlie such an agenda. The title *ICT4D, Information and
Communication Technology for Development* has been chosen in part because
of the widespread use of this term in international forums, but it also deliberately raises the question as to what we actually mean by 'development'.
For many in the early 21st century, development is primarily seen as being
concerned with economic growth, and identifying the ways in which the
economic systems of poor countries can be made more effective (see for
example Easterly, 2001; van der Hoeven and Shorrocks, 2003; Sachs, 2005).
However, this is only one perspective, and others prefer to emphasise the
importance of participation and empowerment in effective development
practice (see for example Crewe and Harrison, 1998; Arce and Long, 2000;
Unwin, 2007). A core theme of this book is that ICTs can have a key role to
play in delivering both of these contrasting interpretations of development.

Understanding precisely how ICTs can make a difference to the lives of
the poor and the marginalised does indeed depend in part on their contribution to economic growth, but it is also concerned with issues to do with the
access that people have to information, about the ways in which those from
different backgrounds communicate with each other, and about the content
requirements that poor people need if they are to be able to transform their
lives and livelihoods. Above all, this book is about the ways in which new
ICTs can contribute to these processes. Such technologies have immense

*Street children with laptop in Ethiopia, 2002 (source:* Tim Unwin).

potential, but they are a two-edged sword. They have the ability to make a fundamental difference to the lives of poor people, but, as Habermas (1974) suggests in the quotation at the start of this chapter, technology has all too often been used mainly to enable the rich and privileged to retain their positions of economic, social and political power. How then can we change things so that poor people and marginalised communities can have fairer access to the great opportunities that ICTs can make available? As will become clear in the pages that follow, this is a profoundly moral and ethical question. How we see ICT4D depends fundamentally on the place from which we are looking.

## Aims and objectives

This book sets out to do three main things. First, it provides readers with a framework for understanding the emergence of ICT4D as a set of situated practices within the broad field of development. Many previous accounts of ICT4D (see for example Weigel and Waldburger, 2004; ITU, 2005; Schware, 2005; Weiler *et al.*, 2005) have concentrated primarily on providing summary accounts of case studies or lessons learnt based on practical experiences, without setting these within a sufficiently broad theoretical context to enable their wider significance fully to be appreciated (but see also Mansell and Wehn, 1998; and Servon, 2002). This book therefore begins with an interpretation of key aspects of relevant contemporary development theory and practice, so that those seeking to implement ICT4D initiatives can understand the constraints and opportunities within which they need to operate.

Second, this book provides accounts of key areas where ICTs have been incorporated into development practices, concentrating particularly on health, education, governance, enterprise and rural development. These chapters have been written by practitioners specifically to combine syntheses of current knowledge with relevant case studies and prognoses of how we can better deliver ICT-based initiatives in the future. The choice of themes reflects the areas where ICTs have begun to be used most widely in a practical development context, but it is also specifically intended to emphasise the links between ICTs and the dominant contemporary motifs of economic growth (enterprise) and liberal democracy (governance), as well as the Millennium Development Goals (http://www.un.org/millenniumgoals) associated with education (goals 1–3), health (goals 4–6) and environmental sustainability (goal 7).

Third, the book also has a distinctly practical intent. It aims to challenge many taken-for-granted assumptions about ICT4D, and to identify the underlying success factors that need to be in place if we are truly to deliver on our strategic objectives. Despite all the rhetoric of success, very few ICT4D activities, especially in Africa, have yet proved to be sustainable. Why is this? What needs to be in place if the poorest and most vulnerable people and communities are to be able to take advantage of the potential benefits that ICTs can provide? This book provides a critique of recent attempts to use ICTs in development so that those working in the interests of poor people and marginalised communities can use these insights in their struggle for empowerment.

## Organisation and structure

In order to deliver this threefold agenda, the book is shaped around four practical dimensions: an emphasis on multidisciplinary collaboration; a specific conceptualisation of the dynamic relationship between theory and practice; the inclusion of short case studies that illustrate key aspects of ICT4D; and a focus on the importance of monitoring and evaluation.

The field of ICT4D is inherently *multidisciplinary*. There is therefore an urgent need for those involved in delivering ICT4D programmes to learn the distinct vocabularies, styles of discourse, practical agendas and means of validation that are adopted in fields other than their own areas of specialisation. Experts in the technical aspects of computer networking may very well not easily understand the needs of rural health workers, let alone the ways in which they express their arguments. However, if wireless technologies are going to be used effectively in delivering rural health services it is important that such people understand each other and are able to work together effectively in teams. One immediate aspect of this multidisciplinary character of ICT4D is thus the need for arguments to be written and expressed clearly in a readily-accessible style that avoids excessive use of disciplinary-specific jargon.

*Child beggars in Bihar, India, 1976: how might ICTs have transformed their lives? (source: Tim Unwin).*

A second characteristic of this book is the way in which it explicitly seeks to combine *theory* and *practice*, building on a tradition of critical theory developed in the work of Jürgen Habermas (1974, 1978). Without an appropriate understanding of both the theoretical and the practical dimensions of ICT4D we will not be able to help people implement changes that will be of practical benefit to them. Theoretical explorations are here combined with practical examples of the use of ICT4D in two main ways. First, the book begins with four largely theoretical chapters and then shifts attention to the practical delivery of ICT4D activities. Second, case studies and commentaries from leading figures in the field of ICT4D are included at appropriate points throughout the text. Another aspect of Habermas's (1974, 1978) notion of critical theory, though, is especially pertinent here. This is his argument that there is an intimate connection between knowledge, self-reflection and practical interest. As he argues: 'in the insights produced by self-reflection, knowledge and the emancipatory interest of knowledge are "one"' (Habermas, 1974, p. 15). This book is thus fundamentally designed to encourage self-reflection on the part of all those involved in ICT4D activities, with the ultimate objective of creating a fairer and more equitable world. Its style is deliberately that of a critique, and its success will ultimately depend on the practical discourses and activities subsequently undertaken by those who read it. Again, as Habermas

*Mobile phone stall in Uganda, 2008 (source:* Tim Unwin).

(1974, p. 15) comments: 'Critique understands that its claim to validity can be verified only in the successful process of enlightenment, and that means: in the practical discourse of those concerned'.

A final practical characteristic of the book is its concern with *evaluation*. It argues that we need to have an honest appraisal of those aspects of ICT4D activities that have really worked in the interest of poor people, and those that have merely reflected the hype of global organisations and private-sector enterprises without generating lasting and substantial change. Too few ICT4D activities, especially in Africa, have yet proved to be particularly successful or sustainable. However, we actually know rather little about this because of the paucity of rigorous monitoring and evaluation studies that have yet been undertaken (Heeks, 2002; although see Wagner *et al.*, 2005). While some good evaluative studies are now beginning to be undertaken (see for example Souter *et al.*, 2005; Cassidy, 2007), very few ICT4D activities actually implement ongoing monitoring into their practical implementation, even when this is specified as an integral part of their original design. Until such transparent, ongoing and self-enhancing monitoring becomes integral to ICT4D practice, we run the risk of deluding ourselves about the real success of our practices.

Two critical areas of recent debate are essential for an understanding of the significance and potential of ICT4D in the world today: the character of contemporary development, especially its intersection with ideas about 'globalisation'; and the implications of whether we are indeed living in a new type of information or knowledge society, transformed by a particular kind of technology. Chapter 2 therefore provides an overview of the most important aspects of these debates in order to situate the subsequent analyses of ICT4D within this wider context. The next chapter explores the meaning and uses of 'information' and 'communication' in development practice in more detail, before Chapter 4 provides an overview of the different types of 'technology' that have come to be associated with ICT4D. Chapter 5 then explores the emergence of ICT4D in both theory and practice, concentrating in particular on the global agendas that have helped to bring it to prominence in the international arena.

## References

Arce, A. and Long, N. (eds) (2000) *Anthropology, Development and Modernities: exploring discourse, counter-tendencies and violence*. London: Routledge

Cassidy, T. (2007) *The Global Education Initiative (GEI) Model of Effective Partnership Initiatives for Education*. Geneva: World Economic Forum

Crewe, E. and Harrison, E. (1998) *Whose Development? An ethnography of aid.* London: Zed Books

Easterly, W. (2001) *The Elusive Quest for Growth: economists' adventures and misadventures in the Tropics*. Cambridge, MA: Harvard University Press

Habermas, J. (1974) *Theory and Practice*, tr. J. Viertal. London: Heinemann

Habermas, J. (1978) *Knowledge and Human Interests*, 2nd edn, tr. J. Shapiro. London: Heinemann

Heeks, R. (2002) Failure, success and improvisation of information systems projects in developing countries (Development Informatics Working Paper Series, no. 11). Manchester: Institute for Development Policy and Management, University of Manchester

ITU (ed.) (2005) *Digital Reach*. Leicester: Tudor Rose for ITU

Mansell, R. and Wehn, U. (1998) *Knowledge Societies: information technology for sustainable development*. Oxford: Oxford University Press

Sachs, J. (2005) *The End of Poverty: how we can make it happen in our lifetime*. London: Penguin Books

Schware, R. (ed.) (2005) *E-Development: from excitement to effectiveness*. Washington, DC: The World Bank Group

Servon, L. (2002) *Bridging the Digital Divide: technology, community and public policy*. Melbourne: Blackwell Publishing

Souter, D. with Scott, N., Garforth, C., Jain, R., Mascarenhas, O. and McKerney, K. (2005) *The Economic Impact of Telecommunications on Rural Livelihoods and Poverty Reduction: a study of rural communities in India (Gujarat), Mozambique and Tanzania*. London: CTO and DFID

Unwin, T. (2007) No end to poverty. *Journal of Development Studies*, 43 (5), pp. 929–53

van der Hoeven, R. and Shorrocks, A. (2003) *Perspectives on Growth and Poverty*. Tokyo: United Nations University Press

Wagner, D.A., Day, B., Kozma, R.B., Miller, J. and Unwin, T. (2005) *The Impact of ICTs in Education for Development: a monitoring and evaluation handbook*. Washington, DC: *infoDev*

Weigel, G. and Waldburger, D. (eds) (2004) *ICT4D – connecting people for a better world*. Berne and Kuala Lumpur: Swiss Agency for Development and Cooperation and Global Knowledge Partnership

Weiler, R., Khan, A.W., Burger, R.A. and Schauer, T. (eds) (2005) *ICTs for Capacity-Building: critical success factors*. Brussels: Nematrix for UNESCO and Club of Rome

# 2 | Development agendas and the place of ICTs
## Tim Unwin

- It is essential to understand what we mean by 'development' before we can explore how ICTs can best contribute to its achievement.
- Particular interests underlie the use of terms such as 'information age' and 'knowledge society', and we need to be aware of the roles of these interests in shaping the processes associated with globalisation.
- ICTs have the potential either to increase inequalities or to reduce them, depending on the social, political and economic contexts within which they are introduced.
- Understanding how ICTs can be appropriated either for individual profit or for communal purposes can help us design appropriate programmes to empower poor and marginalised communities.

## Development agendas

Any account of ICT4D must begin with an understanding of the '4'; what it is intended for, its practical intent, namely 'development'. This is by no means a trivial undertaking, since the notion of 'development' signifies contrasting things to different people. The concept is highly malleable, being readily transformed to suit each current phase of change in the relationships between the rich and the poor. At its core, though, the idea of development is usually understood to involve concepts of 'progress' and of 'growth'.

Such a notion of development is often considered to have emerged during the European Enlightenment of the 18th century (see Gay, 1996; Bronner, 2004). Jeffrey Sachs (2005, p. 351) thus draws on the ideas of Jefferson (1743–1826), Smith (1723–1790), Kant (1724–1804) and Condorcet (1743–1794) to suggest that in the 21st century we can use rational argument and our technological skills to end absolute poverty. According to such arguments, politics, the economy, science and technology can all be brought together to make the world a better place. Such a heroic vision of the Enlightenment sees the 18th century as being the key period for the emergence of the notions that rationality underlies knowledge and ethics, that empirical experimentation should be at the heart of scientific enquiry, and that by combining these it is possible to achieve enlightened progress away from the darkness, superstition and irrationality of the medieval era. The Enlightenment is thus seen as providing the foundation for many of the ideas about democracy, freedom and reason that are at the heart of contemporary development practice.

There are, nevertheless, significant problems with such an interpretation of the role of the Enlightenment in shaping our concepts of development. Above all, it fails sufficiently to understand the significance of earlier intellectual traditions, it places insufficient emphasis on the moral and ethical dimensions of religion, and it remains a profoundly European concept. Very significant intellectual changes took place during the 17th century, prior to what is usually seen as the dominant period of the Enlightenment. The works and ideas of John Locke (1632–1704), René Descartes (1596–1650), Francis Bacon (1561–1626) and Thomas Hobbes (1588–1679) were thus essential to later discourses about rationality, empiricism and the rights and duties of individuals. What is so important about this is that these notions emerged within the social, political and economic context of 17th-century Europe, at a time when communal traditions were being replaced by an increased emphasis on the individual, when capitalist relations of production were replacing feudalism, and when European states were increasingly imposing their political and economic will over other parts of the world. All of these are critical for appreciating our contemporary notions of development, and thus of the role of ICTs in contributing to it.

It is also important to highlight the role that religions, and moral discourses more widely, have played in shaping and sustaining notions about the desirability of development. While some 18th-century philosophers, building in part on the ideas of Descartes, sought to use rationalism to justify the existence of God, the dominant emphasis of the Enlightenment, reflected particularly in the works of Rousseau (1712–1778) and Voltaire (1694–1778), was to challenge the Church and its role in resisting beneficial social and political change. Religion, according to this view, was one of the key factors that had held humanity back from progress in the medieval period. This theme later emerged in Marx's (1970, p. 131) famous dictum that 'Religion is the sigh of the oppressed creature, the heart of a heartless world and the soul of soulless conditions. It is the opium of the people'. Nevertheless, the role of religion in shaping our understandings of development must not be underestimated. At the heart of many of the religions that originated in south-west Asia and the eastern Mediterranean region lies the notion that people have duties and responsibilities to the poor and less able within their midst. This is, for example, as true of Islam as it is of Christianity. According to Islam, it is thus mandatory for financially able believers to give *zakat* (alms) and other support to the neediest of Muslims. Likewise, Christianity's emphasis on giving alms to the poor has provided the basis for a long heritage of work designed to improve the lives of the poor and marginalised, derived in large part from Jesus' second commandment that his followers should love their neighbours as themselves. In addition to such specifically religious emphasis on poverty reduction, the emergence of secular Humanism in the 19th century also played a very significant role in shaping thoughts and practices relating to development, particularly through its interface with discourses on ethics and the duties people have to 'distant others' (see for example O'Neill, 1986; Corbridge, 1998; Smith, 2000).

A final challenge to the emphasis placed on the Enlightenment in understandings of development is that it is a profoundly European concept. Modernist traditions derived from the European Enlightenment have attained global prominence over the last century, and such notions of development now therefore dominate both intellectual discourse and development practice across the world. However, it is crucial to understand that there are many other possible notions of development. Escobar (1995) and other advocates of what has become known as post-developmentalism (see Rahnema and Bawtree, 1997) have thus emphasised the importance of conceptualising alternative models to development and in particular of exploring what we can learn from indigenous autonomous social movements. In this context, it is important to consider precisely what it is that such alternative traditions understand by the notion of development (see for example Saraswati, 1997a). Han (1997), for example, emphasises how Confucianism, Buddhism, Taoism and Shamanism have contributed to social and economic change in Korea, and Saraswati (1997b) has likewise argued convincingly that Western definitions of development are distinctly alien in the Sanskritic traditions of India.

European notions of development have long held that it is about progress and growth towards a greater good, be this economic, social or political. In such a context, ICT4D is therefore often interpreted as being the use of ICTs to deliver such benefits. From at least the 17th century, the use of 'technology' or science has been at the heart of most of the dominant practices and discourses that have been concerned with development, from the industrial 'revolution' of the 19th century to the 'green revolution' of the mid-20th century. However, just as we need to be aware of alternative conceptualisations of development, so too do we need to consider different cultural interpretations of the role of ICTs in such practices. While focusing primarily on the dominant practices and discourses of ICT4D, this book is therefore careful to draw attention to alternative concepts and practices where they are of particular pertinence. In order to understand the context within which the theory and practice of ICT4D has emerged over the last decade, it is crucial to understand more about the dominant development rhetoric over this period, and the ways in which this has been connected to the leitmotif of 'globalisation'. These two themes provide the focus for the next sections of this chapter.

## Liberal democracy and the free market

It is no coincidence that ICT4D emerged as a distinctive field of practice in the latter part of the 20th century at a time when the dominant mode of development discourse was associated with notions of economic growth and liberal democracy. It is, though, important to distinguish between 'doing development' and 'writing about development'. Throughout the last half century, there has been a complex interplay between these two types of activity. In the 1960s, for example, the US economist Walt Rostow's (1960) model of stages of economic growth was highly influential in shaping practitioners' thoughts about the implementation of development planning in the poorer countries of the world, in part because of his role as an adviser on national security affairs to the Kennedy and Johnson administrations in the USA. Nevertheless, his anti-communist views and his advocacy of free enterprise subsequently became subject to much criticism from left-wing academics. Interestingly Rostow's model placed particular stress on the role of technology. Improved technologies and transport were seen as being crucial preconditions for take-off; the take-off stage itself was characterised by rapid economic growth, the development of more sophisticated technology, and investment especially in the manufacturing sector; and the drive to maturity again featured considerable advancements in technology, as economies became more diversified, with increased emphasis on consumer goods and services taking place in the final age of high mass consumption. This connection between technologies and economic growth is closely paralleled in more recent debates about the role of ICTs in economic growth some forty years later.

The diverse radical criticisms of development practice (Peet with Hartwick, 1999; Kothari, 2005) that emerged in the 1970s, influenced heavily by a re-awakening of English-speaking academics to wider European traditions of Marxist theory, were in contrast focused mainly on critique (Frank, 1969; McMichael, 2004). As such, they were not primarily intended to 'improve' development practice, but were designed instead to highlight the fundamental flaws of what their authors saw as the overall programme of capitalist exploitation of poor people living in Africa, Asia and Latin America. As Harris and Harris (1979, p. 576) emphasised at the time, most of these radical positions were 'generally critical of interventionism, even when this involves practical programmes with the apparent objective of ameliorating conditions of poverty' (see also Harris, 2005). These critiques nevertheless did draw attention to the inequalities, both social and spatial, inherent within the existing models of development, as well as the fundamental problems associated with military interventionism during the Cold War conflict between the USA and the Soviet Union for dominance in the so-called 'Third World'. They also began to highlight the diversity of expressions of poverty, and particularly the experiences of women (see for example Momsen and Townsend, 1987; Momsen and Kinnaird, 1993).

One area where there was, though, some practical impact from critiques of the dominant top-down, urban-based, centralised model of development planning was in the increased emphasis that began to be placed on bottom-up (Stöhr and Taylor, 1981) and agropolitan development (Lipton, 1977; Lea and Chaudhri, 1983) in the early 1980s. This was often energised by civil society and non-governmental organisations (NGOs), and was particularly successful where these institutions were based in poor countries themselves. Parnwell (2002) has thus commented:

> NGOs have many theoretical advantages over cumbersome and amorphous institutions of the state in terms of delivering development at the grassroots level. They are seen to be more flexible, adaptable and nimble, have shallower decision making hierarchies and shorter lines of communication, are largely autonomous, and are typically less costly to run because of a high contribution of voluntary inputs into their activities.
>
> (Parnwell, 2002, p. 116)

These are important themes that will be returned to when examining the role of civil society organisations in delivering partnership-based ICT4D initiatives.

The dominance in development practice at the start of the 21st century of the economic-growth agenda enabled by liberal democracy and the free market nevertheless returns us in many ways to some of the arguments of Rostow (1960) and his adversaries in the 1960s. The so-called debt crisis of the early 1980s necessitated leaders of the richer countries of the world to reconsider their interventionist agendas. At the same time, the rise of free-market ideology in parts of Europe and the USA, led particularly by the Thatcher (1979–1990) and Reagan (1981–1989) administrations, created the context within which a very different set of policies began to be 'exported' to the governments of poorer countries of the world. If the economic difficulties of the 1970s in Europe and north America had been 'solved' by deregulating the markets, by reducing state intervention, and by selling off inefficient public-sector enterprises, why should these policies not also work in the poorer countries of the world? Such arguments helped shape the policies of institutions such as the World Bank and the IMF, particularly with respect to their responses to the debt crisis in Latin American countries. These have subsequently come to be known as the Washington Consensus, after Williamson's (1990) formulation of the types of reform that he saw being advocated by institutions in Washington during the 1980s (see also Naím, 2000; Stiglitz, 2002; Sachs, 2005). At their heart lay the three principles of macroeconomic discipline, a market economy and openness to the world. These then came to be adopted as central features of the Structural Adjustment Programmes (SAPs) that were to be implemented by countries wishing to receive assistance from the global donor agencies and banks.

(*continued on page 14*)

# Case study: 'Across the wires th' electric message came, "He is no better; he is much the same"'

Richard Manning

*Chair of the OECD's Development Assistance Committee, 2003–2008; formerly Director General for Policy at DFID*

Does this line from the poem attributed to Alfred Austin, 'Lines on the Illness of the Prince of Wales' – complete with its reference to the information technology of the day – apply to the last 20 years of development cooperation?

The last two decades have seen an unprecedented episode of global growth. Despite the challenges of the Asian financial crisis of 1997, major financial crises in other emerging economies, several prolonged wars and the increasing incidence of natural disasters, developing countries in aggregate have grown faster than at any recorded period, led by the largest countries of all – China and India. This growth, now at last visible in Africa, has gone hand in hand with a prolonged recovery in private investment and trade after the debilitating debt crisis of 1982. Absolute numbers of very poor people are falling for the first time in recorded history, though income disparities between and within countries are wide and often rising.

Development aid has in general become much less significant as a contributor to progress, and much more concentrated on poorer countries. 96% of all aid now goes to Least Developed countries, other Low Income countries and Lower Middle Income countries. The end of the Cold War has encouraged more weight on development objectives. This is enshrined in the Millennium Development Goals agreed by the UN in 2000.

Development aid remains of real significance to the poorer countries, particularly those in sub-Saharan Africa, and small and vulnerable economies everywhere. The number of donors has continued to grow. All EU member states, for example, have accepted targets for aid levels to be reached by 2010, even states still receiving major transfers of assistance within the EU. Countries outside the traditional membership of the OECD Development Assistance Committee, such as South Korea, Turkey, Brazil, India and, above all, China are developing significant programmes. The number of multilateral agencies has been swelled by a new generation of single-purpose funds, notably in environment and in health, and often bringing official and non-official contributors together. Indeed foundations have stepped up very considerably their involvement in global and development issues, and multinational companies have increasingly worked with others in public–private partnerships which address business-related development opportunities, for example in health or in ICT. The internet has facilitated much stronger networking among civil society groups, with direct impacts on policymaking – the Jubilee debt campaign being a striking example.

The effective delivery of aid in this more diverse environment has been much debated. Two important strands have been the reinforcement of a country-based model of development priorities – the Poverty Reduction Strategies required as part of the debt cancellation exercises – and successive attempts at more harmonisation among donors and closer alignment of their aid to country-owned strategies, notably in the Paris Declaration of 2005. Many donors have also increased programmatic forms of aid, notably by flexible support for specific sectors or by general support to country budgets. This approach recognises the reality that many poor countries cannot cover their recurrent spending needs, but presents challenges where governments fail to implement needed reforms.

The year 2005 was marked by new commitments from most donors to step up their aid in support of the Millennium Goals, most of which are set for 2015. Many look very challenging, though the core goal for the reduction of absolute poverty will be met several years early: however, some recent data shows that even in the social sectors, where progress has lagged, rapid progress can be achieved – a 30 per cent reduction in five years of infant mortality in Tanzania and some other African countries being a telling example.

Austin is wrong: the message on the electric wires is one of progress.

*UNDP's office in Rwanda, 2008 (source:* Tim Unwin).

In addition, the collapse of the former Soviet Union at the end of the 1980s brought a new political dimension to development theory and practice in the form of an overt emphasis on 'liberal democracy' (for differing notions of democracy see Held, 1997). The so-called 'transition' economies of central and eastern Europe were thus encouraged to introduce new democratic structures that would enable the energy of individualism to be released from the constraints imposed on it by the centralised authority of the previous communist regimes (see Pickles and Smith, 1998). From 1991, a distinctive combination of liberal democracy and economic growth thus came to dominate international rhetoric of development, especially given the apparent failure of the intellectual Left to contribute any alternative models of development in the aftermath of the collapse of the Soviet Union (Habermas, 1994; Kothari, 2005). This dominant position has given rise to an increasingly hegemonic approach by international donors and financial institutions about how best to support development in the poorer countries of the world, based fundamentally on devising mechanisms to ensure economic growth through the creation of liberal democratic political systems. This is based on the adoption of absolute definitions of poverty, a belief that development is about the elimination of such poverty through economic growth, that this can best be implemented by encouraging a free market, and that good governance is an essential precursor for such growth. Hence, the UN's Millennium Development Goals (MDGs) adopted in 2000 were specifically focused on poverty elimination, and Poverty Reduction Strategy Papers (PRSPs) have now succeeded SAPs as the dominant framework through which international aid is provided for the poorest countries (for a wider critique see Unwin, 2004, 2007). One significant element to be noted about this overall agenda is the increased emphasis that it has placed on so-called 'partnerships', and the role that ICTs can contribute in this respect (Unwin, 2005). MDG 8 is thus to 'Develop a global partnership for development' including the aim 'In cooperation with the private sector, make available the benefits of new technologies – especially information and communication technologies' (http://www.un.org/millenniumgoals). ICTs have thus become central to the development agenda of growth and democracy intended to eliminate poverty. A sense of the vitality and enthusiasm of those committed to delivering this agenda is captured in the case study on pages 12–13.

This dominant approach to development practice is nevertheless not without its critics (see for example Easterley, 2006; Unwin, 2007). Once again, there is something of an impasse between critical academic writing on development, and the policies adopted by global agencies charged with eliminating poverty. As Harris (2005, p. 39) has commented, 'The challenge for development studies... is in renewing its relevance through improved historical understanding of development, and of the moral and practical requirements of global justice... This calls for a *critical* engagement on the part of development scholars with development policy-making'. This returns us to considerations of ethics and morality that were touched on in the previous chapter, and with the definitions of what development is truly about. For many development practitioners today, development has become synonymous with 'poverty elimination'. Poverty is prescribed primarily in economic terms, and it is to be eliminated through good governance and economic growth. However, such agendas ignore the plethora of alternative arguments that see development as something much more subtle, culturally shaped and socially relevant (Crewe and Harrison, 1998; Arce and Long, 2000). ICTs are equally significant in these alternative development agendas, and have the potential to play an important role in enabling the emergence of new forms of political organisation and social movement.

## Interconnected worlds

Interpretations and practices of 'development' in the 1990s were increasingly interwoven with the rhetorics and realities of 'globalisation', especially following the collapse of the former Soviet Union, and the emergence of the USA as the dominant global superpower. Harris (2005, p. 38) thus notes that by the end of the 1990s, only a short while after its inception, the term *globalisation* 'had both entered into popular language and become the vehicle for a whole new academic growth industry' (see in particular Amin, 1997; Wallerstein, 1999; Held *et al.*, 1999; Held and McGrew, 2002). A sound understanding of 'globalisation' is therefore essential for any analysis of ICT4D.

Although 'globalisation' is often seen as an autonomous process with the power to change people's lives, it is better understood as a term used to describe a coalescence of specific economic, social, cultural and political interests. Above all, globalisation refers to the ways in which these have led to increasing interconnectedness of human activity across the world. Typically, the dominant economic characteristics of globalisation are seen as a rapid increase in international trade, the integration of global financial systems, changing systems of industrial production involving increased amounts of outsourcing, growing economic interdependence between states, increased power of global or multinational corporations, increasingly global patterns of consumption, and an increasing complexity of global economic institutions such as the World Trade Organization (WTO). Socially, globalisation has been characterised by increased migration and travel, by new means of social communication such as instant messaging and mobile telephony, and by increasingly complex patterns of human relationships across the world. In the cultural sphere, there has been increased intermixing and hybridisation, the creation of global fashions and crazes, the rise of global media organisations, increasing acceptance of a global set of human values as reflected in the Universal Declaration of Human Rights, and above all a tendency for the artefacts of a few dominant cultures to be spread much more widely across the world. Finally, globalisation can be seen in the political sphere, reflected for example in the expansion of global justice movements and the creation of the International Criminal Court in 2002, the growth of international political alliances, the increasing significance of so-called 'international terrorism', the rise of global environmental movements, the dominant military role of the USA as a global political force, and indeed the existence of a worldwide anti-globalisation movement. In understanding 'globalisation', though, the key issue is to explore what underlies these characteristics, and to unravel the influence of particular events and processes on the subsequent evolution of those features in which we are interested. ICTs have been instrumental in facilitating many of these changes.

There are important contradictions within the concept of 'globalisation'. Indeed, most of the above characteristics can be seen as either positive or negative, as opportunities or threats, depending on the perspective from which they are observed. Globalisation has thus been characterised both by a tendency towards uniformity and also by increased opportunities for local cultures and identities to find global expression, often referred to as 'glocalisation' (see Cox, 1997; Dreher, 2006; http://globalization.kof. ethz.ch). In seeking to disentangle these contradictions it is helpful to explore the diverse accounts that have been used to interpret its evolution in the late 20th century. The first important point to note, though, is that globalisation is actually a very ancient process. Ever since the dawn of humanity, the pace and scale of interaction between people and societies has been increasing (see Menzies, 2002; North and Thomas, 1973). Moreover, throughout history, ICTs have played a crucial role in the processes of globalisation. The development of cartography in the 15th century was thus as essential to European explorations of Africa, Asia and Latin America (see Braudel, 1982) as the emergence of new ICTs in the 20th century for the shaping of the latest manifestations of globalisation. Information and communication have always been valuable, and those in positions of power have regularly sought to develop technologies to ensure that they retain advantageous access to it.

Such arguments are reinforced by Wallerstein (1999), who suggests that we need to consider processes operating in both the short term (the last 50 years) and also over the last 500 years if we are truly to comprehend globalisation. He argues that the view that we are now living for the first time in an era of globalisation is actually 'a deception imposed upon us by powerful groups' (Wallerstein, 1999, p. 1). For Wallerstein (1983; see also Harvey, 1989, 1996, 2000), we cannot understand globalisation without appreciating the way in which it is fundamentally connected with the resolution of the crisis tendencies of capitalism. In particular, capitalist enterprises are driven by the continual need to search for cheaper raw materials and production resources, notably labour, and also to expand their markets so that their profits can be realised. It is these factors that have fundamentally driven the processes associated with globalisation over the last 500 years or so. Although their intensity increased in the latter part of the 20th century, their underlying rationale has remained as true today as it was in the 17th century. Wallerstein (1999) suggests that:

We can think of this long transition as one enormous political struggle between two large camps: the camp of all those who wish to retain the privileges of the existing inegalitarian system, albeit in different forms, perhaps vastly different forms; and the camp of all those who would like to see the creation of a new historical system that will be significantly more democratic and egalitarian.

(Wallerstein, 1999, p. 19)

He goes on to argue that the former 'will assert that they are modernisers, new democrats, advocates of freedom, and progressive' (Wallerstein, 1999, p. 19). It is they who are seeking to deceive us into the belief that we are indeed living in a revolutionary new world, in a new era of globalisation. According to such arguments, the notion of globalisation becomes a self-fulfilling prophecy driven by the interests of capital. As Harvey (2000, p. 69) has stated most clearly, 'The answer to the question "who put globalization on the agenda" is, therefore, capitalist class interests operating through the agency of the US foreign, military and commercial policy' (see also Soros, 1998, 2002).

It is here that it becomes particularly important to explore how the processes associated with globalisation intersect with our experiences of space and time (see Lefebvre, 1974, 1981; Giddens, 1984; Soja, 1989; Harvey, 1996; Unwin, 2000). As Harvey (2000, p. 58) has commented, 'capitalism is always under the impulsion to accelerate turnover time, to speed up the circulation of capital and consequently to revolutionise the time horizons of development'. While historically canals, railways and aeroplanes have all helped to bring people and processes closer together, thereby accelerating the potential for the accumulation of capital, the introduction of new ICTs in the last two decades of the 20th century has played an even more dramatic role in restructuring the potential for ever faster accumulation, and with it the social and cultural structures necessary to maintain it.

ICTs are fundamentally concerned with the ways in which individuals and societies experience space and time. The invention of writing and books, for example, enabled information to be recorded and stored in ways that had previously been impossible in oral cultures. The agreement of a written record of particular events in turn created fundamentally different forms of social discourse from those that had prevailed previously when agreements had been based purely on word of mouth. Likewise, throughout most of human history, the maximum speed that people have been able to travel on land has been restricted to the pace of a horse. Riders for the pony express between 1860 and 1861 were, for example, expected to travel at about 10 miles an hour, with the minimum time for the 2,000 mile journey from St Joseph, Missouri to Sacramento in California being recorded as 7 days and 17 hours (http://www.ponyexpress.org). However, the use of signal fires and other such systems of communication have for millennia enabled limited messages to travel very rapidly over great distances. Information could thus pass very swiftly along the entire 6,700-kilometre length of the Great Wall of China during the Ming Dynasty (1368–1644). Moreover, the simple use of voice relays with people calling to their neighbours over short distances, long before the use of the telephone, could enable people to communicate remarkably swiftly across difficult terrain, even if there was often a decay in the accuracy of such information. Yodelling in the Swiss Alps thus provided a means for people to pass simple messages across deep valleys in mountainous areas without actually having to spend many hours travelling to see each other. These examples are important, because they remind us that people have never actually needed to move physically to be able to communicate with one another, and also that very rapid communication over considerable distances is not a particularly new concept.

What is, of course, new is the scale at which this is possible, with vast amounts of data now being transferred across the globe almost instantaneously through the use of new ICTs. One expression of this has been the way in which many companies now provide internet access for employees at home, thereby enabling them to work ever longer hours. This form of self-exploitation has been particularly evident in the 'encouragement' given to staff to undertake online training at home, and to 'catch up with' their e-mails in the evenings or at weekends, outside 'traditional' working hours. More recently, global corporations have increasingly begun to insist on staff having handheld digital devices so that they can connect to their offices at all hours of the day and night wherever they are in the world. As BlackBerry's website advertises, 'In an ideal world…you could respond faster to customer issues in the field' (http://www.blackberry.com/solutions/index. shtml, accessed 15 June 2006). BlackBerry thus claims to offer four distinctive benefits to businesses: achieving compelling returns on investment, improving decision making, improving customer satisfaction, and improving productivity. This is to be achieved through the combination of e-mail, phone, wireless internet, tethered modem, organiser, SMS, instant messaging, corporate data access and paging technologies all contained within a single handheld device (http://www.blackberry.com/products/blackberry/ index.shtml, accessed 15 June 2006). Employees are now truly at the beck and call of their managers 24 hours a day, seven days a week, 52 weeks a year.

Human cultures have produced many different conceptualisations of the ways that societies both construct and are constructed by space and time, and also of the significant influences that these conceptualisations have had in shaping our material existence (see for example Sack, 1980; Gregory and Urry, 1985; Soja, 1989; Harvey, 2000). In particular, it is often argued that recent changes encapsulated in the notion of globalisation have led to the compression or annihilation of space (Giddens, 1984; Harvey, 2000). This is, though, too simplistic a notion, because space can never be considered purely in isolation; space and time are intimately connected. As the above examples have illustrated, an increasingly globalised world is also one where our experiences and understanding of time have also changed. Just as the effects of distance become less, so too do those of time (see Flood and Lockwood, 1986; Unwin, 1992). We now live in a 24-hour seven-day world, in which those with access to ICTs can gain huge amounts of information and communicate instantly with people anywhere in the world. In less than 50 years we have moved from letters and fixed-line telephones as dominant modes of communication, to faxes, then e-mails, mobile phones, instant messaging, and now video conferencing and TelePresence using the internet (Cisco, 2008). Communication has become much more rapid and ubiquitous, and this has changed our entire lives. Such interplay between societies, ICTs, space and time lies at the heart of this book. If we desire to help empower poor and marginalised communities, it is essential for us to understand something of the complexity of these inter-relationships. The next section therefore turns to an exploration of the suggestion that we may be living in a completely new type of information or knowledge society.

## Information and knowledge societies

Given the changes that have recently taken place in human experiences of space and time across the world, a growing body of literature has argued that we are indeed now living in a fundamentally new era (see particularly Castells, 2000a, 2000b, 2003; UNESCO, 2005; Friedman, 2006). This section suggests that while these changes are indeed important, their significance may have been exaggerated. Just as the notion of globalisation has been coined for a particular set of interests, I argue that the notion of an *information society* also reflects a particular set of theoretical and practical agendas. If we are successfully to identify ways in which ICTs can indeed be used to support poor and marginalised communities, it is essential for us to understand better the underlying principles that have given rise to the concept, as well as the claimed reality, of an information or knowledge society.

### *Mythologies of ages*

One of the most prominent advocates of the notion that we are now living in a distinct 'information age' has been Manuel Castells (1985, 1989, 2000a, 2000b, 2003; but see also Friedman, 2006). In his monumental trilogy *The Information Age: economy, society and culture*, he makes a convincing case that recent technological change has had profound impacts on the way in which societies, economies and culture are shaped and function, to such an extent that this can be characterised as a truly new age. For him, this has been expressed in a fundamental restructuring of capitalism, and in particular 'an accentuation of uneven development, this time not only between North and South, but between the dynamic segments and territories of societies everywhere, and those others that risk becoming irrelevant from the perspective of the system's logic' (Castells, 2000a, p. 2).

If this is indeed so, it presents a fundamental challenge to the concept that ICTs can be used to benefit the poor, since the dominant forces within our global society will continue to ensure that the inequalities to which Castells (2000a) refers are maintained and reinforced. Another conclusion that can be drawn from Castells' arguments is that many of those advocating ICT4D are, often unintentionally, actually part of a global conspiracy in which these new technologies as well as the notion of an information society itself are being used to reinforce the 'differences' and contradictions that remain essential to a thriving capitalist global economy. In contrast, I wish to permit at least the possibility of a more radical agenda, one in which we can indeed hope to use ICTs to empower poor people and marginalised communities.

While few would argue against the view that new technologies have transformed the ways in which we communicate and gain information, a fundamental point of debate is over whether the changes and processes catalogued in such detail by Castells and others are truly as revolutionary as they claim. Harvey (2000, p. 62) thus comments that, 'The idea of an "information revolution" is powerfully present these days, and is often viewed as the dawning of a new era of globalisation within which the information society reigns supreme…It is easy to make too much of this. The newness of it all impresses, but then the newness of the railroad and the telegraph, the automobile, the radio, and the telephone in their day impressed equally'. Castells (2000a, p. 78), though, firmly believes that we are indeed 'witnessing a point of historical discontinuity'. In particular, he argues that:

> The emergence of a new technological paradigm organized around new, more powerful, and more flexible information technologies makes it possible for information itself to become the product of the production process. To be more precise: the products of new information technology industries are information-processing devices or information processing itself. New information technologies, by transforming the processes of information processing, act upon all domains of human activity, and make it possible to establish endless connections between different domains, as well as between elements and agents of such activities.
>
> (Castells, 2000a, p. 78)

For these reasons, he claims that the information age is fundamentally different both from the first industrial revolution of the 18th century in which hand tools were replaced by machines, as well as from the second industrial revolution in the second half of the 19th century, which featured among other technological changes the development of electricity and the internal combustion engine. Science and technology played a leading role in all of these, but according to Castells (2000a, p. 31) only in the information age has there been 'a cumulative feedback loop between innovation and the uses of innovation'.

Deciding whether or not something is truly revolutionary depends on the criteria that one selects for analysis, and on the extent to which one is willing to acknowledge the significance of antecedents in shaping the phenomenon under investigation. There is certainly good evidence that many of the technological changes associated with the information age were first introduced well before the end of the 20th century. Indeed, it can be argued with some force that many of the features of globalisation and contemporary development practice actually reflect the outworking of the long-established structural interests of global capital in minimising production costs, especially labour, and maximising the market, rather than necessarily the revolutionary impact of information technology. One could, for example, just as easily say that the origins of printing in China in the 6th century and its introduction in Europe in the 15th century were also instances where information was the product of the production process, and where there was feedback between innovation and the production of new knowledges.

Alongside attempts to define our contemporary world as being an information age have been others who have preferred the term *knowledge society* or indeed *knowledge economy* (see for example World Bank Institute, 2007). The authors of a recent volume on knowledge societies (UNESCO, 2005, p. 17) have thus commented that 'The idea of the information society is based on technological breakthroughs. The concept of knowledge societies encompasses much broader social, ethical and political dimensions'. It is, though, difficult to reconcile such a view with Castells' (2000a, b) arguments for an information age, which reflect a very broad conceptualisation of the human condition and pay clear attention to the social, moral and political dimensions of the issues with which he was concerned. This therefore begs the question of what is meant by 'information' and by 'knowledge' (see for example Machlup, 1962; Drucker, 1966, 1969; Bell, 1976; Porat, 1977). 'Knowledge' and 'information' are often used synonymously, but at the heart of most practical distinctions between the terms is the sense that 'knowledge' requires higher-order human processing, whereas 'information' is something that is generally only produced and communicated. Accordingly, if 'information' is not understood and actively used it cannot become 'knowledge'. One way of grappling with such concepts is to consider 'information' as processed raw facts or 'data'. 'Knowledge', in turn, can then be understood as a form of processed 'information' that is used for a particular purpose (see Habermas, 1978, for a detailed exploration of the connections between knowledge and human interests). In this sense, knowledge is information that has been incorporated into human understanding based on experience and context. Put another way, information becomes knowledge when it is combined with experience, context, interpretation and reflection so that it can be applied to actions based upon human decision-making (Davenport and Prusak, 1998). Such differences are particularly important in the context of discussions over information and knowledge management, as well as on the ways in which information and knowledge are communicated.

Those preferring the use of the terms 'knowledge societies' or 'knowledge economies' (as with UNESCO, 2005; Britz *et al.*, 2006; World Bank Institute, 2007) do so most frequently with the intention of drawing a distinction between their arguments and those who they see as advocating a more restricted technological definition of 'information'. In particular, many such claims are based on normative arguments about the nature of the type of knowledge society that their proponents would like to see. In particular, such arguments place considerable emphasis on the notion of knowledge as a global public good, on the emphasis within knowledge societies of human-rights agendas, and on the importance of knowledge sharing. As UNESCO (2005, p. 18) thus asserts, 'A knowledge society should be able to integrate all its members and to promote new forms of solidarity involving both present and future generations. Nobody should be excluded from knowledge socie-ties, where knowledge is a public good, available to each and every individ-ual'. UNESCO (2005, p. 18) continues by proclaiming that 'the "information age" knowledge societies differ from older knowledge societies because of the focus on human rights and the inclusive participatory character they inherited from the Enlightenment'. These are powerful aspirations, and an examination thereof is essential for understanding the potential role of ICT4D in delivering them. However, there is as yet little evidence that human societies are actually moving in this direction. Indeed, Britz *et al.* (2006) argue forcefully that 'Africa still has a long way to go to become a true knowledge society'. There are powerful interests that are determined to ensure not only that information and knowledge are carefully controlled but also that they are being used by the rich and powerful to maintain their positions of influence and control. There is thus a fundamental challenge in seeking to use ICTs for development, since they can both enable greater global control and profit generation, while also providing the opportunity for the kinds of global knowledge-sharing communities that people in organisations such as UNESCO (2005) wish to see.

The fundamental problem with UNESCO's (2005) assertions as stated above is that they conflate the positive and the normative. The statement that 'knowledge is a public good' (UNESCO, 2005, p. 18) appears to make a universal claim about what 'should' be that conforms neither to the historical evidence nor to contemporary practical reality. UNESCO (2005, p. 19) goes on to claim that 'information is in many cases a commodity, in which case it is bought or sold, whereas knowledge, despite certain restrictions (defence secrets, intellectual property, traditional forms of esoteric knowledge, for example), belongs of right to any reasonable mind'. The trouble with such an assertion is that it is not only information that has become commodi-tised, but also 'knowledge' itself. Some might claim that knowledge should belong of right to anyone, but one of the fundamental characteristics of con-temporary society is that ICTs seem to be increasing the commodisation of knowledge. In part, this reflects the considerable cost of managing and processing both information and knowledge, and the need for companies that invest in these processes to return profit to their investors. However, as Habermas (1978) has argued, different forms of knowledge have always had different practical interests associated with them. There is no good reason to suppose that contemporary society should be any different. Indeed, later in the argument, UNESCO (2005, p. 22) seems to recognise this by noting that 'knowledge itself has become "commoditised" in the form of exchangeable, and codifiable information'. Hence, we need to lay to rest arguments that claim that knowledge is some kind of universal public good, and instead recognise that it is commoditised and serves particular interests. As Roberts (2000, p. 439) has commented, 'As one element in a broader neoliberal discourse, where the primacy of the market for organising all human activity is taken for granted, "knowledge" becomes just another commodity: Something to be bought, sold, traded and consumed'.

Such debates nevertheless highlight the critical importance of understanding the relationships between information producers and knowledge users, as well as the relationships between individuals and states, if we are to implement effective ICT4D strategies and activities. It is to these issues that the next section turns in more detail.

### Interests in information and knowledge

At the heart of the emergence of capitalism in 17th-century Europe was the idea that investment in production offered the opportunity for individual gain. Old systems of trade were becoming less profitable as a result of more widely available information about prices pertaining in different markets. As a result, people began to invest increasingly in land, and their application of technological innovations in agriculture and industry laid the basis for the so-called agricultural and industrial revolutions. These processes were, though, only enabled by changing understandings of the relationships between individuals and communities, as well as of the rights that both had to different kinds of information and knowledge. In essence, the privatisation of knowledge was, and still is, fundamental to the acquisition of profit. Hence, a complex framework of intellectual property rights has emerged parallel to, and in support of, the emergence of capitalism. Particularly during the latter part of the 20th century, this has, though, been challenged by those advocating a 'return' to more communal forms of knowledge sharing that are based on a fundamentally different kind of logic and argument, drawing validity from moral and ethical standpoints rather than from purely economic ones (see for example UNESCO, 2005, p. 27).

The specific notion of intellectual property rights (IPR) is relatively recent, emerging in the 19th century and not really coming to prominence until the creation of the World Intellectual Property Organization (WIPO, http://www.wipo.int) in 1967 (see also Merges et al., 2003; APC and ITeM, 2007). Such rights, nevertheless, have much older precedents in laws associated with copyright and patents (see Price, 1913; Jaffe and Trajtenberg, 2002). In origin, patents were designed both to enable individual profit and also to permit wider communal access to, and thus benefit from, innovations. Two lasting characteristics of patents can be noted from their origins: first they are of limited duration, and second they pertain to the particular jurisdiction in which they are granted. During the 20th century, the increasingly globalised nature of the economy led to the need for greater consideration to be paid to international agreements concerning patents and the rights that people had more generally to intellectual property, including copyrights, patents, trademarks, design rights and the proprietary knowledge of businesses. As well as the creation of WIPO this trend towards greater harmonisation of intellectual property rights was reflected in the 1994 World Trade Organization's Agreement on Trade-Related Aspects of Intellectual Property Rights (TRIPS). Significantly, this was a result of strong lobbying by representatives of the richer governments of the world, and it has subsequently been much criticised by those who see it as part of the processes associated with globalisation that have led to resources flowing from poorer countries to copyright and patent holders in richer parts of the world (see Steinberg, 1997; Ganguli, 2000).

A contrasting set of arguments has sought to return attention to what is seen as having been lost in the 17th-century shift to individualism, and in particular the perceived benefits of the 'commons'. Debate over the so-called 'tragedy of the commons' was conceived primarily in the context of population pressure on the environment (Hardin, 1968), but it has recently been reinvigorated in discussions over the 'digital commons'. In essence, many of the institutional changes in 16th- and 17th-century Europe associated with increasing private land-ownership led to prescriptions on the rights that poor people previously had to communal land and resources, such as grazing or the collection of fallen timber. The process of enclosure can thus be interpreted as a way in which certain privileged individuals were able to gain private profit at the expense of poor people who were dispossessed of their previous rights and subsequently had to sell their labour power to the emerging class of capitalists. Likewise, today there are concerns that the internet may become privatised, and that the potential communal benefits that it currently provides for poor people will be eliminated. As Poynder (2003, p. 33) has commented, there is 'considerable concern that aggressive use of intellectual property – most notably copyright and patents – threatens to "enclose" the open nature of the internet and therefore privatise it by stealth'. Attempts to counter such trends and to reclaim the digital commons have led to a range of alternative kinds of licensing both for software and for content, notably the GNU General Public License (GPL) (http://www.gnu.org/copyleft/gpl.html), the Open Publication License (OPL) (http://opencontent.org/openpub) and more recently Creative Commons licences (http://creativecommons.org) that enable originators to choose from a range of qualifying conditions that they wish to be assigned to their material. At the heart of many such initiatives is the notion that material should be made commonly available, providing that individual users return any adaptations that they make to that material to the wider community of users. This is also intended to encourage the communal creation processes that the internet has so readily enabled, typified by the open-content encyclopedia Wikipedia (http://www.wikipedia.org). The ways in which such conflict over the institutional ecology of the digital environment are played out over the next decade are likely to have a fundamental impact on how we understand the world around us and on how we communicate and share information with each other (Benkler, 2006; see also Krishna and Madon, 2003).

## A world of differences

There is a very real tension between the arguments of those who see ICTs as being a means whereby poor countries and people can catch up with the economic successes of their richer neighbours, and those who advocate the need for the rich to remain competitive in the global knowledge economy. This applies equally to those in the business community and to politicians. In his letter to the newly appointed Secretary of State for Trade and Industry in the UK, the then Prime Minister Tony Blair (2006) commented that one of the key domestic challenges for the UK was 'to build on our unprecedented record of economic achievement ensuring our country can compete and win in the global knowledge economy'. Likewise, in a speech in 2005 he emphasised that 'It is hard to overstate to Britain's future the importance of knowledge, and the embedding of knowledge throughout society through education, technology and social mobility' (Blair, 2005). In so doing, he stressed in particular the importance of ICT alongside other aspects of science and technology in helping to shape this knowledge economy. This speech emphasised the UK's interest in remaining competitive in the global knowledge economy and the role that ICTs can play in helping to achieve this. However, Blair was by no means alone in his aspirations. Other leaders of the European Union (EU) are equally determined to use the opportunities provided by ICTs to transform their economies and maintain their competitive advantages. The EU's Information Society portal claimed in 2006 that:

> The last few years have witnessed a transformation in the industrial landscape of the developed world. Telecommunications liberalisation, the explosive growth of the internet and the increasingly networked nature of business and society all point to one thing – the birth of the Information Society (IS). Developing a successful European Information Society is at the very heart of the EU's 'Lisbon Goal' of becoming the world's most dynamic and competitive economy by 2010.
>
> (http://europa.eu.int/information_society/text_en.htm, accessed 19 June 2006)

A fundamental question that must be asked is whether such comments are compatible with a vision that sees ICTs as being an important element through which poor and marginalised people and countries can be em-powered. There is little doubt that ICTs can contribute positively to eco-nomic growth and thus to development if this is defined primarily according to such criteria. However, the real issue with which this book seeks to grapple is whether it is actually possible to use ICTs effectively to help transform the lives of poor people and marginalised communities despite the global interests that seek to maintain competitive advantages and thus digital divides at a range of scales. If it is indeed possible, how can this best be achieved?

The evidence to date suggests that although ICTs can make a significant difference to the lives of poor and marginalised communities, many well-intentioned projects have failed (Heeks, 2002; Greenberg, 2005), and the integration of ICTs more widely into the 'globalisation project' may have actually led to an accentuation of inequalities rather than their reduction. Such arguments have been encapsulated in wider discourses about the cre-ation of a 'digital divide', the term introduced during the 1990s to refer to the growing differences in access that communities had to computers and the internet (see for example Norris, 2001; World Bank, 2006). There are indeed substantial differences in access to and use of ICTs at a range of scales, from the local through to the international, and these divides are not merely in terms of networks and connectivity, but also relate to content, access to information, accessibility and literacies (Unwin and de Bastion, 2008). Even in the world's richest countries, there are significant social and spatial divides in terms of access to information and communication (for an example from the UK, see Point Topic, 2005). Such differences are even starker in poorer countries, with readily accessible internet connectivity often only being available in the major urban centres.

Globally, the differences are equally marked. Figure 2.1 shows the stark contrasts in mobile phone use across the world. Likewise, Africa averaged 1.74 personal computers (PCs) per 100 inhabitants in 2004, compared with 50.84 PCs in Oceania (ITU, 2006a). As Figure 2.2 illustrates, the spatial divi-sions within Africa itself are also very significant, with countries such as Burundi, the Democratic Republic of Congo, Ethiopia and Niger all hav-ing less than 1 internet user per 100 people in 2006, compared with 2.7 in Ghana, 7.9 in Kenya, 12.7 in Tunisia and 24.1 users in Mauritius (ITU, 2006a). There is, though, some indication that as many richer countries have become saturated with certain types of ICT, the divisions between them and the poorer countries have begun to decline (ITU, 2006b). Figures 2.3 and 2.4 are particularly interesting in this respect. These show that the number of internet users and mobile phone subscribers per 100 people in the developed world were only 5.7 and 2.7 times those in developing coun-tries respectively in 2006, compared with 14.6 and 9.2 times respectively in 2000. This would indeed suggest a reduction in the differences. However, looked at in another way, the real differences between them have actually expanded. In 2006, the absolute difference between the numbers of internet

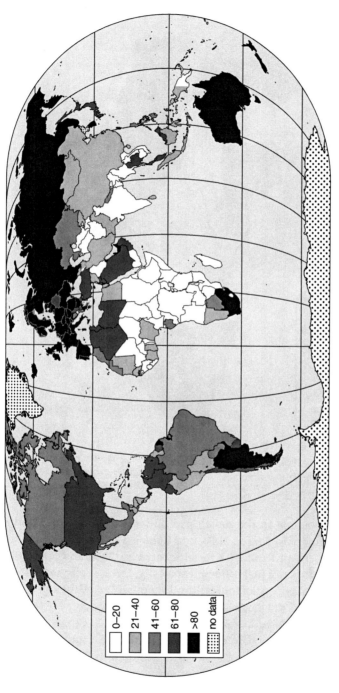

Figure 2.1 *Mobile phone subscribers per 100 inhabitants, 2006 (source: derived from ITU data at http://www.itu.int/ITU-D/icteye/Indicators/Indicators.aspx#).*

0–20
21–40
41–60
61–80
>80
no data

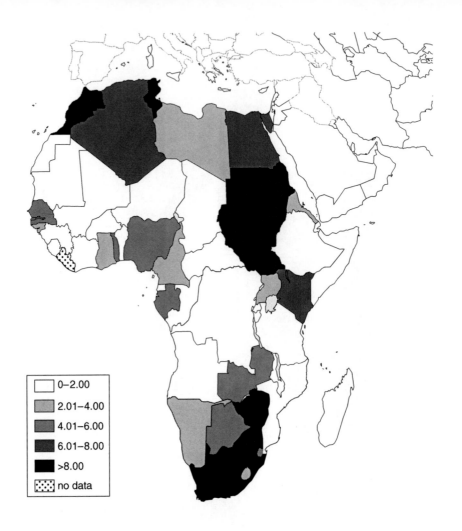

Figure 2.2 *Internet users per 100 inhabitants in Africa, 2006* (*source:* derived from ITU data at http://www.itu.int/ITU-D/icteye/Indicators/Indicators.aspx#).

users per 100 people in the developed and developing world had risen to 48.4 from its figure of 28.6 in 2000, and likewise for mobile phone users the difference had risen from 44.2 to 58.5 between 2000 and 2006. Moreover, the digital divide is not just reflected spatially, but it is also to be seen across the world in terms of social and cultural inequalities. Although statistics are hard to obtain and not necessarily reliable, it is evident, for example, that women frequently have lower levels of access to ICTs than do men. Thus, while 51 per cent of total internet users in the USA and Canada are estimated to be women, this figure falls to 37 per cent in Germany and Italy, 35 per cent in Malaysia, and only 19 per cent and 12 per cent in South Africa and Senegal respectively.

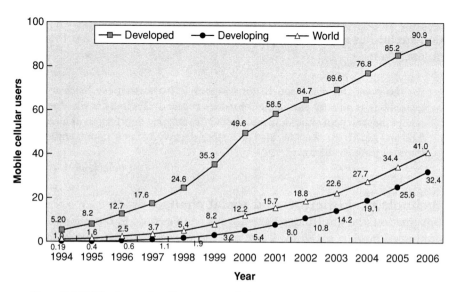

Figure 2.3 *Mobile phone subscribers per 100 inhabitants, 1994–2006* (*source:* http://www.itu.
int/ITU-D/ict/statistics/ict/graphs/mobile.jpg).

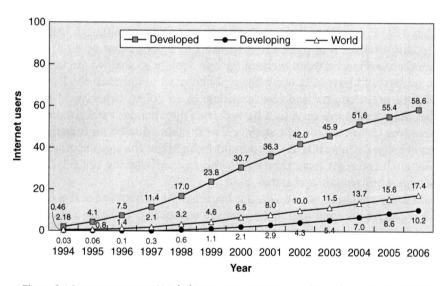

Figure 2.4 *Internet users per 100 inhabitants, 1994–2006* (*source:* http://www.itu.int/ITU-D/
ict/statistics/ict/graphs/internet.jpg).

At the beginning of the 2000s, many of those working for donor organisations argued that poor people and communities had more pressing needs
than for ICTs. However, the rapidity of the changes that have taken place
over the last few years means that it is no longer a question of *whether*
to provide books or ICTs, but rather how we can ensure that ICTs do not

become yet another means whereby large segments of the world's population are further systematically disadvantaged. Weigel (2004) has thus commented that:

> For the poor, the real issue is not whether ICT are desirable because the technology is already part of their broader context. The issue is whether we accept that the poor should, in addition to the existing deprivation of income, food and health service, etc., also be further deprived of new opportunities to improve their livelihoods.
>
> (Weigel, 2004, p. 18)

## Technological interests and social change

Information and knowledge have always been central to the effective functioning of human societies. They are the means through which societies reproduce themselves, through which understanding is passed on to future generations, and through which social relations are established. As such, attempts to describe our contemporary world as being a new information age or a knowledge society seem misplaced. What writers such as Castells (2000a, b; 2003) and Friedman (2006) nevertheless reinforce is that the scale and ways in which information is now used are unprecedented, and that it is particularly in the way that technology has been appropriated to shape these functions that much novelty is to be encountered. In concluding this chapter, it is therefore important to return more generally to this interconnection between technology and society so that we are better able to understand how ICTs can effectively be used to enhance the livelihoods of poor and marginalised communities. In so doing, it is crucial to establish the specific interests that have driven the agendas associated with the practices characteristic of a society that is claimed to be an information or knowledge society. It is also important to highlight the significant influence that such interests have thereby played in restructuring the relationships between individuals and states.

Broadly speaking, writers on the historical links between science and society can be grouped into those who see technology as being a response to social and economic changes, those who see it as determining such changes, and those who claim that technology is somehow neutral (see for example Adas, 1989; Feenberg and Hannay, 1995; McClellan and Dorn, 2006). The fundamental debate is over whether, as Feenberg and Hannay (1995, p. 1) ask, technology is something that is 'socially and ethically neutral, a product of rational problem solving,' or 'a kind of materialised ideology, a prop of the established society?'. The position that I want to develop here is that although technology has been used by elites throughout history to reinforce their status, and is therefore not something that is in any sense neutral, we should nevertheless allow for the possibility that new ICTs might also be used to enable poor and marginalised communities to change their lives. The solution to this is not so much a technical one but a moral one.

Such debates go back to ancient Greece, when the public sphere tended to exalt philosophy over technology (Feenberg and Hannay, 1995). However, the development of a new kind of scientific enquiry in 17th- and 18th-century Europe is widely seen as shifting this balance in the favour of technology as an autonomous force that could be used to advance economic progress (see also Malthus, 1992; Boserup, 1965). McClellan and Dorn (2006) emphasise how a series of technological innovations helped transform Europe from being a relative backwater in the medieval period to a position of global dominance in science and technology in the 20th century. The emergence of a particular connection between the scientific establishment and the creation of 'useful' technical innovations, especially from the 17th century onwards, provided important mechanisms whereby an emerging class of capitalists was able to extract ever greater levels of production from the labourers that they employed. This was premised on the emergence of a particular model of science in which experimentation and hypothesis testing came to be the dominant mode of enquiry, leading to the creation of 'scientific' laws that could be used for both explanation and prediction. By the 19th century, this view of science became formalised in the positive philosophy of Auguste Comte (1798–1857), which sought to do away entirely with human subjectivity and instead argued that social phenomena could be subject to the same rules and methods as natural phenomena (Kolakowski, 1972; Thompson, 1976). It was this positivist model of science that came to dominate the world in the 20th century, and thus provided the foundations for the research and innovation that shaped the development of modern information and communication technologies (see Pippin, 1995, p. 43).

What is so significant about this is that until the end of the 19th century – even in Europe, let alone in other parts of the world – there were many different views of what knowledge was concerned with and of the relationships between epistemology (theories of knowledge) and science. Since then, there has been a gradual rise in European science's belief in itself. This dominance of scientism, 'that is the conviction that we can no longer understand science as one form of possible knowledge, but rather must identify knowledge with science' (Habermas, 1978, p. 4), has meant that for much of the 20th century there was a damaging rupture between philosophy and science. This clear connection between on the one hand 'science and technology' and on the other 'knowledge' is absolutely crucial, because of the significance that 'science' has therefore played in shaping the concept of information and knowledge societies (see Habermas, 1978; Feenberg, 1991). Habermas (1978), for example, has argued that there are three types of science, each associated with a different knowledge-constitutive interest: empirical–analytic science, historical–hermeneutic science and critical science (see also Unwin, 1992). This suggestion provides a useful framework for interpreting recent developments in the field of ICT4D.

The emergence of postmodernism in the latter part of the 20th century sought to shatter the illusion of certainty that modernism in general, and empirical–analytic science in particular, had conveyed, and in so doing challenged the overarching theories of those such as Habermas (for a wider discussion see also Heidegger, 1977; Arendt, 1958; Feenberg, 1991) who had sought to provide cohesive interpretations of our social condition (Harvey, 1989; Bauman, 1997). However, Habermas's arguments remain pertinent in understanding the interests that have lain behind the role of ICTs in an increasingly globalised world, and thus too in how it might be possible to use these technologies to serve the emancipatory interests of the poor.

The dramatic expansion in the use of ICTs in the latter part of the 20th century was driven primarily by the technical interests of global capital, eager to expand both its labour productivity and its markets. Technology, as in the 19th century, but vastly more powerfully in the form of computers, the internet, television and mobile telephony, has thus helped both to increase the productivity of labour, and also to reach distant markets that had previously been inaccessible. These interests lie primarily, although not exclusively, in the hands of those who own the major global corporations, and the politicians in states that have sought to provide environments suitable for the accumulation of capital, notably through the enhancement of liberal democracy and a free market. The hegemonic mode of scientific enterprise in the 20th century has thus been supported both by states and by the private sector. As Habermas argued, these interests are primarily concerned with technical control, with issues to do with productivity of labour and above all with information. Significantly, Habermas also draws attention to the importance of individual learning processes; information itself, as argued by Castells (2000a), becomes integral to the productive forces that a society accumulates. In many ways, therefore, this knowledge-constitutive interest can be seen as paralleling the emerging dominance of the concept of information technology (IT) during the late 1980s and 1990s. The focus was primarily on using technologies to process and generate content and to develop systems capable of managing large amounts of information. The dominant interests in this context were those of the private sector, not only in providing the technologies to manage this information but also in producing and selling content itself as, for example, with e-learning resources. States too had a powerful interest in acquiring and managing information about citizens living within their territories, an emphasis that has continued to this day, with ever more sophisticated technologies now being used to monitor their activities, from health-service databases to digital surveillance systems.

Habermas's (1978) second type of knowledge-constitutive interest has a practical orientation towards understanding and communication, with a particular emphasis on language. This can be paralleled by the shift in focus that occurred during the late 1990s and early 2000s to a concern not so much with information alone, but also to an understanding of the equal importance of communication. In a representational sense, this was reflected in the increased use of the term ICT, which many now chose in preference to IT. At a practical level, this shift was enabled by the rapid expansion of mobile telephony and broadband connectivity, but more subtly it was also apparent in the greater emphasis placed on the value of networks and knowledge communities more widely. In part this resulted from a critique of what was seen as an over-emphasis on 'information', but it was also underlain by a fundamentally different conceptual framework. This distinction can clearly be seen in the contrasting arguments and usage of the terms 'information society' and 'knowledge society' discussed above. It was also reflected in a shift in the educational sector from a tendency primarily to use technologies to access information, to the placing of much greater emphasis on the value of collaborative learning through networks and the creation of knowledge communities. In part, this shift was led by civil society and international organisations such as UNESCO, with its emphasis on culture and education, but there were also clearly economic interests in maximising the profits to be gained both from the human desire to communicate and from the potential that increased networking opportunities offered for productivity gains.

One of the key significances of Habermas's framework of knowledge-constitutive interests is his suggestion that each of the modes through which we apprehend reality is grounded in different interests, is reflected in different social media, and is associated with different forms of scientific enquiry. In particular, Habermas derives his third approach from a critique of the previous two. He suggests not only that empirical–analytic science 'directs the utilisation of scientific information from an illusory viewpoint, namely that the practical mastery of history can be reduced to technical control of objectified processes', but also that hermeneutic science 'defends sterilized knowledge against the reflected appropriation of active traditions and locks up history in a museum' (Habermas, 1978, p. 316). In response, he proposes that we engage in a critical science that encourages a form of self-reflection that will enable the systematically distorted patterns of communication in society to be revealed for the benefit of all (see also Habermas, 1984, 1987). It is with such an agenda that ICT4D is primarily concerned. Unlike IT and ICT, where the main focus is on what *is* and what *can* be achieved, ICT4D is about what *should* be done and *how* we should do it. ICT4D therefore has a profoundly moral agenda. It is not primarily about the technologies themselves, but is instead concerned with how they can be used to enable the empowerment of poor and marginalised communities. This is a shared agenda and involves reflection on behalf of all those who aspire to make the world a fairer and better place. The challenge is to create effective partnerships that will enable this to be achieved. The remainder of this book explores how we might deliver such an agenda.

## Key readings

Castells, M. (2000a) *The Rise of the Network Society* (*The Information Age: economy, society and culture*, vol. 1, 2nd edn). Oxford: Blackwell

Habermas, J. (1978) *Knowledge and Human Interests*, 2nd edn, tr. J. Shapiro. London: Heinemann

Held, D. and McGrew, A. (2002) *Globalization/Anti-Globalization*. Cambridge: Polity

Mansell, R. and Wehn, U. (1998) *Knowledge Societies: information technology for sustainable development*. Oxford: Oxford University Press

Stiglitz, J.E. (2002) *Globalization and its Discontents*. London: Penguin

UNESCO (2005) *Towards Knowledge Societies*. Paris: UNESCO

Weigel, G. and Waldburger, D. (eds) (2004) *ICT4D – connecting people for a better world*. Berne and Kuala Lumpur: Swiss Agency for Development and Cooperation and Global Knowledge Partnership

## References

Adas, M. (1989) *Machines as the Measure of Men: science, technology, and ideologies of Western dominance*. Ithaca, NY: Cornell University Press

Amin, S. (1997) *Capitalism in the Age of Globalization: the management of contemporary society*. London: Palgrave Macmillan

APC and ITeM (Association for Progressive Communications and Third World Institute) (2007) *Global Information Society Watch 2007*. Uruguay: Association for Progressive Communications and Third World Institute

Arce, A. and Long, N. (eds) (2000) *Anthropology, Development and Modernities: exploring discourse, counter-tendencies and violence*. London: Routledge

Arendt, H. (1958) *The Human Condition*. Chicago: Chicago University Press

Bauman, Z. (1997) *Postmodernity and its Discontents*. New York: New York University Press

Bell, D. (1976) *The Coming of Post-Industrial Society: a venture in social forecasting*, 2nd edn. New York: Basic Books

Benkler, Y. (2006) *The Wealth of Networks: how social production transforms markets and freedom*. New Haven, CT: Yale University Press

Blair, T. (2005) Labour Party: the party of wealth creation. Speech on the economy and extending opportunity for all at Canary Wharf, London, 14 April 2005 (http://www.labour.org.uk/index.php?id = news2005&ux_news%5Bid%5D = tbspeech14 04&cHash = 3a8a5d5f0d, accessed 19 June 2006)

Blair, T. (2006) Letter from PM to Alistair Darling, 16 May 2006 (http://www.number10.gov.uk/output/Page9463.asp, accessed 19 June 2006)

Boserup, E. (1965) *The Conditions of Agricultural Growth: the economics of agrarian change under population pressure*. London: Allen and Unwin

Braudel, F. (1982) *The Wheels of Commerce (Civilization and Capitalism 15th–18th Century. Volume II)*. tr. S. Reynolds. London: William Collins and Harper & Row

Britz, J.J., Lor, P.J., Coetzee, I.E.M. and Bester, B.C. (2006) Africa as a knowledge society: a reality check. *International Information and Library Review*, 38, pp. 25–40

Bronner, S.E. (2004) *Reclaiming the Enlightenment: toward a politics of radical engagement*. New York: Columbia University Press

Castells, M. (1985) *High Technology, Space and Society*. Beverly Hills, CA: Sage

Castells, M. (1989) *The Informational City: information technology, economic restructuring, and the urban-regional process*. Oxford: Blackwell

Castells, M. (2000a) *The Rise of the Network Society* (*The Information Age: economy, society and culture*, vol. 1, 2nd edn). Oxford: Blackwell

Castells, M. (2000b) *The End of Millennium* (*The Information Age: economy, society and culture*, vol. 3, 2nd edn). Oxford: Blackwell

Castells, M. (2003) *The Power of Identity* (*The Information Age: economy, society and culture*, vol. 2, 2nd edn). Oxford: Blackwell

Cisco (2008) *TelePresence Overview*. (http://www.cisco.com/en/US/solutions/ns669/networking_solutions_products_genericcontent0900aecd80546cd0.html)

Corbridge, S. (1998) Development ethics: distance, difference, plausibility. *Ethics, Place and Environment*, 1 (1), pp. 35–54

Cox, K.R. (ed.) (1997) *Spaces of Globalization: reasserting the power of the local*. London: Guilford Press

Crewe, E. and Harrison, E. (1998) *Whose Development? An ethnography of aid*. London: Zed Books

Davenport, T.H. and Prusak, L. (1998) *Working Knowledge: how organizations manage what they know*. Cambridge, MA: Harvard University Press

Dreher, A. (2006) Does globalization affect growth? Evidence from a new Index of Globalization. *Applied Economics*, 38 (1), pp. 1091–1110

Drucker, P. (1966) *The Effective Executive*. New York: HarperBusiness

Drucker, P. (1969) *The Age of Discontinuity: guidelines to our changing society*. New York: Harper and Row

Easterly, W. (2006) *The White Man's Burden: why the West's efforts to aid the rest have done so much ill and so little good*. New York: Penguin

Escobar, A. (1995) *Encountering Development: the making and unmaking of the Third World*. Princeton, NJ: Princeton University Press

Feenberg, A. (1991) *Critical Theory of Technology*. Cambridge: Cambridge University Press

Feenberg, A. and Hannay, A. (eds) (1995) *Technology and the Politics of Knowledge*. Bloomington and Indianapolis: Indiana University Press

Flood, R. and Lockwood, M. (eds) (1986) *The Nature of Time*. Oxford: Basil Blackwell

Frank, A.G. (1969) *Latin America: underdevelopment or revolution*. New York: Monthly Review Press

Friedman, T.L. (2006) *The World is Flat: the globalized world in the twenty-first century*. London: Penguin

Ganguli, P. (2000) Intellectual property rights. Imperatives for the knowledge industry. *World Patent Information*, 22 (3), pp. 167–75

Gay, P. (1996) *The Enlightenment: an interpretation*. New York: W.W. Norton

Giddens, A. (1984) *The Constitution of Society: outline of the theory of structuration*. Cambridge: Polity Press

Greenberg, A. (2005) *ICTs for Poverty Alleviation: basic tool and enabling sector*. Stockholm: Sida

Gregory, D. and Urry, J. (eds) (1985) *Social Relations and Social Structures*. London: Edward Arnold

Habermas, J. (1978) *Knowledge and Human Interests*, 2nd edn, tr. J. Shapiro. London: Heinemann

Habermas, J. (1984) *The Theory of Communicative Action. Vol. 1: Reason and the Rationalization of Society*. Boston, MA: Beacon Press

Habermas, J. (1987) *The Theory of Communicative Action. Vol. 2: Lifeworld and System*. Cambridge: Polity Press

Habermas, J. (1994) *The Past as Future, Jürgen Habermas Interviewed by Michael Haller*, tr. M. Pensky, introduction by P. Hohendahl. Cambridge: Polity Press

Han, Sang-Bok (1997) The role of endogenous culture in socio-economic development of Korea. In Saraswati (ed.) (1997a) (http://www.ignca.nic.in/cd_05011.htm)

Hardin, G. (1968) The tragedy of the commons. *Science*, 162, pp. 1243–8

Harris, J. (2005) Great promise, hubris and recovery: a participant's history of development studies. In Kothari (ed.) (2005), pp. 17–46

Harris, J. and Harris, B. (1979) Development studies. *Progress in Human Geography*, 3, pp. 576–94

Harvey, D. (1989) *The Condition of Postmodernity*. Oxford: Blackwell

Harvey, D. (1996) *Justice, Nature and the Geography of Difference*. Oxford: Blackwell

Harvey, D. (2000) *Spaces of Hope*. Oxford: Blackwell

Heeks, R. (2002) Failure, success and improvisation of information systems projects in developing countries (Development Informatics Working Paper Series, no. 11). Manchester: Institute for Development Policy and Management, University of Manchester

Heidegger, M. (1977) *The Question Concerning Technology*, tr. W. Lovitt. New York: Harper and Row

Held, D. (1997) *Models of Democracy*. Stanford, CA: Stanford University Press

Held, D. and McGrew, A. (2002) *Globalization/Anti-Globalization*. Cambridge: Polity

Held, D., McGrew, A., Goldblatt, D. and Perraton, J. (1999) *Global Transformations: politics, economics and culture*. Cambridge: Polity Press

ITU (2006a) ITU market information and statistics (http://www.itu.int/ITU-D/ict/statistics)

ITU (2006b) World Telecommunication/ICT Development Report 2006 – summary page (http://www.itu.int/ITU-D/ict/publications/wtdr_06/index.html)

Jaffe, A.B. and Trajtenberg, M. (2002) *Patents, Citations, and Innovations: a window on the knowledge economy*. Cambridge, MA: The MIT Press

Kolakowski, L. (1972) *Positive Philosophy: from Hume to the Vienna Circle*. Harmondsworth: Penguin

Kothari, U. (ed.) (2005) *A Radical History of Development Studies: individuals, institutions and ideologies*. London and Cape Town: Zed Books and David Philip

Krishna, S. and Madon, S. (eds) (2003) *The Digital Challenge: information technology in the development context*. Aldershot: Ashgate

Lea, D.A.M. and Chaudhri, D.P. (eds) (1983) *Rural Development and the State: contradictions and dilemmas in developing countries*. London: Methuen

Lefebvre, H. (1974) *La production de l'éspace*. Paris: Anthropos

Lefebvre, H. (1981) *Critique de la vie quotidienne, III: de la modernité au modernisme (pour une metaphilosophie du quotidian)*. Paris: L'Arche

Lipton, M. (1977) *Why Poor People Stay Poor: a study of urban bias in world development*. London: Temple Smith

Machlup, F. (1962) *The Production and Distribution of Knowledge in the United States*. Princeton, NJ: Princeton University Press

Malthus, T.R. (1992) *An Essay on the Principle of Population*, selected and introduced by D. Winch. Cambridge: Cambridge University Press

Marx, K. (1970) *Critique of Hegel's Philosophy of Right*, tr. A. Jolin and J. O'Malley. London: Cambridge University Press (originally published in Deutsch-französische Jahrbücher, Paris, February 1844)

McClellan III, J.E. and Dorn, H. (2006) *Science and Technology in World History: an introduction*, 2nd edn. Baltimore, MD: Johns Hopkins University Press

McMichael, P. (2004) *Development and Social Change: a global perspective*, 3rd edn. Thousand Oaks, CA: Pine Forge

Menzies, G. (2002) *1421: the year China discovered the world*. London: Bantam Books

Merges, R.P., Menell, P.S. and Lemley, M.A. (2003) *Intellectual Property in the New Technological Age*, 3rd edn. Frederick, MD: Aspen Law and Business

Momsen, J.H. and Kinnaird, V. (eds) (1993) *Different Places, Different Voices: gender and development in Africa, Asia and Latin America*. London: Routledge

Momsen, J.H. and Townsend, J.G. (eds) (1987) *Geography of Gender in the Third World*. Albany, NY: State University of New York Press

Naím, M. (2000) Washington consensus or Washington confusion? *Foreign Policy*, 118, pp. 86–103

Norris, P. (2001) *Digital Divide: civic engagement, information poverty, and the internet worldwide*. New York and Cambridge: Cambridge University Press

North, D.C. and Thomas, R.P. (1973) *The Rise of the Western World: a new economic history*. Cambridge: Cambridge University Press

O'Neill, O. (1986) *Faces of Hunger: an essay on poverty, justice and development*. London: George Allen & Unwin

Parnwell, M. (2002) Agropolitan and bottom-up development. In *The Companion to Development Studies*, ed. V. Desai and R. Potter. London: Arnold, pp. 112–116

Peet, R. with Hartwick, E. (1999) *Theories of Development*. New York: Guilford Press

Pickles, J. and Smith, A. (eds) (1998) *Theorizing Transition: the political economy of change in Central and Eastern Europe*. London: Routledge

Pippin, R.B. (1995) On the notion of technology as ideology. In Feenberg and Hannay (eds) (1995), pp. 43–61

Point Topic (2005) Broadband, the internet and the election (http://www.point-topic.com/content/dslanalysis/UK %20election%20guide.htm)

Porat, M. (1977) *The Information Economy: definition and measurement* (Publication 77-12(1)). Washington, DC: US Department of Commerce, Office of Telecommunications

Poynder, R. (2003) Reclaiming the digital commons. *Information Today*, 20 (6), pp. 33–6

Price, W.H. (1913) *The English Patents of Monopoly*. Cambridge, MA: Harvard University Press

Rahnema, M. and Bawtree, V. (eds) (1997) *The Post-Development Reader*. London: Zed Books

Roberts, P. (2000) Knowledge, information and literacy. *International Review of Education*, 46 (5), pp. 433–53

Rostow, W. (1960) *The Stages of Economic Growth: a non-communist manifesto*. Cambridge: Cambridge University Press

Sachs, J. (2005) *The End of Poverty: how we can make it happen in our lifetime*. London: Penguin Books

Sack, R.D. (1980) *Conceptions of Space in Social Thought: a geographic perspective*. Cambridge: Cambridge University Press

Saraswati, B. (ed.) (1997a) *Integration of Endogenous Cultural Dimension into Development*. New Delhi: D.K. Printworld (http://ignca.nic.in/cd_05.htm)

Saraswati, B. (1997b) Cultures and development: guideline questions. In Saraswati (ed.) (1997a) (http://www.ignca.nic.in/cd_05005.htm)

Smith, D.M. (2000) *Moral Geographies: ethics in a world of difference*. Edinburgh: Edinburgh University Press

Soja, E. (1989) *Postmodern Geographies: the reassertion of space in critical social theory*. London: Verso

Soros, G. (1998) *The Crisis of Global Capitalism: open society endangered.* New York: PublicAffairs

Soros, G. (2002) *George Soros on Globalization.* New York: PublicAffairs

Steinberg, R.H. (1997) Trade–environment negotiations in the EU, NAFTA, and WTO: regional trajectories of rule development. *The American Journal of International Law,* 91 (2), pp. 231–67

Stiglitz, J.E. (2002) *Globalization and its Discontents.* London: Penguin

Stöhr, W.B. and Taylor, D.R.F. (eds) (1981) *Development from Above or Below? The dialectics of regional planning in developing countries.* Chichester: John Wiley

Thompson, K. (1976) *August Comte: the foundation of sociology.* London: Nelson

UNESCO (2005) *Towards Knowledge Societies.* Paris: UNESCO

Unwin, T. (1992) *The Place of Geography.* Harlow: Longman

Unwin, T. (2000) A waste of space? *Transactions of the Institute of British Geographers,* new series, 25 (1), pp. 11–29

Unwin, T. (2004) Beyond budgetary support: pro-poor development agendas for Africa. *Third World Quarterly,* 25 (8), pp. 1501–23

Unwin, T. (2005) *Partnerships in Development Practice: evidence from multi-stakeholder ICT4D partnership practice in Africa.* Paris: UNESCO

Unwin, T. (2007) No end to poverty. *Journal of Development Studies,* 43 (5), pp. 929–53

Unwin, T. and de Bastion, G. (2008) Bridging the digital divide. In *International Encyclopedia of Human Geography,* ed. R. Kitchin and N. Thrift. Oxford: Elsevier (in press)

Wallerstein, I. (1983) *Historical Capitalism.* London: Verso

Wallerstein, I. (1999) Globalization or the age of transition? A long-term view of the trajectory of the world system (http://fbc.binghamton.edu/iwtrajws.htm)

Weigel, G. (2004) ICT4D today – enhancing knowledge and people-centred communication for development and poverty reduction. In Weigel and Waldburger (eds), pp. 16–42

Weigel, G. and Waldburger, D. (eds) (2004) *ICT4D – connecting people for a better world.* Berne and Kuala Lumpur: Swiss Agency for Development and Cooperation and Global Knowledge Partnership

Williamson, J. (ed.) (1990) *Latin American Adjustment: how much has happened?* Washington, DC: Institute for International Economics

World Bank (2006) *2006 Information and Communications for Development (IC4D): global trends and policies.* Washington, DC: World Bank

World Bank Institute (2007) *Building Knowledge Economies: advanced strategies for development.* Washington, DC: World Bank Institute

# 3 | Information and communication in development practices

## Tim Unwin

- Different stakeholders in 'development' have varying information and communication needs. It is essential to understand these needs before we identify how they may be delivered effectively through the use of new ICTs.
- Lessons learnt from the long history of using diverse media in development practices remain highly relevant for the implementation of contemporary ICT4D initiatives.
- Successful communication is multidimensional and complex; it is much more than simply the dissemination of information.
- It is important to focus especially on the needs of poor people and marginalised communities when implementing information and communication strategies that are intended to have a significant development impact.

Information and communication are central to the implementation of development, however we choose to define it. In undertaking any development activity it is thus essential for information about the activity to be produced and for communication between participants to occur. The purpose of this chapter is to provide an overall framework through which we can interpret the role of information and communication in development practice. Only then can we explore the ways in which new information and communication technologies (ICTs) can be used in support of this agenda.

A fundamental failing of many previous approaches to ICT4D has been that they have tended to concentrate first on the technologies and only later have they addressed the potential that ICTs might offer to poor and marginalised communities (see for example Baldwin and Thomas, 2005; Schware, 2005). Many initiatives that have been implemented within such a framework have tended to be supply-led rather than demand-driven. As a result, they have often insufficiently delivered on the real information and communication needs of poor people, and have therefore been unsustainable once initial external funding and support has been consumed. By beginning explicitly with an exploration of the information and communication needs and practices that are important *for* development, it will then be possible more clearly to identify how we can use ICTs most effectively in delivering these needs. More generally, it is essential for the successful implementation of any ICT4D initiatives that they are driven by the interests of poor and marginalised people. Academics and practitioners therefore need to begin by seeking to understand better the development objectives that these people choose to define (see for example World Bank, no date; Schilderman, 2002).

## Information and communication in development

Each of the diverse participants and stakeholders involved in ICT4D initiatives has their own particular needs, and such needs vary depending in part on how we choose to define development. The information and communication needs of those involved in top-down and supply-led development initiatives are thus very different from those working in bottom-up empowerment-focused activities. However, the important point to emphasise is that new ICTs can be highly effective in delivering both of these sets of needs. Moreover, there is a long history of usage of 'information and communication' in development practice, from which those seeking to use ICTs effectively in delivering such objectives have much to learn.

### *A framework for understanding information and communication needs*

The ways in which we choose to think about development as a process have a fundamental influence over the groups of people we consider to be important in its implementation. As was stressed in Chapter 2, the top-down modernisation models of development that dominated the 1960s were fundamentally different in focus and intent from bottom-up and participatory approaches that came to be adopted in many parts of the world in the 1980s and especially in the 1990s (Richardson and Paisley, 1998; Coldevin, 2003). Mchombu (2004) thus differentiates between two very different types of information flow for development: the modernisation model and the people-centred model. In the former:

> To produce the change from underdevelopment to development, information needed to be communicated to peasants and small farmers through the mass media. It was believed that radio, newspapers, television and books would change their culture, attitudes, and the traditional way of life. The result would be a new type of people who would be interested in accepting modern Western ideas of development.
>
> (Mchombu, 2004, p. 16)

In contrast, as he goes on to say:

> The role of information services in the people-centred or human development approach is very different from the role of information in the modernization or economic growth model of development. Some of the major differences are:

a  Access to information is for all groups in the population (including women, youth, and rural and urban poor people);

b  Information is a tool and access to information is a process for building self-reliance, empowerment, civil society, participation and gender equality;

c  Indigenous or traditional knowledge and locally-generated information are given high status;

d  Traditional channels of communication are respected and not regarded as barriers to development.

(Mchombu, 2004, p. 19)

There are many other variations around these two poles, but Mchombu's summary usefully characterises the fundamental difference that exists between on the one hand a model in which information is to be communicated from those who know (the experts) to those who do not (the ignorant), and on the other a model in which communities share information in a much more open and flexible manner for the benefit of all concerned. The former is predicated on an assumption that some information, often derived from European or North American science, is more significant for the development process than other, more traditional kinds of knowledge. Accordingly, the essence of development is to persuade less knowledgeable people to accept this new information because it will then benefit them in their pursuit of whatever it is that is considered to be development. Such an instrumental logic has lain behind much of the research and practice on innovation diffusion (Binswanger and Ruttan, 1978; Brown, 1981; Rogers, 1983; Unwin, 1987), as well as the models of agricultural extension that pervaded the practice of rural development in the 1960s and 1970s, finding particular expression in the dissemination of the technological innovations associated with the green revolution (Pearse, 1980; Bayliss-Smith and Wanmali, 1984). There is little doubt that this transfer of information and scientific knowledge, primarily from 'developed' to 'less developed' countries, did enable considerable strides to be taken in increasing food production across the world, but at the same time there was also an underlying interest in encouraging people in poorer countries to adopt 'Western' ideas and consequently also to become increasingly engaged in a global economy dominated by the interests of European and North American capital. As Mchombu (2004, p. 16) goes on to note, within this model 'All traditional forms of information and communication (music, dance, poetry, theatre and indigenous knowledge) were condemned because they sustained cultural forms of social structure and authority' and were thus inimical to these expansionist economic interests. There was thus an intellectual and a practical elitism that dominated both the types of information and the media used to disseminate them. Such elitism is still a characteristic of much intellectual discourse about development to this day, particularly in the field of ICT4D.

In contrast, community-based and participatory approaches to development have focused much more on a bottom-up and shared experience of information. Indeed, if the modernising approach concentrated primarily on ensuring that the optimal *information* was transmitted to potential adopters of these new technologies, people-centred human development approaches have instead concentrated mainly on the *communication* aspects of information sharing (see also Melkote and Steeves, 2001). These latter have been typified by the participatory approaches to development championed by Chambers (1983, 1997, 2004; but more critically see also Mohan, 1999, and Hickey and Mohan, 2006), as well as more recent practical guides to communication, such as Bessette's (2004) handbook entitled *Involving the Community: a guide to participatory development communication*. This, for example, asserts that:

> Communication is an essential part of participatory research and development. As the researcher working with a community or as a development practitioner, you are first of all a communication actor. The way you approach a local community, the attitude you adopt in interacting with community members, the way you understand and discuss issues, the way you collect and share information, all involve ways of establishing communication with people.
>
> (Bessette, 2004, p. 7; see also Tacchi *et al.*, 2003)

Regardless of the particular approach taken, all stakeholders involved in development activities have an interest in information and communication. Broadly speaking, such stakeholders can be grouped into seven main categories: poor individuals and marginalised communities; the majority of consumers and producers within a population; governments; donor agencies; civil society; the private sector; and academics. Despite the present rhetoric of emphasis on the importance of information and communication for poor people, it is surprising how little rigorous empirical research has actually been undertaken specifically on this subject (but see Standing, 2000; Melkote and Steeves, 2001; Coldevin, 2003; Souter *et al.*, 2005). For the very poorest, the most important information needs are those concerned with the basics of survival: where to find food at times of famine; how to avoid armed gangs seeking to steal during times of civil unrest; where to find shelter from violent storms; where rich tourists might be found from whom to beg. For children living and working on the streets, the information they need likewise includes such things as when a police raid might occur, who might have a job that they could do, or where best to find safe shelter for the night. Rarely do the priorities of development 'experts', focusing as they do on themes such as Education For All or Sustainable Development, address these essential information needs of the very poorest. What, for example, are the information needs of the group of out-of-school youths in the Philippines shown in the photograph below?

*Out-of-school youths in the Philippines, 2006: what are their information and communication needs? (source: Tim Unwin).*

Nalaka Gunawardena, Director of the non-profit media organisation TVE Asia Pacific, in criticising much media reporting of poverty, has argued passionately that:

> The information needs — and wants — of the poor are as wide and varied as everybody else's. Sarvodaya, Sri Lanka's largest development organisation, once surveyed the information needs of poor people in rural and semi-urban areas.
>
> It was found they wanted information on health and nutrition, as well as details of bank loans, foreign jobs and insurance policies. There was also considerable interest in world affairs, new books and movies, national politics, and questions being asked in parliament. To ignore this diversity and assume that farmers only want to know about the weather and crop prices is grossly insulting. We must stop treating poor people as some kind of subhuman species with a simpler set of living needs and aspirations.
>
> (Gunawardena, 2005)

All too frequently, donors, governments and civil society organisations think that they already know what poor people need and then try to find ways of delivering it (although for a contrasting view, see World Bank, no date). Leaders of the world's countries, supported by numerous academic researchers and consultants, have thus identified the Millennium Development Goals (MDGs) as being essential for the elimination of

*(continued on page 46)*

**Table 3.1** *An indicative framework for understanding the information and communication needs of stakeholders in development*

| | Economic | Social | Political | Ideological/cultural |
|---|---|---|---|---|
| **The poorest individuals and marginalised communities** | | | | |
| Information about | Sources of food<br>Shelter<br>Education | Health<br>Education | State welfare systems<br>Institutions of oppression<br>Education | Religion<br>Education |
| Communication with | Employers<br>Those providing means of survival | Family and relatives<br>Friendship groups<br>Civil society groups | Governments<br>Human rights organisations | Prayer and meditation |
| **The majority of the population (seen primarily as producers and consumers)** | | | | |
| Information about | Employment opportunities<br>Prices of goods in different markets<br>Education | Health information<br>Accepted norms of social behaviour<br>Education | Electoral information<br>Systems of representation<br>Legal systems<br>Education | Religion<br>Cultural activities<br>Education |
| Communication with | Labour organisations<br>Employers<br>Sellers of commodities | Family and relatives<br>Friendship groups | Government at various scales<br>Political parties | Entertainment<br>Religious/cultural groups<br>Prayer and meditation |
| **Governments (including state organisations)** | | | | |
| Information about | The economy (production, consumption and exchange)<br>Taxation revenue | Social and demographic statistics | National political opinion polls<br>International institutions and treaties | Cultural statistics<br>Ethical agendas |
| Communication with | Private sector corporations<br>Trade unions | Different government departments and agencies<br>Rural extension workers meeting with farmers | International organisations<br>Systems of monitoring and surveillance<br>Members of their own and other political parties | Religious organisations<br>Cultural organisations |
| **Donor agencies (multilateral and bilateral)** | | | | |
| Information about | Global and national economic growth policies<br>Their own government's agendas<br>Needs of recipient countries | Social conditions in recipient countries | Global and national governance agendas<br>International treaties and entities<br>National and international political agendas | Ideological conditions in recipient countries |

|  | | | | |
|---|---|---|---|---|
| Communication with | Governments and management boards | Sharing a sense of community within the organisation, and between organisations | Recipient governments / Other donors and international agencies | Religious organisations and faith communities / Cultural organisations |

**Civil society and non-governmental organisations**

|  | | | | |
|---|---|---|---|---|
| Information about | Sources of funding / Economic needs of beneficiaries | Social needs of beneficiaries | Political needs of beneficiaries | Cultural needs of beneficiaries |
| Communication with | Donors / Beneficiaries / Global communities | Other civil society organisations | Governments / International agencies | Religious organisations and faith communities |

**Private sector (international and local)**

|  | | | | |
|---|---|---|---|---|
| Information about | Commodity prices / Market information / Tax regimes / Wage rates | Good practices to maintain labour force | Regulatory environment / News about political stability and instability in different parts of the world | Cultural factors influencing the market / Cultural practices in doing business |
| Communication with | Customers and employees / Marketing organisations / Shareholders / Suppliers | Employees / Civil society organisations and trade unions | Government officials / Donor agencies | Peer communities advocating particular ideological stances |

**Universities / research institutions (including science and technology organisations)**

|  | | | | |
|---|---|---|---|---|
| Information about | International student market / National and international funding opportunities | Demographic and social trends in market countries | Politics of university funding agencies and governments / Political attitudes to education | Public attitudes to research and higher education |
| Communication with | Students and research networks / Funding agencies | Staff and students / Research and learning communities | Governments and international agencies | Academic communities |

*Note:* The examples of information and communication within this table are chosen to be indicative, rather than a comprehensive listing of all possible types of information and communication

*Source:* Tim Unwin

poverty (see for example Sachs, 2005). Donors have in turn sought how best to deliver on the various MDG targets such as universal primary education and reducing child mortality. Among the available means, ICTs have been identified as offering potentially powerful solutions, and numerous ICT4D initiatives have thus been launched (Weigel and Waldburger, 2004; Greenberg, 2005; Schware, 2005). All too frequently, though, these initiatives have failed to make a significant impact on poverty, usually because they have insufficiently considered the real practical needs of poor people.

Table 3.1 provides an outline framework for considering the information and communication needs of different stakeholders in terms of their economic, social, political and ideological or cultural dimensions. This is only indicative. Its central purpose is to provide a conceptual checklist for those involved in designing ICT4D activities, and the specific examples given are merely suggestive. While the dimensions and categories overlap, such a framework is helpful in that it focuses on the specific requirements that different groups of people and organisations have. For example, most people like to have some economic information about their employment opportunities, wage rates and the prices of goods for sale in the shops. Politically, it is useful for them to know about the legal system of the country in which they live, as well as the system of electoral representation. They communicate socially with their friends and families, and culturally they may participate in a diversity of religious ceremonies or festivals. In contrast, the interests of private-sector companies are rather different, focusing mainly on the need for economic information about such things as the markets in which they are operating, the prices of commodities to be found therein and the minimum wages that they need to pay. They are also, though, interested in cultural information about the practices that should be followed in conducting business in different parts of the world, as well as political details of the regulatory environment and tax regimes in which they are going to be operating. In terms of communication, the private sector is particularly concerned with means of interacting with employees, customers, suppliers and shareholders, as well as influencing the political decisions made by government officials and obtaining feedback from customers about ways in which they can further develop specific markets. Within the private sector, the media industry plays a very specific role, in that it both facilitates the flow of information and also benefits from the demand for increasing amounts of communication across the world.

There is increasing recognition among many involved in the practice of development that more attention needs to be paid to the information and communication needs of each of these diverse stakeholders. In 2006, the team in the UK's Department for International Development (DFID) responsible for information and communication thus justified its role by emphasising the following six points:

- Access to information (e.g. free media) is a critical driver of social and political change.
- The acquisition and use of knowledge is critical to the development process.
- Improving the content of what is communicated, and including poor people in communication processes are important factors in strengthening service delivery and the accountability of governments, as well as in empowering poor people to make better decisions about their livelihoods and participate in public debate and dialogue.
- Participative and accountable policy making requires improved information.
- Improved communications is in many countries a pre-condition for peace & reconciliation.
- Improved communications and information is in many countries a pre-condition for economic growth.

(http://www.dfid.gov.uk/aboutdfid/organisation/icd.asp, accessed 28 June 2006)

Such an approach clearly indicates the significance of both information and communication across the economic, political and social dimensions of development.

It is important to recognise that there are nevertheless many different types of information and communication. In particular, information once created can simply gather dust and not be used: the fate of most academic papers published in international journals! In contrast, communication is a dynamic process that involves both producers and recipients. Moreover, while most studies focus on the visual and the aural aspects of communication in development, we must remember that communication involves all of our senses of sight, hearing, touch, smell and taste. This is particularly important when working with people with disabilities, as for example with blind people using the sense of touch through Braille to read. All too often these other senses are ignored in our analyses of communication, and we need to reinsert them if we are to gain a full understanding of how best to serve the communication needs of marginalised people.

Another important point to emphasise is that each category of stakeholder identified within Table 3.1 is itself highly diversified. In particular, there are significant gender, ethnic and cultural differences within each of the categories mentioned, and these have considerable influence over the types of information needed and the ways in which communication is undertaken. Numerous studies (see for example Derbyshire, 2003; Souter et al., 2005) have shown not only the differential access that women and men have to particular kinds of ICT, but also the varying ways in which people of different gender or cultural background choose to use the same hardware or software. Despite this, it is remarkable that many standard texts on human–computer interaction or digital design (see for example

Dix *et al.*, 2004; Benyon *et al.*, 2005) fail to pay sufficient heed to the importance of these differences, thereby helping inadvertently to ensure that technology reinforces rather than changes their impact. If this is to alter, it is critically important that those involved in designing ICTs pay specific attention to the gendered and culturally specific dimensions of their use.

Table 3.1 also highlights the overarching importance of education and learning in responding to the information and communication needs of people in all of the different stakeholder categories. Education not only provides access to information content across all the four domains of human experience, but it also provides one of the most important contexts through which we learn how to communicate effectively. While much learning takes place informally, formal education is becoming increasingly important in helping people to master the requirements of modern systems of communication, as with the use of the communication aspects of learning management systems or even the internet. In the implementation of ICT4D programmes, it is therefore essential to ensure that sufficient attention is paid to the provision of appropriate training in the acquisition of information and the mechanisms through which communication takes place.

As a reminder of this diversity of information and communication, and also to provide a setting within which the use of new ICTs can be interpreted, the next section briefly reviews the importance of traditional knowledge systems in development practice. This is followed by an overview of the diversity of ways in which various media have been used to communicate and to share information in such systems, focusing especially on theatre.

### *Traditional knowledge systems*

The top-down model of information dissemination that dominated much development practice in the 1960s and 1970s placed little emphasis on the traditional knowledge systems of indigenous peoples. Development was thus premised on the transfer of 'useful' information from knowledgeable 'experts' to 'peasants' who were by and large assumed to be ignorant (see Harriss, 1992). Increased research since then on traditional knowledge systems has emphasised the inappropriateness of such simplistic approaches (see for example Chapman, 1983). This in turn has necessitated recognition of the diversity of ways in which various kinds of information are evaluated and acted upon by stakeholders in development activities. Increasingly, emphasis is being placed not only on recording such traditional knowledge systems, but also on exploring how they can be used to deliver contemporary development objectives. In South Africa, for example, the National Research Foundation has 'indigenous knowledge systems' as one of its key focus areas. As the Foundation argues:

> We need to understand IK (Indigenous Knowledge) and its role in community life from an integrated perspective that includes both spiritual and material aspects of a society as well as the complex relation between them. At the same

time, it is necessary to understand and to explore the potential contribution of IK to local development. Further, research into the protection of IK and its utilisation for the benefit of its owners and the communities where it is practised is also needed. The present status of IK is that these forms of knowledge have hitherto been misunderstood and as such suppressed.

(http://www.nrf.ac.za/focusareas/iks, accessed 26 June 2006)

At a global scale, the World Bank has also initiated an exciting Indigenous Knowledge Program (http://www.worldbank.org/afr/ik) intended both to ensure that awareness is raised about the role that community-based practices can play in enriching the development process, and also to 'help development practitioners to mainstream indigenous/traditional knowledge into the activities of development partners and to optimize the benefits of development assistance, especially to the poor' (see for example Prakash, 2002; Dava et al., 2002).

Such initiatives highlight the importance of understanding the traditional knowledge systems within which any ICT4D practice is to be implemented. Without sufficient understanding of, and adaptation to, these systems, it is unlikely that such interventions will be successful, and the probability of unanticipated consequences will be much higher than if such practices are tailored to the specific needs of the communities with whom they are designed. The Food and Agriculture Organization (FAO) of the United Nations has, for example, recognised that much of its early work in using communication for development had concentrated either on 'information dissemination and motivation' or on providing 'education and training for field workers and rural producers' (Coldevin, 2003, p. 3). As Coldevin (2003, p. 3) goes on to emphasise, the former of these was 'mainly concerned with simply informing rural people of new ideas, services and technologies, and changing attitudes toward improving their quality of life'. It was scarcely surprising therefore that so many of these initiatives were not as successful as had originally been hoped. As a result, the FAO and the World Bank (2000) have more recently recommended a new framework for agricultural knowledge and information systems which places the farmer at the centre of a 'knowledge triangle', consisting of education, research and extension (see Figure 3.1). These are each then treated as complementary services that are designed to respond to farmers' needs for enhanced productivity, income, welfare and sustainable development.

### Theatre, dance and cinema in development

So far, this chapter has argued that there have broadly been two strategies in the use of information and communication for development: one that is top-down, concerned with communicating beneficial development information from those who know to those who need to know; and the other that is participatory and community-based, with its focus on shared learning and communication about mutual development needs and solutions.

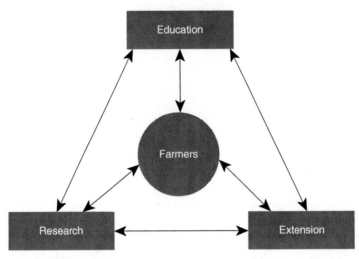

Figure 3.1 *Framework for agricultural knowledge and information systems for rural development (AKIS/RD)* (*source:* FAO and World Bank, 2000, http://www.fao.org/sd/EXdirect/EXre0027.htm).

These distinctions are particularly well illustrated by the changes in the use of theatre, dance and cinema in development practice over the last fifty years. These are discussed here both to illustrate that information and communication have been important in development practice long before the advent of ICTs, and also to emphasise that those implementing ICT-based programmes have much to learn from the successes and failures of previous such media-based initiatives.

Many different kinds of media were well established as means of disseminating information during the first half of the 20th century under colonial regimes across the world. This was particularly so in the context of education in general, and agricultural development in particular. Books, magazines and pamphlets have always been of fundamental importance to those seeking to encourage improvements in agriculture. It is thus no coincidence that the one book the Romans are reputed to have saved from the burning of the Carthaginian libraries in their destruction of the city in 146 BC was an agricultural treatise by Mago probably written in the 4th century BC (Mahaffy, 1890). Agricultural works, from Cato (243–149 BC), Varro (116–27 BC) and Columella (1st century AD) (Unwin, 1991) to the writings of Arthur Young in the 18th century (Mingay, 1975), have played a central part in encouraging people to adopt new agricultural techniques and thereby to enhance levels of food production and profit. However, in the late colonial period, other media increasingly began to be used to convey development agendas. Gibbs (1999) thus describes the role of Alec Dickson (1950a, b) in using a wide range of media in the late 1940s to encourage community development in the Gold Coast, later Ghana, focusing particularly on drama. Such an emphasis in this part of Africa has been long-lasting, with Okagbu (1998, p. 25) for example commenting much more recently that the Ghanaian government's Non-Formal Education Division had initiated an adult literacy programme 'in which theatre, especially role-play, had featured prominently'.

Much traditional use of theatre in development practice has tended to concentrate on the way in which it could be used by those in power and with knowledge to convey messages to those that they wanted to encourage to make changes to their behaviour (more widely see Richmond et al., 1990; Versényi, 1993; Banham et al., 1999; Bhatia, 2004). Indeed, this concept of theatre for development (TfD) has generated a wide range of literature and practices (see for example Kidd, 1982; Levert and Mumma, 1995; Salhi, 1998; van Erven, 2001; Nicholson, 2005). Since the 1970s, earlier approaches to the use of theatre simply as a vehicle through which information could be conveyed have increasingly been criticised, building especially on the work of two Brazilians, the pedagogic philosophy of Paulo Freire (1970 and 1972) and the theatrical theory of Augosto Boal (1979) (de Costa, 1992). Freire emphasised in particular the role of liberation through education, and the way that critical dialogue can contribute to empowerment. Building in part on such ideas, Boal (1979) advocated ways in which theatre could be placed at the service of the oppressed, especially through bringing spectators and performers together to establish new senses of community. As a result, as Okagbu (1998) has commented, there has been a shift from a product-based theatre for development that focused merely on the transmission of ideas, to a much more process-oriented practice that models itself on input from indigenous communities, on local solutions rather than external 'expert' advice, and on self-reliance in development.

This increasing emphasis on local practices and solutions has led to a much greater emphasis on traditional styles of performance and theatre practice from across the world, typified for example by 'the *Pungwe* in Zimbabwe, the *Kwaghir* in the Katsina-Ala projects in Benue and the *Lifela* by the Marotholi Theatre Group in Lesotho', all of which involve communities in theatre (Okagbu, 1998, p. 36). It has also helped to develop innovative ways of using theatre to contribute to the resolution of wider social agendas and issues, as with the effects of HIV/AIDS, especially in Africa (Elliott et al., 1996; Bagamayo College of Arts et al., 2002), and responses to environmental disasters such as the 1999 earthquake in Taiwan (Chang, 2005). While such community-based theatre can enable people to gain a better understanding of their conditions, it is not without its problems. Chang (2005) notes the difficulties in undertaking such practices, especially where the family is paramount over the individual as with Confucianism, and in which people are afraid of exposing intimate family information more widely within a community. Such concerns over the use of theatre are also evident in the way in which it has been used as a means both of coercion and of empowerment at times of war. Plastow (1999, p. 111) has noted the importance of theatre in reaching illiterate communities without access to mass media, but in her study of the conflict between Eritrea and Ethiopia she emphasises that it has been used not only 'as a tool of rebellion and empowerment' but also 'as a means of controlling and repressing the people'. There are therefore complex issues that need to be addressed surrounding the ethics of practice in the use of theatre for development, some of which have usefully been considered by Joseph (2005) in the context of Kenya, where he draws attention to the need for the interests of the many different stakeholders to be made transparent.

This ambivalent role of theatre in development practice has been particularly well explored by Ahmed (2002) in his study of Bangladesh. Here, since the late 1970s, NGOs such as Proshika have been putting on plays designed to address critical social issues such as injustices, polygamy, gender discrimination, arbitrary divorce, environmental issues and various health practices. 'These issues supposedly come from the people themselves', but as Ahmed (2002, p. 211) comments, they 'are selected by the village co-ordination committee, the union co-ordination committee of the troupe and each play projects a clear top-down message'. More significantly, he notes that almost all of the funding for such initiatives comes from international donor organisations, and that such activities therefore serve 'globalisation in the name of poverty reduction': 'the NGOs are caught in the contradiction of either empire building for self-sustenance or serving as pseudo-mercenaries for survival. Through subtle manipulation, the interests of multi-national capital determine the donor's agendas, which in turn determine the issues taken up by the NGOs in their plays – all in the name of the people' (Ahmed, 2002, p. 211).

There are three significant lessons for those engaged in ICT4D practices to learn from this brief exploration of the use of theatre in development. First, the use of information and communication in development practice has been well established over many years. The application of new ICTs should therefore not be seen as representing a totally new departure, but rather we should examine how it can build on previous experiences in the use of information and communication in development, as exemplified by theatre, music and dance. Second, any modality of development practice, be it theatre or the use of new ICTs, can have both positive and negative repercussions, depending on the purposes for which it is used and the cultural context in which it is applied. Third, there is good evidence that the most transformatory experiences, especially for poor people, are encountered when there is plural reflexivity, with communication being seen as a multiple process of exchange rather than merely as the one-way transfer of information.

## Information in development practice

To appreciate the ways in which new ICTs can have a positive influence on development practice, it is essential to begin by understanding the information needs of those involved in development. As outlined in the previous section, these needs vary enormously depending on the kind of development that is being promoted, and on the groups of people who have interests in such information. In Chapter 2, 'information' was defined as processed raw 'facts' or data, and was differentiated from 'knowledge', which was interpreted as information that had been incorporated into human understanding and action. However, if we are fully to appreciate the significance of information in development we need to delve a little deeper beneath these definitions.

### What is information for development?

In much literature on ICT4D the concept of 'information' is not seen as being at all problematic (see for example Weigel and Waldburger, 2004; Greenberg, 2005). Information is something that exists; it is 'out there', for use in a diversity of ways. But even this implies at the very least that information must somehow be produced, stored and accessed if it is to be of any value. Information needs to be received and understood. Very rapidly, a discussion of the meaning and significance of 'information' becomes much more complex.

Floridi (1999a, b, 2002) has usefully drawn attention to four different ways in which the notion of information is used: information *about* something, as with statistical data about a country or the information contained within a travel guide; information *as* something, referring for example to the information contained within DNA or fingerprints; information that is used *for* something, such as algorithms or the instructions that tell computers what to do; and finally information contained *in* something, as with a pattern or constraint. One of the particularly interesting things about the interface between information and technology, as Floridi (1999a) has noted, is that recent advances in computing, such as artificial intelligence (Russell and Norvig, 2002), ontology engineering (Maedche, 2002) and the semantic web (Daconta *et al.*, 2003), have opened up a whole new array of philosophical agendas that await detailed exploration.

Not only is information of interest to philosophers, but it is also central to the interdisciplinary fields of informatics and information science (see Munasinhe, 1989), as well as to information theory. *Informatics* is a term that emerged in the 1950s and 1960s in Germany (*Informatik*), France (*informatique*) and Russia (*informatika*) to refer to what in the English-speaking world was becoming known as computer science. A widely accepted definition of informatics is that it is the 'study of the structure, behaviour, and interactions of natural and engineered computational systems' (http://www.inf.ed.ac.uk/about/vision.html). In the USA, the term informatics became adopted by computer scientists to distinguish what they did from the work of library scientists who had begun to adopt the term information science to describe their own work. Increasingly, the term informatics is being used in association with particular sub-disciplinary branches, especially with health or medical informatics (van Bemmel and Musen, 1997), but also in social informatics (Kling, 1999), bio-informatics (Baldi and Brunak, 2001) and ecological informatics (Recknagel, 2006).

In contrast, information theory is a branch of applied mathematics that emerged initially in the 1940s, focusing particularly on the quantification of data and utilising probability theory and statistics (Shannon and Weaver, 1949; Ash, 1965; Mackay, 2003). Today, it is particularly concerned with cryptography (or information security) and with coding theory (involving the compression of data into as few bits as possible). Although often ignored in works on ICT4D, these are all issues that have as much importance in poor countries as they do in the major economies of the world. Indeed, access to the benefits of advanced, but often expensive, systems of encryption and authentication will become increasingly significant across Africa and Asia if poor countries and people are fully to benefit from the potential of ICTs in fields such as electronic commerce and e-government. There is therefore considerable opportunity for the development of indigenous open-source information security solutions in such contexts.

For the purposes of this book, it is important to recognise three particular characteristics of information: it is produced, it needs to be stored, and it is consumed. Each of these raises important issues that all those involved in ICT4D activities need to consider in implementing their initiatives. Many different kinds of information are produced every moment of the day, and new ICTs have greatly facilitated this process leading to an ever-increasing amount and diversity of information generation. The process of information production is embedded within the societies in which it takes place, and therefore reflects their gendered, ethnic, political and social structures. Traditionally, for example, information produced by elites has generally been deemed to be of more importance and value than that produced by those seen to be of less social or political importance. In a market economy, information is valued largely in terms of its utility, and in the past this has closely reflected the balance of supply and demand. Information for which there is little demand has thus usually been considered to be of low value, whereas people have been willing to pay large amounts for information that they deem to be important. In implementing ICT4D initiatives, it is therefore important to reflect on issues such as who produces information, the reasons why they do so, the audience for which it is intended, and the format in which it is produced.

One of the most recent changes that the internet has enabled, for example, has been a transformation in the traditional structures of power in the production of information. This is best typified in the production of weblogs, or blogs. These emerged as recently as the late 1990s, and were developed using new Web technologies from the earlier online diaries that had begun to appear at the start of that decade. From only some 100 Web diaries in existence in 1996, over 51.3 million weblogs had been created by August 2006 (http://www.technorati.com, accessed 16 August 2006). The rapid expansion of this entirely new form of information is of particular interest given the way in which blogs transcend most traditional forms of information dissemination, and have enabled novel forms of political activism to take shape. They are widely seen as being one of the main ways in which the Web has become increasingly democratised in recent years.

All of these factors are closely related to the ways in which information is stored. Traditionally, libraries, record offices and filing cabinets have been the main means through which physical information has been stored. However, it is also important to emphasise that for an individual it is their own human brain that is the most important information storage system. For societies without a written form of language, oral traditions are likewise the means through which information is stored and passed on to future generations. This highlights the considerable importance not only of the location of information storage but also of the format in which it is stored. Language and literacy are essential elements of information storage and retrieval (more widely see Roberts, 2000). As with the production of information, new ICTs have completely transformed the storage of information, in terms of both where and how it is kept. Digital publications and records are largely replacing the keeping of information in paper format, although predictions that books would disappear in the face of a digital revolution have, at least for the time being, proved to be wide of the mark. While most libraries still retain hard copies of books and journals, their role is rapidly changing so that they now place much greater emphasis on the provision of access to digital resources and networks. The sheer scale at which the amount of information has increased in recent years is quite staggering. Lyman and Varian (2003) have suggested that some 5 exabytes of new information was produced in print, film, magnetic and optical storage media in 2002 alone. (One byte is equivalent to 8 digital bits, which is sufficient to represent a single alphanumeric character. A terabyte is $2^{40}$ bytes, and an exabyte is $2^{60}$ bytes.) As with the production of information, so too does the storage of information reflect the character of the society in which it is stored. In most societies, power has usually been in the hands of those who have access to most information and who are able to use it to maintain their systems of control and surveillance. In our contemporary world, those who store information and are thus able to control its use and dissemination through the internet are in very considerable positions of power.

This information explosion has precipitated the need for new storage systems and has also been enabled by their creation (see Sweeney, 2001). In this context Lyman and Varian (2003) have produced a useful classification that distinguishes between four main types of physical storage (print, film, magnetic and optical) and four flows through electronic channels (telephone, radio, TV and the internet). The existence of huge databases of information has required completely new ways of managing and accessing them. Whereas in the past the reputation of the producer of information and the place where it was published were generally seen to be good indicators of its reliability and worth, this can no longer be taken entirely for granted. The dominance of information stored in magnetic forms has led to the increased importance of search engines in enabling people to access and consume information. Hence Google, which began as a research project as recently as 1996, was estimated in 2006 to have some 450,000 servers located in data centres across the world designed to enable people to access the information that they need (http://en.wikipedia.org/wiki/Google, accessed 16 August 2006; see also Vise, 2005). The company then had some 54 per cent of market share, and received around a billion search requests each day. However, while such means are necessary for people to access and consume information in an increasingly digital world, they also reflect a darker side of new ICTs in that they permit much greater surveillance of such usage. Google thus keeps a record of all internet searches done through its facilities, and it can access these at any time. This has raised considerable ethical debates concerning privacy as well as over intellectual property rights. Whereas in the past no one kept records of what books one might have browsed in a library, details of the searches made with the IP address of the computer one uses are being added inexorably to the world's store of information. As more and more information is stored and accessed digitally, those who for whatever reason are unable to access it are becoming increasingly marginalised. This is not just an issue of cost of access, but it also concerns the means of access to information. If the dominant mode of information access in the richer countries of the world is now a computer terminal, ICT4D initiatives need to provide relevant training in such usage, need to ensure sufficient bandwidth and connectivity, and need to make this available at affordable prices if poor and marginalised communities are to be able to access the benefits of digital information.

### Information needs in development

Table 3.1 provides an indicative framework for exploring the information needs associated with different groups involved in development processes. The poorest individuals and marginalised communities are deliberately placed at the top to emphasise that it is the needs of these people that we should address first if we are to use ICTs to make the world a fairer and more equitable place. It should nevertheless be highlighted that the needs of different groups of people often coalesce, and it is therefore important to adopt a holistic approach to the production, storage and consumption of information in a development context. One of the key tasks that must then be undertaken is to identify the specific technologies that can best be used to deliver these needs for different groups of people. It is unlikely that a single solution will suit everyone, and for ICT4D programmes to be successful it is usually necessary for them to adopt a diversity of approaches in their delivery.

As has already been emphasised, Table 3.1 is schematic rather than comprehensive. Rather than exploring all of the boxes in turn, this section focuses instead on two contrasting examples of information needs, those of poor people and of donors, to highlight the kinds of issues that have to be addressed by those seeking to implement programmes using new ICTs in support thereof. Most studies of information in poor countries have concentrated much more on the supply-side than they have on the demand that poor people have for information. This is scarcely surprising, since people cannot ask for things of which they are not aware or have not yet experienced. An important exception, though, is the work undertaken by the Intermediate Technology Development Group (ITDG, now known as Practical Action) and funded by DFID, which focused explicitly on the needs of poor urban people in Peru, Sri Lanka and Zimbabwe (Schilderman, 2002). This not only highlighted that there are important similarities in the information needs of poor people in different parts of the world, but it also emphasised that there are significant local differences in what they need and how they gain access to it. Typical needs in all three countries included the need for information on income generation, healthcare, education, housing, water and sanitation. However, local and national needs varied and included such diverse requirements as information on electricity supply, prostitution and resident registration. Furthermore, 'women are often disadvantaged in terms of access to information compared to men; the needs of other marginalized groups, such as the disabled or homeless, are not well served either' (Schilderman, 2002, p. 4). The report goes on to emphasise the diversity of sources of information that people turned to, including friends and key individuals, civil society organisations, local political leaders, government institutions and community-based organisations. People's own social networks were the dominant source of most information relevant to their needs. The report also notes that the most important characteristics that poor people thought that informants should have were the need for them to present information in an accessible format, that they should be willing to share it, that it should be reliable and that it should be relevant to their needs. These requirements are also highly pertinent for those seeking to make such information available through the use of new ICTs. One of the particularly significant findings of this research, though, was that poor people rarely found the media to be a useful source of information, and there was much uncertainty as to whether ICTs could play a bigger role in delivering the information needs of those surveyed. For example, while radio and TV provided entertainment, they were not generally seen as focusing on the real needs of poor people. As Schilderman (2002, p. 5) concludes, 'So far, modern Information and Communication Technologies (ICTs) have not played a major role in getting livelihood information to the urban poor. The poor rarely have direct access to them, a factor which some think does increase their exclusion'.

The information needs of international donors are very different, but are also of critical importance if we are to ensure that ICT4D can contribute better to the needs of poor and marginalised communities. The overload of e-mails from which many people working in international donor organisations now suffer is but one example of the negative impact that ICTs can have on the development process! Such systems need to be effectively managed, and all too frequently donors fail to have sufficiently strict e-mail policies and management systems in place, thereby increasing the unproductive workload of their staff on often trivial and unimportant issues. More substantively, it is interesting to note how few bilateral donors have developed comprehensive and effective formal information management strategies and procedures of their own. One of the donors that has developed such a policy is the Canadian International Development Agency (CIDA) which has an Information Management and Technology Branch (IMTB), alongside a Communications Branch and a Performance and Knowledge Management Branch (PKMB), all reporting to the Executive Vice-President's Office (http://www.acdi-cida. gc.ca/cidaweb/acdicida.nsf/En/NIC-54101940-JTC). The PKMB's role is to provide 'the Agency with credible, timely and useful information, which supports more effective and efficient international development programming. As well, information gathered from PKMB's performance management activities (that is, evaluations, internal audits, results-based management approach, monitoring, and reporting) enables CIDA to demonstrate accountability and transparency to Canadians' (http://www.acdi-cida.gc.ca/cidaweb/acdicida.nsf/En/NIC-54121044-LYW). The remit of the Communications Branch is then to lead on CIDA's external communication strategy about development, issues and results, and it also manages the Development Information Program which focuses on recognising and promoting the efforts of Canadians through mass media and educational initiatives. Although logical in concept, it has yet to be seen whether this somewhat top-down information management structure will effectively deliver on the information and communication needs of the organisation as a whole.

The example of CIDA's information strategy highlights three key needs that bilateral donors have with respect to information. First, they require good organisational information, both internally and also so that they can report on their delivery targets to the leaders of their governments. Second, they need to provide information to external communities, including the mass media, people living in their own countries, civil society and potential recipients of their funding. Third, they need to acquire information about development issues so that their staffs are better able to undertake their work and thus deliver their development objectives. Ideally, bilateral donors should also have in place effective knowledge management systems that can enable those living in poorer parts of the world to benefit from the potential of the latest ICTs through shared information and communication (for an alternative example, see DFID's information and communication framework at http://www.dfid.gov.uk/aboutdfid/organisation/corporate-performancedivision.asp).

Many donors have sought to outsource much of their information generation and dissemination activities to agencies, universities and research institutes. In the USA, for example, the Global Workforce in Transition (GWIT) team has been established to support USAID missions in developing sound workforce development systems designed to enhance economic growth and reduce poverty (http://www.gwit.us/overview.asp). Likewise, DFID in the UK has funded the development of research consortia to address particular needs that it has identified, and the work of its Central Research Department is in part disseminated through its R4D site (http://www.research4development.info). Donors also fund other information dissemination vehicles, as with DFID's support for id21 (http://www.id21.org) to disseminate information about research to policymakers and practitioners worldwide, focusing especially on health, education, global issues, urban development, rural development and natural resources (see also CAB International's work at http://www.cabi.org/InformationForDevelopment.asp).

### Accessing and managing information

The above discussion of the information needs of the urban poor and of bilateral donors has emphasised the need for information to be effectively managed. It is also essential for it to be accessible to those who need it wherever they are located. This, once again, forces us to recognise the critical importance of equality of access to information if we are to use ICTs effectively for development.

In examining these issues, it is important to begin by returning briefly to the distinctions made between information and knowledge in Chapter 2, since these have become particularly significant in discussions about both information management and knowledge management. Indeed, recent research and practice has focused much more on the latter than the former (see for example Schwartz, 2005; Suresh and Mahesh, 2006). There is considerable overlap in meaning and usage between information and knowledge (Roberts, 2000) and thus between information management and knowledge management. For the present purposes, the key distinction is that knowledge is information that has been processed by individual human understanding. In the 1980s and 1990s, information management became an important field of study, precipitated in part by the explosion of information permitted by new digital technologies (see Laudon and Laudon, 2005), but by the late 1990s attention shifted increasingly to knowledge management (Schwartz, 2005). In part this reflected an increased understanding of the importance that human engagement played in the management of information, but it also represented a deliberate attempt to create a new discipline by groups interested in the more human dimensions of information management. Thus, in the late 1990s and early 2000s, there was widespread use of terms such as management information systems (MIS), education management information systems (EMIS) (as with UNESCO's OpenEMIS) and health management information systems (HMIS) (see for example WHO, 2004), whereas by 2005 the term knowledge management became much more widely used for development purposes, pioneered in large part by the important work done by organisations such as Bellanet (http://home.bellanet.org) and its support for km4dev (http://www.km4dev.org). The km4dev wiki thus describes *information management* (IM) as:

> an interdisciplinary field which focuses on information as a resource with an emphasis on collection... Practitioners select, describe, classify, index, and abstract this information to make it more accessible to a target audience, either within or outside their organization. In a development context, IM is concerned to provide transparent and standardized access to information both within and outside the organization. IM has been often framed in terms of tools and technologies to store and organize information... ,

whereas *knowledge management* (KM):

> makes sense of information in the context of [its] users. Practitioners summarize, contextualize, value-judge, rank, synthesize, edit and facilitate to make information and knowledge accessible between people, either within or outside their organization. It concerns itself with the social interactions around the sharing and use of knowledge. KM is largely based on tacit interpretation and less on rules.
>
> (http://www.km4dev.org/wiki/index.php/
> Difference_between_IM_and_KM)

Another subtle but important effect of the increased use of the term 'knowledge' rather than 'information' has been the greater emphasis that it has placed on knowledge *sharing*. This has been closely allied with the deliberate focus of many involved in knowledge-sharing activities on the importance of 'knowledge' as a global common good, in contrast to those who tend to see 'information' as a commodity to be bought and sold (although see earlier discussion of these themes in Chapter 2). The concept of *knowledge and communication technologies for development* (KCT4D) has nevertheless not yet become popularised, and although this book is fundamentally concerned with both knowledge and information, it therefore continues to use the more familiar ICT4D to refer to the interface of technologies with both information and knowledge.

The ways that information and knowledge are managed at both a global and an institutional level have profound importance, and new ICTs have played a very significant part in changing how we think about these concepts. Globally, the advent of the World Wide Web (the WWW or Web) as a publicly available service on the internet in 1991 (Berners-Lee with Fischetti, 1999), created the opportunity for a fundamental shift in the way in which people accessed information and shared the knowledge that they created. In essence, the Web permits people to access and contribute to the information stored on computers across the world. The increased use of mobile phones and other small devices now also enables access without even the use of a computer. The Web is thus a very powerful tool in potentially democratising and opening up the use of information, but this is only the case if three conditions are met: people have access to devices that enable them to use the Web; information relevant to their needs is actually uploaded onto servers with access to the internet; and search engines enable them to find relevant information. In much of the world poor people and marginalised communities still do not have access to hardware and connectivity that is sufficiently cheap and reliable for them to access information that could be of use to them. Moreover, most of the sites dedicated to ICT4D remain difficult for poor people to use, because their search facilities are but poorly developed. This once again reiterates the importance of the effective management of knowledge and information if ICT4D initiatives are to be successful.

## Effective communication in development practice

The discussion of knowledge sharing above indicates the importance of communication in development practice; information without communication is of little value. Poor people need to communicate their needs so that policymakers can determine how best these can effectively be met. Agricultural extension officers and farmers need to communicate their knowledge to each other so that more sustainable agricultural practices can be implemented. People in divided communities need to communicate their hopes and fears so that they can work together towards peace. Just as the fields of information and knowledge have spawned huge literatures, so too has the field of communication (see for example Fiske, 1990; Melkote and Steeves, 2001; Singhal and Rogers, 2001; Singhal *et al.*, 2004; Coldevin, 2003). This section seeks to provide an overview of this literature, by focusing on three main issues: the conditions required for successful communication; the diverse means through which people communicate; and the purposes of communication in development practice.

### *Theorising effective communication*

Communication is one of the defining aspects of humanity. It is a means through which people express their identity and participate in social activity. As Buckley (2000, p. 180) has commented, 'Communication is the means by which people create their identity. It underlies our sense of community, our sense of belonging and our sense of difference'. Given its importance, it is scarcely surprising that numerous different approaches to an understanding of communication have been proposed. Melkote and Steeves (2001, p. 143) thus identify four distinct approaches to the social-scientific foundations of communications in the context of development: the communication effects approach; the mass media and modernisation approach;

the diffusion of innovations approach; and the social marketing approach. Each of these has its own history and geography. As Melkote and Steeves (2001, p. 44) go on to comment, 'The role of communication in society cannot be understood apart from other processes and structures of society, and their unique histories and circumstances'.

As with approaches to the use of information in development, so too is it possible to identify two broad approaches to the ways in which communication has been used in development practice: those that are designed to deliver a particular message; and those that are more participatory, focusing on discussion and networking. The existence of such a division has been well described by Melkote and Steeves (2001, p. 43) who note that, '*Communication* has often been used to refer to a linear process of information exchange, resulting in knowledge acquisition or persuasion. However, we prefer a definition that emphasizes a process of shared meaning that takes place in a cultural and political-economic context and is inseparable from that context'. In many ways, this conceptualisation can be linked to Habermas's (1978) framework of different types of knowledge-constitutive interest as discussed in Chapter 2. In such a framework, the first type of communication can be seen as being conceived essentially within a modernist and positivist context, using an empirical–analytic scientific approach to convey particular kinds of information. In contrast, the second approach is closely related to the interests of historical–hermeneutic science, with its emphasis on interpretation and shared understanding.

In general terms, there has been a shift in communication studies from the former to the latter over the last half century. The 1960s were dominated by the use of communication to support technology transfer. It was soon realised that simply providing information about such technologies was not going to lead to their adoption, and so the emphasis shifted to communication that was focused more on skills and ideas, persuading people of the reasons why they should adopt these innovations. Gradually, through the 1970s, greater attention came to be placed on the importance of literacy in enabling people to learn from the information being provided, and there was also a shift towards much greater use of the mass media in propagating development-related messages. However, these approaches still remained within an overtly top-down model of communication. By the late 1970s, a much more nuanced approach that increasingly emphasised participation and networking in the context of communication came to be practised alongside this earlier top-down model. This focused especially on two-way communication, on the encouragement of grassroots initiatives, and a return to traditional media as a means for communication (see pp. 48–9).

One of the more interesting approaches to communication, particularly in the field of rural development, has been the development support communication (DSC) model, proposed initially by Coldevin (1995) for the FAO in Sierra Leone during the mid-1980s, but also subsequently implemented in the Philippines. As originally designed this was intended to be applicable both 'to top-down or "push" strategies for technology transfer as well as to participatory, "demand" or "pull" approaches initiated at the farmer level' (Coldevin, 1995, unpaginated). It was also meant to be flexible enough to cater for short intensive communication campaigns as well as longer-term programmes. The DSC model involves 11 operational steps, divided into two stages: the front-end analysis and the support communication process. Despite Coldevin's claim that the model was intended also to be relevant to participatory approaches, it nevertheless remains largely a top-down and supply-led framework concerned with using communication to convey particular messages, rather than encouraging dynamic communication so that people might have a greater understanding of particular development-related issues (but see also Coldevin, 2003).

Participatory models of communication are one alternative to the top-down emphasis that still dominates much of the use of communication in development practice and literature. However, all too often the encouragement of such networking grassroots approaches has failed to empower poor people sufficiently to enable them to overcome the conditions that have impoverished them. In contrast to top-down and participatory models, therefore, it is possible to conceive of a third kind of framework that builds on Habermas's (1978) notion of critical science and focuses instead much more explicitly on the use of communication in the empowerment and enlightenment of poor and marginalised communities. This is the kind of approach advocated by Melkote and Steeves (2001, p. 327), who emphasise the need to 'examine how the organizational value of communication (as opposed to its transmission value) may be harnessed to help empower marginalized groups and communities'. In so doing they develop what they call a communitarian theory, that builds on liberation theology, feminism, environmentalism and participatory action research, with the intention of enabling poor people to have a greater voice in the political, ideological and economic processes prevalent in their societies. This approach could usefully be developed further into a practical framework for a critically aware ICT4D practice drawing on Habermas's (1984, 1987) own theory of communicative action. Habermas (1984, 1987) is of particular importance in this respect because of his core focus on human emancipation and a moral framework based on universal pragmatics. In essence, his project is to explain social disorder through an understanding of the ways in which communication is structured and organised. He does this by postulating the existence of three worlds (objective, social and subjective) in which people interact when they speak, and by emphasising that actors raise three validity claims in making any statement: that it is truthful; that it conforms to the existing normative context; and that what is said is indeed meant (see McCarthy, 1984; Unwin, 1992).

Habermas's ultimate aim in his theory of communicative action is to reassert the importance of the public sphere in which citizens are able actively to engage in political processes that determine their future. It is here that communication practices are of such fundamental importance, not only in enabling communities of shared interest to express themselves, but also in involving them directly in practical political action based on shared moral principles. The potential of ICTs to support such processes, not least through mechanisms such as blogs and wikis, offers an unprecedented opportunity for the emergence of new trans-global communities and consequently for them to engage in political processes in ways that have not yet fully been realised. There are undoubtedly challenging dimensions to these new means of communication, as with the use of the internet to enable those intent on murder and bloodshed to communicate more effectively both among themselves and also to global audiences, or the use of mobile phones to detonate explosives. The enhanced surveillance potential that these technologies likewise offer to states for the monitoring of their citizens is also frightening if abused. However, the potential for these new means of communication to be used creatively by poor and marginalised communities is one that needs to be grasped fully and effectively if they are truly to empower themselves.

### *Means of communication*

Humans communicate through all of their senses, and yet until recently ICTs have tended to concentrate on only a limited range of the communication means at our disposal, notably the written and spoken word. With the advent of television in the mid-1930s, visual imagery first became widely used in mass communication, and much more recently the emergence of IP-based videoconferencing in the 1990s has dramatically extended the combination of the visual and the aural in personal communication. One of the latest expressions of this desire to share integrated audio-visual communication more widely was the creation of YouTube in 2005. This permits users to upload short video clips, and within 18 months of its creation it claimed that 100 million videos were being accessed each day with 65,000 new videos being uploaded over the same time period (http://www.youtube.com, accessed 22 August 2006).

Despite this exponential growth in audio-visual communication, it is important to emphasise that human communication actually involves all of our senses. Although there are varying estimates of the different roles that these play in our interpretation and recollection of information, there is quite general agreement that non-verbal communication accounts for about 50 per cent of the message, voice characteristics some 40 per cent, and actual content only about 10 per cent in the context of a lecture or presentation (for a wider discussion of non-verbal communication see Knapp, 1978; Malandro and Barker, 1989). Moreover, we need to recall that alongside hearing, speaking and seeing, the senses of touch and smell are also critical to our communicative lives. While the use of digital communication systems can satisfactorily enable audio-visual communication to take place from one part of the globe to another, they do not convey the physicality of a touch or a kiss. Moreover, many of these other more subtle and frequently forgotten aspects of communication are highly culturally specific. Thus, in many parts of Europe friends greet each other with a kiss, something that would not be deemed appropriate in most traditional Asian societies (Axtell, 1991). While much has been said about the dominance of the English language as a means of digital communication, particularly on the Web, the ways that these more nuanced cultural aspects of body language translate into our digital lives remain to be explored in much greater depth. Furthermore, their significance for those with disabilities, such as impaired hearing or sight, is also of critical importance. For blind people, being able to 'read' a webpage through 'feeling' the words on a Braille keyboard, or for the deaf, the use of voice-to-text phones, can transform their communicative lives. Much more attention needs to be paid to these aspects of digital communication than has heretofore been the case (for an example of the incorporation of non-verbal communication in a digital context see Guye-Vuillème *et al.*, 1999).

The concept of literacy is central to discussions about effective communication. Indeed, one of the basic definitions of literacy is that it is the combination of skills that are essential for people to be able to communicate in a particular format. In the past, this format was generally considered to be reading and writing. However, as Roberts (1995) points out, there is enormous controversy as to exactly how the notion of literacy should now be defined. In particular, there is substantial debate over whether literacy merely involves the acquisition of technical skills or in contrast whether it is something that is culturally defined (see Street, 1984, 2001). Increasingly, a much broader definition of literacy is therefore being advocated, that moves beyond simply the acquisition of reading and writing skills. Terms such as digital literacy and e-literacy are now becoming much more widely used, emphasising that people need to have a wide range of communication skills if they are effectively to be able to communicate in a world dominated by the use of ICTs (see for example Wagner, 1999; Collins and Blott, 2003). Such arguments are of central importance to discussions of ICT4D, and given the cultural specificity of traditional forms of literacy they raise interesting questions about the extent to which the acquisition of ICT skills is also culturally and socially embedded. Indeed, a strong argument can be made that the need to learn a particular set of ICT skills, as exemplified for example by qualifications such as the European (ECDL) and International (ICDL) Computer Driving Licences (http://www.ecdl.com), is yet another way in which the culturally dominant practices of the USA and Europe are being imposed on people living in other parts of the world. More interestingly, it is also possible to conjecture that the use of ICTs may be reducing the dependency that people have on the traditional literacy skills such as reading and writing. Voice conversion software packages such as IBM's ViaVoice (http://www-306.ibm.com/software/voice/viavoice, accessed 23 August 2006) can, for example, transform the spoken word into text, thus possibly negating the need for people in the future even to learn to write. Likewise, most word-processing packages such as Microsoft Word now have sophisticated grammar and spelling checking facilities, and text-messaging (SMS) has led to the emergence of completely new kinds of language. More widely, there is increasing interest in the two-way relationship between the use of these new technologies and the self. García-Montes *et al.* (2006, p. 78) thus write about the 'dialectical relationship between the self and the mobile phone', noting in particular the fact that mobile phones are not linked to any specific space, and that this can be related to what they term the notion of an 'empty self' (García-Montes *et al.*, 2006, p. 76; see also Plant, 2002).

Understanding the overall function of literacy, both as traditionally defined and in its more recent plural definition, is also of particular importance in the field of ICT4D. Literacy is far more complex a notion than merely the acquisition of a set of specific reading and writing skills. The advent of mass reading and writing campaigns in the education systems of Europe in the 19th century was fundamentally connected with the emergence of very specific social and economic relations of production. Capitalist entrepreneurs required an increasingly 'literate' labour force that was able to function effectively in the newly created factory systems of industrial Europe. Moreover, these newly acquired literacy skills enabled the publishers of newspapers and books to generate profit from entertainment, as increasing numbers of people turned to reading as a source of information and enjoyment. The acquisition of digital literacy skills can be seen in just the same way in the 21st century. Computer literacy is essential for much contemporary economic production, and the acquisition of basic computer skills has likewise enabled substantial profits to be generated from entertainment software in the form of computer games. This is not to deny the wider social and cultural benefits of literacy, but it is to emphasise that all forms of literacy are also fundamentally embedded in the profit motives of contemporary capitalism. Roberts (2000) has written convincingly about the need for a critical literacy that:

> involves a form of meta-awareness, as far as this is possible under any circumstances, of the reasons for becoming literate (in new ways), and the transformative limits of reading and writing. Taking such a stance does not mean turning one's back on the new information technologies; to the contrary, such technologies might have a decisive role to play in enabling precisely the sort of critical debate and dialogue across nations and cultures necessary to stimulate and promote alternative futures. The Internet has retained something of an anarchic character to date, even if the growing commercialisation of networked communication poses challenges to this.
>
> (Roberts, 2000, p. 447)

At a more practical level, it is also important to note that there are many ways in which people communicate, and this diversity should also be something that those involved in ICT4D practices should try to replicate. Melkote and Steeves (2001, p. 322), for example, emphasise that 'the most basic and fundamental expressions of religious practice, including prayer and meditation, *are* forms of communication. Most people globally do find these modes of communication perhaps the most empowering in sustaining faith and hope, and providing the inspiration and strength for action'. Likewise, Singhal and Rattine-Flaherty (2006) have re-emphasised the way in which much research concentrates on the use of text alone, and they highlight the importance that tools such as pencil sketches and photographs can play in communication, without there needing to be any text associated with them.

One of the ways in which ICTs have helped to transform communication in recent years has been their ability to enable synchronous communication to take place at a distance and involving a multiplicity of users. Historically, the only way that people have been able to communicate with each other at the same time, or synchronously, has been when they have been together in the same place. Other forms of communication, such as letter writing, were asynchronous, meaning that there was a delay between someone sending a message and receiving a reply. The advent of telephony in the second half of the 19th century transformed this, for the first time enabling people to transmit and receive messages sequentially in a short space of time but over a long distance. The use of new ICTs, particularly video-conferencing and chat rooms, is rapidly transforming our means of communication, and the start of the 21st century has witnessed the emergence of relatively cheap and effective means of synchronous communication throughout most of the world. This distinction between synchronous and asynchronous communication has become of particular interest in distance education, especially when facilitated by the use of ICTs (see Chapter 7). Asynchronous communication still dominates much distance learning, either in the form of written text or the use of e-mail and electronic mailing lists, when teachers and learners interact at different times of their own choice. The emergence of chat rooms, instant messaging services and Web-based synchronous communication software, however, is rapidly transforming the character of distance education and opening up novel opportunities for learners and educators alike to explore. The notion of virtual schools and universities is now becoming a reality, bringing with it considerable implications for the transformation of human behaviour and educational delivery systems across the world.

### Communication in development practice

Effective communication is a two-way process, involving both listening and speaking. With multiple stakeholders, effective communication therefore becomes highly complex, necessitating creative structures that permit a multiplicity of messages to be conveyed and understood. Despite this, it is remarkable how often communication strategies in development practice remain concerned primarily with the unidirectional dissemination of information. As Mozammel (2005, p. 23) has acknowledged, 'Communication approaches in development interventions are often looked at as a mechanism for information dissemination, a campaign, public education to a feedback system'. He goes on to note that 'In addition, communication activities are often occasional and temporary interventions planned or implemented in reaction to a certain situation or challenge' (Mozammel, 2005, p. 23; see also Myers *et al.*, 2005). This top-down, information-dissemination approach to communication arises from many causes: an aspiration to apply the best scientifically generated knowledge in development practice; the arrogance of many donor organisations who believe that only they truly know how to deliver development; the interests of the private sector in marketing their products; the dominance of unidirectional mass media in the field of communication; and a belief that poor and uneducated people do not know how to implement beneficial development initiatives. To be sure, these are widely recognised flaws, but the fact that so much communication remains focused primarily on information dissemination is one of the main reasons that development initiatives fail. A multidimensional communication strategy that involves all relevant stakeholders in listening to each other and implementing shared strategies in true partnership would do much to transform the practice of development. It is here that new ICTs have such a significant role to play, not only in conveying information, but also in enabling new communities of practice to emerge. We are only at the beginning of this process, but if these technologies can be used to encourage new kinds of participatory practice, in which all those stakeholders with interests in delivering a particular development intervention can be involved, we may be able to create more sensitive and effective initiatives that will truly begin to help poor and marginalised communities make a difference to their lives. For this to be effective, it is essential that these communities are able to express their voices in a global context, and that they are then listened to by those in positions of power.

The growing importance of communication in development practice has been reflected in the creation and expansion of significant global initiatives in this field since the mid-1990s. Three of the most interesting of these have been The Communication Initiative (http://www.comminit.com), the International Institute for Communication and Development (IICD) (http://www.iicd.org), and the Panos Network (http://www.panos.org.uk). The Communication Initiative was established in 1998 as a partnership between the Rockefeller Foundation, UNICEF, USAID, WHO, BBC World Service, CIDA, Johns Hopkins University's Center for Communication Programming, UNFPA, Soul City and Panos, and it has since expanded considerably with 28 partner organisations being involved in its work in August 2006. In essence, The Communication Initiative seeks to create an online space for those involved in using communication to support economic and social development, and it is involved in four main types of activity: maintenance of an extensive website in English and Spanish of more than 17,000 pages related to communication and development; e-publications, notably *The Drum Beat* which is a weekly electronic magazine featuring information included on its website;

issue- and region-specific windows as points of entry into its processes and information; and particular projects through which the partners support development communication. More broadly, it has five core goals:

- To debate development communication issues and programmes
- To improve strategic communication analysis and action
- To support a stronger voice for the communication experiences and learning in The South
- To expand communication and development networks in The South, and
- To promote the importance of communication in Development

(http://www.comminit.com/mission.html)

In contrast, the IICD is much more focused on the practical delivery of communication initiatives on the ground in the nine countries where it is currently working (see also pp. 130–1). Established in the late 1990s, IICD focuses on helping developing countries to assess the potential uses of ICTs and then to realise their own locally owned sustainable development practices through the use of a roundtable methodology (http://www.iicd.org/countries/roundtable). IICD's emphasis is on the use of ICTs to support existing development activities, and it therefore focuses in particular on education, governance, health, agriculture and environment.

The Panos network consists of eight different institutes, and has an overall mission 'to ensure that information is effectively used to foster public debate, pluralism and democracy' (http://www.panos.org.uk/files/councilmission.doc). Panos London was originally established as a charity in 1986, and the network as a whole is now funded by a range of international donors. At its core, Panos is concerned with stimulating informed debate around key development agendas, and works to promote an enabling media and communications environment. Unlike many other initiatives, it is particularly concerned to ensure that 'the perspectives of the people whose lives are most affected by development (the poor and marginalised) are included within decision-making' (http://www.panos.org.uk/about/mission.asp). Communication agendas thus lie at the heart of Panos's work, and its portfolio of activities includes encouraging participatory and inclusive communication within the information society, seeking to ensure that poor and marginalised people are put first in the development of policy on communication, and supporting the media in peace-building after conflicts.

## Access, understanding and relevance

This chapter has highlighted the complexity that needs to be addressed when considering the information and communication needs associated with ideas of 'development'. The many development stakeholders all have their own particular information and communication needs regardless of whether development is seen as being driven by the demands of global capital for an expanded market and more cost-effective labour, or whether instead it is envisaged as being the empowerment of poor individuals and marginalised communities. In conceptualising these requirements, it is important to consider the different stakeholders involved and their various economic, social, political and ideological needs (Table 3.1). Such a framework highlights both the diversity of issues that need to be considered, and also that information and communication are fundamentally different categories of concept. All too often in development practice, communication is simply seen as the delivery of information instead of as the multidimensional interaction between the many stakeholders in development processes that it is. The chapter has also stressed that there is a long history of attention being paid to the use of information and communication in development. These past experiences offer much of value to those seeking to implement ICT4D initiatives that truly empower the people they are working with. All too often recent initiatives have been driven by technology-focused agendas, and as a result they have failed to understand sufficiently many of the basic principles that ought to be addressed in considering the information and communication requirements of poor people. In particular, there needs to be an appropriate balance between supply and demand, between the aspirations of those seeking to implement the initiatives and the needs of those who will be using and implementing them.

A further feature that should be emphasised is the importance that access to means of communication and information acquisition plays in determining the success of any development initiatives. Even if the needs of the relevant stakeholders are sufficiently identified and appropriate means of delivering them secured, the users still need to be able to access them effectively. Access can be seen in terms of not only the physical presence of a particular technology, but also its reliability, its cost, its cultural acceptability, the ability of people to use it and the relevance of the content that is available to them. The challenge facing those who aspire to make available the benefits of new ICTs to poor and marginalised communities is to ensure that all of these conditions of access are met. All too frequently the reality of ICT4D programmes is that they fail to deliver on one or another of these critical requirements.

## Key readings

Bessette, G. (2004) *Involving the Community: a guide to participatory development communication.* Ottawa: International Development Research Centre

Mchombu, K.K. (2004) *Sharing Knowledge for Community Development and Transformation: a handbook*, 2nd edn. Ottawa: Oxfam Canada

Melkote, S.R. and Steeves, H.L. (2001) *Communication for Development in the Third World: theory and practice for empowerment*, 2nd edn. New Delhi: Sage

Roberts, P. (2000) Knowledge, information and literacy. *International Review of Education*, 46 (5), pp. 433–53

# References

Ahmed, S.J. (2002) Wishing for a world without 'theatre for development': demystifying the case of Bangladesh. *Research in Drama Education*, 7 (2), pp. 207–19

Ash, R.B. (1965) *Information Theory*. New York: Interscience

Axtell, R.E. (1991) *Gestures: the do's and taboos of body language around the world.* Chichester: John Wiley & Sons

Bagamayo College of Arts, Tanzania Theatre Centre, Mabala, R. and Allen, K.B. (2002) Participatory action research on HIV/AIDS through a popular theatre approach in Tanzania. *Evaluation and Program Planning*, 25 (4), pp. 333–9

Baldi, P. and Brunak, S. (2001) *Bioinformatics: the machine learning approach*, 2nd edn. Cambridge, MA: MIT Press

Baldwin, P. and Thomas, L. (2005) *Promoting Private Sector Investment and Innovation to Address the Information and Communication Needs of the Poor in Sub-Saharan Africa.* Washington, DC: International Bank for Reconstruction and Development for *info*Dev and Alcatel

Banham, M., Gibbs, J. and Osofisan, F. (eds) (1999) *African Theatre in Development.* Oxford: James Currey

Bayliss-Smith, T. and Wanmali, S. (eds) (1984) *Understanding Green Revolutions: agrarian change and development planning in South Asia: essays in honour of B.H. Farmer.* Cambridge: Cambridge University Press

Benyon, D., Turner, P. and Turner, S. (2005) *Designing Interactive Systems: people, activities, contexts, technologies.* Harlow: Pearson

Berners-Lee, T. with Fischetti, M. (1999) *Weaving the Web: the original design and ultimate destiny of the world wide web by its inventor.* San Francisco, CA: HarperCollins

Bessette, G. (2004) *Involving the Community: a guide to participatory development communication.* Ottawa: International Development Research Centre (http://www.idrc.ca/openebooks/066-7)

Bhatia, N. (2004) *Acts of Authority/Acts of Resistance: theater and politics on colonial and postcolonial India.* Ann Arbor: University of Michigan Press

Binswanger, H.P. and Ruttan, V.W. (1978) *Induced Innovation: technology, institutions and development.* Baltimore, MD: Johns Hopkins University Press

Boal, A. (1979) *Theatre of the Oppressed*, tr. C.A. and M.-O. Leal McBride. London: Pluto

Brown, L. (1981) *Innovation Diffusion: a new perspective.* New York: Methuen

Buckley, S. (2000) Radio's new horizons: democracy and popular communication in the digital age. *International Journal of Cultural Studies*, 3 (2), pp. 180–7

Chambers, R. (1983) *Rural Development: putting the last first.* London: Longman

Chambers, R. (1997) *Whose Reality Counts? Putting the last first.* London: ITDG

Chambers, R. (2004) *Ideas for Development: reflecting forwards.* Brighton: Institute of Development Studies

Chang, I.I. (2005) Theatre as therapy, therapy as theatre transforming the memories and trauma of the 21 September 1999 earthquake in Taiwan, *Research in Drama Education*, 19 (3), pp. 285–301

Chapman, G.P. (1983) The folklore of the perceived environment in Bihar. *Environment and Planning A*, 15, pp. 945–68

Coldevin, G. (1995) *Farmer-First Approaches to Communication: a case study from the Philippines.* Rome: FAO (http://www.fao.org/docrep/V8911E/v8911e00.htm)

Coldevin, G. (2003) *Participatory Communication: a key to rural learning systems.* Rome: FAO (ftp://ftp.fao.org/docrep/fao/005/y4774e/y4774e00.pdf)

Collins, J. and Blott, R.K. (2003) *Literacy and Literacies: text, power and identity.* Cambridge: Cambridge University Press

Daconta, M.C., Obrst, L.J. and Smith, K.T. (2003) *The Semantic Web: a guide to the future of XML, web services, and knowledge management.* New York: John Wiley & Sons

Dava, F., Ahmad, Z. and Easton, P. (2002) Managing natural resources along the Mozambican shoreline: the role of myths and rites. *IKNotes*, 45. Washington, DC: World Bank (http://siteresources.worldbank.org/EXTINDKNOWLEDGE/Resources/iknt46.pdf)

de Costa, E. (1992) *Collaborative Latin American Popular Theatre: from theory to form, from text to stage.* New York: Peter Lang

Derbyshire, H. (2003) *Gender Issues in the Use of Computers in Education in Africa.* London: Imfundo (DFID) (http://imfundo.digitalbrain.com/imfundo/web/learn/genderissues)

Dickson, A. (1950a) Mass education in Togoland. *African Affairs*, 49, pp. 136–50

Dickson, A. (1950b) Training community leaders in the Gold Coast. *Overseas Education,* 22 (1), pp. 8–21

Dix, H., Finlay, J., Abowd, G.D. and Beale, R. (2004) *Human–Computer Interaction,* 4th edn. Harlow: Pearson

Elliott, L., Gruer, L., Farrow, K., Henderson, A. and Cowan, L. (1996) Theatre in AIDS education – a controlled study. *AIDS Care*, 8 (3), pp. 321–40

Fiske, J. (1990) *Introduction to Communication Studies*, 2nd edn. London: Routledge

Floridi, L. (1999a) *Philosophy and Computing: an introduction.* London: Routledge

Floridi, L. (1999b) Information ethics: on the theoretical foundations of computer ethics. *Ethics and Information Technology*, 1 (1), pp. 37–56

Floridi, L. (2002) What is the philosophy of information? *Metaphilosophy*, 33 (1/2), pp. 123–45

Food and Agriculture Organization and World Bank (2000) *Agricultural Knowledge and Information Systems for Rural Development.* Rome: FAO

Freire, P. (1970) *Pedagogy of the Oppressed.* New York: Seabury Press

Freire, P. (1972) *Cultural Action for Freedom.* London: Penguin

García-Montes, J.M., Caballero-Muñoz, D. and Pérez-Álvarez, M. (2006) Changes in the self resulting from the use of mobile phones. *Media, Culture and Society*, 28 (1), pp. 67–82

Gibbs, J. (1999) Propaganda and mass education: Alec Dickson and drama for development in the Gold Coast. In Banham, Gibbs and Osofisan (eds) (1999), pp. 13–23

Greenberg, A. (2005) *ICTs for Poverty Alleviation: basic tool and enabling sector.* Stockholm: Sida

Gunawardena, N. (2005) Communication rights and communication wrongs. (http://www.scidev.net/Opinions/index.cfm?fuseaction=readopinions&itemid=447&language=1)

Guye-Vuillème, A., Capin, T.K., Pandzic, A., Magnenat Thalmann, N. and Thalmann, D. (1999) Nonverbal communication interface for collaborative virtual environments. *Virtual Reality*, 4 (1), pp. 49–59

Habermas, J. (1978) *Knowledge and Human Interests*, 2nd edn, tr. Jeremy Shapiro. London: Heinemann

Habermas, J. (1984) *The Theory of Communicative Action. Vol. 1: Reason and the Rationalization of Society.* Boston: Beacon Press

Habermas, J. (1987) *The Theory of Communicative Action. Vol. 2: Lifeworld and System.* Cambridge: Polity Press

Harriss, J. (ed.) (1992) *Rural Development: theories of peasant economy and agrarian change*. London: Routledge

Hickey, S. and Mohan, G. (eds) (2006) *Participation – from tyranny to transformation*. London: Zed Books

Joseph, C.O. (2005) Theatre for development in Kenya: interrogating the ethics of practice. *Research in Drama Education*, 10 (2), pp.189–99

Kidd, R. (1982) Popular theatre and popular struggle in Kenya: the story of the Kamiriithu Community Educational and Cultural Centre. *Theaterwork*, pp. 47–61

Kling, R. (1999) What is social informatics and why does it matter? *D-Lib Magazine*, 5 (1), unpaginated (available at http://webdoc.gwdg.de/edoc/aw/d-lib/dlib/january99/kling/01kling.html)

Knapp, M.L. (1978) *Nonverbal Communication in Human Interaction*. New York: Holt, Rinehart and Winston

Laudon, K. and Laudon, J. (2005) *Management Information Systems*, 9th edn. New York: Pearson

Levert, L. and Mumma, O. (eds) (1995) *Drama and Theatre: communication in development*. Nairobi: KDEA

Lyman, P. and Varian, H.R. (2003) How much information 2003? (http://www2.sims.berkeley.edu/research/projects/how-much-info-2003)

Mackay, D.J.C. (2003) *Information Theory, Inference and Learning Algorithms*. Cambridge: Cambridge University Press

Maedche, A. (2002) *Ontology Learning for the Semantic Web*. Dordrecht: Kluwer

Mahaffy, J.P. (1890) The work of Mago on agriculture. *Hermathena*, 7, pp. 29–35

Malandro, L.A. and Barker, L.L. (1989) *Nonverbal Communication*. New York: Random House

McCarthy, T. (1984) *The Critical Theory of Jürgen Habermas*. Cambridge: Polity

Mchombu, K.K. (2004) *Sharing Knowledge for Community Development and Transformation: a handbook*, 2nd edn. Ottawa: Oxfam Canada (http://www.oxfam.ca/news-and-publications/publications-and-reports/sharing-knowledge-handbook-2/file)

Melkote, S.R. and Steeves, H.L. (2001) *Communication for Development in the Third World: theory and practice for empowerment*, 2nd edn. New Delhi: Sage

Mingay, G.E. (1975) *Arthur Young and his Times*. London: Macmillan

Mohan, G. (1999) Not so distant, not so strange: the personal and the political in participatory research. *Ethics, Place and Environment*, 2 (1), pp. 41–54

Mozammel, M. (2005) Strategic communication in PRSPs: principles, challenges and applications. In *With the Support of Multitudes: using strategic communications to fight poverty through PRSPs*, ed. M. Mozammel and S. Odugbemi. London: DFID

Munasinhe, M. (ed.) (1989) *Computers and Informatics in Developing Countries*. London: Butterworth

Myers, M. with Woods, N. and Odugbemi, S. (2005) *Monitoring and Evaluating Information and Communication for Development Programmes*. London: DFID (Information and Communication for Development Team)

Nicholson, H. (2005) *Applied Drama: the gift of theatre*. Basingstoke: Palgrave Macmillan

Okagbu, O. (1998) Product or process: theatre for development in Africa. In Salhi (ed.) (1998), pp. 23–41

Pearse, A. (1980) *Seeds of Plenty; Seeds of Want: a critical analysis of the green revolution*. Oxford: Clarendon Press

Plant, S. (2002) *On the Mobile: the effects of mobile telephones on social and individual life*. Libertyville, IL: Motorola (http://www.motorola.com/mot/doc/0/234_MotDoc.pdf)

Plastow, J. (1999) Uses and abuses of theatre for development: political struggle and development theatre in the Ethiopia–Eritrea war. In Salhi (ed.) (1998), pp. 97–113

Prakash, S. (2002) Using indigenous knowledge to raise agricultural productivity: an example from India. *IKNotes*, 45. Washington, DC: World Bank (http://siteresources.worldbank.org/EXTINDKNOWLEDGE/Resources/iknt45.pdf)

Recknagel, F. (ed.) (2006) *Ecological Informatics: scope, techniques and applications*, 2nd edn. Berlin: Springer

Richardson, D. and Paisley, L. (eds) (1998) *The First Mile of Connectivity – advancing telecommunications for rural development through a participatory approach*. Rome: FAO (http://www.fao.org/documents/show_cdr.asp?url_file=/docrep/x0295e/x0295e00.htm)

Richmond, F.P., Swann, D.L. and Zarrilli, P.B. (eds) (1990) *Indian Theatre: traditions of performance*. Honolulu: University of Hawaii Press

Roberts, P. (1995) Defining literacy: paradise, nightmare or red herring? *British Journal of Educational Studies*, 43 (4), pp. 412–32

Roberts, P. (2000) Knowledge, information and literacy. *International Review of Education*, 46 (5), pp. 433–53

Rogers, E.M. (1983) *Diffusion of Innovations*. New York: The Free Press

Russell, S. and Norvig, P. (2002) *Artificial Intelligence: a modern approach*, 2nd edn. Englewood Cliffs, NJ: Prentice Hall

Sachs, J. (2005) *The End of Poverty: how we can make it happen in our lifetime*. London: Penguin Books

Salhi, K. (ed.) (1998) *African Theatre for Development: art for self-determination*. Exeter: Intellect

Schilderman, T. (2002) *Strengthening the Knowledge and Information Systems of the Urban Poor*. London: DFID and ITDG

Schware, R. (ed.) (2005) *E-Development: from excitement to effectiveness*. Washington, DC: The World Bank Group

Schwartz, D. (ed.) (2005) *Encyclopedia of Knowledge Management*. Hershey, PA: Idea Group Reference

Shannon, C.E. and Weaver, W. (1949) *The Mathematical Theory of Communication*. Champaign, IL: University of Illinois Press

Singhal, A. and Rattine-Flaherty, E. (2006) Pencils and photos as tools of communicative research and praxis. *International Communication Gazette*, 68 (4), pp. 313–30

Singhal, A. and Rogers, E.M. (2001) *India's Communication Revolution: from bullock carts to cyber marts*. New Delhi: Sage

Singhal, A., Cody, M.J., Rogers, E.M. and Sabido, M. (eds) (2004) *Entertainment-Education and Social Change: history, research and practice*. Mahwah, NJ: Laurence Erlbaum

Souter, D. with Scott, N., Garforth, C., Jain, R., Mascarenhas, O. and McKerney, K. (2005) *The Economic Impact of Telecommunications on Rural Livelihoods and Poverty Reduction: a study of rural communities in India (Gujarat), Mozambique and Tanzania*. London: CTO and DFID

Standing, H. (2000) Gender impacts of health reforms – the current state of policy and implementation. Paper for ALAMES meeting, Havana, Cuba, July 2000

Street, B. (1984) *Literacy in Theory and Practice*. Cambridge: Cambridge University Press

Street, B. (ed.) (2001) *Literacy and Development: ethnographic perspectives*. London: Routledge

Suresh, J.K. and Mahesh, K. (2006) *Ten Steps to Maturity in Knowledge Management: lessons in economy.* Oxford: Chandos

Sweeney, L. (2001) Information explosion. In *Confidentiality, Disclosure, and Data Access: theory and practical applications for statistical agencies,* ed. L. Zayatz, P. Doyle, J. Theeuwes and J. Lane. Washington, DC: Urban Institute (http://privacy. cs.cmu.edu/people/sweeney/explosion2.pdf)

Tacchi, J., Slater, D. and Hearn, G. (2003) *Ethnographic Action Research: a user's handbook developed to innovate and research ICT applications for poverty eradication.* New Delhi: UNESCO

Unwin, T. (1987) Household characteristics and agrarian innovation adoption in north-west Portugal. *Transactions of The Institute of British Geographers,* new series, 12, pp. 131–46

Unwin, T. (1991) *Wine and the Vine: an historical geography of viticulture and the wine trade.* London: Routledge

Unwin, T. (1992) *The Place of Geography.* Harlow: Longman

van Bemmel, J.H. and Musen, M.A. (eds) (1997) *Handbook of Medical Informatics.* Heidelberg: Springer

van Erven, E. (2001) *Community Theatre: global perspectives.* London: Routledge

Versényi, A. (1993) *Theatre in Latin America: religion, politics and culture from Cortés to the 1980s.* Cambridge: Cambridge University Press

Vise, D.A. (2005) *The Google Story.* London: Macmillan

Wagner, D. (ed.) (1999) *The Future of Literacy in a Changing World.* Cresskill, NJ: Hampton Press

Weigel, G. and Waldburger, D. (eds) (2004) *ICT4D – connecting people for a better world.* Berne and Kuala Lumpur: Swiss Agency for Development and Cooperation and Global Knowledge Partnership

WHO (2004) *Developing Health Management Information Systems: a practical guide for developing countries.* Geneva: World Health Organization for the Western Pacific (http://www.wpro.who.int/NR/rdonlyres/3A34C50D-C035-425A-8155-65E8AD3CB906/0/Health_manage.pdf)

World Bank (no date) *Voices of the Poor* (http://go.worldbank.org/H1N8746X10)

# 4 | The technologies: identifying appropriate solutions for development needs

## Tim Unwin

- ICT4D initiatives need to be driven by the provision of appropriate technological solutions for the challenges faced by poor and marginalised people and communities, rather than by an interest purely in these physical technologies themselves.
- The choice of the optimal hardware and software solutions in any particular circumstance depends on a range of economic, social, political and ideological factors that need to be properly understood before any ICT4D initiatives are implemented.
- Convergence, miniaturisation and the shift from analogue to digital solutions have all created new opportunities that can be used creatively to empower poor people and marginalised communities.
- Those implementing technological solutions need to ensure that they are context specific and adapted to local needs and conditions.

Chapters 2 and 3 have explored the reasons why information and communication are central to 'development' processes. This chapter turns to an examination of the technologies that can be used to support these information and communication needs. Two key issues must be emphasised right at the beginning. First, it is essential to recognise that the actual technologies by themselves have little development impact. It is only when they are used effectively to deliver on the aspirations of poor people and marginalised communities that they may be able positively to influence their lives and livelihoods. Indeed, ICTs are often a financial drain on communities until there is sufficient wealth generated for them to provide enough profit for their continued use. Second, ICT4D initiatives are not sustainable or effective unless the technologies embedded within them deliver on the demands of users in appropriate ways. There is little point simply in introducing the technologies if users cannot see any economic, social or political benefit in paying for them. For this to happen, it is essential that potential users have a sound understanding of how they can use new ICTs beneficially. One of the most important challenges facing those implementing ICT4D initiatives is therefore to identify how best to respond to the needs of poor and marginalised communities once they have recognised this potential, and then to help them to develop innovative solutions that will enable them to achieve their aspirations.

This chapter provides a broad introduction to the diverse technologies that are referred to by those working in the field of ICT4D. The first section suggests that we need to be flexible in our definitions and approaches if we are to create effective technological solutions for the problems faced by the poor. The chapter then proposes a fourfold conceptualisation of ICTs, focusing on the technologies used in the *production*, *storage* and *sharing* of information and knowledge, as well as the *infrastructures* used to support them. Underlying the practical usage of these technologies, it is crucial to recognise that there are also important regulatory issues that determine the social, economic and political context within which they are introduced. The chapter ends by emphasising the importance of the debate between those advocating 'proprietary' and 'open' technological solutions for development agendas. Throughout, the aim is to highlight both the potential and the challenges associated with the use of specific technologies, so that those charged with implementing ICT4D programmes can have a realistic understanding of the contributions that each can make.

## ICTs: a conceptual framework

There have been many approaches to the definition and classification of the technologies associated with information and communication. Frequently, the term ICTs is used primarily to refer to the use of computers and the internet. The Wikipedia Information Technology Portal thus refers to IT (or ICT) as the subject that deals with 'electronic computers and computer software to convert, store, protect, process, transmit and retrieve information' (http://en.wikipedia.org/wiki/Portal:Information_technology). In contrast, the online TechTarget definition places emphasis on the different types of technology themselves, claiming that ICT 'is an umbrella term that includes any communication device or application, encompassing: radio, television, cellular phones, computer and network hardware and software, satellite systems and so on, as well as the various services and applications associated with them, such as videoconferencing and distance learning' (http://searchsmb.techtarget.com/sDefinition/0,290660,sid44_gci928405,00.html). Weigel and Waldburger (2004, p. 19) similarly use the term to refer 'to technologies designed to access, process and transmit information. ICT encompass a full range of technologies – from traditional, widely used devices such as radios, telephones or TV, to more sophisticated tools like computers or the Internet' (see also von Braun and Torero, 2006). Hamelink (1997) has usefully sought to clarify this complexity, by distinguishing between capturing technologies (such as cameras and digital video recorders), storage technologies (such as CD-ROMs and film), processing technologies (such as application software), communication technologies (such as Local Area Networks) and display technologies (such as computer monitors or the screens of mobile phones).

## A digital world

In the past it was possible to distinguish between separate ICTs such as telephones and radios, but since the late 1990s such distinctions have become increasingly blurred as a result of the widespread introduction of technologies that have enabled text, image and sound to be broken down into binary formats. This has allowed them all to be accessed through a range of new electronic devices. Digital processing, for example, has fundamentally transformed the practice of photography, enabling users to do away with film and instead access their photographs immediately. They can then 'post' them on the internet through sites such as http://www.flickr.com (see also social networking sites such as http://www.bebo.com or http://www.facebook.com) so that anyone in the world can see and access them almost instantaneously. This introduction of digital technologies has had two fundamentally important effects: first, it has enabled single devices, such as the new generation of portable media players and phones, to receive and display text, image and sound together; and second, it has permitted such multi-functional devices to become very much smaller and more mobile. The combination of miniaturisation with better use of power, enhanced compression of data and digitalisation has led to a transformation in the potential of ICTs.

Traditionally, communication systems such as telephones, radio and TV functioned through the use of analogue technologies, with the term 'analogue' being used to refer to an analogy between cause and effect; as sound increases, for example, so too might the voltage of an analogous electrical system. Importantly, an analogue signal is one that continuously varies both through time and in amplitude, and therefore all changes in the signal are meaningful. Using analogue systems, communication is enabled because small fluctuations in a signal can be conveyed by changes in the properties of the medium being used to transmit it. Transducers are used to convert energy of one type into energy of another that can then be transmitted. Thus, with the analogue recording of sound, a microphone is used to pick up variations in pressure caused by the sound, and these are then converted into changes in the current passing through it or the voltage across it. The main problem with analogue systems, though, is that they are subject to random variations and disturbance known as noise. This is particularly the case, for example, when multiple copies of a recording are made, since the noise leads to a reduction in the quality of the signal. Likewise, radio or TV signals can pick up interference from other such sources, and this noise then leads to a diminution in the quality of the sound.

In contrast, digital systems quantise signals into discrete blocks, and any slight variations are treated as the values nearest to them, thus minimising the effects of noise and distortion. Historically, there have been numerous systems of digital communication, perhaps best seen with the use of beacons that could convey messages over long distances by line-of-sight connections simply by being lit or unlit. Likewise, Morse code and Braille are both forms of digital communication, the former using dots, dashes and different lengths of gaps between letters, the latter using a six-bit code in the form of raised dot patterns. However, the term is now most frequently used to refer to digital electronic systems, in which information is encoded into binary digital format through the use of complex systems of switches. The underlying principle, though, remains the same, in that information is converted into a presence/absence format, and can be stored and accessed through a diversity of media.

Although digital electronic systems have increasingly come to dominate the market since their widespread introduction in the music industry in the 1980s, it remains important to recognise that both digital and analogue systems have their own particular strengths and weaknesses (Beards, 1996; Crecraft and Gergely, 2002). Their key differences are in the ways in which information is encoded, processed and represented. However, the easier design and smaller size of digital electronic circuits have made them much cheaper to produce, and they have therefore come to dominate the mass market in ICTs in the late 1990s.

### A framework for conceptualising ICTs

In conceptualising ICTs in this rapidly changing and ever more dominantly digital world, it is helpful to think about these technologies as being associated with three main sets of interconnected processes: the capture of information, its storage, and the ways in which people access and share it. Underlying all these, there has to be a physical infrastructure in place that enables them to operate and be connected, and a regulatory mechanism to ensure that there are common standards in place for communication to be possible between devices (Figure 4.1). This chapter focuses primarily on the physical technologies and infrastructure, while the next includes a discussion of regulation in the context of policy formulation and the implementation of ICT4D partnership initiatives.

Means of information capture were traditionally discrete and quite large in size. Large typewriters and bulky cameras have now, for example, been replaced by ever more powerful slimline digital cameras and keyboards. The complexity of recording music and voices onto the analogue sound medium of gramophone records has likewise been dramatically transformed into the contemporary process of digital recording through which people can readily capture their own voices and music using small electronic devices. The size of devices for storage has likewise been transformed, largely through the introduction of digital circuits. Moore's Law, propounded by Gordon Moore, one of the co-founders of Intel, as long ago as 1965, asserted that the number of transistors per unit area on an integrated circuit was at that time doubling every two years. Today, the law has been reinterpreted to assert that data

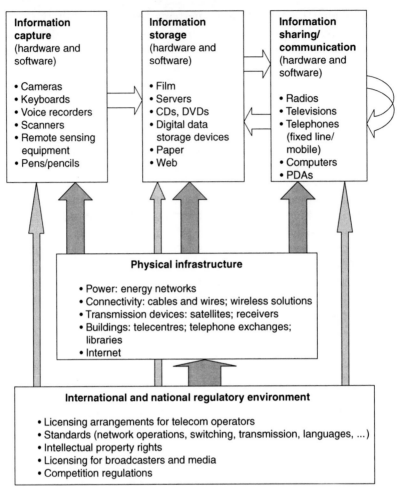

Figure 4.1 *Framework for conceptualising information and communication technologies* (*source:* Tim Unwin).

density is now doubling approximately every 18 months. The technological advances that have underlain this mean that the size of storage devices has been reduced dramatically, while it has been possible to increase their capacity at the same time. As Intel's website asserts: 'Moore's Law also means decreasing costs. As silicon-based components and platform ingredients gain in performance, they become exponentially cheaper to produce, and therefore more plentiful, more powerful, and more seamlessly integrated into our daily lives' (http://www.intel.com/technology/mooreslaw/index. htm). In 1971, Intel's first processor, the 4004, had 2300 transistors in it; in 2006, Intel's Core 2 Duo Processors had more than 291 million transistors. The 4004's circuit line width was 10 microns, whereas the latest generation microprocessors have widths of 0.065 microns, fifteen hundred times smaller than the diameter of human hair (http://www.intel.com/museum/archives/4004facts.htm).

Figure 4.1 emphasises the diversity of options that people can use to communicate and to manage information. This chapter aims to give a balanced overview of some of the most important of these, focusing particularly on the ways in which poor and marginalised communities can use them to gain information and to communicate more effectively. It begins by examining the increasingly sophisticated ways in which information is captured and stored, concentrating on three particular issues: the use of printed material for libraries; the role of multimedia material; and the increasing significance of the internet. None of these technologies would be of any use unless there were appropriate physical infrastructures available to enable them to function effectively. The third main section of this chapter therefore focuses explicitly on four key aspects of infrastructure provision: cables and wires; satellites; wireless networks; and appropriate energy solutions. This is followed by a section that explores the benefits and challenges associated with the use of specific user interfaces, both for accessing information and for communicating more generally, concentrating on telephones, computers, new handheld devices, and the role of radio, television and film. In addressing these particular technologies, however, it must be emphasised once again that they are already all closely interconnected and the boundaries between them will become ever more blurred in the future. In particular, the distinction between users and suppliers of information is one that is rapidly changing. The internet has enabled a much more fluid world of communication in which people can share information with each other, instead of having to rely primarily on the 'supply' of information by privileged organisations such as broadcasters and publishers, be they public service organisations or private companies.

### Individual and communal technologies

Different types of technology, both hardware and software, have varying potential uses in ICT4D initiatives. Figure 4.2 illustrates three dimensions of these technologies: their costs to end users, their ease of access, and the extent to which they are communal or individual (see also Weigel and Waldburger, 2004). In general, to the right of the figure there are low-cost, easy to use and communal solutions such as radio, and to the left there are high-cost, complex and individual solutions such as personal computers linked to the internet. While these categories are by no means mutually exclusive, it is often the case that easier-to-use technologies are indeed cheaper, and have wider communal use than expensive and complex technologies. This is typified, for example, by the success of Grameenphone's Village Phone Program (http://www.grameenphone.com) started in 1997 in Bangladesh, which was designed to provide universal access to telecommunication services in remote rural areas through a network of some 200,000 village phone operators, most of whom are women (for communal

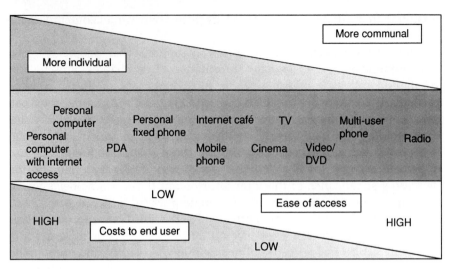

Figure 4.2 *Costs to end user and ease of access of ICTs* (*source:* derived in part from Weigel and Waldburger, 2004).

aspects of mobile phones, see also Geser, 2004; Souter *et al.*, 2005). While expanding the market for high-cost individualised technological solutions may contribute to the economic growth seen by many as being central to development processes, alternative communal solutions may prove to be much more sustainable and relevant to the needs of poorer communities. These issues are explored further in the section 'Individuals and communities: debates over software and content' (p. 114), which focuses particularly on the different software solutions available and the potential of open learning resources.

## The capture and storage of information

The introduction of small and relatively cheap information capture and storage devices has transformed the world in which we live. Not only is this a remarkable technical transformation, but importantly it also offers a rare opportunity to change the traditional balances of power associated with the provision of access to information. New ICTs have provided an increased chance for the democratisation of knowledge in ways that have not yet fully been grasped. This section explores these issues in three main arenas: libraries, multimedia technologies, and the internet.

### The changing place of libraries

Historically, library buildings have been the main place where information has been stored and made available for people to read. Indeed, as Klugkist (2001, p. 197) has commented: 'until the 1980s and 90s, libraries virtually had a monopoly on the provision of information to students, teachers and researchers'. Libraries served a public good in that they were usually free to use and they frequently offered a range of additional services including the provision of information about the local community as well as other learning opportunities. Libraries, in essence, served the needs of those individuals unable to afford to purchase their own books and information.

During the last twenty years of the 20th century, two fundamental changes took place that transformed libraries: first, the dramatic increase in the number of books, journals and other printed media being published has meant that it is impossible physically for most libraries to store it; second, the availability of digital technologies has enabled much of this information to be accessed in entirely new ways. The provision, for example, of both hard-copy and digital versions of publications is completely transforming the world of publishing and academic research. While there are undoubted cost savings and presumed environmental benefits in the shift from hard-copy books and journals to digital publication, there nevertheless still remain problems in accessing such information in a sufficiently flexible and user-friendly manner. Thus, although digital book downloads are readily available, most people still prefer to read 'real' rather than 'virtual' books. This is particularly the case with elderly people, whose eyesight might be failing.

In exploring what libraries will be like in the future, Klugkist (2001, p. 197) has usefully suggested that they will be a gateway to information, an expertise centre, a physical entity, and a collection centre for printed material. According to such arguments (see also Saunders, 1999), digital information will not replace libraries as places where information is accessed, but rather the means of accessing this information within libraries will change. As Dendrinos (2005, unpaginated) has commented: 'The library as a building has been transformed to the library as an environment of electronic services established on a computer server or a network of cooperating servers'.

The emergence of digital libraries has required the development of new systems of cataloguing and searching publications so that information about them can readily be searched and made accessible to potential users (Lesk, 2005). In 1994, the USA established a Digital Libraries Initiative (http://www.dli2.nsf.gov/dlione), funded by the National Science Foundation, with a remit to 'collect, store, and organize information in digital forms, and make it available for searching, retrieval, and processing via communication networks – all in user-friendly ways'. Likewise, in the latter part of the 1990s, the New Zealand Digital Library Project began at the University of Waikato, and with the collaboration of UNESCO and the Human Info NGO from 2000, this led to the production of the Greenstone multilingual suite of open-source software for building and distributing digital library collections either on the internet or on CD-ROM (http://www.greenstone.org;

(*continued on page 86*)

# Case study: The Greenstone Digital Library Software

Ian H. Witten

*Professor of Computer Science, University of Waikato, New Zealand*

David Bainbridge

*Department of Computer Science, University of Waikato, New Zealand*

The New Zealand Digital Library Project (Witten and Bainbridge, 2003, 2007) was established in 1995 and grew out of research on text compression (Bell *et al.*, 1990) and, later, index compression (Bell *et al.*, 1994; Witten *et al.*, 1994). Initially, it consisted of a collection of 50,000 computer science technical reports downloaded from the internet (Witten *et al.*, 1995). We were assisted by one-off equipment funding from the New Zealand Lotteries Board and operating funding from the New Zealand Foundation for Research, Science and Technology (1996–1998 and 2002–present).

In 1997 we began to work with Human Info NGO to help them produce fully searchable CD-ROM collections of humanitarian information. The first publicly available CD-ROM, the Humanity Development Library 1.3, was issued in April 1998. A French collection, UNESCO's Sahel point Doc, was issued a year later. The first multilingual collection appeared six months later: the Spanish/English Biblioteca Virtual de Desastres/Virtual Disaster Collection. Since then about 40 CD-ROM collections have appeared. At this point we realised that we did not aspire to be a digital library site ourselves, but rather to develop software that others could use for their own digital libraries.

Towards the end of 1997 we adopted the term Greenstone: we decided that 'New Zealand Digital Library Software' was not only clumsy but could impede international acceptance and so sought a new name. 'Greenstone' turned out to be an inspired choice: snappy, memorable, and un-nationalistic but with strong national connotations within New Zealand. A form of nephrite jade, greenstone is a hallowed substance for Māori, valued more highly than gold. Early releases were posted on our website greenstone.org (which was registered on 13 August 1998), but in November 2000 we moved to the SourceForge site for distribution.

We became acquainted with UNESCO through Human Info's long-term relationship with them. Although they supported Human Info's goal of producing humanitarian CD-ROMs and distributing them in developing countries, UNESCO was really interested in sustainable development, that is, empowering people in those countries to produce and distribute their own digital library collections. We began to aspire to put the power to build collections into the hands of non-technical people (Witten *et al.*, 2001; Bainbridge *et al.*, 2003). From the outset, UNESCO's goal was to distribute the entire Greenstone software (not just individual collections plus the run-time system, as in Human Info's products) on CD-ROM, so that it could be used by people in developing countries without ready access to the internet. These CD-ROMs contained all the auxiliary software needed to run Greenstone as well, which is not included in the internet distributions because it can be obtained from other sources. When we and others started to give workshops, tutorials and courses on Greenstone, we adopted a policy of putting all instructional material – PowerPoint slides, exercises, sample files for projects – on a workshop CD-ROM, and began to include this auxiliary material on the UNESCO distributions.

Good documentation was (rightly!) seen by UNESCO as crucial. They were keen on making the Greenstone technology available in Spanish, French and Russian. The cumbersome process of maintaining up-to-date translations in the face of continual evolution of the software led us to devise a scheme for maintaining all language fragments in a version control system so that the system could tell what needed updating. This resulted in the Greenstone Translator's Interface, a web-based interface where officially registered translators can examine the status of the language interface for which they are responsible and update it (Bainbridge *et al.*, 2003).

With UNESCO's encouragement, we have worked to enable developing countries to take advantage of digital library technology by running hands-on workshops. Recognising that devolution is essential for sustainability, we are now attempting to distribute this effort by establishing regional Greenstone Support Groups. One for South Asia was launched in 2006 and another for Southern Africa in 2007.

*This toki (adze) was a gift from the Maori people of New Zealand in recognition of our project's contributions to indigenous language preservation. It resides in the project laboratory at the University of Waikato.*

see also Bainbridge *et al.*, no date, and http://www.nzdl.org). This has pro-vided a valuable tool for development-related work, enabling the creation of digital libraries such as the Bibliothèque pour le développement durable library in 1999 (http://nzdl.sadl.uleth.ca/cgi-bin/library?a = p&p = about&c = tulane) as well as the UNAIDS library (http://nzdl.sadl.uleth.ca/cgi-bin/library?a = p&p = about&c = unaids) (see the case study 'The Greenstone Digital Library Software' on p. 84). Similar initiatives include the EU's Dig-ital Libraries Initiative and eContent*plus* Programme (http://ec.europa.eu/information_society/activities/digital_libraries/index_en.htm, http://ec.europa.eu/information_society/activities/econtentplus/index_en.htm). Moreover, Google Book Search now provides a facility whereby users can read and search an array of books online, and the Google Books Library Project enables people to gain information about books not yet available online (http://books.google.com/googlebooks/library.html).

Accessing many of these new bibliographic resources nevertheless re-mains a challenge for the poor. While university libraries in the world's rich countries subscribe to vast collections of online journals, the costs of such access remain prohibitively high for institutions in many of the poorer countries of the world. Likewise, having sufficient bandwidth as well as appropriate terminals from which to access these materials gives rise to serious challenges, particularly for marginalised communities. Much work remains to be done in ensuring that appropriate content is developed and made available as extensively as possible to users who cannot afford it.

### *Multimedia materials*
As Chapter 3 highlighted, the use of film and audio in development prac-tice has a long tradition. However, recent advances in digital technologies have transformed the production and storage opportunities associated with such media. Whereas in the past it was complex, costly and bulky to make films or audio-tapes, the use of small digital recorders has brought this opportunity to many people in a relatively easy-to-use and low-cost con-text. Moreover, the explosion of interest in sharing still and video images among friends and communities through the internet, using sites such as http://www.flickr.com, http://www.youtube.com or http://www.myspace.com, reflects the scale of the social demand for such practices. YouTube, which was launched only in February 2005, was bought by Google for US$ 1.65 billion in October 2006, at which point some 100 million videos were being viewed each day. Such potential has not yet, though, been widely used for development purposes, with a search on YouTube on 22 Decem-ber 2006 listing only 214 videos for the words 'Africa' and 'development', including a seven-minute video entitled *Achieving the Millennium Develop-ment Goals* (http://www.youtube.com/watch?v = ReRx12QUv54, accessed 22 December 2006) which had at that date been viewed by 1,400 people. By 7 January 2008, there had been a considerable increase in interest in de-velopment agendas, with 948 videos being revealed in a search for 'Africa'

and 'development', and 9,670 people having viewed the MDG video. These figures nevertheless remain paltry beside the 60,000 videos posted with reference to George Bush or 81,400 on Britney Spears; there were also 28 videos on ICT4D.

The production of multimedia resources has enormous potential for development practice. Paradoxically, though, much of this potential has yet to be realised in full. In part this reflects the expense of developing and editing really high-quality multimedia resources. However, it also reflects a general focus on the use of text-based resources in most learning and teaching environments. Among the most important advantages that film, video and audio can bring to information sharing and knowledge creation in the development context are: their ability to incorporate several senses in the learning experience; an opportunity to provide information that cannot easily be shown in other ways; the use of a story line that can link issues to emotions; their ability to be shown on widely available television sets or even projected onto a sheet hung between trees; and their use as a catalyst for discussion.

Traditional film and video-tape production and storage had four main drawbacks: cameras, processing equipment and projection facilities tended to be very bulky and complex to use; the materials and equipment were relatively expensive; the video-tapes or films did not last long in harsh environments; and they were not conducive to interactivity because the tapes ran in sequence from beginning to end, and were therefore not easy to search for particular scenes or sequences that participants might want to return to for discussion. Many of these issues have now been overcome through the introduction of digital technologies. Cameras today are much cheaper and smaller; there are no expensive film processing costs; relatively little training is required for people to learn how to edit digital video on a computer; CDs or DVDs are cheap and robust in harsh environments; and content is readily searchable and playable for group discussion purposes (see GTZ and inWent, 2003). Good examples of such material include the 20-minute video *Understanding Livelihoods: complexity, choices and policies in Southern India* produced by Catcher Media (no date) for DFID (High *et al.*, 2001; see also http://www.livelihoods.org/info/tools/UL_video.html), and the film *A Mother's Story* made by the Mediae Trust in Kenya in 2000 for the National Malaria Control Programme, which was shown at the annual Roll Back Malaria Global Partners Meeting in Geneva that year, was subsequently incorporated into a CD by Imfundo's partners (http://imfundo.digitalbrain.com), and was later made accessible online (http://www.gg.rhul.ac.uk/ict4d/Malaria.html).

It is important to distinguish between two different types of use of film, video and audio resources: those developed and made by external agents for a particular development learning or dissemination purpose; and those

(*continued on page 90*)

# Case study: The internet of things

Marco Zennaro

*Abdus Salam International Centre for Theoretical Physics, Trieste, Italy*

The internet began in the 1960s as a link between a few university computer centres; in the 1970s and 1980s the users were counted in thousands, and the predominant applications were e-mail and file transfer; in the 1990s, Web browsing became dominant and users were counted in millions. Today, in the 2000s, we are at the start of a new era, in which computer devices will be embedded in everyday objects, invisibly at work in the environment around us. Communication networks will connect these devices together to facilitate anywhere, anytime, always-on communications. The users of the internet will be counted in billions, with humans becoming a minority.

Key technological enablers for the success of this so-called *internet of things* have been identified as radio-frequency identification (RFID) and wireless sensor networks. RFID is an automatic identification method, relying on storing and remotely retrieving data using devices called RFID tags or transponders. A RFID tag is an object that can be attached to or incorporated into a product, animal or person for the purpose of identification using radio waves. In order to connect everyday objects and devices to databases and networks, a system of item identification is necessary. Anything, from a house key to a human being, has the potential to become a node of the internet.

Wireless sensor networks are one of the key building blocks of the internet of things. A sensor node or 'mote' is an electronic device which detects, senses and measures physical phenomena such as heat, motion or light, and responds in a specific way. Being wireless devices, they can easily be deployed even in hostile environments. Sensors collect data from the environment, generating information about their context that can be used to adapt the computing system. The sensors are portable, reliable and low-cost, and can be battery operated. RFID and sensors can create an environment in which the status of objects can readily be determined, monitored and communicated.

These emerging technologies have the potential to offer economic, social and environmental benefits, and the developing world merits special attention. RFID, for example, has been used to track and monitor containers of frozen beef and chicken exported from Namibia to the UK. For Namibia, beef is one of the main items of export to the EU, and tagging containers with RFID sensors ensures the quality of meat. In India, the emerging apparel industry has likewise started to look into RFID to improve its supply-chain efficiency and to comply with international standards.

Smart sensors have much to offer to developing countries. The deployment of a wireless sensor network can enable the measurement of environmental data and its forwarding to the internet, thus allowing researchers to analyse it at a distance. The development of water quality control technologies is essential: in many developing countries, both surface and ground water contain biological and chemical contaminants but the appropriate technology for measuring the type and degree of contaminants in water is lacking. The advantage of wireless sensor networks (WSN) is that they can determine the quality of water with a dense spatio-temporal resolution. A WSN to monitor water quality has been deployed in Bangladesh, where people in the Ganges Delta drink ground water that is contaminated with arsenic. A manual arsenic sensor, combined with the data collected from the sensor network, has been used to get a better understanding of the groundwater chemistry at shallow depths. A WSN has similarly been deployed in Ethiopia to monitor antiretroviral drug therapies for AIDS. The system is expected to replace paper-based handwritten data collection systems currently used to track the progress of the disease. The sensors used in the project were initially developed for use in monitoring vital signs of astronauts in space. These will now help collect information, transfer the data via wireless systems to a base station connected to the internet and facilitate tracking of disease outbreaks.

*Use of radio in a roadside market, Uganda, 2008 (source:* Tim Unwin).

used in a participatory way as part of a self or communal learning process. Both have value in development practice. The former category includes most materials made as contributions to the enhancement of development practices as mentioned above. As Bohmann (2003, unpaginated) has commented, 'These media are usually used in group work to arouse interest in a topic, to transfer certain information, and as a didactic instrument at the micro level'. They can also be used to raise general awareness of development issues among people in richer countries and more privileged societies. However, an alternative and important use of video, and some-times also audio, is in participatory methods (see White, 2003), and notably in the regular monitoring of performance (Lunch, 2007). The use of video by teachers to monitor their own teaching performance, or by doctors in the way in which they respond to patients, can thus be extremely helpful in enhancing the delivery of education and health provision.

### *The power of the internet and the World Wide Web*
It is important to distinguish between two often confused terms: the internet and the World Wide Web (or Web). The internet is essentially a connection of interconnected computers, or a network of networks (Abbate, 1999), where-as the World Wide Web is the body of resources accessed by hyperlinks, commonly called uniform resource locators (URLs), that is accessed over the internet. As the number of computers increases, so too does the power of the internet, but only if these computers are effectively and efficiently connected. Hence the amount of computer memory and the channel capac-ity between computers, often referred to as the bandwidth, are absolutely essential components of the internet. The modern Web provides the world's greatest source of information storage, combining the memory contained in all of the computers of the internet. Moreover, because anyone with a computer terminal and the appropriate software can now upload material, it has transformed traditional processes of information capture, sharing and retrieval (see the case study 'The internet of things' on pp. 88–9).

For the internet to function at all, some computer systems, known as servers, need to run permanently, so as to provide the required services to other computers within a given network that wish to access them. These servers include mail servers that handle e-mails, application servers that run applications, and file servers that store files and databases. The inter-net then works by enabling data to be transmitted in 'packets' through a range of mechanisms, such as through wires, fibre-optic cables or by radio waves (see 'The physical infrastructure', below). So that users can know what data they want to access, a system of rules for addresses has been constructed that enables computers to communicate, and this is known as the Internet Protocol or IP; each computer is allocated a unique IP address that enables it to communicate with any other computer on a network. The dominant IP version in use for the internet today is IPv4, which was released in 1981 (ftp://ftp.rfc-editor.org/in-notes/rfc791.txt) and uses 32-bit binary addresses (usually written as four groups of decimal numbers each representing eight bits as in 213.207.6.42) enabling it to have some 4 billion potential addresses. With the rapidly increasing number of computers, it has been necessary to expand this, and its successor is likely to be IPv6 which uses 128-bit addresses and therefore has the potential for $3.4 \times 10^{38}$ addresses (Loshin, 1999; Miller, 2004). In enabling computers to access data from other computers, it is crucial for data packets to be routed efficiently, and hence much attention has been paid to the design and development of 'routers' that enable path selection to be optimised.

Much of the early development of the internet (Leiner *et al.*, 2003) and its associated protocols and technologies was undertaken within the Defense Advanced Research Projects Agency (DARPA) of the US Department of Defense, evolving from the ARPANET project in the late 1960s. It is therefore no coincidence that most of the control of the internet remains in the hands of US institutions. The system of assigning IP addresses has been particularly controversial. It was embedded in the early work of DARPA, and by the late 1980s the US government had established an Internet Assigned Numbers Authority (IANA, http://www.iana.org) to fulfil this role. Then in 1998 the Internet Corporation for Assigned Names and Numbers (ICANN, http://www.icann.org) was established as a non-profit corporation based in California to manage these and other internet-related functions, particularly the assignment of domain names and IP addresses. This dominance of the USA in internet governance has become a topic of considerable debate, and was one of the key issues discussed during the Tunis phase of the World Summit on the Information Society in 2005 (see pp. 142–3; Huston, 2005).

The amount of traffic using the internet has increased dramatically since its origins in the late 1960s (see Amateur Computerist, 2007). By the start of 2008, it was estimated that there were more than 1.26 billion users, representing more than a doubling in use since 2000 (Internet World Stats, http://www.internetworldstats.com/stats.htm, accessed 7 January 2008). However, as Table 4.1 emphasises, such usage is highly variable across the world. Asia, for example, has the most internet users, but this largely reflects its huge population, of which only 13.7% were actually internet users at the end of 2007. In contrast, North America has the highest percentage of internet users among its population (71.1%), but the lowest usage growth rate (120.2%). The fundamental point to note about these figures is that internet access is still low in Africa, Asia, Latin America, the Caribbean and the Middle East, and even within these regions it is primarily the rich who benefit most from its potential. While many innovative ICT4D projects have been developed, and the pace of change is accelerating rapidly in these regions, the fundamental conclusion that must be drawn is that at present other technologies have much greater potential to deliver the information and communication needs of poor people. If we are truly to aspire to digital equality, with poor people indeed being empowered through the internet, we still have a very long way to go. Indeed, Table 4.1 is a reminder that,

**Table 4.1**  *Internet usage statistics, December 2007*

|  | Internet users (millions) | Internet users as % of population | Internet usage growth 2000–2007 | Usage as % of world use 2007 |
|---|---|---|---|---|
| Africa | 44.3 | 4.7% | 882.7% | 3.4% |
| Asia | 510.5 | 13.7% | 346.6% | 38.7% |
| Australia/ Oceania | 19.2 | 57.1% | 151.6% | 1.5% |
| Europe | 348.1 | 43.4% | 231.2% | 26.4% |
| Latin America/ Caribbean | 126.2 | 22.2% | 598.5% | 9.6% |
| Middle East | 33.5 | 17.4% | 920.2% | 2.5% |
| North America | 238.0 | 71.1% | 120.2% | 17.9% |
| World total | 1,319.8 | 20.0% | 265.6% | 100% |

*Source:* Internet World Stats (http://www.internetworldstats.com, accessed 19 February 2008)

however much work has been done over the last decade in seeking to implement beneficial internet-based learning and health initiatives, these are only scratching the surface of poverty and marginalisation in the poorest regions of the world.

It is not only at a global level that there are striking differences in internet usage. As Figure 2.2 (p. 28) illustrates, even within the poorest regions of the world, there are vast differences. While north African countries such as Tunisia (15.7%) and Egypt (7.5%) generally have more than 5% of their populations being internet users, this figure falls to as low as 0.03% in Liberia, and most sub-Saharan countries have less than 1% of their populations using the internet in 2007 (http://www.internetworldstats.com). Moreover, even where there is access, the quality of access may be extremely poor, reflected in slow download and upload times, unreliable connectivity and high cost. Only when the internet can be reliably available at a price that poor people can afford will it become a powerful tool for their empowerment.

## The physical infrastructure

All communication systems require a physical infrastructure to be in place to provide energy and to generate and receive signals. Without such infrastructure, none of the complex systems of computers, radios or mobile phones that exist today would be able to function. The provision of physical infrastructure, though, is often one of the least considered aspects of ICT4D programmes. On more than one occasion, ambitious programmes have been developed to introduce computers into schools, only for it to be realised subsequently that the absence of electricity has meant that only a few such schools would actually be able to benefit. Indeed, much of the inequality in the distribution of the benefits of ICTs can be attributed to a spatially differentiated supply of basic infrastructure. One of the reasons why China's initiatives to introduce educational television into schools have, for example, been so successful, is that they were preceded by a substantial programme of rural electrification (Pan *et al.*, 2006) with the launching of appropriate satellites then enabling television signals to be relayed throughout the country. In contrast, the lack of a basic and reliable electricity supply across much of Africa today remains one of the greatest handicaps to the continent's development.

In exploring the most relevant infrastructural needs, it is useful to distinguish between two different main types of system, those that use wires or cables and those that do not. Within the latter group it is common to differentiate between terrestrial wireless technologies and the use of satellites. As well as the actual media used, this section of the chapter also pays explicit attention to the energy needs associated with ICTs and questions surrounding their sustainability. It is important to recognise that the choice of infrastructure depends on many factors, including the physical environment in which one is seeking to provide a solution, the distances involved, the security that is required, as well as the need for flexibility in response to future changes in capacity, and the regulatory environment within which the technology is to be deployed (McQuerry, 2004).

### Cables and wires

Until recently, most telecommunication systems used wires as the medium to connect transmitters and receivers using analogue systems. Voice was converted by a microphone to electrical signals that were transmitted down a wire to a speaker that would then convert the waves back to sound. The earliest telephone lines were simply wires made of iron or steel. These rapidly corroded, and it was not until the introduction of hardened copper wires in the late 19th century that a successful basis for effective telephony was established. Bell then introduced a two-wire circuit to replace the single grounded wire system in 1881, and in essence this principle remained the basis of most telephone systems throughout the 20th century, although numerous subsequent innovations enabled increasing capacity to be carried. The original telephones were connected in pairs, but as demand grew individual telephones were connected to exchanges, so that they could then use shared lines between exchanges to connect to any number of other telephones. Initially human operators would connect people to those with whom they wanted to speak. However, advances in telecommunications technology by the mid-1960s enabled electrical switches controlled by pulses sent by the caller's phone to connect the user's line with the number required.

By the late 20th century, the introduction of digital systems transformed telephony, permitting digital signal processing over existing twisted-pair telephone wires. This enabled people with modems to connect these to their normal telephone lines to carry digital signals as well as voice. Digital subscriber lines (DSL), using frequencies above those needed in voice telephone conversations, in conjunction with standards and protocols known as integrated services digital network (ISDN) systems were then introduced to enable complex voice, text and video over normal copper telephone wires. In particular, asymmetric digital subscriber line (ADSL) technology, with flows of data greater in one direction than the other, have now enabled copper wires to retain their place in the market.

As with all technologies, copper wires and cables have both advantages and disadvantages. With copper prices being relatively cheap, and with new algorithms and hardware enabling ever-faster transfer of voice and data, it is likely that traditional telephone cables will continue to be used in this way for some time to come. However, with the dramatic expansion in mobile telephony and in areas where existing cables have not already been laid, it may well be that alternative solutions will become much more popular. This is especially so given the ease with which copper cables can be tapped, and the extent to which they are stolen in many poor countries (Mbarika, 2002).

Fibre-optic technology has recently provided a fundamental challenge to telecommunications systems based on copper wires. It has the particular advantages of being able to carry very much more traffic and of being much less possible to tap into than traditional copper cables. Fibre optics, based on the passing of light through a glass or plastic fibre, were first used in the communications industry in the 1970s, and the field has expanded very rapidly since (Hecht, 2002). The first transatlantic cable using fibre optics went into operation in 1988, and during the 1990s the introduction of photonic crystal fibre, which uses diffraction from a periodic structure rather than total internal reflection to transmit light, led to a considerable increase in capacity. Fibre optics have four key advantages over copper cable: they have much less loss on transmission, and therefore permit long distances to be covered without repeaters or amplifiers; they have very much greater data-carrying capacity or bandwidth; when laid alongside each other, they do not suffer from the 'cross-talk' associated with copper cabling; and they are also very much lighter. Although the costs of production and deployment of fibre-optical cable are higher than for traditional copper cabling, these advantages mean that many of the richer countries of the world are now providing broadband access with previously undreamt-of capacity through the use of fibre optics (see for example http://billaut.typepad. com). As yet, though, only a very small percentage of the total fibre-optical capacity in the world is used, and it is likely to be several more years before it comes to replace traditional copper cabling. If sufficient funding can be made available, though, there is a strong case for poorer countries of the world to install fibre-optic cables from the very beginning in areas that are not yet served, so that they will have the bandwidth capacity for the delivery of services in the future as they become available.

An alternative wired solution to the provision of digital connectivity is through the use of electric power lines, known as power line communication

(PLC) (see for example International Powerline Communications Forum, http://www.ipcf.org and http://www.powerlinecommunications.net; Dostert, 2001). In essence, this can provide communication links wherever electricity flows, by impressing a modulated carrier signal onto the wiring system. This can apply equally through the wiring system of a house, or across a national electricity transmission network. Such systems eliminate the need for separate digital wiring, and have the distinct advantage that they can provide broadband connectivity wherever there are power lines (BPL – broadband over power lines). However, the lack of standardisation in the provision of electricity services, the noisy environment of power lines, and existing regulatory frameworks have all limited the expansion of BPL to date. In the future, particularly in rural areas, there is nevertheless potential for power lines to provide a service backbone with wireless systems then providing wider connectivity from transmitters along the route of a power line.

### Wireless solutions

Wireless technology replaces the need for the medium of cables and wires by using parts of the electromagnetic spectrum to transmit signals. An alternating current is applied to an antenna to produce the waves, and these can then be picked up by a receiver which converts them back into sound, pictures or data. Wireless technologies are often divided into three types: short-range communication between devices; broadcast distribution; and last-mile solutions (Panos, 2006). Wireless technologies use 'radio' frequencies (those electromagnetic waves that lie in the range of 3 Hz to 300 GHz). These can be subdivided into specific groups according to their frequency and wavelength. As frequency increases, wavelength decreases, and these properties mean that different parts of the spectrum are suitable for particular purposes. Thus very low to extremely low frequencies between 3 Hz and 30 kHz, with wavelengths of 100,000 km to 10 km, often known as sonar (sound navigation and ranging), are used for communicating with submarines and geophysics. Radio and television broadcasting generally uses the range from 30 kHz to 300 MHz, and microwave ovens, mobile phones, wireless local area networks (LANs) and Bluetooth use ultra high frequencies of 300–3,000 MHz, with wavelengths generally between 1 m and 100 mm. Three general principles underlie the use of these different spectra:

- the longer the wavelength, the further it goes;
- the longer the wavelength, the better it travels through and around things;
- the shorter the wavelength, the more data it can transport.

(Alchele et al., 2006, p. 16)

Thus radio broadcasting uses longer wavelengths than television since it needs to send less data, and digital broadband – which needs to transport very large amounts of data – uses much shorter wavelengths.

At present, there are two main wireless technologies of interest for data transfer: Wi-Fi (first standards in 1997) and WiMAX (since 2001). Until recently, there were three main Wi-Fi (Wireless Fidelity) standards in use: 802.11 b and g for frequencies between 2.412 and 2.484 GHz, and 802.11 a operating between 5.170 and 5.805 GHz (Gast, 2005). These were largely replaced in 2007 by 802.11-2007. For WiMAX (Worldwide Interoperability for Microwave Access), the original standard was 802.16 for the 10 to 66 GHz range, and this was updated in 2004 (802.16-2004, also known as 802.16d) to add specifications for the 2 to 11 GHz range, being further amended in 2005 to the 802.16e-2005 standard (Andrews *et al.*, 2007). There are important differences between the Wi-Fi and WiMAX standards. In essence, signals from all those wishing to use Wi-Fi must pass through a wireless access point on a random access basis, whereas WiMAX uses a scheduling algorithm which not only makes it more stable but can also ensure that appropriate bandwidth is allocated to control the quality of service delivered. Generally speaking, Wi-Fi is more appropriate for small networks requiring shorter ranges of several hundred metres (although for longer distances see WiLDNet, http://tier.cs.berkeley.edu/wiki/Wireless). In contrast, WiMAX provides solutions over several kilometres typically with a point-to-point connection between an internet service provider (ISP) and an end user (http://www.wimaxforum.org/technology).

All wireless technologies need some kind of transmitter, or antenna, as well as a receiver. One of the key differences between radio and television broadcasting on the one hand and wireless digital technologies on the other is that because of their longer wavelengths the former can pass around obstacles whereas the latter generally cannot. This is why, when designing wireless networks for high bandwidth data transmission, it has until recently been essential to have line-of-sight visibility between the antenna and the receiver. The longer wavelengths of the WiMAX standard are now making this less of a restriction. In designing wireless internet networks, three different configurations are often identified: point-to-point, where a single remote site is linked to a central hub; point-to-multipoint, where a central hub links to a number of remotes; and multipoint-to-multipoint, where all of the points can interconnect with each other. Each of these alternatives can have applications in different circumstances depending on the particular needs of the user, and the constraints placed on them. Likewise, it is important to emphasise that the initial internet connection to the central antenna can be provided in a variety of ways, either through cable or via satellite.

Wireless technologies have immense potential in poor countries and communities, especially where good line-of-sight visibility is possible (for a wide discussion see Castells *et al.*, 2007). In flat areas, a mast can be erected, and in mountainous parts of the world point-to-point connections can be provided by locating antennae on the highest ground. Where there are fears over theft, it is generally also far easier to protect antennae than it is to keep an eye on lengths of cabling over long distances. There are, though, different security concerns with respect to wireless, because the networks are based on a shared medium and their traffic is therefore visible to all users. Where data security is of importance, it is thus essential to use encrypted systems and to maintain effective authentication procedures. Another critical factor that needs to be considered in the use of wireless is the regulatory environment in place, not only within a country but also globally. Without a clearly defined set of rules to control the use of different wavelengths, only those with the most powerful transmitters, or in closest proximity to an antenna, would be able to send or hear a signal. Hence, complex systems of regulation and standards have been put in place to enable these issues to be managed effectively (Bekkers and Smits, 1999; see also Chapter 5).

### Satellites

Satellites are a central part of modern wireless technology. As well as providing means for disseminating radio and television broadcasts widely across the globe, they have increasingly also been used for telephony and multimedia data services. Satellites provide a very important mechanism for enabling digital connectivity in parts of the world poorly served by traditional wired infrastructures, but the initial cost of launching them means that the provision of these services by satellite is an expensive option. Vanbuel (2003, p. 7) has highlighted five key advantages that satellites can provide:

- 'Reception is possible with small antennae.'
- It is possible to have instant connection almost anywhere within the footprint of a satellite, without the need for any cabling or other terrestrial infrastructure.
- The equipment that consumers need to purchase is relatively low cost.
- 'Internet connectivity can be combined with traditional broadcasting technologies such as digital TV and Radio, enabling content providers to select the most appropriate delivery means according to the type of content.'
- The use of satellites for one-way multimedia push services such as data broadcasting is very efficient, because they do not require a modem and internet connection for the return link.

Satellites reflect wireless signals from a transmitter on the ground, the uplink, to receivers somewhere else in the world, the downlink. They do this through transponders, which receive the signals from the transmitting earth station, translate them, and then relay them to an antenna that transmits them back to earth. Satellites in general have several transponders on board, and they can therefore deliver various communication channels together at the same time. Broadly speaking, there are two main kinds of satellite: geosynchronous ones that travel 36,000 km above the earth, making one orbit every 24 hours, thus appearing stationary above a particular part of the earth's surface; and those that travel much faster at less distance from the earth in either medium or low orbits. The advantage for users of geostationary satellites is that earth stations can be fixed in their orientation to pick up their signals, but these satellites require more power to transmit the signal than do low or medium orbiting satellites that are nearer the earth's surface.

One particular application of satellite technology, very small aperture terminal (VSAT) systems, has become particularly prevalent in recent years to provide communication services for a range of uses, from corporate banks to rural telecommunications. VSAT solutions, using dish antennae less than 3 m in diameter, 'provide very efficient point-to-multipoint communication, are easy to install, and can be expanded at low extra cost' (Vanbuel, 2003, p. 31). VSAT is very flexible, and can provide any digital services, including telephony, broadband internet and video-conferencing. For this reason, they have become a popular development solution, exemplified in contexts as diverse as the World Bank's Global Development Learning Network (GDLN) (http://www.gdln.org), which now has some 120 learning centres in nearly 80 countries, and the contracts won by Gilat (http://www.gilat.com) for providing telecommunication services in India and Africa. Problems in implementing the latter have, however, highlighted the costs and complications of using VSAT in rural areas of poor countries.

The type of equipment needed on the ground to receive satellite signals varies with the type of intended usage. Key considerations for users of satellite services are the cost of the ground equipment and the amount paid for the services provided. Cost calculations can be extremely complex (see Vanbuel,

*Satellite solutions in rural Kenya, 2007 (source:* Tim Unwin).

2003), and it has been difficult to find models that enable poor communities to afford the undoubted potential that satellite technology can provide.

### *Energy and environmental sustainability*

None of the above elements of the infrastructure required for ICT4D would be possible without electricity. This applies as much to the power needed to make a radio work, as it does to the energy requirements of a group of servers in the headquarters of an international bank. Unlike many other industrial sectors, ICTs are almost completely dependent on electricity. Other fuels, such as oil and gas, or the energy provided by flowing water or wind, cannot directly power a computer or television transmitter; they first need to be converted into electricity. It is not easy to obtain data on electricity availability globally, but consumption and availability are closely related, and Figure 4.3 therefore provides an important reminder of the dramatic differences between electricity supply in different parts of the world. Despite an almost six-fold increase in electricity generation since 1971, Africa still only produced around 540,000 GWh in 2004, representing a mere 0.62 MWh per person, compared with around 14.25 MWh per person in the USA (figures derived from http://www.iea.org). It is not only at a global scale that these issues make a difference, because in most poor countries there is also a marked difference between electricity supply in urban and rural areas; 60 per cent of households in Africa do not have access to their national grids (Bertolini, 2004, p. 3).

Without electricity there can be no ICT4D. Electricity can, however, be generated in a variety of ways, and recent innovations with solar power and the use of human energy, as with 'wind-up radios' (see for example http://www.freeplayenergy.com), illustrate the diversity of solutions that are available, especially to the most marginalised communities. Central to any consideration of electricity supply in the poorer countries of the world is not only its presence or absence, but also its reliability. For effective implementation of ICT4D programmes, it is essential that there is an appropriate and consistent source of electricity, and this usually means that back-up generators or some form of energy storage is required. Four main scales of electricity supply for ICT4D can be identified: national mains supplies, or the electricity grid; locally produced electricity from solar, wind, water and human energy; generators producing electricity from fuel such as oil or natural gas for specific organisations or institutions; and batteries, both rechargeable and otherwise. One of the fundamental difficulties in delivering ICT4D projects at a large scale is that such projects almost always rely on a mains supply. Using solar power at a single-school level is a costly solution. Nevertheless, as Greenstar (http://www.greenstar.org) have shown, it is possible to build effective solar-powered community centres that deliver electricity, purified water, health and education information, and a wireless internet connection as illustrated in their projects in villages in Jamaica, India, Ghana and Brazil. One of the advantages that many of the poorer countries of the world located between

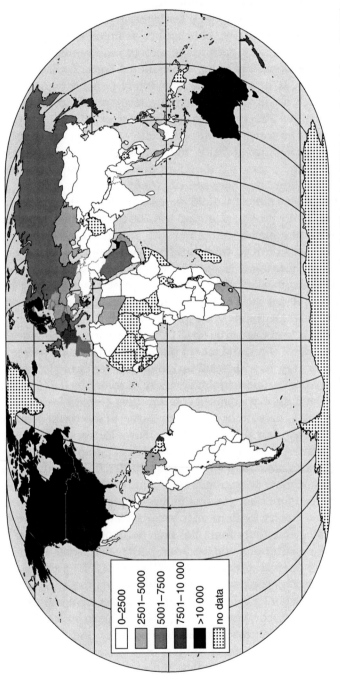

Figure 4.3 *Electricity consumption per head (kWh/capita), 2005 (source: derived from OECD/ IEA data, 2007).*

Legend:
- ☐ 0–2500
- 2501–5000
- 5001–7500
- 7501–10 000
- ■ >10 000
- ▦ no data

the Tropics possess is abundant sunlight, and if photovoltaic technology can increase in efficiency and decline more rapidly in cost in the future then it may offer a viable solution for implementing ICT4D initiatives in locations not served by national grids. Few initiatives have yet experimented with the use of small-scale locally produced wind and water power to provide electricity to marginally located ICT4D programmes, but the potential of these sources of energy, especially in mountainous and coastal regions, is worthy of greater investigation. Critical to all such initiatives is the need to have energy-efficient batteries that can store the electricity that is not immediately used, thereby helping to provide greater continuity of supply. At a smaller scale, the Freeplay Foundation (http://www.freeplayfoundation.org) has been developing and implementing human-powered electricity generation, such as the Weza, a foot-powered portable energy source, that can be used to provide sustainable rural energy solutions for ICTs (see the case study 'Radio for education' on pp. 102–3).

Any discussion of energy would be incomplete without some mention of the environmental sustainability issues surrounding the use of ICTs. There is no doubt that the dramatic global increase in the use of ICTs has led to a considerable surge in energy demand. Moreover, many of the components used in computers are highly toxic and until recently little attempt has been made by suppliers to minimise their use or to initiate recycling programmes (Kuehr and Williams, 2003). Indeed, there have been very few rigorous attempts to analyse the total environmental impact of ICTs. Such research would need to factor in the costs of launching and decommissioning the satellites used for telecommunication purposes, apportioning the full costs of energy infrastructure provision, and the impacts that these technologies have had on human physical mobility through, for example, the use of video-conferencing instead of face-to-face meetings. Campaigning organisations such as AsYouSow (http://www.asyousow.org/sustainability/ewaste.shtml) have nevertheless recently begun to have an impact, with computer companies now beginning to provide recycling solutions for their hardware. Civil society organisations such as Computer Aid International (http://www.computer-aid.org) and Digital Links International (http://www.digital-links.org) have also begun to provide refurbished computers for use in poorer parts of the world, and there is clearly a demand for such products. Nevertheless, there is considerable debate about the costs and benefits of such initiatives. On environmental grounds, the use of refurbished computers prolongs the life of perfectly usable hardware, and thus helps to reduce the wastage resulting from the obsolescence caused by the rapid rate of technological innovation in the ICT industry. However, against this, it can be argued that the shipping of old computers from the richer countries of the world to the poorer ones is actually also shifting the responsibility for their eventual disposal to those who can least afford

(continued on page 104)

# Case study: Radio for education

David Hollow

*ICT4D Collective, Royal Holloway, University of London, UK*

The role of ICTs in enhancing education in Africa has received considerable attention in recent years, with much activity centred on how best to utilise the rapid expansion of computer and internet availability across the continent. Despite the clear educational potential of these technologies, many such initiatives have been influenced by a top-down, supply-led mentality and strong private-sector agendas, with the result that alternative and potentially more appropriate educational technologies have tended to be overlooked. This case study considers how educational development can be catalysed through radio, the ICT that currently has the greatest penetration levels across Africa.

Despite current efforts within African primary education to provide universal access, there are still significant challenges surrounding enrolment, completion rates and overall levels of attainment. The role of radio in providing education within such a context has traditionally been inhibited by two key barriers: the medium's inherent lack of interactivity, leading to the perpetuation of didactic approaches to teaching; and unreliable electricity supplies combined with the prohibitive cost of batteries, leading to a failure to access the most marginalised communities.

These longstanding constraints, compounded by the rise of other in-vogue technologies, have led to radio being somewhat ostracised within current ICT for education agendas. However, the Zambian Ministry of Education initiative Learning at Taonga Market (LTM) demonstrates that, when deployed within an appropriate framework, the radio remains a valuable educational tool in the 21st century. The programme has shown the potential to overcome the recognised limitations of the technology, offering widespread access to high-quality and low-cost education for both economically and geographically marginalised children. The effectiveness of LTM is due to the combination of two distinctive elements: the use of the interactive radio instruction (IRI) teaching methodology and the Lifeline radio.

The IRI methodology is dependent upon a central team of educationalists to design content for the daily radio broadcasts, and a mentor in each community to gather the children and facilitate the local learning environments. This combination develops the radio from a simple rote-learning device into a tool that promotes a student-centred approach based on a constructivist, dialogical pedagogy.

As a dual-powered device utilising both wind-up and solar technology, the Lifeline radio circumvents dependency on traditional sources of power, thus minimising maintenance costs and ensuring widespread and equitable access. The radio was developed by the Freeplay Foundation (*http://www. freeplayfoundation.org*, accessed 20 November 2007) for specific use in the humanitarian sector. It is now deployed in numerous educational contexts across Africa, and is popular because of its simplicity, durability and distinctive design.

LTM was launched with the objective of combining the potential of IRI and the Lifeline radio in order to provide access to good-quality education for the 800,000 Zambian children not currently attending school. Since its launch in 2000, over 160,000 children have received education through the programme. In addition to the curricular broadcasts, a daily life-skills session provides an opportunity for broader learning, encouraging behavioural change among the students and instigating wider discussion among community members. Exam results from Lusaka province in 2007 indicated a significant improvement in educational quality among LTM students compared with those in mainstream schools, leading to a decision by the Ministry of Education to expand the programme to supplement teaching in an additional 4,000 government primary schools during that year.

The scaling-up of ICT for education initiatives to operate sustainably at a national level remains a widespread challenge. However, the case study of LTM in Zambia demonstrates the potential for achieving this transition successfully when certain fundamental components are in place. Programmes must be demand-driven, employ appropriate technology and have support from both local community and government, remaining focused on the primary role of ICTs in education as catalytic tools for instigating progressive reform.

*Zambian schoolgirl listening to a Lifeline radio (source:* http://www. freeplayfoundation.org).

it, especially since older computer parts are also more likely to fail than younger ones. On the socio-economic side, there are likewise strong arguments that giving poor people the opportunity to learn how to use computers is of real benefit, regardless of the quality of the actual computers themselves. Much high-quality educational software, for example, can run on very basic computers, and does not require the use of the latest high specification and expensive machines. On balance, provided that the quality of the refurbished computers is of a high standard, and particularly where people in recipient communities enhance their own skills and expertise by undertaking the refurbishment work themselves, there does seem to be some value in such initiatives. However, as a report by SchoolNet Africa (2004) summarises, many well-meaning initiatives have failed because of faulty computers, a lack of planning, and poor quality of post-supply support. In contrast, where refurbishing and maintenance skills can be developed within Africa, where the schemes are coordinated and implemented coherently, and where in-school ICT capacity is explicitly enhanced, then they can indeed bring benefits to people who could not otherwise afford to access computers.

## User interfaces and information sharing

People require some kind of physical interface if they wish to gain information and communicate with each other at a distance. Whereas in the past there were distinct types of interface for various such interactions, the advent of digital technologies has meant that single multi-functional devices now combine most of the required functionality. The use of fixed-line telephones transformed traditional means of face-to-face communication, enabling people in the 20th century to communicate with others in any part of the world. Nevertheless, telephones were rarely used primarily to gain vast amounts of information; their fundamental purpose was to enable two people to communicate effectively together at a distance. In contrast, televisions were used to broadcast information and entertainment; few people ever imagined that they could be an interface for two-way communication. Today, Voice over Internet Protocol (VoIP) and wireless technologies have enabled computers to become hugely powerful interfaces both for the gathering of information and also for communication purposes (see for example http://www.skype.org). This convergence of technologies has had a profound impact on human society, but remains spatially constrained. For many of the world's poorest people, telephones, radios and computers remain distinct and separate. This section therefore continues to draw a distinction between these main types of user interface.

### *Telephones*

Fixed-line telephones dominated the world of telephony during the 20th century. Although radio was in use as early as the 1920s to enable communication on trains and with aeroplanes, it was not until the 1960s that advances in electronics enabled the first primitive mobile phones to be produced. These operated in a specific zone, or cell, accessible from a base station. By the 1980s, the technology had advanced sufficiently for the first generation of commercial mobile phones to be produced, taking advantage of networks of cells and base stations situated relatively close together. Such phones, however, were extremely bulky, and it was not until the 1990s that second generation (2G) phones were introduced (commonly known as GSM), using different frequencies and much more advanced signalling between phones and networks, as well as improvements in battery design and circuitry that made them smaller. The subsequent dramatic rise in the use of mobile phones was enabled by the construction of numerous base stations to increase cell density and thus permit users seamlessly to access networks wherever they wanted to. The success of such mobile phones led to a plethora of new innovations and competing technologies, which in turn required a complex system of standards to be introduced to enable users to communicate effectively with each other. Most recently, third generation (3G) mobile phones have been developed to combine voice data with digital video and e-mail. These required the use of new radio frequencies, the licensing of which in many countries has been seen by governments as a source of substantial revenue generation. The consequent high costs of implementation, as well as uncertainties over whether users actually want the services provided, has therefore led to some delay in the worldwide roll-out of 3G telephony.

Over the last decade, mobile phones have transformed the world of telephony (Table 4.2), both technically and also socio-spatially (Taylor and Harper, 2003). The impact of mobile telephony has been greatest in regions that previously had the lowest levels of fixed-line connectivity. Thus, although Africa still has by far the lowest density of telephone subscribers, some 87.2 per cent of all telephone lines on the continent were mobile subscribers in 2006, compared with a mere 57.5 per cent in the USA. This indicates not only

Table 4.2   *Fixed-line and mobile telephone subscribers, 2005–2006*

|  | Total telephone subscribers per 100 inhabitants | | Mobile phone subscribers per 100 inhabitants | | Mobile subscribers as a % of total phone subscribers |
|---|---|---|---|---|---|
|  | 2005 | 2006 | 2005 | 2006 | 2006 |
| Africa | 18.48 | 24.32 | 15.34 | 21.77 | 87.2 |
| Americas | 86.14 | 94.72 | 53.04 | 62.27 | 65.7 |
| USA | 130.23 | 134.55 | 71.43 | 77.40 | 57.5 |
| Asia | 38.45 | 45.20 | 22.98 | 29.73 | 65.2 |
| China | 56.53 | 62.62 | 29.90 | 34.83 | 55.6 |
| India | 12.67 | 18.47 | 8.16 | 14.83 | 80.3 |
| Europe | 125.12 | 135.14 | 85.35 | 99.27 | 70.5 |
| Oceania | 106.55 | 109.33 | 68.78 | 73.43 | 66.5 |

*Source:* derived from ITU (http://www.itu.int/ITU-D/icteye/Indicators/Indicators.aspx#)
*Note:* Figures are as given by ITU in separate tables, and do not always necessarily compute accurately

the problems and costs of installing and maintaining fixed-line services in Africa, where theft of copper cabling has been rife, but also the huge demand that exists for such communication services. Table 4.2 also emphasises the very rapid changes currently taking place globally in the balance between fixed and mobile telephony. These generalisations, nevertheless, hide many spatial inequalities, and as Figure 2.2 highlights (p. 28), there remain huge differences in the density of mobile phone subscribers in different countries. Thus, in states such as Ethiopia, where the government tightly regulates the telecommunications sector, there were on average only 0.53 mobile subscribers per 100 people in 2005, whereas in South Africa the figure was as high as 71.6 subscribers per 100 people (http://www.itu.int, accessed 26 March 2007). Viewed from another perspective, the average annual cost of mobile telephony for a user in Ethiopia is approximately 1/10th of the average annual income, whereas in South Africa it is 1/150th (Vanbuel, pers. comm.). Furthermore, within most of the poorer countries of the world, rural areas still have much less accessibility than do urban areas, once again reinforcing the disadvantages between the urban rich and the rural poor.

The very rapid adoption of mobile telephony in many of the poorer countries of the world, and particularly in Africa, has given rise to much interest in its use for broadly defined development purposes (see for example Kukulska-Hulme and Traxler, 2005). Typical potential uses, for example, have been explored particularly with respect to the opportunities that they can provide for farmers to gather market information, for mobile banking, for the provision of health services, and in teacher education. However, despite such potential value, much evidence suggests that mobile phones as yet are still used primarily for social networking rather than for any more specific poverty elimination purposes. Souter *et al.* (2005, p. 8) draw five important conclusions about the use of telephones in Gujarat, Mozambique and Tanzania:

- they are very important in emergencies so that people can contact one another;
- they are used widely to maintain social networks, particularly within the family;
- 'they are valued more for saving money than for earning money';
- richer and better-educated people place more value on phones than do poorer people;
- they were 'considered unimportant for information gathering'.

Although these conclusions relate to the use of telephones in general, and not just mobile phones, they provide a salutary warning for those who see this particular technology as offering significant potential for the elimination of poverty.

This is not, though, to suggest that enabling poor people to have access to telephony is not of value in itself. Social networking is of extreme importance to human empowerment, and the ability of poor people to use mobile phones for social and political purposes can be of great value to their sense of being and identity (see also Brown *et al.*, 2001). Socially, there is much evidence that the advent of mobile telephony has fundamentally changed the ways in which people interact with each other. In the past, people had to move to fixed locations in order to communicate at a distance by phone, whereas now they have the freedom to communicate anywhere that they have a signal. This has led to profound changes in social interaction, and to very different kinds of human movement in space. Furthermore, the introduction of text messaging on mobile phones has led to the emergence of entirely new modes of behaviour, especially among young people, who have developed many new and culturally distinct forms of communication (see for example Taylor and Harper, 2003; Castells *et al.*, 2007). The political use of mobile phones is especially interesting, because they can be used both by those seeking to impose the rule of law, as well as by those eager to engage in political protest against that law. The richer governments of the world thus see their tracing of the global flow of phone conversations as a permissible means to fight the so-called 'war against terror', whereas others see it as an infringement of individual human liberties. As with so many technologies, the ability of those in power to control and regulate their use suggests that ultimately the advantage lies with them rather than with those eager to use such technologies to create alternative social and political structures.

### *Computer technologies*

The modern computer has until recently been one of the most powerful tools in transforming the ways in which we communicate, gain information and share knowledge. While computational machines have been in existence for centuries, it was only in the 1960s that the invention of integrated circuits and microprocessors paved the way for the rapid dissemination of home and workplace computers from the 1970s onwards (Ceruzzi, 2003; for timeline see http://en.wikipedia.org/wiki/Timeline_of_computing). Central to the success of this transformation has been the dramatic increases in memory and processing speed (see pp. 79–80). Three main types of device associated with modern computers are usually distinguished: the processing part of the computer itself; input devices; and output devices. Broadly speaking, the hardware necessary for a computer to function consists of the following: the motherboard, holding the central processing unit (CPU) and random access memory (RAM), as well as other parts such as the basic input/output system (BIOS); a storage device, usually known as a hard disk; a power supply and fan to keep it cool; video and audio cards in order to enable sound and visual displays; buses which transfer data or power between components; and a means of enabling the computer to interact with the internet, such as a modem. Input devices are becoming increasingly diverse, moving beyond the traditional mouse and keyboard, to include microphones, cameras, gaming sticks, tablets, image scanners and screens that also act as input devices. Output devices include screens, printers, loudspeakers or touchpads for people with visual impairments. Many of these can be integrated into a single notebook computer, but more often than not the computational, output and input devices remain separate, as with desktop computers that also require external power supplies.

While hardware provides the basic functionality of computers, it is the software that runs on them that enables users to take advantage of this. Most people have little knowledge of the processing functionality of computers, and their use tends to be restricted to five main functions: information gathering (most frequently on the internet, but also from data storage devices such as CDs or DVDs); communication (traditionally via e-mail, but now increasingly frequently through social networking sites, such as http://www.facebook.com, and VoIP); information processing (from basic calculations, to image processing, and database applications); the production of information and knowledge (as in the writing of reports, or graphic design and simulations); and entertainment (in the form of music, films and games).

The most important point to be made here is that the particular conjuncture of hardware and software can be configured very differently to serve the needs of varying users. Unfortunately, all too often users are provided with standardised hardware and software that may not actually be of direct benefit to their development needs. For example, almost all basic ICT training programmes such as the European/International Computer Driving Licence (ECDL/ICDL) (http://www.ecdl.com) focus largely on the provision of a standardised set of 'office' packages, such as word processing, spreadsheets, databases and presentations. While these are indeed relevant to business environments, they are invariably of little direct use to poor and marginalised communities. Teachers, for example, do not need to learn how to use the word-processing functions of an office package in order to be able to use good educational software to help students learn. Likewise, Sugata Mitra's (2003) work on minimally invasive education has shown conclusively that young poor people can benefit from using computers placed in readily accessible places in their communities without any formal training at all (see the case study in Chapter 10, pp. 340–1, and http://www.hole-in-the-wall.com). Moreover, people with disabilities, including visual and hearing impairments as well as those who have difficulty controlling their fine motor skills, can benefit enormously from input and output devices designed to suit their needs, such as Braille readers and specially designed keyboards and mice. Unfortunately, because of the relatively small demand for such devices, they are much more expensive than the standardised hardware available to other users.

One distinction in the architecture or configuration of computer systems that is of particular importance in the field of ICT4D is that between what are known as 'fat' client and 'thin' or 'lean' client systems. Because of the relative cheapness of personal computers (PCs), most computer laboratories in schools, libraries, universities, businesses and community centres in the richer parts of the world effectively consist of a large number of fully functional individual computers, linked together by cabling to a central server that then provides connectivity to the outside world as well as other networking services. Most of the processing is actually done on the individual desktop or notebook computers, with data only being passed to a server for networking, and sometimes storage. This is what is known as a 'fat client' solution. However, for most uses it is not necessary to have large amounts of processing power within all of the computers in a lab, and a single powerful server can do most of the necessary processing for a large number of 'dummy' terminals. These terminals need only contain an input (keyboard, mouse) and an output (screen) device, as well as a limited amount of processing sufficient to run a web browser or some kind of remote desktop software. They are therefore generally cheaper, and can be of much lower specification than the desktops to be found in most computer labs across the world. Such 'thin client' architectures therefore have much potential in delivering appropriate solutions in contexts where the cost of hardware is a major concern. Other benefits that thin client systems offer for development contexts include their lower energy costs, their ability to be used effectively in dirty environments because the terminals do not have moving parts, lower maintenance costs because everything can be managed from the server, and the fact that because the terminals are of low value they are less appealing to thieves. Despite these advantages, and the ardent advocacy of organisations such as NetDay South Africa (http://www.netday.org.za), it is surprising that not more thin client solutions are being promoted in Africa and Asia. In part this is because such solutions require careful and organised deployment and support, and work best where there can be institution-wide implementation, which is not often possible in small-scale community-based installations.

### Convergence and the new generation of mobile devices

One of the key features of the ICT industry over the last decade has been the rapid convergence in technologies. The latest generation of mobile phones and personal digital devices, for example, not only provide telephony, but also contain cameras, radios and calendars as well as having quite powerful computational abilities and connectivity to the Web. Thus, in 2007 Nokia's advertising campaign for their recently launched N95 mobile phone described it as 'It's what computers have become' (http://shop.nokia.co.uk/invt/0027027, accessed 4 May 2007). Such technology nevertheless comes at a price, with the N95 costing £459 from Nokia at the start of 2008 (http://shop.nokia.co.uk, accessed 7 January 2008), compared with the lower cost of a Dell Inspiron 6400 laptop at only £329 (http://www.dell.com, accessed 7 January 2008). In the not-too-distant future it is possible to imagine a single small combined device that will have all of the basic information and communication functionality that most people will need. To date, the key restrictions on most mobile devices have been the size of the screen and the difficulties of using the keyboard. However, external keyboards are already available, and as voice-controlled software improves, it is likely that inputting information will become much easier. More of a challenge is the problem of the screen size, but even this is becoming less of an issue, as shown in the quality of videos and movies on devices such as the latest generation of iPods from Apple (http://www.apple.com/ipod/ipod.html).

Already, there is a wealth of expertise on mobile- or m-learning (see for example http://www.m-learning.org; Attewell, 2005; Kukulska-Hulme and Traxler, 2005; Leech *et al.*, 2005), but much of this remains ambivalent in terms of its real development benefits for poor and marginalised communities. Enthusiasts are eager to show that it is indeed possible to use small digital devices such as mobile phones and PDAs to provide useful materials for teachers and learners, but their use has not yet caught on as swiftly as might have been expected. In part this can be explained by the findings of Souter *et al.*'s (2005) study which emphasise that people in Asia and Africa still tend to want to use their phones primarily for communication, rather than actually to gather information. It may also reflect quite simply the lack of relevant content and educational software that has as yet been made available for these devices. The size of the screens on these small devices, especially for those with poor eyesight, is nevertheless likely to remain a serious drawback to their wider use for learning purposes.

This problem of size can, however, be approached from another direction by thinking about reducing the size as well as the cost of notebook computers. The One Laptop per Child initiative (OLPC), launched by Nicholas Negroponte in 2005 with a group of colleagues from the MIT Media Lab (http://www.laptop.org), provides one such vision for the future (see also Intel's Classmate project http://download.intel.com/intel/worldahead/pdf/classmatepc_productbrief.pdf?iid = worldahead + ed_cmpc_pdf, accessed 4 May 2007). The OLPC initiative in part seeks to reduce the cost of specially designed laptops for children by purchasing very large numbers of parts at discounted prices. Initially, it was announced that the laptop would cost $100 but by April 2007 this figure was revised to $175, which has reduced its appeal. Although the OLPC project specifically claims that it is an education initiative rather than a laptop one, with its goal being 'To provide children around the world with new opportunities to explore, experiment and express themselves' (http://www.laptop.org/en/vision/index.shtml, accessed 11 May 2007), the pedagogic model upon which it is based is seriously flawed (Kozma, 2007) and its real educational usages in poor countries have not yet been sufficiently proven. Moreover, the cost of providing such laptops to every poor child in Africa would be prohibitively expensive, and there is a strong argument that such money could better be spent on training good teachers to inspire a new generation of African learners. Interestingly, India has rejected the OLPC project, and in May 2007 its Ministry of Human Resource Development announced that it was exploring the production of even cheaper laptops, costing an estimated $47 per unit, possibly coming down to only around $10 (http://timesofindia.indiatimes.com/TOIonline/India/HRD_hopes_to_make_10_laptops_a_reality/articleshow/1999849.cm, accessed 11 May 2007). If this price mark is indeed even approximately achievable, then there do seem to be very real possibilities for extensive deployment of a new generation of small but powerful user interfaces that could become of real value to poor people and marginalised communities. We urgently therefore need to be engaging much more pro-actively in exploring the potential of these hardware 'solutions', identifying how best they might serve the needs of such communities. We must also develop and share better understandings of the total cost of deployment of such technologies before foisting them on unsuspecting governments and educational systems.

### Radios and television
Much of the ICT4D literature and practice, while espousing the notion that ICTs are indeed much more diverse than just the use of computers and the internet, has tended to ignore the real contribution that more traditional forms of mass media can make to contemporary development. Indeed, it is often the case that the most appropriate and effective means of communication can be radio and TV, particularly since they are generally most accessible for the poorest and most marginalised communities (Figure 4.2) (Buckley, 2000; Girard, 2003; Skuse et al., 2004; Mozammel and Odugbemi, 2005).

The use of TV and radio for development objectives has not, though, been unproblematic (de Fossard, 1996). By definition, mass media has tended to be centrally driven, with the intention of broadcasting a particular set of messages to a large number of intended recipients. Indeed, many radio-for-development initiatives in Africa and Asia initially drew their impetus from the use of radio programmes in the post-1945 period in Europe to encourage a particular path of social and economic change. Similar initiatives in the poorer countries of the world have, as Melkote and Steeves (2001, p. 268) comment, been 'criticized for (i) their trivial and irrelevant content; (ii) giving rise to a *revolution of rising frustrations* in developing nations; and (iii) increasing the knowledge gap between the advantaged and disadvantaged sectors of the population'.

National centralised public broadcasting has often been used to convey particular messages through which governments have sought to influence and control their populations. Indeed, the character of broadcasting largely reflects the character of the society that produces it. Centralised states, most notably the Soviet Union and fascist Germany, used film and radio directly and effectively in the 20th century to seek to impose the will of their leaders on the minds of their populations (Taylor, 1998). Nevertheless, all publicly or government-owned radio and TV broadcasting does have this potential to convey only the messages that rulers want their people to hear. As Barnett (2004, p. 251) has emphasised: 'Modern understandings of the relationships between media and citizenship have developed in a specific context in which broadcasting was institutionalized as an assemblage of technologies, organizations, markets and social practices that articulated two spatial scales of activity: the private domestic home and the nation state'. One of the most striking examples of the use of radio in recent times to mobilise people to do the will of their leaders was thus its use in the Rwandan genocide that took place in 1994. As reported by Fahamu (http://www.fahamu. org/rwanda.php): 'Prior to the genocide, radio stations and newspapers were carefully used by the conspirators to dehumanise the potential victims, Rwanda's Tutsi minority. During the genocide, radio was used by the Hutu extremist conspirators to mobilise the Hutu majority, to coordinate the killings and to ensure that the plans for extermination were faithfully executed' (see also http://news.bbc.co.uk/1/hi/world/africa/3257748.stm; and Windrich, 2000, for an Angolan example).

Nevertheless, as Buckley (2000, p. 180) has also emphasised: 'Democracy and communication are inextricably linked, so much so that the existence or otherwise of certain forms of communications can be a measure of the limits to which democracy itself has developed or is held back'. Where the mass media is independent from government control, and ensures a plurality of voice, it can do much to provide opportunities for effective democratic processes to emerge. Moreover, local and community radio can be used highly effectively not only to convey particular information messages but also to engage and involve people in beneficial development practices (see for example Mano, 2004; Papa *et al.*, 2000; Jayaprakash, 2000; Vaughan *et al.*, 2000a, b; Villaran and Caistor, 2000). In developing such programmes, it is crucial for script writers and producers to draw upon the advantages of radio as a medium, such as its basis in oral tradition, its appeal to the imaginations of listeners, and its ability to be heard en masse and individually at the same time. Likewise, they need to overcome problems with the medium, notably that most listeners tend to use radio as background, that it is usually only heard once, that there are some subjects that radio alone cannot teach, and that it can only use the medium of sound to try to create an impression of the scenes that are being represented (de Fossard, 1996).

It is often thought that radio is merely a one-way transmission of information and ideas, but the use of telephones and the internet have transformed the potential for interactivity in radio usage. This is typified in some of the initiatives that have sought to introduce community radio for empowering poor people. As Jewel (2006) has commented in the context of Bangladesh:

Community Radio is radio for the people and by the people. The main objective of such a radio station is to enhance democratic process at a local level by giving voice to the voiceless. Also such an outlet helps in increasing diversity of content and information at the local level in order to promote culture. It also encourages participation, sharing information and innovation...It can reach people who live in areas with no phones and no electricity. Radio reaches people who can't read and write. It can be a main vehicle to distribute information, discuss issues and define our culture.

(Jewel, 2006, p. 5)

(For a wealth of resources on community radio, see http://www.communityradionetwork.org.)

Reducing the costs of equipment and opening up licensing to the spectrum of broadcasting airwaves have enabled local communities to produce radio programmes that can be of real relevance to their needs, be they farmers in parts of rural India, or teachers in Africa (see UNDP and VOICES, 2004a, b). However, the origin of community radio in the illegal pirate radio stations of the 1970s has given rise to some concerns over its use (Sakolsky and Dunifer, 1998). Hence, the conditions under which community radio stations are emerging are generally being very tightly regulated by national governments. In the long run, though, it seems likely that the increasing use of podcasts and the ease of dissemination of digital broadcasting over the Web will lead to much more general acceptance of the value that community radio stations can provide.

The added realism provided by the visual dimension of television has also been used extremely powerfully in delivering empowerment and development-related programmes that move beyond the mere sound of radio. However, the costs of television production and broadcasting are much higher than those for radio. To produce a 15-minute radio-soap episode in Kenya cost around £800 in 2007, whereas to produce a high-quality 30-minute episode of a TV-soap cost around £20,000. Moreover, the costs of TV airtime are also very high, being £2,000 for a 30-minute slot for TV in Kenya as compared with Kenya Broadcasting Corporation's charge of around £800 for 15 minutes on their Kiswahili radio service. However, if the TV or radio programme is popular and relevant, the costs can be met by advertisers. The value of TV for conveying important development-related messages is particularly striking, especially since it can often be used to reach much larger audiences than radio. In Kenya, for example, three main TV stations compete for a seven million audience, whereas there are 48 FM radio stations competing for a 20 million audience.

The benefits of both TV and radio are well illustrated by the work of Soul City, which first began programmes on HIV/AIDS and mother and child health in South Africa in 1994, and by 2007 was regularly reaching some 16 million South Africans. Key factors in the success of Soul City have been its multimedia format, the drama 'edutainment' format that has been sustained over time, and its thorough development process grounded in local contexts (Scheepers *et al.*, 2004). Another example of the value of TV in South Africa has been *Yizo Yizo*, an educational programme first shown in 1999 which focuses on youth issues, and is described by its producers as 'a gritty, uncompromising television drama series set in a township school that has achieved record-breaking audiences and cult status among South Africa's youth. Rape, murder, prostitution, abuse, HIV/AIDS. Serious issues. We wanted to contextualize them for people with the power of music, laughter, friendship and glamour to match the gritty authenticity of the work' (http://www.thebomb.co.za/yizo1.htm; see also Barnett, 2004).

The value of TV and radio is not, though, only through the impact that it has among the world's poorer communities. Media events such as Live Aid in 1985 (Geldof, 1986) and Live 8 in 2006 (http://www.live8live.com), which it is claimed was watched by 3 billion people, have a very significant effect in raising issues associated with poverty in the minds of people living in the richer countries of the world. This, in turn, contributes to political campaigns, and to the policies adopted by donor countries with respect to development agendas. Nevertheless, the imagery and sounds broadcast on TV and the radio, as well as those used more widely in advertising campaigns, are far from neutral, and are chosen to represent the views of those producing the programmes. This was particularly well brought home in a report by VSO (2002) that explored the impact of events such as Live Aid on the UK population's perceptions of development. It highlighted that: 'Many UK consumers retain an essentially one-dimensional view of developing countries. The stereotypes are primarily driven by images of drought and famine in African countries – "the Live Aid Legacy"' (VSO, 2002, p. 15). As the VSO (2002, p. 15) report went on to comment: 'While these stereotypes are not completely false, they are only part of the picture. They generate and reinforce a relationship of powerful giver and helpless recipient. This relationship pigeonholes and constrains developing countries, creating the impression of a one-way, rather than two-way relationship. In turn, this limits our capacity to learn and benefit from such countries and cultures'.

## Individuals and communities: debates over software and content

Chapters 2 and 3 highlighted the contrasting logics of different approaches to development practice, and placed particular emphasis on the need to consider relative aspects to poverty as well as the currently more popular focus on economic growth as a solution to absolute poverty. These different approaches also underlie one of the fundamental conceptual distinctions in the use of ICTs for development, one that has crucial practical implications. At the heart of this debate is the way in which we conceptualise the value of knowledge, and whether it is something that should be individually or communally 'owned' (Figure 4.2).

This has particular resonance for any consideration of ICT4D, especially since the new technologies discussed in this chapter have the potential to make information much more accessible and more widely distributed than ever before. Two, often conflated, aspects need to be distinguished: the actual information *content*; and the mechanisms through which this is distributed, including both the *channel* and the *software*. Models and practices exist whereby each of these can be subject to payment, or can be free to end users. There is, though, as yet little agreement as to which options are actually best for different communities (see for example Rangachari, 2006; Yusof, 2007), in part because advocates of the different propositions usually base their arguments on very different premises and assumptions.

### Software solutions

For the purposes of this discussion, the term software is used to refer to the programs that enable hardware, including not only computers but also phones and other digital devices, to function effectively. For long, software designed by programmers working for the private sector has been developed and sold by companies such as Microsoft (with its Windows and Vista operating systems) that have kept the programming code confidential. The operating systems and application programs that run on it, such as Microsoft Office, are sold at a profit to enable the programmers to be paid, new products to be developed and shareholders to reap financial benefit. In contrast, there has also been a parallel movement that has sought to develop software on a shared basis for the common good (Gay, 2002). This 'free software movement' was officially founded by Richard Stallman in 1983 when he initiated the GNU (GNU's Not Unix) Project, and it became fully functional in 1992 when Linux (developed by Linus Torvalds) was released as a completely independent and free operating system (Moody, 2002). If proprietary systems are essentially about economic gain, free software is much more of a social and ethical movement, and this distinction is one of the main reasons why advocates of these contrasting positions frequently seem to have difficulty in agreeing on any basis for reaching consensus decisions.

The creation of 'free' software has necessitated the creation of new types of licence that seek to permit how people are allowed to use it. The Free Software Foundation has thus defined four freedoms:

- The freedom to run the program, for any purpose (freedom 0).
- The freedom to study how the program works, and adapt it to your needs (freedom 1). Access to the source code is a precondition for this.
- The freedom to redistribute copies so you can help your neighbor (freedom 2).
- The freedom to improve the program, and release your improvements to the public, so that the whole community benefits (freedom 3). Access to the source code is a precondition for this.

(http://www.gnu.org/philosophy/free-sw.html)

During the late 1990s, alternative models emerged, particularly the Open Source Initiative, which has not been so opposed to proprietary software, and has instead promoted the use of the term 'open source software' as an alternative to free software. In turn, FOSS (Free and Open Source Software) and FLOSS (Free/Libre Open Source Software), the latter ensuring the incorporation of a French dimension, have emerged as generic terms to refer to alternatives to proprietary software.

The critical question for those advocating the development and use of FOSS (see for example Ouédraogo, 2005) is how to generate sufficient revenue to cover the costs involved in developing the software. Sometimes this is done by providing services in support of the programs that have been developed, such as training or maintenance, but few such models have as yet been proven to be particularly profitable or sustainable. Much FOSS development is actually undertaken by programmers who generate income from other activities, even working for companies selling proprietary software, and treat their FOSS work as a 'spare-time' activity, thus in a sense self-exploiting their labour for the common good. There is extensive debate as to the relative advantages of open source and proprietary software. Advocates of open source point out that:

- it is much cheaper for end users than proprietary software, and therefore it is particularly relevant for poorer communities;
- it is less susceptible to viruses, because potential assailants are less interested in damaging a communal project;
- it is of potentially higher quality, because a whole community of developers is available to enhance it and solve any problems that emerge, unlike the case of proprietary software which is developed by a smaller number of paid programmers;
- it has the moral high ground, because it is developed and shared for the common good rather than individual profit; and
- those involved in the community are among the most gifted and committed programmers who are involved primarily because of their interest rather than any income that it generates.

In contrast, advocates of proprietary software argue that you get what you pay for, and that to develop high-quality software requires very considerable investment that must be financed through an appropriate market mechanism. Moreover, they also argue convincingly that certain highly specialist types of software, especially where secrecy is involved, can only be developed through focused research and development that must in turn be paid for.

In trying to resolve these apparently contradictory positions, it can be suggested that different types of solution are preferable in different contexts. A comparative study by bridges.org (2005), for example, has emphasised that many other factors than simply cost must be taken into consideration in reaching any decision, and local context and needs are crucially important. However, if an organisation, be it a small NGO or an entire country's education system, simply cannot afford licences for Windows operating systems, then a Linux-based alternative may well make a lot of sense. Likewise, with applications software, Open Office (http://www.openoffice.org) is a completely free multiplatform alternative to Microsoft Office. Recognising this threat to their position, but also determined to help reduce the digital divide, Microsoft announced the release of a cut-down version of its Vista operating system and Office software called the Microsoft Student Innovation Suite early in 2007, to be made available for students in developing countries for the sum of only $3 (http://www.microsoft.com/emerging/transformingeducation/MicrosoftStudentInnovationSuite.mspx). An alternative approach has been that adopted by Apple, which deliberately sought to bring together different development environments, and combined the work of its own programmers alongside the strengths of the FOSS movement in creating its Mac OS X operating system (see http://www.kernelthread.com/mac/oshistory). Crucial to the ability of users to work across several environments has been the incompatibilities involved in using different operating systems. As a result, regulators and indeed many application software developers have been keen to ensure consistency of standards across the industry, and those operating on behalf of consumers have also sought to limit the monopolistic tendencies of some global corporations. In one of the best known of these, the European Commission concluded in 2004 that Microsoft had broken European Union competition law, by leveraging its near monopoly for its operating system 'onto the markets for work group server operating systems and for media players' (European Commission, 2004).

### Open content

A similar but distinct debate has arisen over the cost and means of production of content, usually with reference to educational content, but also of relevance to health-related content and indeed market information (see for example http://topics.developmentgateway.org/openeducation and http://www.hewlett.org/Programs/Education/OER). Traditionally, most published 'content' was developed by authors who entered contracts with publishers to produce books or articles, the income from which funded the publishing houses, defrayed the authors' expenses, and if the author was lucky might generate a small profit. However, by the end of the 20th century this model began to break down, with new ICTs enabling knowledge to be shared much more readily across the world, and a completely new international market in higher education provision also beginning to emerge. This has given rise to profound challenges to traditional models of higher education and knowledge production. In particular, authors and publishers have been forced to question the continued value of academic journals as the optimal means of knowledge dissemination for the former and as a source of profit for the latter. Likewise, universities have had to rethink their models of learning provision, with MIT for example leading the way in making the content of its lectures freely available on the Web (http://ocw.mit.edu; see also http://openlearn.open.ac.uk), and many institutions now providing the opportunity for students to undertake courses through distance-based modalities.

These changes have been brought to the fore in discussions about open educational resources (OER), and the value of collaborative authoring projects, enabled by the use of software such as wikis that allow many users to edit content (see especially http://oerwiki.iiep-unesco.org; but also Downes, 2007; Tapscott and Williams, 2006). As with FOSS, discussions concerning OER are similarly charged, and derive from fundamentally different conceptualisations of the world: on the one hand, the individualistic view, where knowledge is seen as a commodity, the purchase of which can give rise to greater earning potential and is thus a good investment; and on the other, the view that knowledge is a collectively produced social good, that should therefore be shared communally and indeed globally. The former is based once again primarily on economic arguments, whereas the latter is derived from rather different social and philosophical premises.

Three aspects of OER are particularly pertinent to their use in the context of ICT4D. First, there is already a wealth of content that is freely available on the Web for educational and health-related purposes. To be sure, not enough of this is specifically relevant and in a format usable by many poor people, and more work should be done in developing such resources by, for example, making them accessible in local languages. However, given the existence of so much material, it seems more important to develop effective mechanisms through which the good resources that already exist can be accessed in a user-friendly way by poor and marginalised communities than it is to fund the generation of yet more resources that people will have to sift through to find what they really want. Second, the facilitation of collaborative authoring projects through the use of software such as wikis provides a powerful mechanism through which shared understandings and communal knowledge creation can take place. Colleagues can now work together on knowledge creation from locations across the world, and if used creatively this can enable high-quality material to be developed that is of direct relevance to the needs of specific communities. The key advantage of wikis is that it is possible for others to benefit from the acquired wisdom of many authors and thereby to gain a richer understanding than that provided by one person alone (Tapscott and Williams, 2006; although see Keen, 2007, for a critical perspective). Nevertheless, a third issue with OERs concerns the mechanisms whereby authors are remunerated for their contributions. Various models exist for such provision (see for example Downes, 2007), but as yet most OER content development is enabled by people whose main source of income is generated from other activities. It is all very well encouraging groups of teachers or health workers to develop and share learning resources, but if this is to be done outside normal school or hospital hours, when many such people in poor countries have to undertake other forms of employment just to make a living, some form of additional remuneration must be provided. Likewise, there is a strong case for bilateral and multilateral donors to ensure that the results of any activities that they fund should be made available in the form of OER. Where donors finance the publication of textbooks in poor countries, for example, they should insist that these are made available in digital format for use in the diverse new learning contexts that are becoming increasingly accessible, even to some of the poorest communities.

## Conclusions

This chapter has provided an overview of some of the more important technologies that can be used to address the information and communication needs of poor and marginalised communities. Four key issues can be highlighted in conclusion. First, there are many different technologies that can be applied to any one particular problem or situation. The most appropriate solution will depend on a wide range of factors, including cost, local context, infrastructural provision, the regulatory environment, and the specific needs of stakeholders and user communities. Far too often, externally generated solutions have been imposed without sufficient attention being paid to these crucial factors, and this is one of the main reasons why so many ICT4D projects have failed to deliver sustainable outcomes. Second, and linked to this, the provision of basic infrastructure, most notably electricity but also digital connectivity, is a fundamental prerequisite for the successful implementation of all ICT4D programmes. Without electricity even telephones and radios are useless. Far too often, ambitious ICT4D programmes have simply failed to recognise the huge obstacles that the lack of infrastructure creates for innovative solutions that can indeed help to empower poor people. Invariably, this is also caused by a concentration on technological solutions rather than on the real problems that need to be addressed. Third, the processes of convergence and miniaturisation have important implications for the sorts of hardware solutions that can best be developed for delivering effective ICT4D programmes. Once the complexities associated with screen size and the inputting of content are overcome, small low-cost multifunctional digital devices will offer enormous potential for those who wish to reshape the conditions that create poverty across the world. Finally, it seems likely that debates between those advocating open source and proprietary software solutions will persist for some time to come, since they are based on profoundly different sets of arguments and ideologies. While many would like to claim that knowledge should indeed be a global common good to which all should have equality of access, the reality of the early 21st century is that knowledge is increasingly becoming a commodity. Those seeking to engage in delivering ICT4D agendas that will truly bring equality of opportunity to poor and marginalised communities

must therefore engage actively in arenas well beyond the realm of technology alone, and ensure that they can create powerful arguments that will
shape the global social, economic and political agendas of the next fifty
years.

## Key readings

Castells, M., Fernández-Ardèvol, M., Qiu, J.L. and Sey, A. (2007) *Mobile Communication and Society: a global perspective.* Cambridge, MA, and London:
MIT Press

Keen, A. (2007) *The Cult of the Amateur: how today's internet is killing our culture.* New York: Currency

Kukulska-Hulme, A. and Traxler, J. (eds) (2005) *Mobile-learning: a handbook
for educators and trainers.* London: Routledge

Melkote, S.R. and Steeves, H.L. (2001) *Communication for Development in
the Third World: theory and practice for empowerment,* 2nd edn. New Delhi:
Sage

Souter, D. with Scott, N., Garforth, C., Jain, R., Mascarenhas, O. and McKerney,
K. (2005) *The Economic Impact of Telecommunications on Rural Livelihoods
and Poverty Reduction: a study of rural communities in India (Gujarat),
Mozambique and Tanzania.* London: CTO and DFID

Weigel, G. and Waldburger, D. (eds) (2004) *ICT4D – connecting people for a
better world.* Berne and Kuala Lumpur: Swiss Agency for Development and
Cooperation and Global Knowledge Partnership

## References

Abbate, J. (1999) *Inventing the Internet.* Cambridge, MA: MIT Press

Alchele, C., Flickenger, R., Fonda, C., Forster, J., Howard, I., Krag, T. and Zennaro,
M. (2006) *Wireless Networking in the Developing World: a practical guide to planning
and building low-cost telecommunications infrastructure.* Seattle, WA: Hacker
Friendly LLC (http://wndw.net)

Amateur Computerist (2007) On the origin of the Net and the Netizen. *The Amateur
Computerist,* 15 (2), pp. 1–61

Andrews, J., Ghosh, A. and Muhamad, R. (2007) *Fundamentals of WiMAX:
understanding broadband wireless networking.* Upper Saddle River, NJ: Prentice
Hall

Attewell, J. (2005) *Mobile Technologies and Learning: a technology update and m-
learning project summary.* London: Learning and Skills Development Agency

Bainbridge, D., Thompson, J. and Witten, I.H. (2003) Assembling and enriching
digital library collections. *Proceedings of the 3rd ACM/IEEE-CS joint conference on
Digital Libraries,* Houston, Texas, May. IEEE Computer Society, pp. 323–33

Bainbridge, D., Buchanan, G., McPherson, J., Jones, S., Mahoui, A. and Witten,
I.H. (no date) Greenstone: a platform for distributed digital library applications
(http://www.cs.waikato.ac.nz/~ihw/papers/01-DB-GMcP-etal-Aplatformfor.pdf)

Barnett, C. (2004) *Yizo Yizo:* citizenship, commodification and popular culture in
South Africa. *Media, Culture and Society,* 26 (2), pp. 251–71

Beards, P.H. (1996) *Analog and Digital Electronics: a first course.* London: Prentice
Hall

Bekkers, R. and Smits, J. (1999) *Mobile Telecommunications: standards, regulation, and applications*. London: Artech House

Bell, T.C., Cleary, J.G. and Witten, I.H. (1990) *Text Compression*. Englewood Cliffs, NJ: Prentice Hall

Bell, T.C., Moffat, A. and Witten, I.H. (1994) Compressing the digital library. *Proceedings of the First Annual Conference on the Theory and Practice of Digital Libraries*, College Station, Texas, June. ACM, pp. 41–46

Bertolini, R. (2004) Making information and communication technologies work for food security in Africa. *International Food Policy Research Institute, 2020 Africa Conference Brief* 11, Washington, DC: International Food Policy Research Institute

Bohmann, K. (2003) Media overview. In GTZ (Deutsche Gesellschaft für Technische Zusammenarbeit) and inWent (Internationale Weiterbildung und Entwicklung gGmbH) *Use of Media in Rural Development: guidelines and examples for practitioners based on the proceedings of a workshop*. Eschborn and Feldafing: GTZ and inWent

bridges.org (2005) Comparison study of free/open source and proprietary software in an African context (http://www.bridges.org/publications/21)

Brown, B., Green, N. and Harper, R. (eds) (2001) *Wireless World: social and interactional aspects of the mobile age*. Heidelberg: Springer Verlag

Bruns, N., Mingat, A. and Rakotomalala, R. (eds) (2003) *Achieving Universal Primary Education by 2015: a chance for every child*. Washington, DC: World Bank

Buckley, S. (2000) Radio's new horizons: democracy and popular communication in the digital age. *International Journal of Cultural Studies*, 3 (2), pp. 180–7

Castells, M., Fernández-Ardèvol, M., Qiu, J.L. and Sey, A. (2007) *Mobile Communication and Society: a global perspective*. Cambridge, MA, and London: MIT Press

Catcher Media (no date) *Understanding Livelihoods: complexity, choices and policies in Southern India*. Video. London: Catcher Media for DFID

Ceruzzi, P.E. (2003) *History of Modern Computing*, 2nd edn. Boston, MA: MIT Press

Crecraft, D. and Gergely, S. (2002) *Analog Electronics: circuits, systems and signal processing*. Oxford: Butterworth-Heinemann

de Fossard, E. (1996) *Radio Serial Drama for Social Development: a script writer's manual*. Baltimore, MD: The Johns Hopkins University School of Public Health (http://www.jhuccp.org/pubs/fg/3/3.pdf)

Dendrinos, M. (2005) From the physical reality to the virtual reality in the library environment. *Library Philosophy and Practice*, 7 (2), unpaginated (http://libr.unl.edu:2000/LPP/dendrinos.htm)

Dostert, K. (2001) *Powerline Communications*. Upper Saddle River, NJ: Prentice Hall

Downes, S. (2007) Models for sustainable open educational resources. *Interdisciplinary Journal of Knowledge and Learning Objects*, 3, pp. 29–44 (http://www.ijklo.org/Volume3/IJKLOv3p029-044Downes.pdf)

European Commission (2004) Press Release: Commission concludes on Microsoft investigation, imposes conduct remedies and a fine. (http://europa.eu/rapid/pressReleasesAction.do?reference=IP/04/382&format=HTML&aged=1&language=EN&guiLanguage=en)

Gast, M. (2005) *802.11 Wireless Networks: the definitive guide*, 2nd edn. Sebastopol, CA: O'Reilly

Gay, J. (ed.) (2002) *Free Software, Free Society: selected essays of Richard M. Stallman*. Boston, MA: GNU Press

Geldof, B. (1986) *Is That It?* London: Sidgwick and Jackson

Geser, H. (2004) Towards a sociological theory of the mobile phone (http://socio.ch/mobile/t_geser1.pdf)

Girard, B. (ed.) (2003) *The One to Watch: radio, new ICTs and interactivity*. Rome: FAO

GTZ (Deutsche Gesellschaft für Technische Zusammenarbeit GmbH) and inWent (Internationale Weiterbildung und Entwicklung gGmbH) (2003) *Use of Media in Rural Development: guidelines and examples for practitioners based on the proceedings of a workshop*. Double Multimedia CD. Eschborn and Feldafing: GTZ and inWent

Hamelink, C.J. (1997) *New Information and Communication Technologies, Social Development and Cultural Change*. Geneva: United Nations Research Institute for Social Development (Discussion Paper no. 86)

Hecht, J. (2002) *Understanding Fiber Optics*, 4th edn. Upper Saddle River, NJ: Prentice Hall

High, C., Goldsmith, R. and SPEECH (2001) *Understanding Livelihoods: Complexity, Choices and Policies in Southern India*. Hereford: Catcher Media

Huston, G. (2005) Opinion: ICANN, the ITU, WSIS, and Internet Governance. *The Internet Protocol Journal*, 8 (1), unpaginated (http://www.cisco.com/web/about/ac123/ac147/archived_issues/ipj_8-1/internet_governance.html)

Jayaprakash, Y.T. (2000) Remote audiences beyond 2000: radio, everyday life and development in South India. *International Journal of Cultural Studies*, 3 (2), pp. 227–39

Jewel, G.N. (2006) *Community Radio: ready to launch in Bangladesh*. Dhaka: Bangladesh NGOs Network for Radio and Communication

Keen, A. (2007) *The Cult of the Amateur: how today's internet is killing our culture*. New York: Currency

Klugkist, A.C. (2001) Virtual and non-virtual realities: the changing role of libraries and librarians. *Learned Publishing, the Journal of the Association of Learned and Professional Society Publishers*, 14 (3), pp. 197–204

Kozma, R.B. (2007) One laptop per child and education reform (http://www.olpcnews.com/use_cases/education/one_laptop_per_child_education.html)

Kuehr, R. and Williams, E. (eds) (2003) *Computers and the Environment: understanding and managing their impacts*. Dordrecht: Springer

Kukulska-Hulme, A. and Traxler, J. (eds) (2005) *Mobile-learning: a handbook for educators and trainers*. London: Routledge

Leech, J., Ahmed, A., Makalima, S. and Power, T. (2005) *DEEP Impact: an investigation of the use of information and communication technologies for teacher education in the Global South*. London: Department for International Development

Leiner, B.M., Cerf, V.G., Clark, D.D., Kahn, R.E., Kleinrock, L., Lynch, D.C., Postel, J., Roberts, L.G. and Wolff, S. (2003) A brief history of the Internet (http://www.isoc.org/internet/history/brief.shtml)

Lesk, M. (2005) *Understanding Digital Libraries*, 2nd edn. San Francisco, CA: Morgan Kaufmann

Loshin, P. (1999) *IPv6 clearly Explained*. San Francisco, CA: Morgan Kaufmann

Lunch, C. (2007) The most significant change: using participatory video for monitoring and evaluation. *Participatory Learning and Action*, 56, pp. 28–32

Mano, W. (2004) Renegotiating tradition on Radio Zimbabwe. *Culture, Media and Society*, 26 (3), pp. 315–36

Mbarika, V.W.A. (2002) Re-thinking information and communications technology policy focus on internet versus teledensity diffusion for Africa's least developed countries. *Electronic Journal on Information Systems in Developing Countries*, 9 (1), pp. 1–13

McQuerry, S. (2004) *CCNA Self-Study: introduction to Cisco networking technologies (INTRO) 640-821, 640-801*. Indianapolis, IN: Pearson Education, Cisco Press

Melkote, S.R. and Steeves, H.L. (2001) *Communication for Development in the Third World: theory and practice for empowerment*, 2nd edn. New Delhi: Sage

Miller, M.A. (2004) *Internet Technologies Handbook: optimizing the IP network*. New York: Wiley

Mitra, S. (2003) Minimally invasive education: a progress report on the 'hole-in-the-wall' experiments. *British Journal of Educational Technology*, 34 (3), pp. 367–71

Moody, G. (2002) *Rebel Code and the Open Source Revolution*. New York: Basic Books

Mozammel, M. and Odugbemi, S. (eds) (2005) *With the Support of Multitudes: using strategic communications to fight poverty through PRSPs*. London: DFID (Information and Communication for Development)

OECD/IEA (2007) *Key World Energy Statistics, 2007*. Paris: International Energy Agency

Ouédraogo, L.-D. (2005) *Policies of United Nations System Organizations Towards the Use of Open Source Software (OSS) for Development*. Geneva: United Nations Joint Inspection Unit

Pan, J., Peng, W., Li, M., Wu, X., Wan, L., Zerriffi, H., Victor, D., Elias, B. and Chi, Z. (2006) Rural electrification in China 1950–2004. Stanford, CA: Program on Energy and Sustainable Development, Working Paper 60 (http://iis-db.stanford.edu/pubs/21292/WP_60,_Rural_Elec_China.pdf)

Panos (2006) *Going the Last Mile: what's stopping a wireless revolution?* London: Panos (Panos Media Toolkit on ICTs no. 4)

Papa, M., Singhal, A., Law, S., Pant, S., Sood, S., Rogers, E.M. and Shefner-Rogers, C.L. (2000) Entertainment-education and social change: an analysis of parasocial interaction, social learning, collective efficacy, and paradoxical communication. *Journal of Communication*, 50 (4), pp. 31–55

Rangachari, R. (2006) Open source vs. proprietary management tools. *IT Managers Journal* (http://www.itmanagersjournal.com/articles/11403, accessed 11 May 2007)

Sakolsky, R. and Dunifer, S. (eds) (1998) *Seizing the Airwaves: a free radio handbook*. Oakland, CA: AK Press (http://infoshop.org/texts/seizing/toc.html)

Saunders, L.M. (ed.) (1999) *The Evolving Virtual Library II: practical and philosophical perspectives*. Medford, NJ: Information Today

Scheepers, E., Christofides, N.J., Goldstein, S., Usdin, S., Patel, D.S. and Japhet, G. (2004) Evaluating health communication – a holistic overview of the impact of Soul City IV. *Health Promotion Journal of Australia*, 15 (2), pp. 121–33

SchoolNet Africa (2004) *'Treat Refurbs and Africa with Respect': towards a framework on refurbished computers for African schools*. Johannesburg: SchoolNet Africa (available at http://www.schoolnetafrica.net/fileadmin/resources/Refurbished_computers_ResearchReport.pdf)

Skuse, A., with Butler, N., Power, N. and Woods, N. (2004) *Radio Broadcasting for Health: a decision maker's guide*. London: DFID (Information and Communication for Development)

Souter, D. with Scott, N., Garforth, C., Jain, R., Mascarenhas, O. and McKerney, K. (2005) *The Economic Impact of Telecommunications on Rural Livelihoods and Poverty Reduction: a study of rural communities in India (Gujarat), Mozambique and Tanzania*. London: CTO and DFID

Tapscott, D. and Williams, A.D. (2006) *Wikinomics: how mass collaboration changes everything*. New York: Penguin Group, Portfolio

Taylor, A.S. and Harper, R. (2003) The gift of the gab? A design-oriented sociology of young people's use of mobiles. *Computer Supported Cooperative Work*, 12, pp. 267–96

Taylor, R. (1998) *Film Propaganda: Soviet Russia and Nazi Germany*, 2nd edn. London: I.B. Tauris

UNDP and VOICES (2004a) *Community Radio in India: step by step*. New Delhi: UNDP and VOICES (http://www.communityradionetwork.org/leftlinks/comm_radio_ hdbk/leftlinks/comm_radio_hdbk/content_list, accessed 2 January 2007)

UNDP and VOICES (2004b) *Capacity Building Through Radio*. New Delhi: UNDP and VOICES (http://www.communityradionetwork.org/leftlinks/comm_radio_hdbk, accessed 2 January 2007)

Vanbuel, M. (2003) *Improving Access to Education via Satellites in Africa: a primer*. London: Imfundo, DFID. Revised edition

Vaughan, P.W., Regis, A. and St. Catherine, E. (2000a) Effects of an entertainment-education radio soap opera on family planning and HIV prevention in St. Lucia. *International Family Planning Perspectives*, 26 (4), pp. 148–57

Vaughan, P.W., Rogers, E.M., Singhal, A. and Swalehe, R.M. (2000b) Entertainment-education and HIV/AIDS prevention: a field experiment in Tanzania. *Journal of Health Communication*, 5 (supplement), pp. 81–100

Villaran, S. and Caistor, N. (2000) Peru: the experience of IDEELE Radio. *International Journal of Cultural Studies*, 3 (2), pp. 219–26

von Braun, J. and Torero, M. (2006) Introduction and overview. In *Information and Communication Technologies for Development and Poverty Reduction*, ed. M. Torero and J. von Braun. Baltimore: The Johns Hopkins University Press for the International Food Policy Research Institute

VSO (2002) *The Live Aid Legacy: the developing world through British eyes – a research report*. London: VSO (http://www.vso.org.uk/Images/liveaid_legacy_tcm8-784. pdf)

Weigel, G. and Waldburger, D. (eds) (2004) *ICT4D – connecting people for a better world*. Berne and Kuala Lumpur: Swiss Agency for Development and Cooperation and Global Knowledge Partnership

White, S.A. (2003) *Participatory Video: images that transform and empower*. London: Sage

Windrich, E. (2000) The laboratory of hate: the role of clandestine radio in the Angolan war. *International Journal of Cultural Studies*, 3 (2), pp. 206–18

Witten, I.H. and Bainbridge, D. (2003) *How to Build a Digital Library*. San Francisco, CA: Morgan Kaufmann

Witten, I.H. and Bainbridge, D. (2007) A retrospective look at Greenstone: lessons from the first decade. *Proceedings of the 2007 Conference on Digital Libraries*, Vancouver, Canada. ACM, pp. 147–56

Witten, I.H., Moffat, A. and Bell, T.C. (1994) *Managing Gigabytes: compressing and indexing documents and images*. New York: Van Nostrand Reinhold

Witten, I.H., Cunningham, S.J., Vallabh, M. and Bell, T.C. (1995) A New Zealand digital library for computer science research. *Proceedings of the Second Annual Conference on the Theory and Practice of Digital Libraries*, Austin, Texas, June. ACM, pp. 25–30

Witten, I.H., Bainbridge, D. and Boddie, S.J. (2001) Power to the people: end-user building of digital library collections. *Proceedings of the 1st ACM/IEEE-CS joint conference on Digital Libraries*, Roanoke, VA. ACM, pp. 94–103

Yusof, K. (2007) *FOSS Education Primer*. UNDP-APDIP International Open Source Network: Software Freedom for All (http://www.iosn.net/education/ foss-education-primer)

# 5 | ICT4D implementation: policies and partnerships

## Tim Unwin

- The roles and actions of key institutions and individuals in shaping the emergence of ICT4D as a distinct field of theory and practice need to be understood if we are effectively to promote its value in development.
- Many ICT4D initiatives have not yet been taken to scale or become sustainable, despite their potential to contribute significantly to enhancing the lives of poor and marginalised communities.
- Balancing the supply and demand dimensions of ICT4D is essential if we are to implement effective programmes that will be of lasting benefit to poor people and marginalised communities.
- Effective multi-stakeholder partnerships are central to the implementation of ICT4D initiatives, but the complexity of their implementation is one of the reasons why they are not always as successful as anticipated.
- The role of high-level champions is crucial in the success of ICT4D initiatives at all scales.

During the late 1990s, a coalescence of interests precipitated the emergence of a specific new focus on the potential that the latest information and communication technologies could contribute to development practices. These interests heralded an entirely different conceptualisation of the ways in which poverty might be reduced through the use of technology, and brought together organisations and institutions that had previously often had little engagement with each other. This chapter explores the complex interplay between the private sector, donor agencies, governments of poor countries, civil society organisations and international bodies that has created and shaped this new field of ICT4D. It begins by tracing the chronology of ICT4D-related events convened by global institutions over the last decade, and against this background then provides an overview of the design and implementation of specific ICT strategies in different parts of the world. One of the underlying reasons why so many ICT4D initiatives have failed is because they have insufficiently addressed the highly complex issues surrounding the balance between supply and demand. The next section of this chapter therefore teases out some of these complexities, before providing a framework for considering the effective delivery of multi-stakeholder partnerships in ICT4D practice.

## Global ICT4D initiatives

Until the late 1990s there was little explicit focus on the use of new ICTs in development practice. However, a coalescence of interests had come together over the previous decade that swiftly led to a dramatic awakening of interest in the potential of ICTs for development, both through their role in economic growth and also through the empowerment of poor people and communities. This section explores three main periods in the evolution of global initiatives concerned with promoting ICT4D activities: their origins in the 1990s and expansion in the early 2000s; the impact of the World Summit on the Information Society in 2003 and 2005; and the role of bilateral and multilateral donors during the 2000s (see Table 5.1 for an overview).

### *The institutional origins of ICT4D initiatives*

The origins of interest in the role of ICTs in development is often seen as lying in the work of the Independent Commission set up by the International Telecommunications Union (ITU) in 1982 to examine worldwide telecommunication development (Milward-Oliver, 2005; Souter, 2005). During the 1970s there had been growing pressure from developing countries to create a new world information order, and by the 1980s their increased share of ITU membership enabled them to redirect the activities of the ITU towards much greater development cooperation. The work of this commission can in part therefore be seen as an outcome of the changing structure of the ITU (Tegge, 1994). Its final report, widely known as the Maitland Report after its Chairman Sir Donald Maitland, was entitled *The Missing Link*, and emphasised the key importance of ensuring that effective global telecommunications networks were created so that all could benefit from them. As the report concluded, 'Given the vital role telecommunications play not only in such obvious fields as emergency, health and other social services, administration and commerce, but also in stimulating economic growth and enhancing the quality of life, creating effective networks world wide will bring immense benefits' (Maitland, 1984, p. 65). The report particularly highlighted the need for governments across the world to redress the imbalance that existed in the distribution of telecommunications; developing country governments were encouraged to ensure that sufficient emphasis in development plans was placed on communications, and those offering development assistance were likewise recommended to provide specific provision for supporting such plans. Higher priority for investment in telecommunications, and the need to attract foreign entrepreneurs were its two crucial messages (Maitland, 2005).

**Table 5.1** *Global institutional events in the evolution of ICT4D*

| | |
|---|---|
| December 1984 | Report of the Independent Commission for World Wide Telecommunications Development (The Maitland Report) (http://www.itu.int/osg/spu/sfo/missinglink/index.html) |
| 1990 | Foundation of the Association for Progressive Communication (http://www.apc.org/english/about/history/index.shtml) |
| February 1995 | G7 Global Information Society meeting in Brussels (http://europa.eu.int/ISPO/intcoop/g8/i_g8conference.html) |
| 1995 | The World Bank Group's *infoDev* program launched (http://www.infodev.org) |
| May 1996 | African Information Society Initiative launched at the 22nd meeting of the Economic Commission for Africa's Conference of Ministers (http://www.uneca.org/aisi) |
| May 1996 | Information Society and Development Conference, South Africa (http://www.ucalgary.ca/newcurrents/Vol3.4/SouthAfrica.html) |
| 1996 | International Institute for Communication and Development established (http://www.ftpiicd.org/files/temp/IICD-anniversary-booklet.pdf) |
| June 1997 | Global Knowledge Conference '97 in Canada (Global Knowledge Partnership) (http://www.globalknowledge.org/gkps_portal/GK97/97+Program.pdf) |
| 1998/1999 | World Development Report 1998/1999 *Knowledge for Development* (http://www.worldbank.org/wdr/wdr98) |
| January 2000 | World Economic Forum launches its Global Digital Divide Initiative |
| March 2000 | Global Knowledge Conference 2000: Building Knowledge Societies, in Malaysia (Global Knowledge Partnership) (http://www.globalknowledge.org/gkii/conf_prog.htm) |
| July 2000 | Creation of the G8's DOT Force at Kyushu-Okinawa Summit in Japan (http://www.g7.utoronto.ca/summit/2001genoa/dotforce1.html) |
| September 2000 | Millennium Summit acclaiming Millennium Development Goals (http://www.un.org/millenniumgoals); Goal 8 'Develop a global partnership for development' includes: 'In cooperation with the private sector, make available the benefits of new technologies—especially information and communications technologies' |
| 2001 | UNDP Human Development Report, *Making Technologies Work for Human Development* (http://hdr.undp.org/reports/global/2001/en) |
| November 2001 | Creation of UN ICT Task Force, having been suggested earlier in the year by ECOSOC (http://www.unicttaskforce.org/about; http://en.wikipedia.org/wiki/UN_ICT_Task_Force) |
| June 2002 | Final Report of DOT Force at G8 Summit in Kananaskis, Canada (http://www.ictdevagenda.org/frame.php?dir=07&sd=10&id=227) |
| December 2003 | World Summit on the Information Society (WSIS) I in Geneva, organised by ITU (http://www.itu.int/wsis/index-p1.html) |
| December 2003 | Global eSchools and Communities Initiative (GeSCI) created (http://www.gesci.org) |
| July 2004 | SPIDER (Swedish Program for ICT in Developing Regions) formally constituted (http://www.spidercenter.org) |
| November 2005 | WSIS II in Tunis, organised by ITU (http://www.itu.int/wsis/index-p2.html) |
| December 2005 | UN ICT Task Force mandate ends; much of work to be continued by Global Alliance for ICT and Development (GAID) |
| June 2006 | Inaugural Meeting of Global Alliance for ICT and Development in Malaysia (GAID) (http://www.un-gaid.org) |
| July 2006 | Launch of the UN Group on the Information Society (UNGIS) (http://www.ungis.org) |
| May 2007 | Cluster of WSIS events in Geneva (http://www.itu.int/wsis/implementation) |
| December 2007 | Global Knowledge Conference GK3, Malaysia (Global Knowledge Partnership) (http://www.gkpeventsonthefuture.org/gk3) |

*Source:* Tim Unwin

The Maitland Report concentrated primarily on the telecommunications sector, and was influential in shaping the changes that took place therein over the next decade (Souter, 2005). Prime among these was the introduction of much greater competition, designed both to open the sector up to investment from international companies, and also to reduce prices through market forces so that the benefits of telephony could become more widely available. The success of this latter aim has depended heavily on the power of regulators to ensure that services have indeed been made available to rural and otherwise marginalised populations, and the Maitland Report was an important beacon in highlighting the importance of such equity issues.

However, the initial pace of change was slow, and during the late 1980s the ITU was widely criticised for lack of direction and leadership, with many people predicting the end of the institution (Tegge, 1994). It was therefore not until the mid-1990s, by which time other developments in the field of ICTs were also occurring, that sufficient impetus had been achieved to catalyse the global community into further action. Key individuals and institutions, particularly in north America and Europe, began to explore the impact that these technological innovations might have on development agendas. One of the first major events that specifically addressed the ways in which 'developing countries' could benefit from the emerging 'information society' was a Ministerial Conference of the Group of Seven Industrialised Nations (G7), hosted by the European Commission in Brussels in February 1995 (Table 5.1). This was designed to 'encourage and promote the innovation and development of new technologies, including, in particular, the implementation of open, competitive, and world-wide information infrastructures' (http://europa.eu.int/ISPO/intcoop/g8/i_g8conference.html, accessed 3 August 2007, unpaginated), and initiated 11 projects where international cooperation was seen as being an asset. Significantly, it also included senior figures from industry alongside government officials, thus setting in place the basic pattern of 'public–private' partnership that was central to many subsequent ICT4D initiatives. As guest speaker at a dinner for senior delegates at the conference, Thabo Mbeki, then Executive Deputy President of South Africa, challenged the audience to ensure that the developing world was also able to benefit from the changes currently taking place so that there would be a truly global information society, and he offered South Africa as the location for a follow-up conference that would involve the developing world with the G7 countries and the European Commission (http://europa.eu.int/ISPO/docs/promotion/past_events/isad_conclusion.doc, accessed 3 August 2007). This led to the Information Society and Development Conference (ISAD) held in Midrand in May 1996, which was attended by representatives from 40 countries and 18 international organisations, with the aim of launching a dialogue, initiating the process of defining a shared vision for the global information society, and beginning to work towards common principles and collaborative action. Earlier that May, the Economic Commission for Africa's (ECA) Conference of Ministers had also met in Addis Ababa, where they launched the Africa Information Society Initiative (AISI) (http://www.africa.upenn.edu/ECA/aisi_implmt. html), which was designed 'to create effective digital opportunities to be developed by Africans and their partners, and to speed the continent's entry into the information and knowledge global economy' (http://www.uneca. org/aisi, accessed 3 August 2007, unpaginated). These two events provided significant impetus for the creation of dialogue and partnerships intended to enable the poorer countries of the world, especially in Africa, to benefit from the technologies associated with the rapid social and economic changes then occurring in the most developed countries of the world.

The G7 countries, notably Canada, took a leading role in driving these global agendas forward (http://www.ucalgary.ca/newcurrents/Vol3.4/ SouthAfrica.html). By the mid-1990s, staff at Canada's International Development Research Centre (IDRC) (http://www.idrc.ca/en/ev-43441-201-1-DO_TOPIC.html) had become increasingly interested in the potential of new technologies to have a significant development impact, and following discussions in Italy in 1993 and 1994 they launched the Bellanet initiative in 1995 with the purpose of using ICT to implement a global forum for sustainable development research and capacity development (http://home. bellanet.org). Further discussions during the 1996 Information Society and Development Conference gave rise to the Acacia initiative (http://www. idrc.ca/acacia), which was designed to focus on empowering poor African communities through research, development and demonstration. This has subsequently provided an important vehicle through which Canadian support has been delivered for the ECA's AISI (http://network.idrc.ca/en/ev-8455-201-1-DO_TOPIC.html). Shortly thereafter, Canada hosted the first Global Knowledge conference in Toronto in June 1997 on the theme of 'Knowledge for Development in the Information Age', one of the outcomes of which was the creation of the Global Knowledge Partnership (GKP) designed to bring together governments, the private sector and civil society to deliver knowledge for development (K4D) and ICT4D activities. Initially hosted in the World Bank, the GKP's secretariat moved to Kuala Lumpur in 2001 (http://www.globalknowledge.org), and since then Malaysia has become another important player in the ICT4D arena.

The mid-1990s were also significant for the creation of other ICT4D-related initiatives, notably the Information for Development (*info*Dev) programme within the World Bank Group, and the International Institute for Communication and Development (IICD) based in the Netherlands. *info*Dev was initially founded as a multilateral fund by the World Bank in 1995 to co-finance ICT initiatives in developing countries and countries in so-called transition (http://www.europaworld.org/week109/infodev131202.htm; see also World Bank Development Grant Facility, 2002). Key initial funders of the programme were France, Japan, Canada, Italy, Finland, Sweden and the United Kingdom, reflecting the strong influence of the G7, together with Finland and Sweden, both of which had significant corporate interests in the field of ICT through their companies Nokia and Ericsson. By June 2002, *info*Dev had provided $52.9 million in support of 355 projects that had a total cost of $112.5 million, and had also created other initiatives such as the Africa Connection Program, the Y2K initiative to address potential problems facing developing countries at the turn of the millennium, and country gateways. Its core aims were threefold: to encourage the development of policies that would benefit the poor; to build human capacity; and to pilot innovative aspects of ICT application. In 2002, the donors recommended that *info*Dev's core programme should be phased out at the end of 2003, and that it should then concentrate on a small number of flagship initiatives (World Bank Development Grant Facility, 2002). One of *info*Dev's core modalities was to operate through partnerships, notably with global institutions such as the ITU, UNDP and UNESCO, research centres such as IDRC and IICD, ICT-related organisations such as ICANN and the OECD, and the private sector, notably IBM, Telecom Italia and Motorola. Since 2002, *info*Dev has continued to evolve, with a new governance framework being put in place in 2005 that focused its remit on helping to maximise the impact of ICTs in achieving the Millennium Development Goals, through enabling access for all, mainstreaming ICTs as tools of development and poverty reduction, and supporting innovation, entrepreneurship and growth (http://www.infodev. org/en/Page.Themes.html). Today, its website (http://www.infodev.org) provides one of the most useful sources of comprehensive and rigorous information on ICT4D. As a recent review by Universalia (2007, p. ii) reported, '*info*Dev appears to have established a distinct niche for itself as a provider of authoritative knowledge products and services in the ICT4D domain. Its uniqueness stems from its global reach, its proximity to the knowledge and operational resources of the World Bank, and its role as an aggregator of ICT4D-related expertise and experience'.

Meanwhile, in Europe, a group of Dutch scientists had also been engaged in exciting initiatives that were exploring ways that the newly emerging ICTs might be of benefit in developing countries. In 1993 Rutger Engelhard (2000), based in Amsterdam and with a long history of research in agricultural extension in Africa, had co-initiated TOOLnet, a FidoNet e-mail provider for developing countries. In 1995, the Dutch Minister of Development Cooperation, Jan Pronk, determined to create a communications institute, and initiated discussions within his ministry to explore ways in which the Dutch government might support ICT-based development initiatives. Engelhard, who had by then moved to the ministry, contributed significantly to these debates, and was asked in 1996 by Pronk to take forward plans to create a communication institute that would focus on the future rather than the past. Pronk not only had the insight to see how the internet could contribute, but was also eager to use the opportunity to create a public–private partnership, inviting his friend Koos Andriessen, the entrepreneur, former Minister of Economic Affairs and champion of ICT, to become Chairman of IICD's Board. This was formally established in 1998 (http://www.iicd.

org/articles/changes-within-iicd2019s-international-advisory-board-iab; IICD, 2006). As IICD's (2006, p. 5) ten-year anniversary publication comments, 'Pronk set IICD the task of initiating, stimulating and supporting collaboration with partners in developing countries, and then linking demands from these partners in the South to the knowledge and finance resources that could be provided by institutions in the North'. This example not only reinforces the significance that partnerships were seen as playing in ICT4D initiatives, but also highlights the importance of having champions at the highest level to drive forward successful programmes. On his appointment as IICD's Interim Director and first Programme Director, Engelhard initiated what was to become a key feature of the institute's work, namely round-table workshops, that were designed to bring together multi-stakeholder partners to identify information and communication needs that IICD could then help facilitate delivery of through its partners in the richer countries of the world (see also pp. 159–71). This methodology has provided a consistent focus for IICD's work in subsequent years, as it has developed into one of the world's leading ICT4D centres.

By the late 1990s, there was thus a growing coalescence of interest among governments of both donor and recipient countries, the private sector, academics and civil society organisations that ICTs could play a critical role in delivering on their shared 'development' objectives. This was reflected in part by the emphasis that the World Development Report for 1998/99 (World Bank, 1999) placed on *Knowledge for Development*. This comprehensive report focused on narrowing knowledge gaps, ways of addressing information problems, and what international institutions and governments could do. The scene was therefore set for four important events that occurred in 2000: the formation of the World Economic Forum's Global Digital Divide Initiative (GDDI); the second Global Knowledge Conference, held in Malaysia; the creation of the Digital Opportunities Task Force (DOT Force) by the G8; and the Millennium Summit at the end of the year (Table 5.1). At the start of 2000, in the annual meeting of the World Economic Forum at Davos, chief executives in the communications and technology, and media and entertainment sectors launched the Global Digital Divide Initiative, with the aim of spreading access to the internet and digital technologies more widely across the world, focusing particularly on 'education, entrepreneurship and policies/strategies' (World Economic Forum, 2001, p. 9). This not only highlighted the economic interests that the private sector had in expanding their markets, but also recognised the corporate sector's belief in the development benefits that ICTs could bring for poor countries. Soon afterwards, the second Global Knowledge Conference took place in Malaysia, with one of its key features being a Global Knowledge Forum where participants from government agencies, companies, civil society organisations and international agencies were able to pool their resources to build an international framework for ICT4D. The conference focused especially on issues to do with access, empowerment and governance, and culminated in a global action plan of 17 items that the Global Knowledge Partnership (GKP) would take forward (GKP, 2001).

The third key event in 2000 was the creation by the G8 heads of state of the Digital Opportunity Task Force (DOT Force) at their Kyushu-Okinawa Summit. As the DOT Force's report to the G8's 2001 meeting in Genoa noted, this was the result of 'a unique international collaboration' and 'brought together forty three teams from government, the private sector, non-profit organizations, and international organizations, representing both developed and developing countries, in a cooperative effort to identify ways in which the digital revolution can benefit all the world's people, especially the poorest and most marginalized groups' (http://www.g7.utoronto.ca/summit/2001genoa/dotforce1.html, unpaginated; see also G8 Information Centre, 2001) (Table 5.2). The report from the DOT Force's first year of work highlighted the challenges facing the achievement of digital opportunities for all and the ways in which these challenges could be met, concluding with a Genoa Plan of Action that addressed nine main agendas (http://www.g7.utoronto.ca/summit/2001genoa/dotforce1.html).

The DOT Force secretariat was hosted by the World Bank and UNDP, and its report for the Genoa meeting provides a fine summary of shared wisdom at that time concerning the role of ICTs in development. In particular, the report recognises not only the potential of ICT4D, but also the pitfalls that are inherent in its application:

> ICT can thus help to ignite a virtuous circle of sustainable development. But misapplied, they can result in marginalisation of the poor and the unconnected. In order for their development potential to be realised, all stakeholders – governments and their citizens, business, international organizations, civil society groups and individuals – need to work together towards achieving real change. As with all other development challenges, ownership by developing countries themselves and other relevant stakeholders will be indispensable.
> 
> (http://www.g7.utoronto.ca/summit/2001genoa/dotforce1.html, unpaginated)

Following the Genoa summit, the DOT Force created implementation teams for each of the action points, and these formed the basis of a report card presented to the next summit at Kananaskis, hosted by the Canadians. This drew attention to four main action areas:

- strengthening readiness for e-development;
- increasing access and connectivity;
- developing skills for the information economy; and
- fostering local content and applications.

Under each of these headings, the DOT Force had highlighted and promoted initiatives that were designed to implement its recommendations

**Table 5.2** *Membership of the G8 Digital Opportunity Task Force*

| | | |
|---|---|---|
| Government representatives (17: G8 + 1, 8 other countries) | Bolivia<br>Brazil<br>Canada<br>Egypt<br>European Commission<br>France<br>Germany<br>India<br>Indonesia | Italy<br>Japan<br>Russia<br>Senegal<br>South Africa<br>Tanzania<br>UK<br>USA |
| International/multinational organisations (7) | ECOSOC<br>ITU<br>OECD<br>UNCTAD | UNDP<br>UNESCO<br>World Bank |
| Private sector (11, including 3 global networks) | Accenture (UK)<br>Communications Authority (Italy)<br>GBDe<br>GIIC<br>Hewlett-Packard Co (USA)<br>Microsoft Research Ltd (Russia)<br>Siemens Business Services (Germany)<br>Telesystem Ltd (Canada)<br>Thomson Multimedia (France)<br>Toshiba (Japan)<br>WEF | |
| Non-profit sector | Centre for Global Communications<br>  (GLOCOM) (Japan)<br>IDRC (Canada)<br>Markle Foundation (USA)<br>MATTEI (Italy)<br>OneWorld International Foundation (UK)<br>Russian Union of Internet Providers<br>University of Bonn (Germany)<br>VECAM (France) | |

*Source:* http://www.ictdevagenda.org/frame.php?dir = 07&sd = 10&sid  = 1&id = 49

(CTO, 2002). However, with the conclusion of its work at the Kananaskis summit, it was unclear exactly how the momentum that had been created would be taken forward. As the report card concluded, 'The first and most essential task is to maintain the sense of political leadership and accountability that have characterised the work and mandate of the DOT Force' (Digital Opportunity Task Force, 2002, p. 6). It is somewhat ironic, therefore, that the DOT Force's own original domain name is now host to a pornography site designed for mature appeal.

Meanwhile, September 2000 saw the hosting of the Millennium Summit, when heads of state agreed to a set of 'goals and targets for combating poverty, hunger, disease, illiteracy, environmental degradation and discrimination against women' (http://www.un.org/millenniumgoals/

MDGs-FACTSHEET1.pdf). Although there was not a specific goal for ICT4D, the eighth Millennium Development Goal (MDG), advocating the development of a global partnership for development, does indeed include an objective to 'In cooperation with the private sector, make available the benefits of new technologies – especially information and communications technologies' (http://www.un.org/millenniumgoals). This positioning of ICTs is particularly significant for two main reasons: first, it once again highlights the role of the private sector and partnerships; and second, it emphasises the way in which ICTs were identified primarily as an enabler of development, rather than as an end in themselves. These two features have been fundamentally important in shaping subsequent donor attitudes towards ICT4D, because they have provided the grounds for them to argue that primary attention should be paid to the education, health, gender and environment MDGs, and also that the private sector should contribute much of the resourcing for any ICT4D initiatives that may be developed in support of these (see 'Donor attitudes to ICT4D' below, pp. 145, 148–9).

The mention of ICTs in the MDGs reflected a growing awareness within the UN and its agencies of the significant importance that ICTs could play in development. This was, for example, highlighted by the Human Development Report for 2001 which was entitled *Making New Technologies Work for Human Development* (UNDP, 2001), the front cover of which boldly stated that 'Technology networks are transforming the traditional map of development, expanding people's horizons and creating the potential to realize in a decade progress that required generations in the past'. The report reiterated many of the familiar themes that had featured in the previous decade's discussion, notably the potential that the network age offered for development, the risks that are nevertheless involved in technological change, and the importance of national ICT strategies in ensuring that everyone can benefit from their effects. The report was also important because it argued that there were two main ways in which technology can benefit human development: first, by enhancing human capabilities, as with the use of the internet directly to improve people's health; and second, by contributing to economic growth. It therefore placed ICTs centrally within the increasingly hegemonic agenda associated with the belief that economic growth is indeed the solution to poverty (see Sachs, 2005; for a critique, see Unwin, 2007). One of its key recommendations was that expanding access was critical to overcoming the digital divide. To this end, the World Bank launched the Development Gateway initiative in July 2001 (http://www.developmentgateway.org) as a portal for development information. This was initially widely criticised, especially by civil society organisations, merely for being a means through which the World Bank could disseminate its ideas and information. Partly in response to such criticisms, the World Bank then established the international non-profit Development Gateway Foundation (http://www.dgfoundation.org/about.html) to oversee the initiative, and by 2007 it had gained funding support from 15 governments, three international organisations (UNDP, UNFPA and World Bank), and nine private-sector companies, foundations and individuals. Today the Development Gateway focuses on three main areas: effective government; knowledge sharing and collaboration; and the creation of local partner programmes that now exist in almost 50 countries. Despite its attempts to be more open and collaborative, its origins in the World Bank have meant that many civil society organisations are still suspicious of its role. This is unfortunate, because it does share a wealth of useful information, and its dgCommunities have created environments for engaging partners in discussion about critical ICT4D issues.

More important than the publication of the 2001 Human Development Report, though, was the increasingly central role that the UN began to take in driving forward the ICT agenda more generally (see Annan, 2001). Previous initiatives, such as the G8's DOT Force, had sometimes been seen as having been driven by the world's richest countries and the private sector, even though they had involved participation from Latin American, African and Asian governments. With the wider involvement of UN agencies in the ICT4D arena, it was argued that there would be more opportunity for the voices of the poorer countries to be heard. In parallel with the ongoing work of other initiatives, the UN had therefore convened a group of high-level experts to prepare a report for the General Assembly's 55th Session (http://www.un.org/documents/ecosoc/docs/2000/e2000-55.pdf) to be held in May 2000. ICT4D was also addressed by the UN's Economic and Social Council (ECOSOC) in its substantive session on the role of information technology in the context of a knowledge-based global economy that took place in June 2000, one of the outcomes of which was a request to the Secretary-General Kofi Annan that a UN ICT Task Force should be created. There followed a period of close discussion with other existing initiatives, notably the DOT Force and the World Economic Forum, that led in November 2001 to the official launching of the ICT Task Force with an initial three-year mandate (UN ICT Task Force, 2001). Interestingly, the Task Force was 'the first body created by a intergovernmental decision of a United Nations in which members, representing governments, civil society (including the private sector, not-for-profit foundations, NGOs and academia) and organizations of the United Nations system have equal decision-making power' (http://www.unicttaskforce.org/about, unpaginated). At the heart of the Task Force's remit was the challenge of combining the profit motives of the private sector with the human development goals of the UN, and to this end it was also charged with contributing to the preparations of the World Summit on the Information Society (WSIS) to be held in 2003 and 2005. The Task Force created working groups around four familiar themes (ICT policy and governance; enabling environment; human resource development and capacity building; and ICT indicators and MDG mapping), and also initiated five regional networks (Africa; Latin America and the Caribbean; Asia; Arab States; and Europe and Central Asia). Ten six-monthly meetings were held, with the final Task Force meeting taking place at the WSIS Summit in Tunis in November 2005. One of the lasting contributions of these meetings was the series of publications that resulted from the fora associated with them, on key themes of importance such as internet governance (MacLean, 2004a) and ICTs as an enabling environment for the MDGs (Gilhooly, 2005).

Three broad issues can be highlighted from this review of global ICT4D initiatives prior to WSIS. First, the notion of partnerships was a central theme of almost all ICT4D initiatives, seeking to combine the different interests and expertise of global institutions, the private sector, donors, governments of 'developing' countries, civil society and academic institutions. Balancing these interests and creating a supportive environment in which all can work effectively together has been a huge challenge, and yet in the cases where initiatives have managed to do this effectively they have been successful (see pp. 159–71). Second, a small number of influential countries have played a key role in promulgating the ICT4D agenda. The G8 countries were crucial to the success of the DOT Force, and have continued to play an important role since its demise. More recently, countries such as Sweden (particularly through the Swedish Program for ICT in Developing Regions – SPIDER), Finland, Switzerland (through its hosting of the first phase of WSIS and its chairing role in the GKP), the Netherlands (in part through the role of IICD) and Ireland (Development Cooperation Ireland, 2003) have also joined the group of donors supporting ICT4D. Among countries in Asia and Africa, Malaysia and South Africa have likewise played an important role in championing the cause of ICT4D. Finally, it should be emphasised that there has been a remarkable lack of consistency in the global structures designed to support ICT4D. Although many individuals and organisations have participated with similar agendas in the various different fora that have so far been discussed, this lack of consistency has meant that new institutions have had a tendency to duplicate work that has previously been done elsewhere, and to create new structures that do not go much beyond the findings of previous initiatives.

### The World Summit on the Information Society and its aftermath

The origins of the World Summit on the Information Society are usually identified as being in a proposal from the government of Tunisia at the ITU Plenipotentiary Conference in 1998 (Kelly, 2004). However, this idea was not formally endorsed by the UN until 2001 and, as Souter with Jagun (2007, p. 8) comment, 'It is doubtful if ITU delegates expected this to be a global summit of the kind which the United Nations holds regularly on different issues, but that is what WSIS became when it won the backing of other UN agencies'.

Han Seung-soo, the President of the 56th General Assembly of the UN, commented in his opening remarks to the Assembly in 2001 that:

With the rapid growth of information and communication technologies – or ICT, the 'digital divide' has moved to the top of the development agenda. ICT has the potential to become a powerful new engine of social and economic development, lifting hundreds of millions of human beings out of poverty and into the mainstream of the world economy. These technologies constitute a major force driving the whole phenomenon of globalization. By utilizing and mastering them, mankind can transform that phenomenon from a double-edged sword into a multi-purpose tool of human development.

However, insufficient resources, inadequate knowledge, and lack of infrastructure, prevent the vast majority of human beings on the wrong side of the digital divide from bridging the gap.

(Han Seung-soo, 2001, unpaginated)

With this in mind, the UN formally endorsed the convening of a two-phase World Summit on the Information Society (WSIS) to be held in Switzerland in 2003 and Tunis in 2005. The International Telecommunications Union (ITU) was given the task of leading the organisation of WSIS, and cynical observers suggested that this was primarily to give it a purpose at a time when its role was lacking direction and focus. The PrepCom process began officially in July 2002, with five regional meetings in 2002 and 2003 in advance of the opening of the first phase of the summit in Geneva in December 2003. These prior meetings were designed primarily to clarify the agenda of the summit, and also to prepare the procedures, draft declaration of principles and plan of action. While it was relatively easy to agree on common principles, based largely on the conclusions of previous initiatives such as the DOT Force and ICT Task Force, two matters caused particular problems and were left unresolved by the conference: internet governance, and funding mechanisms. In essence, despite there being strong pressure for internet governance to become a matter of global responsibility, the USA was unwilling to relinquish its existing controls, specifically over ICANN (see Chapter 4; APC and ITeM, 2007). In the end, a compromise solution was adopted in Geneva, and the Plan of Action recommended that the Secretary-General should set up a Working Group on Internet Governance (WGIG, http://www.wgig.org), to report to the next phase of the summit in Tunis (MacLean, 2004a, 2005; Drake, 2005). The second basic area of disagreement concerned mechanisms through which the recommendations that were emerging could be funded. On the one hand were many civil society organisations and the private sector who were eager to see very large sums of money being made available to deliver on the plan of action through a digital solidarity fund; arrayed against them were the donor governments and agencies, most of whom were against the creation of any new funding mechanism. At a time when many bilateral donors were concentrating on seeking to support countries, particularly in Africa, through an increasingly integrated approach based on the creation of Poverty Reduction Strategy Papers (PRSPs) and budget support mechanisms to fund them, the proposal for a new and separate fund for ICT4D initiatives, which in any case were not seen by most of them as being a central element of the MDGs, was never likely to be a realistic outcome for WSIS. Indeed, problems that had recently been encountered with the management and disbursement of funds through the Global Fund to Fight AIDS, Tuberculosis and Malaria (http://www.theglobalfund.org; for more recent accusations of fraud see http://www.timesonline.co.uk/tol/news/uk/article2461274.ece) which had been launched with strong US influence in 2001, made the bilateral donors even more reluctant to consider creating such a fund. The subsequent lack of other 'global funds' in support of any specific development agendas makes this reluctance even more understandable than it may have appeared at the time to some of those clamouring for additional funding to be made available for ICT4D through the WSIS process.

The Geneva phase of WSIS in December 2003 achieved much more than many of the sceptics had predicted. Although civil society groups had been highly critical about the process (see http://www.worldsummit2003.de/en/nav/14.htm, and http://www.nethics.net/nethics_neu/n3/quellen/wsis/CS-press-statement-14-11-03.pdf; see also Souter with Jagun, 2007), more than 11,000 delegates from 176 countries participated, and agreed on a far-reaching declaration of principles designed to create a common vision for the information society (http://www.itu.int/wsis/docs/geneva/official/dop.html), and a plan of action that focused on means to deliver the 11 key principles that had been agreed (Table 5.3) (http://www.itu.int/wsis/docs/geneva/official/poa.html). These principles reiterated many of the areas of ICT4D discussion that had emerged over the previous decade, focusing on themes such as security, capacity building, an enabling environment, relevant applications, access and international cooperation, but they also addressed some newer themes such as the ethical and cultural dimensions of ICT4D. The plan of action was based on the 11 principles, included specific targets for the use of ICTs and concluded with a digital solidarity agenda, that emphasised that 'To overcome the digital divide, we need to use more efficiently existing approaches and mechanisms and fully explore new ones, in order to provide financing for the development of infrastructure, equipment, capacity building and content, which are essential for participation in the Information Society' (http://www.itu.int/wsis/docs/geneva/official/poa.html, unpaginated, Section D1). The specific targets contained within paragraph 6 of the WSIS Phase One plan of action were:

> 6. Based on internationally agreed development goals, including those in the Millennium Declaration, which are premised on international cooperation, indicative targets may serve as global references for improving connectivity and access in the use of ICTs in promoting the objectives of the Plan of Action, to be achieved by 2015. These targets may be taken into account in the establishment of the national targets, considering the different national circumstances:

a  to connect villages with ICTs and establish community access points;

b  to connect universities, colleges, secondary schools and primary schools with ICTs;

c  to connect scientific and research centres with ICTs;

d  to connect public libraries, cultural centres, museums, post offices and archives with ICTs;

e  to connect health centres and hospitals with ICTs;

f  to connect all local and central government departments and establish websites and email addresses;

g  to adapt all primary and secondary school curricula to meet the challenges of the Information Society, taking into account national circumstances;

h  to ensure that all of the world's population have access to television and radio services;

i  to encourage the development of content and to put in place technical conditions in order to facilitate the presence and use of all world languages on the Internet;

j  to ensure that more than half the world's inhabitants have access to ICTs within their reach.

(http://www.itu.int/wsis/docs/geneva/official/poa.html)

This confirmed the lack of progress made on funding, but also emphasised the importance of integrating e-strategies within national development plans and the PRSP process. It encouraged developing countries to attract foreign investment in ICT, and for donor countries to help mainstream ICT in their work programmes in support of development agendas. Another practical element of the Geneva phase was the parallel ICT for Development Platform that was organised by the Swiss Agency for Development and Cooperation and the Global Knowledge Partnership, which over five days attracted some 35,000 visitors. This provided an important opportunity to showcase the human and development aspects of ICT4D alongside the political process that was occurring at the summit itself, and one of its lasting impacts was the production of an authoritative book based on the debates that took place at the forum, entitled *ICT4D – connecting people for a better world* (Weigel and Waldburger, 2004).

The first phase of WSIS had concluded with a request to the Secretary-General of the UN to initiate action on the two key areas of a Digital Solidarity Fund and Internet Governance. These were taken forward by a Task Force on Financial Mechanisms under the auspices of the UNDP and the WGIG (MacLean, 2005), whose work fed into the PrepCom meetings in 2004 and 2005, leading up to the Tunis summit in November 2005. The main emphasis of this second summit was to resolve the outstanding issues, and to consider progress that had been made on the declaration of principles and action plan agreed at Geneva (Kelly, 2004). In the end, these tasks were over-ambitious, and it was not able to resolve the key difficulties that had emerged. In terms of outputs, the Tunis summit delivered the Tunis Commitment that largely reaffirmed commitments made in Geneva, and

**Table 5.3** *Action lines from the first phase of the World Summit on the Information Society, and possible moderators/facilitators agreed at second phase*

| Action lines agreed in Geneva phase of WSIS[1] | Possible moderators and facilitators confirmed in Tunis phase of WSIS[2] |
| --- | --- |
| 1 The role of governments and all stakeholders in the promotion of ICTs for development | ECOSOC/UN Regional Commissions/ ITU **[UN DESA]** |
| 2 Information and communication infrastructure: an essential foundation for the information society | **ITU** [APC] |
| 3 Access to information and knowledge | ITU/**UNESCO** [FAO/UNIDO] |
| 4 Capacity building | **UNDP**/UNESCO/ITU/UNCTAD [UN DESA/FAO/UNIDO] |
| 5 Building confidence and security in the use of ICTs | **ITU** |
| 6 Enabling environment | ITU/**UNDP**/UN Regional Commissions/ UNCTAD [UN DESA/UNIDO/APC] |
| 7 ICT applications: benefits in all aspects of life | |
| E-government | UNDP/ITU **[UN DESA]** |
| E-business | WTO/**UNCTAD**/ITU/UPU |
| E-learning | **UNESCO**/ITU/UNIDO |
| E-health | **WHO**/ITU |
| E-employment | **ILO**/ITU |
| E-environment | WHO/**WMO**/UNEP/UN-Habitat/ ITU/ICAO |
| E-agriculture | **FAO**/ITU |
| E-science | **UNESCO**/ITU/UNCTAD [WHO] |
| 8 Cultural diversity and identity, linguistic diversity and local content | **UNESCO** |
| 9 Media | **UNESCO** |
| 10 Ethical dimensions of the information society | **UNESCO**/ECOSOC [WHO/ECPAT] |
| 11 International and regional cooperation | UN Regional Commissions/UNDP/ ITU/UNESCO/ECOSOC **[UN DESA]** |

*Sources and notes:*
[1]Plan of Action from Geneva Phase of WSIS (http://www.itu.int/wsis/docs/geneva/official/poa. html, accessed 7 August 2007)
[2]Report of the Tunis Phases of WSIS (http://www.itu.int/wsis/docs2/tunis/off/9rev1.doc, accessed August 2007); agencies in bold were identified as provisional focal points; subsequent additions suggested in February 2006 are in square brackets (see also APC and ITeM, 2007)

the Tunis Agenda for the Information Society which sought to move from principles to action (http://www.itu.int/wsis/documents/doc_multi.asp? lang = en&id = 2331|2304). On financial mechanisms, the agenda highlighted the importance of appropriate funding for ICT4D, but also recognised the many difficulties involved in achieving this. In the end, it was only able to recommend that 'further cross-sectoral and cross-institutional coordination should be undertaken' (paragraph 24), and came up with some specific recommendations concerning improvements that could be made to existing financial mechanisms, including support for the Digital Solidarity

Fund (paragraphs 27 and 28). This fund, with its secretariat in Geneva, has nevertheless so far failed to gather any momentum, and by 2007 had only two international organisations, two city and local authority organisations, three civil society organisations, and two private-sector companies among its partners (http://www.dsf-fsn.org/cms/content/view/20/54/lang,en).

Shortly before the Tunis summit began, controversy over the issue of internet governance had once again threatened to derail the process. In part this was precipitated by the Association of Progressive Communications (APC), which had been established back in 1990 as a means of allowing grassroots groups to contribute to policy development in the field of ICTs (O'Brien, 2000). Just before the summit, the APC had issued a powerfully worded statement, emphasising that the internet should be open and accessible to all, that there should be further extensive multi-stakeholder debate on the links between internet governance and international human rights, and that ICANN should be transformed into a global body. This reflected the deep tensions and distrust that existed between many civil society organisations on the one hand, and private-sector and government agencies on the other, concerning the wider agendas associated with ICT4D, and especially relating to internet governance. Just before the 2003 summit in Geneva, civil society groups had also identified human rights as one of the main problems impeding progress (http://www.nethics.net/nethics_neu/n3/quellen/wsis/CS-press-statement-14-11-03.pdf) along with a lack of commitment to funding, and in the lead-up to the Tunis summit they expressed increasing concern that the meeting was taking place in a country that did not have universal freedom of expression (International Freedom of Expression Exchange Tunisia Monitoring Group, 2005). The situation was tense, with the USA still refusing to give ground over its control of ICANN. In the end, although wider civil society unrest over holding the conference in Tunisia did simmer under the surface, the summit was able to reach a compromise by agreeing to set up a consultative international Internet Governance Forum (IGF) (paragraph 72 of Tunis Agenda for the Information Society). The IGF (http://www.intgovforum.org) began work in 2006, with its second meeting taking place in Brazil in November 2007. It remains to be seen whether it will be able to resolve the many complexities associated with internet governance, in terms of not only the political interests involved, but also the very different meanings attributed to the concept by the various stakeholders involved (for an excellent review, see MacLean, 2004b).

In summarising the outcomes of WSIS, Souter with Jagun (2007, p. 9) have commented that 'it was always going to be difficult for the secretariat, managed by the ITU, and the summit process as a whole to meet the different aspirations and expectations of different stakeholder groups'. They identify four main problems with the WSIS process: that 'the interaction between WSIS and other decision-making fora was poor'; that the central

(*continued on page 144*)

# Case study: The World Summit on the Information Society – a reflection

Mohamed Abida

*Member of the Cabinet of the Tunisian Minister of Communication Technologies, 2003–2005*

The World Summit on the Information Society (WSIS), held under the patronage of the Secretary-General of the United Nations in Geneva 2003 and Tunis 2005, was the first real opportunity to place the ICT4D agenda at the highest global level. The summit witnessed unprecedented participation of representatives from governments, the business sector, civil society and international organisations. It also generated a large amount of dialogue in its preparatory process (PrepCom, regional and thematic meetings), the creation of working groups and the establishment of online fora.

In the aftermath of the summit, though, a recurrent question is often asked: was it worth organising the conference? In other words, does the enormous time and money spent on an event like WSIS produce any political, social or economic change? In answering this, it is helpful to put the summit into its context. We must first recall its objectives, its framework and the expectations of its results. The idea behind organising this summit came mainly from the need, at the highest political level, to marshal the global consensus and commitment required to promote the urgently needed access of all countries to information, knowledge and communication technologies for development so as to reap the full benefits of the ICT revolution, and to address the whole range of relevant issues related to the information society.

The summit had some unique features that differentiated it from other UN summits. First, WSIS was on a very broad subject because building an information society is not a single-issue problem. Second, WSIS was a double summit, with the first meeting in Geneva in 2003 and the second in Tunis in 2005. In addition to the political dimension in having a phase in the North and another in the South, the two-phase process offered opportunities for more prolonged policy-making. Third and most important, WSIS adopted a multi-stakeholder approach. WSIS rules for participation broke new ground by granting civil society and the private sector formal standing comparable to that of governments.

It is nevertheless important to ask whether the outcome documents (principles and commitments; action plan; and agenda for building an inclusive, people-centred and development-oriented information society) met the expectations of the participants and the international community at large. Opinions vary on whether the summit made a real change. Some consider the summit to have been a waste of effort, time and money. Others, as stated in the civil society statement, believe that much more could have been achieved. There is also a third group who consider that the summit was indeed a success, achieving as much as it was realistically possible to achieve.

In my opinion, as an active participant in shaping the delivery of the Tunisian phase of the summit, both WSIS process and outcome were valuable for three main reasons. First, the summit succeeded in creating a higher level of public awareness about the challenges of the information age and of the value of ICT in development. Second, it has adopted a framework of guiding principles and processes for further action. Third, it has developed a new level of collaboration among governments, the private sector and civil society, introducing the use of 'multi-stakeholder' partnerships as a new principle for global diplomacy.

On the substantive level, and regardless of the degree of satisfaction of different parties who participated in the summit, the consensus reached on the outcome document can be considered as a positive result, even though diplomats at the last moment introduced some magic words, such as 'when appropriate' or 'if justified', to help them overcome the obstacles that they encountered. WSIS should be seen as an event that created an important momentum and initiated a process. The road towards building a global, inclusive and equitable information society is very long. The key recommendation of WSIS is that an information society cannot be built without collaboration, partnerships and solidarity among all stakeholders. This concept will nevertheless remain idealistic, unless a minimum of trust is reinforced among these actors, based on the values of transparency, accountability and respect.

*The World Summit on the Information Society, Tunis, 2005: (top) poster, (bottom) the closing ceremony (source:* Tim Unwin).

role of the ITU, as a technical agency, meant that 'governments also tended to give lead responsibility for their own participation to ministries of communication rather than to central or developmental ministries'; that the two-phase process was costly and stifled discussion of key issues, especially given that so much was changing over the four-year period involved; and fourth, that there were organisational issues with respect to the involvement of the private sector and civil society (Souter with Jagun, 2007, p. 9). Despite these concerns, the lead agencies involved in WSIS, particularly the ITU, UNESCO and UNDP, have continued to take forward the discussions initiated in Geneva and Tunis (Table 5.3), and other organisations, such as the Commission on Science and Technology for Development (CSTD), have additionally contributed to these debates. New organisations have also been spawned, such as the Global Alliance for ICT and Development (GAID) approved in March 2006, and the UN Group on the Information Society (UNGIS, http://www.ungis.org) launched in July 2006.

GAID's stated aim is to transform the spirit and vision of WSIS into action, and to this end it has brought together many of the organisations that have previously been central to ICT4D global initiatives, such as the World Bank, the Swiss Agency for Development and Cooperation, the GKP, IDRC and the Malaysian government, all of which are leading its networks and initiatives (Khan, 2007). A key feature of GAID is its emphasis on bringing together partners from the private sector, global institutions, national governments, civil society organisations and research institutes (http://www.un-gaid.org; Celik, 2007). Its governing bodies consist of a Strategy Council, Steering Committee, Group of High Level Advisors and a Network of Champions, and it seeks to function as a network of fora, institutions and think-tanks under the patronage of the Secretary-General and ECOSOC (Celik, 2007). GAID has also identified five flagship initiatives: telecentre.org (http://community.telecentre.org/en-tc/history; see Case Study 5.2), Better Connectivity with Broadband to Africa, Cyber Development Corps, the Global Initiative for Inclusive Information and Communication Technologies, and Free Access for All Schools to the Net (http://www.un-gaid.org). The precise direction in which GAID will evolve nevertheless remains unclear, as is the added value that it will bring to existing initiatives in the field of ICT4D. There seems considerable danger that unless it identifies where its precise niche role really lies, it will remain a high-level talking shop, and that without sufficient funds to implement substantial initiatives it will be unable effectively to deliver on its espoused mission.

Ultimately, the WSIS process raised awareness of the importance of ICT4D and laid out important key principles for the implementation of strategies to use ICTs to help achieve development objectives, but it failed to agree on substantial new funding mechanisms, and got bogged down in somewhat acrimonious debates about internet governance. As Abida has commented in his personal account of the Tunis Phase of WSIS (see p. 143), there is no doubt that WSIS helped to raise awareness of the importance of ICT4D, but its agenda remains unreal unless more trust is established between the many partners involved in delivering ICT-based initiatives that will empower poor and marginalised communities. Despite this rather downbeat appraisal, many exciting outcomes, such as telecentre.org (see p. 146), did indeed emerge from WSIS, albeit at a level lower than the organisers had initially hoped for. Han Seung-soo's (2001, unpaginated) claim that 'insufficient resources, inadequate knowledge, and lack of infrastructure, prevent the vast majority of human beings on the wrong side of the digital divide from bridging the gap' nevertheless remains as true today as it did when he first said it in 2001.

### Donor attitudes to ICT4D

A lack of bilateral and multilateral donor funding is often seen by civil society and the private sector as constraining the implementation of effective ICT4D initiatives. The Development Assistance Committee (DAC) of the OECD undertook a major survey of its members' contributions to ICT4D initiatives in 2003 (DAC, 2003) and also prepared a report for the UN Task Force on Financial Mechanisms for ICT for Development in 2005 (DAC, 2005). While the DAC does not represent all donors, it is a unique forum where leading donor countries seek to work together to contribute more effectively to delivering development objectives, and by the late 1990s DAC countries provided some 95 per cent of all known Official Development Assistance (ODA). It is extremely difficult to measure precise levels of donor support for ICT4D, but during the 1990s ODA commitments to ICT infrastructure projects declined from US$1.2 billion in 1990 to US$194 million in 2002 (DAC, 2005). The logic for such a shift was that donors expected the private sector to contribute more to such initiatives as part and parcel of the deregulation of the telecommunications sectors in developing countries. Although their contributions to infrastructure declined, the wider portfolio of donor support for ICT4D programmes increased. By 2005, the DAC (2005, pp. 26–7) was thus able to identify five key features of donor strategic orientations towards ICT4D:

- the creation of an enabling environment that will encourage private-sector investment in ICT4D is crucial;
- international or regional cooperation is essential since many aspects of ICT infrastructure are cross-border in nature;
- 'Most donors have abandoned supporting ICT infrastructure, leaving the job to the private sector';
- the policy environment has to be right to persuade the private sector to invest in developing countries; and
- governments and civil society need to ensure that the poor also benefit from ICTs because market forces alone will not deliver this.

These conclusions support the view that donors see their role primarily as helping to create the right environment through which the private sector

(continued on page 148)

# Case study: Telecentre 2.0. What's next? Almost anything

Mark Surman

*Open Philanthropy Fellow at the Shuttleworth Foundation*

I often stop to ask: why all the excitement about computers and the internet? Why do we invest these things with so much potential? Why do we so often and effortlessly link them to empowerment, and power?

As a child at the cusp of the personal computer age, my answer was clear. It lay in the fact that these curious, shiny objects designed to do nothing in particular actually lent themselves to doing almost anything. They made it easy to be a teenage poet, playing with my e.e. cummings layouts deep into the night. They let me publish books with pretty pictures at a time when bookmaking still seemed the domain of kings and titans. And, when these shiny things finally connected to the internet, they became windows onto a wide world of activism and creativity I could barely have imagined. Of course, the real magic didn't come immediately, or even quickly. It came only when I realised that computers and the internet could do almost anything, and started doing it.

It feels like we are on the edge of this kind of magic with telecentres, and with the telecentre movement. Over the past 20 years, more than 100,000 community computing centres have been set up around the world. Most have been very much like early personal computers: shiny and intriguing, but not designed to do anything in particular. If you visited these centres a few years back, you'd probably find people – especially young people – driven by a sense of curiosity and invention. They had the magic. Yet many of the telecentres themselves did not. They were just friendly and helpful places where people could come to use computers. They had not yet figured that they had the power to do almost anything.

As I travel around and visit telecentres today, I see that this is changing. The telecentre movement is buzzing with invention and innovation. There are telecentres that offer agricultural testing and information services in Bangladesh, and that will bring their information to poor rural people by bicycle if they need to. There are telecentres that have become skill- and confidence-building engines for kids living in Brazilian favelas. Collectively, we are finding out that these centres, with their combination of computers, connectivity and community space, can be used to do amazing things.

This is natural, really. It's like the evolution from the 'computer as fancy typewriter' age to the age of successful basement filmmakers and micro-national companies run from bedrooms. It is the evolution from an initial (and very good) instinct to create community computing centres to 2.0 telecentres that are built around concrete service and community engagement concepts. This evolution looks something like the diagram on the next page.

Unfortunately, this evolution doesn't happen overnight. Despite dozens of great inventions and innovations – and a rapidly growing number of telecentres – most centres still focus on computer access. Or they offer a very narrow, prescribed list of services prescribed by government, a funder or a franchise owner. There aren't enough telecentre innovations and they aren't spreading fast enough.

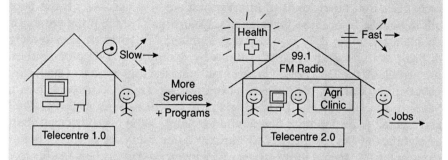

This is one of the main things that we've tried to address by setting up telecentre.org: helping new inventions and ideas travel, and catalysing more 'telecentre 2.0' thinking. The good news is that grassroots leaders in almost 30 countries have taken up the cause of building telecentre networks and associations. And, through these networks, the telecentre 2.0 is starting to spread. But there is still a long way to go.

Why does this telecentre 2.0 concept matter? Mostly because we are seeing telecentres – often scoffed at as development red herrings – mature into a myriad of useful and practical things. The best telecentres are becoming places where we invent what computing can mean for people who are at the very edges of the information society, and where these people are often involved in the invention process. It is this potential for invention that makes 'not designed for anything in particular' platforms like computers – and telecentres – so special. They unlock curiosity, invention and connection, things that are sorely missing from what we typically call 'development'. If more telecentres can tap into this spirit of invention, great things are possible. Almost anything at all.

can then implement ICT4D programmes. However, the final bullet point recognises that other kinds of intervention are also necessary if the poor are to benefit from these investments. Unfortunately, given the emphasis on mainstreaming ICTs in wider development initiatives, it is extremely difficult to measure precise allocations by donors to ICT4D programmes. Nevertheless, the DAC (2005) report highlights the importance of such contributions by Canada, the European Commission, France, Germany, Japan, Sweden, the UK and the USA. In addition, countries such as Switzerland and Ireland (Development Cooperation Ireland, 2003) have also contributed significantly to specific ICT4D initiatives (for summary details of donor support for ICT4D see http://www.infodev.org/en/Publication.186.html).

One significant feature of donor support for ICT4D programmes has been their emphasis on collaborative funding for particular initiatives. One of the most prominent of these has been the Building Communication Opportunities (BCO) Alliance (http://www.bcoalliance.org), which in 2004 replaced the Building Digital Opportunities (BDO) programme that had been running since 2001. BCO brings together donor agencies from Canada, The Netherlands, Switzerland and the UK, with civil society organisations (World Association of Community Radio Broadcasters, APC, Hivos, IICD, OneWorld) and research institutes (IDRC, Panos) to seek to:

- integrate ICT4D in development sectors such as health, agriculture, education, and environmental sustainability;
- strengthen the voice of poor and excluded communities and facilitate debate and dialogue through the use of ICTs; and
- demonstrate the impact of ICT4D on poverty.
        (http://www.bcoalliance.org/node/52, accessed 7 August 2007)

While these are laudable objectives, the fundamental challenge facing many people in poor countries is how to turn the experience gained from such alliances into scalable and sustainable initiatives on the ground.

One of the difficulties for those seeking to understand and influence ICT4D practices is that, despite years of supposed partnership and collaboration, different kinds of stakeholder still remain largely ignorant about the agendas and interests of those working in different sectors from their own. In particular, bilateral donors and senior executives in the private sector still display a remarkable lack of understanding about each other's motives and directions. Three key features of bilateral donor policy seem to be particularly pertinent in this arena. First, delivery on the MDGs has become central to donor policy, allied with a focus on absolute definitions of poverty, and a belief that economic growth will help to eliminate it (Sachs, 2005; Unwin, 2007). Because ICTs do not feature directly at the core of any of the MDGs, but merely as one element within MDG 8, it is not surprising that most donors fail to give it the attention that is paid to sectors such as education or health. Nevertheless, bilateral and multilateral donors are indeed aware that the private sector is crucial for economic growth, and given the importance of the ICT sector within the global economy they have expressed willingness to help support structures to enable ICT companies to invest in delivering appropriate services within developing countries. For most donors, though, this will not amount to the provision of substantial levels of funding specifically allocated to the implementation of nationwide ICT4D programmes.

This is allied to a second feature of donor policy, which is that many donors have shifted their focus from supporting specific projects or programmes to providing a much more integrated approach to development assistance. Over the last decade, particularly in the light of the Monterrey Consensus of 2002 (see World Economic Forum, 2006; and http://www.un.org/esa/ffd) and the Paris Declaration of 2005 (http://www.oecd.org/document/18/0,2340,en_2649_3236398_35401554_1_1_1_1,00.html), most donors have increasingly sought to integrate their support in four main ways: working collaboratively to deliver aligned agendas; reducing transaction costs; providing development assistance in support of clearly defined poverty reduction strategies (PRSPs) that are owned by the peoples of developing countries; and providing untied aid, primarily in the form of budget support mechanisms where the fiduciary risks are minimal (see Unwin, 2005a, for a critique). It should be noted here, though, that not all bilateral donors have signed up to this agenda, with USAID being a notable exception in its continuing emphasis on tied and project-based aid mechanisms. Likewise, one of the few donor governments that has continued specifically to support ICT4D initiatives has been Sweden, with Sida creating the Swedish Program for ICT in Developing Regions (SPIDER) in 2004, hosted within the Royal Institute of Technology in Stockholm (http://www.spidercenter.org). The net outcome of the widely shared donor agenda is that support for ICT4D initiatives will in the future need to come primarily from the governments of developing countries themselves, since they should have much greater control over the budgets necessary to implement such programmes. Hence, it is critically important that these countries have in place coherent and realistic ICT4D strategies, a topic that the next section of this chapter will therefore address.

A third, less tangible aspect of donor policy remains the deep suspicion that many staff working in these organisations still have about the agendas and interests of the private sector in engaging in 'development' practice. While donor governments might well espouse a rhetoric of support for economic growth and therefore for the role of the private sector, the reality on the ground is often that their staff have sparse knowledge of the private sector and see little beyond what they identify as being the profit motive of global corporations in maximising their markets and reducing labour costs (Friedman, 2006). While this culture is changing, many donor organisations still employ people educated in the heyday of the left-wing critique of development during the 1970s (Kothari, 2006), who thus retain a healthy scepticism for the excesses of the neo-conservative agenda associated with economic growth and liberal democracy.

## ICT4D national policies and strategies

All of the major global initiatives discussed in the previous section have emphasised that effective national ICT policies and strategies need to be in place for ICT4D initiatives to be successful. There are three fundamental reasons for this: first, the market alone will not deliver effective mechanisms through which the benefits of ICTs can be gained by poor and marginalised communities; second, the private sector needs to be convinced that it can invest safely in a country with a realistic expectation of generating reasonable profits; and third, there needs to be a forum in which civil society organisations can actively engage with governments at a national scale in determining the roll-out of ICT programmes. While these three objectives might at first sight appear to be incompatible, they nevertheless represent the essential requirements of all national ICT4D strategies. Moreover, it is only the government of a country that can make any attempt to regulate the balance of interests between these competing agendas. This section therefore provides an overview of progress in, and lessons learnt from, the development of ICT4D strategies and policies in the three contrasting regions of Asia, Latin America and Africa.

It is important to begin by distinguishing between the terms *strategies* and *policies* with respect to ICTs, since these are often used interchangeably. Labelle (2005, p. 29) defines ICT strategies as being concerned with the overall strategic approach to the use of ICTs in development, whereas he suggests that the term ICT policies is most usually used to refer to the implementation of policies geared to specific issues. As he goes on to summarise, 'There are several parts to an e-strategy: the assessment, the vision, the strategic plan itself, the action plan or master plan for implementation and the consultation plan. Also included are the institutional mechanisms for implementation and supervision, as well as monitoring and evaluation' (Labelle, 2005, p. 30). Specific policies then emerge from these overall national strategies. Generally, three particular areas of ICT policy have been distinguished, namely telecommunications, broadcasting and the internet, and these can function at global, regional and national levels. As Nicol (2003, p. 10) has emphasised, 'Each level may have its own decision-making bodies, sometimes making different and even contradictory policies'. It is important to emphasise that the strategic and policy issues facing different parts of the world are very varied (see also Tipson and Frittelli, 2003). Latin American countries, for example, have much more advanced telecommunications and broadcasting sectors than do most African countries. There cannot therefore be a single one-size-fits-all solution to ICT policy development. Most policies nevertheless involve three stages: the creation of a vision that is translated into a policy; the formal drafting of legislation; and then the creation of a regulatory agency to license operators and oversee tariff structures (ITU, 2006). Once national policies have been put in place, specific sector ICT policies are usually then designed, with e-strategies created to implement them (see Figure 5.1 based on UNDP-APDIP's experiences).

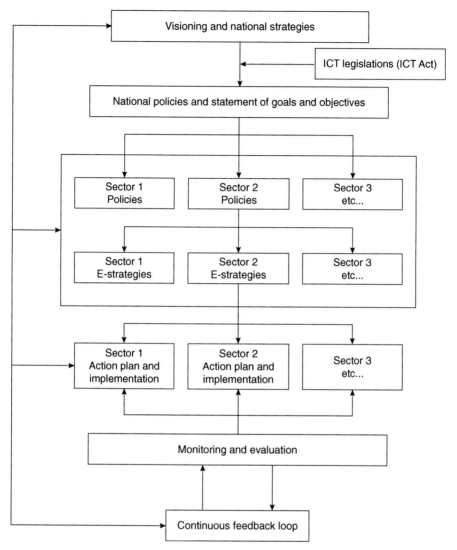

Figure 5.1 *UNDP-APDIP's design for visioning and national ICT strategies* (*source:* Ulrich *et al.*, 2004, p. 3).

Nicol (2003, p. 52) emphasises that individual countries do not act in a vacuum, and 'Powerful intergovernmental organisations are setting the agenda on ICT issues that penetrate all aspects of life – from policy, legislation and regulation to cultural development and the delivery of health and education'. Many of these intergovernmental agencies have produced indices to monitor the efficacy of ICT policies and strategies. The most comprehensive of these is the ITU's ICT Opportunity Index first published in 2007 (ITU, 2007). This was a specific outcome of the WSIS plan of action, which included the recommendation to combine statistical indicators with analytical work on the implementation of ICT policies, and it provides measurements for 183 economies of the world, using ten indicators. The other main indices produced in the mid-2000s have been: the Knowledge Economy Index produced by the World Bank's Knowledge for Development Programme, which is based on the four pillars of economic incentive and institutional regime, education and human resources, the innovation system, and ICT; the World Economic Forum's Networked Readiness Index based on environment, readiness and usage; UNCTAD's Index of ICT diffusion, focusing on connectivity and access; the UN's e-Government readiness index, based on a web measure, telecommunications and human capital sub-indices; and the Economist Intelligence Unit's e-Readiness Index (for full details of all of these indices, see APC and ITeM, 2007). Such indices do indeed provide a measure whereby governments can gauge the efficacy of their policy initiatives, the private sector can make investment decisions, and civil society can lobby for change. However, they can also detract attention from the successful delivery of ICT4D programmes on the ground. Excessive attention to indices can lead governments to invest considerable sums merely in trying to identify why their countries feature higher in some indices than in others, rather than actually in implementing productive changes in practice.

One of the undoubted influences of the WSIS process was that it provided an opportunity to review and highlight progress with the implementation of ICT policies and strategies as they had evolved in the first few years of the 21st century. The next three sections draw on some of the material produced in the course of that review, and highlight key issues that have emerged in the Asia-Pacific region, Latin America and Africa.

### Asian-Pacific e-strategies

The UNDP's Asia Pacific Development Information Programme (UNDP-APDIP) was established in 1997, specifically to work in collaboration with national governments 'to improve access, knowledge-sharing, networking, and management, and application of ICTs for social and economic development' (http://www.apdip.net/about). As well as mobilising support, it has played a key role in helping countries in the region develop strategic visions, and in assisting them to implement appropriate policies (Harris, 2004; Lallana, 2004). In 1998, for example, it delivered ICT policy training seminars in China, Iran, Mongolia, Nepal and Thailand, to be followed in subsequent years by many other such events across the region. A key event in the run-up to WSIS was the Asian Forum on ICT Policies and e-Strategies convened by UNDP-APDIP in Kuala Lumpur in 2003. This adopted a 17-point declaration which 'emphasizes the needs for specific policies on poverty reduction, governance, gender, infrastructure and access, human resources, content and applications, enterprises and entrepreneurs, and regional cooperation' (Sayo et al., 2004, p. vii).

Lallana (2004) highlights the fundamental differences between the evolution of ICT strategies and policies in the high-income economies of the region, such as Japan, South Korea and Singapore, compared, for example, with those of the low-income countries of India, Nepal and Vietnam. He nevertheless suggests that there are five main policy areas that need to be addressed in the evolution of e-strategies in the region: information infrastructure; security in cyberspace; the development and control of content; the creation of effective regulatory agencies; and the need for effective education policies that recognise and use ICTs. He also emphasises that the experiences of the Asia-Pacific countries indicate the need for a light touch by governments in the regulatory environment, the importance of competition as a means of generating better infrastructure and service provision, and the need for strategies to be sufficiently flexible to be able to adapt to changing circumstances. Ulrich *et al.* (2004) likewise emphasise that there is no single model for the development of effective ICT policies and e-strategies in the Asia-Pacific region, but they do conclude that five common principles for success have emerged: the need for the setting of specific goals; the need to avoid reinventing the wheel, and instead to draw on effective practices from elsewhere; the importance of prioritising objectives; the need for patience; and ensuring that governments drive ICT initiatives, particularly through policies that encourage private capital and entrepreneurship (Table 5.4). These are well exemplified in the case study below (pp. 156–7), which highlights the complexities of delivering effective ICT strategies for education in the small Pacific Island states (for a detailed analysis of Sri Lanka, see Hanna, 2007).

### ICT strategies and policies in Latin America

In contrast with many of the poorer countries of Asia and the Pacific, the telecommunications sector in Latin America has a much longer history of development. Hilbert *et al.* (2005) emphasise that the first policies relating to information and telecommunications in the region were put in place in countries such as Brazil and Mexico in the 1960s and 1970s. Nevertheless, many of the same conclusions can be drawn about the evolution of effective ICT strategies. Hilbert and Katz (2003) thus note five particular features that are required: the need for these strategies to embrace the entire government of a country; the importance of a single overarching national authority; the creation of a common vision between the private sector, civil society and the state; the need for the strategy to create synergies, linkages and cooperation among different stakeholders; and the importance of precise goals and objectives.

The United Nations Economic Commission for Latin America and the Caribbean has played an important role in seeking to coordinate and share good practices in the development of ICT policies and strategies in the region (Hilbert and Katz, 2003; Hilbert *et al.*, 2005; ECLAC, 2005). Table 5.5 summarises the recent evolution of ICT strategies in Latin America and the

**Table 5.4** *Selected Asia-Pacific national ICT policies and e-strategies, 2004*

| Country | Teledensity as an indicator of level of ICT usage | ICT policy and strategy key dates | Regulatory framework dates |
|---|---|---|---|
| Bhutan | Teledensity 3.1% | Bhutan Information Technology Strategy 1999<br>ICT Master Plan 2001 | Bhutan Telecom Act 1999 |
| Brunei | Teledensity almost 100% | Brunei Information Technology Council | Authority for Info-Communications Technology<br>Industry Order 2001 |
| Indonesia | Target by 2005 50% villages connected | ICT Policy and Strategy 2004 | Draft laws in existence |
| Lao PDR | Teledensity 1.31% | Strategy Task Force in place | |
| Maldives | Teledensity 10.85% | National Centre for Information Technology policy implementation 2003 | |
| Mongolia | Teledensity 5.4% | ICT Policy and Coordination Department 2003<br>IT Policy 2000 | Communication Law 2001 |
| Nepal | Teledensity 1.4% | Telecommunications Policy 1999 | Telecommunication Regulations Act 1997 |
| Pakistan | Teledensity 2.87% | IT Policy 2000 | Telecommunications Act 1996 |
| Philippines | Teledensity 6.6% | IT and e-Commerce Council 2000<br>National IT Plan 1998 | Public Telecommunications Policy Law 1995<br>IPR Code 1998 |
| Samoa | Teledensity 6.6% | Communications Action Plan 1999<br>National ICT Policy 2002 | Internet Act 1997 |
| Singapore | Mobile teledensity 81.7% | National IT Plan 1986<br>Connected Singapore MasterPlan 2003 | Electronic Transaction Act 1998<br>Computer Misuse Act 1993<br>Internet Code of Practice 1997 |
| Sri Lanka | Teledensity 8.0% | National Computer Policy 1983<br>eSL initiative 2003 | ICT Act 2003 |
| Thailand | Teledensity 13.1% | IT 2010 Policy 2002<br>Ministry of ICT established 2002<br>National ICT Master Plan 2002–2006 | Telecommunication Business Act 2001 |
| Timor-Leste | | Lack of human resources preventing ICT policy development | |

*Source:* Derived from Ulrich *et al.*, 2004; see also http://www.apdip.net/asian-forum/country.asp
*Notes:* Gaps indicate that no dates are given in original. This should not be taken to mean that initiatives to develop policies and strategies are absent, rather that they have not yet been legislated for or officially implemented.

**Table 5.5** *The emergence of recent national ICT policies and strategies in Latin America and the Caribbean*

| Country | Year in which ICT strategy was launched | Whether ICT strategy programmes existed beforehand | Three main thematic priorities |
|---|---|---|---|
| Argentina | 2004 | Yes | E-government, infrastructure, e-learning |
| Bolivia | 2002 | No | E-government, infrastructure, e-learning |
| Brazil | 1999 | Yes | E-government, general services, infrastructure |
| Chile | 1998 | No | E-government, infrastructure, e-learning |
| Colombia | 2000 | No | E-government, infrastructure, e-commerce |
| Dominican Republic | 2002 | Yes | E-government, infrastructure, e-learning |
| Ecuador | 2001 | No | Infrastructure, e-government, e-learning |
| Jamaica | 2002 | No | E-government |
| Mexico | 2001 | No | E-services, infrastructure, policy integration |
| Panama | | Yes | E-government, e-learning, e-infrastructure |
| Peru | 2003 | Yes | Infrastructure, e-government, e-learning |
| Trinidad and Tobago | 2002 | No | Infrastructure, e-government, e-learning |
| Venezuela | 2000 | No | Infrastructure, e-learning, human capital |

*Source:* derived from data in Hilbert *et al.* (2005, pp. 26–7)

Caribbean, and it is immediately apparent from this that the main thematic priorities across the region have been remarkably similar, concentrating primarily on infrastructure, e-government and education. Interestingly, faced with the cost and difficulty of implementing ICT policies across all aspects of their societies and economies, many countries have chosen to focus on the one thing that they can actually do something about, namely e-government, and are hoping to use this as an incentive to encourage change in other sectors. As Hilbert *et al.* (2005) emphasise, most countries already have an overall vision in place, and at the time of WSIS were focusing particularly on the formulation of policies. Among the most advanced in terms of implementation were Chile, Colombia and Mexico, and Trinidad and Tobago. While each of these has adopted rather different approaches, one feature they share has been that the head of state has played a prominent

(*continued on page 158*)

# Case study: ICT and education strategies in the Pacific

Michael Trucano

*Senior ICT and Education Specialist, The World Bank*

The small island developing states of the Pacific face many profound developmental challenges related to their small size, limited economic and natural resources, geographic remoteness, population migrations, and a variety of environmental issues, not least of which is climate change that threatens to put many islands underwater (see also Chapter 9). The potential for ICTs to help address such challenges is of growing interest to many, especially in the education sector (Pacific Archive of Digital Data for Learning and Education, http://www.paddle.usp.ac.fj/paddle/cgi-bin/paddle.exe; Pacific Plan: Pacific Regional Digital Strategy, http://www.pacificplan.org/tiki-page.php?pageName=Digital+strategy1).

With few exceptions, the use of ICT in education in Pacific island nations is still in the very early stages. Computers are expensive and remain a novelty in most schools. Throughout the region, internet connectivity is quite poor – and expensive! Few educators have first-hand experience in using ICTs, both in their professional and personal lives. That said, there is an incipient and growing awareness among governments and education policymakers about the potential relevance of ICT use in teacher training, access to distance education opportunities, increasing ICT literacy, and building stronger ties between schools and their surrounding communities. Ministries of Education are slowly becoming computerised, and select staff are being trained in the use and relevance of ICT for both administrative and pedagogical purposes. Nevertheless, links between central authorities and schools on outlying islands remain a real challenge, especially as Pacific nations have not experienced the explosion in mobile phone use seen in many other parts of the world.

At the grass-roots level, computers are appearing in some communities and schools on major islands, much as they have done in the initial stages of ICT penetration in other parts of the world. At the same time, more systematic and typically community-focused initiatives have been and are emerging, the most famous and notable of which is the People First Network (PFnet) of the Solomon Islands (http://www.peoplefirst.net.sb). This was initiated in 2001 as a key element of the Solomon Islands Development Administration Planning programme, and is an e-mail system that provides access to the internet and e-mail to remote islands across thousands of square kilometres using computers, short-wave radio and solar power. Telecentres have also emerged in places like Fiji as locations for formal and informal learning activities. At the other end of the spectrum, the tiny island of Niue is fully wireless, but, given its close economic ties to Australia and very small population, it is an outlier in the region.

In education as in other sectors, interest in strategies for regional solutions to shared challenges is growing, and indeed it is difficult to see how such solutions might emerge if they do not make extensive use of a variety of ICTs. The PRIDE Project at the University of the South Pacific (USP) (http://www.usp.ac.fj/pride) is the most prominent regional organisation facilitating the sharing of best practice and experience. USPNet, a satellite-communications network connecting all 12 member-countries of the university through a live video feed, is the leading regional provider of distance learning on a wide variety of topics, including those related to health and governance.

Regional, multilateral and bilateral organisations, including the Pacific Islands Forum, UNESCO, *info*Dev, AusAid, NZAid, the Commonwealth of Learning, JICA and the Hawaii-based Pacific Resources for Education and Learning (PREL), have conducted outreach and capacity-building activities related to ICT use in education in recent years. The potential to connect to diaspora communities, especially in Australia, New Zealand and the United States, has helped fuel interest and activity in utilising ICTs to link to education opportunities and content abroad.

Few would argue against the promise that ICTs hold for development in the Pacific in general, and for education in particular. Yet many question whether ICT-related projects and initiatives to benefit education should be given high priority, especially given the high costs of connectivity, computer hardware, software and support services and, more fundamentally, scores of pressing needs to provide basic infrastructure and services to far-flung, isolated populations. There are no easy answers to such questions, but the introduction of ICTs into education throughout the world appears inexorable, for better and for worse, and processes and investigations to help separate the hope from the hype regarding ICT use in the education sector are slowly getting under way throughout the Pacific.

(*Note:* The findings, interpretations and conclusions expressed are entirely those of the author and do not necessarily reflect the view of the World Bank and its affiliated organisations or the governments they represent.)

role in driving the strategy forward. Two other important differentiating factors in the policy process across the region have been the existing technical expertise available for the development of national strategies, and also the sources of funding (Hilbert *et al.*, 2005). In contrast to Asia, the participation of the private sector, academics and civil society in policy formulation has been rather limited in Latin America.

### *The African context*

In contrast to both Latin America and Asia, Africa has by far the least developed ICT sector, and can least afford the costs associated with duplication of effort and the implementation of flawed ICT strategies. The continent has, though, been able to benefit from considerable opportunities to share good practices through the work of organisations such as the UNDP, the AISI and the APC. Despite such initiatives, progress in the formulation of coherent and effective strategies and policies has been slower here than in other regions of the world. At an important conference on the development of African e-strategies convened by UNDP in Mozambique in 2003, Dandjinou (2003) provided a comprehensive overview of the state of such strategies on the eve of WSIS. Although this emphasised that there had indeed recently been progress, some 16 African countries had no ICT policy development process in place, and only 17 actually had e-strategies in 2003. Even among those with a strategy process, few had coherent implementation plans in place. Among the reasons for the lack of implementation, Dandjinou highlighted that common problems included poor infrastructure, a lack of clear financing strategy and a poor regulatory environment. Moreover, in many instances there was little effective national ownership, with many policy initiatives being largely donor-led. In tackling these issues, he suggested that the main issues that required addressing included identifying how best to ensure political will and commitment, how to forge effective partnerships, how to prioritise ICT as an enabler or an industry, and how to finance these strategies. As in Latin America, having an ICT champion at the highest level has been a key success factor in the development of African ICT policies. This was particularly well illustrated in Mozambique, where President Chisano championed the creation of the country's ICT policy, which was launched in 2000 and developed with the support of IDRC, UNECA, UNDP and the World Bank. As a result, Mozambique was recognised as the country with the best ICT policy framework at the ICT Africa Investment Summit in 2004, but despite this the country still languishes at 13th from the bottom of the ITU's ICT-OI index, with a lower average growth rate than that of many other African countries. Having the best policy in place is of little use unless there is sufficient human capacity to implement it, and sufficient resources to make it effective.

The effects of poor policy implementation in Africa will continue to have a lasting impact on the continent in the years ahead. This is well typified by the reorganisation of the telecommunications sector in South Africa.

South Africa passed legislation in 1994 to restructure the sector, in line with the widely held belief that deregulation of the telecommunications sector would necessarily reduce costs to consumers and also widen access. As Horwitz and Currie (2007, p. 1) nevertheless illustrate, 'The Government sold a 30 percent stake in the state-owned incumbent network operator, Telkom, to expand telephone service to under-serviced areas and populations. Ten years on, the reform has largely failed. Telkom, granted a 5-year period of exclusivity to expand the network, has used its monopoly power to thwart competition. It has raised prices so high as to be damaging to the economy'. Horwitz and Currie (2007) identify three inter-related themes that underlie this failure: an emphasis on privatisation over liberalisation; distrust by the government of independent regulation, and thus a lack of sufficient funding for this crucial element of reform; and an inability to control rent-seeking behaviour through which a few people have been able to benefit disproportionately at the expense of the majority. These are lessons that need to be learnt much more widely as other African countries grapple with the complexities of implementing ICT strategies.

Despite such concerns, African countries are making progress, albeit slowly, towards the framing and implementation of effective strategies. As a counter to the frequently top-down emphasis of ICT policies, civil society organisations such as APC and the Southern African NGO Network (SANGONeT, http://www.sangonet.org.za) have played an important role in monitoring such policy development, and in providing advice and support for social justice and development agendas. The APC's Africa ICT Policy Monitor, for example, provides resources and information to support effective civil society engagement in policy development, and it has played an active role in supporting specific initiatives in countries such as Kenya, the Democratic Republic of Congo and Nigeria. Likewise, SANGONeT, founded in 1987, has sought to strengthen the capacity of NGOs to use ICTs effectively in support of their agendas, and in so doing has helped promote understanding about the need for effective strategies and policies.

## Multi-stakeholder partnerships and the implementation of ICT4D initiatives

A recurring theme in this chapter has been that many different kinds of organisation have interests in the delivery of effective ICT4D policies and strategies at all levels. The processes leading up to WSIS thus witnessed a complex interplay between governments, international organisations, the private sector and civil society organisations, each seeking to position themselves to best advantage. Likewise, multi-stakeholder partnerships are frequently seen to be essential for the delivery of effective ICT4D initiatives at all scales from the international meetings of GAID to the local implementation of projects to provide internet access to schools. In recent years there has been a plethora of publications seeking to identify the optimal means to deliver such partnerships (see for example DAC, 2001; GKP, 2003;

Mercer, 2003; Tennyson, 2003; Warner and Sullivan, 2004; Unwin, 2005b; World Economic Forum, 2005, 2006; USAID, 2006; Martens, 2007). However, despite such interest, there remains little agreement on the value of such partnerships, nor on how best they should actually be implemented.

## The role of the private sector in development practice

Martens (2007, p. 4) has neatly summarised the present fascination with partnerships: 'In recent years, a new form of multilateral cooperation beyond intergovernmental diplomacy has gained increasing importance. In this new paradigm of international cooperation, "global partnerships", "multistakeholder initiatives" and "global public policy networks" are perceived as the future of international cooperation'. As he goes on to say:

> The root causes of this general tendency are manifold and include both general dissatisfaction on the part of governments, international organisations and NGOs with the agonizingly slow pace of the cumbersome global negotiation process, and the lack of will and capacity on the part of many governments to engage in binding financial commitments to achieve global agreements, or to translate such existing commitments into practice.
>
> (Martens, 2007, p. 4)

The origins of such a shift of emphasis towards partnerships are complex, but lie in part in changes in the economic re-organisation of societies in North America and Europe in the latter part of the 20th century. During the 1980s, and particularly in the USA under President Reagan and in the UK under Prime Minister Thatcher, there was a fundamental shift towards lower direct involvement of the state in economic activity. Old state-run enterprises and utilities were privatised, and attempts were also made to reduce rates of direct taxation. As a result, the role of the private sector grew significantly in areas that had previously been thought of as the preserve of the state. Not even the domains of education and health, long considered to be inviolable arenas of state involvement, were to be immune from this shift (see for example Sen, 2006; Webster, 2002). This shift of opinion has had two fundamentally important implications. One has been to raise the prospect that the private sector might actually be able to deliver other aspects of a state's functions, such as the provision of development assistance, more effectively than has heretofore been the case. Another has been to re-emphasise the importance of the private sector in delivering what had previously been considered to be public goods in other parts of the world, such as Africa. When these considerations are allied to the important role that the private sector must play in generating economic growth, a powerful new coalition of interests emerges.

With reference specifically to ICT4D, the second half of the 1990s saw rapid growth in the value of the newly emerging internet companies, fuelled in part by the ready availability of venture capital at the time. The meteoric rise and success of these companies helped shape the notion that they really could change the world, and such euphoria began to influence global leaders seeking to identify new ways in which the problems of poverty could be addressed. Although the collapse of this dot-com bubble in March 2000 (Cassidy, 2003) led to some dampening of enthusiasm for the value of ICTs, the seeds had been sown. With charismatic leaders at the helm of the major technology corporations that survived, such as Bill Gates at Microsoft, John Chambers at Cisco and Craig Barrett at Intel, the scene was set for a new kind of engagement between the private sector and governments in the field of ICT.

The private sector has specific interests in being involved in ICT4D programmes, both for commercial reasons and also in support of their corporate social responsibility agendas. As Chapter 2 highlighted, the ICT sector has been a key agent in the processes of globalisation, and has likewise benefited greatly in terms of expanded markets and reduced labour costs (see also Ó Riain, 2004; Hudson, 2005). It is therefore very much in the interests of private capital to see an expanded take-up of ICTs across the world. In the richest countries, increasing market saturation of mobile phones and computers means that companies involved in their production have to innovate ever more creatively in order to continue to expand their revenues. An alternative, though, is for them to seek to expand their markets more extensively in countries where take-up of their technologies has so far been limited (see Figures 2.1 and 2.2). Hence, global ICT corporations have a real interest in encouraging governments and international organisations to facilitate their penetration into such markets, and one way in which they do this is by engaging actively in programmes that propound the benefits of their technologies for 'development'. In the end, such companies must make careful judgements over the balance of investment that they will make in innovation and in expanding global market share, but it is clear that the increased attention that they are now paying to markets in poorer countries of the world is in large part because they can see value in supporting the growth of the ICT sector there in expectation of future financial returns. Cisco's Networking Academy Programme (http://www.cisco.com/web/learning/netacad/index.html) thus explicitly states that it is a 'global education initiative that helps students develop information and communication technology skills to encourage socioeconomic advancement in communities around the world'. Likewise, Microsoft's Partners in Learning initiative 'supports the dual commitment by Microsoft to advance the quality of education and provide alternative channels for economic progress. By building partnerships with governments and schools around the globe, Partners in Learning works to integrate technology into daily teaching, learning, and research' (http://www.microsoft.com/education/partnersinlearning.mspx). Such assertions clearly illustrate the ways in

(continued on page 164)

# Case study: LifeLines India

Melissa Gabriel

*Communications Specialist, Cisco Corporate Affairs*

Adrian Godfrey

*Director, Cisco Corporate Affairs*

'We wanted to help the rural farming community by linking voice to web technology, giving these people the chance to get answers by phone to the questions that are key to improving their lives' (Naimur Rahman, Director of OneWorld South Asia).

India has achieved remarkable economic growth and rapid progress in the area of ICT development, but the benefits of these advancements are largely restricted to urban areas and the most affluent members of society. The vast majority of India's citizens still grapple with poverty, limited communication facilities and high levels of illiteracy, particularly within villages and agrarian communities. These conditions have prompted several private- and public-sector organisations to collaborate on projects that aim to extend the benefits of ICT to all citizens. One such organisation, OneWorld South Asia (http://southasia. oneworld.net), uses ICT-based strategies to help alleviate poverty and promote sustainable development.

In India, OneWorld South Asia hoped to broaden the reach of their Open Knowledge Network initiative by adding a telephone dimension for rural farmers, who are generally unable to access information through the internet. 'The rural farming community in India suffers from poor levels of literacy,' explains Naimur Rahman, director of OneWorld South Asia. 'Many people cannot read and language can also be a barrier since information is often only available in English. Voice is therefore the most powerful medium for information service delivery.'

OneWorld South Asia formed a partnership with British Telecom and Cisco to launch the LifeLines India service in November 2006. This integrates the Cisco Unified Messaging platform and an online application to enable rural farmers to receive timely, expert advice on agriculture and animal husbandry issues. To use the service, farmers dial the LifeLines India number, submit their queries through an automated voicemail system, and call back after 24 hours to hear responses provided by specialists from the Indian Society of Agribusiness Professionals. All queries entered into the system are processed by a OneWorld knowledge worker, who searches through an online database of approximately 145,000 frequently asked questions. If a solution is found in the database, the knowledge worker attaches the response for the farmer to access. If the issue is new, the knowledge worker will seek the advice of a specialist and update the database before submitting a response. The farmer pays just 5 Rupees ($0.12) to use the LifeLines India service. According to Geeta Malhotra, head of grassroots communications at OneWorld South Asia, 'This small charge serves a dual purpose. First, the farmers value and respect the information they get because it is not totally free. Second, it enables us to create a sustainable business model.'

Initially, the LifeLines India service was launched in 85 villages, primarily in the region of Bundelkhand, central India, where irrigation facilities are generally inadequate, and diseases and pests are common problems. Due to the success of the initial launch, LifeLines India is now used by more than 100,000 farmers in 2066 villages, who have embraced the service as a valuable tool for improving crop efficiency and earning potential. An independent study of the programme impact in three villages showed a consistent increase in product quality and productivity, leading to 25 to 150 per cent profit growth for farmers. 'The social return of such an improvement is immense,' says Naimur Rahman. 'A better harvest can mean increased income, which will mean a better quality of life for families, enabling children to be better educated and have a brighter future. This is good for the individual and good for India.' Plans are currently in place to expand the LifeLines India service to 3,000 villages and 15 million people by March 2010. Based on the proven success and sustainability of the service model, the programme will also be adapted and scaled to address additional topics such as education, healthcare, microcredit, employment and disaster relief.

*Farmers who have benefited from LifeLines India (source:* OneWorld South Asia).

which these companies are seeking to ally themselves with the international emphasis that has recently been placed on economic growth as the main means of eliminating poverty. Alongside such economic agendas, however, many of those working in global ICT corporations have a real passion and commitment for using their technologies specifically to support initiatives that they know can make an impact on reducing poverty in the world. Unfortunately, all too often such altruism is misinterpreted somewhat cynically as being merely a cover for the economic interests of these corporations. While this can often be the case, it is by no means always so, and the very genuine concerns of many people within ICT corporations to use technology to improve the lives of poor people should be built upon enthusiastically. We need to recognise that there are indeed many different interests involved in delivering ICT4D initiatives, and work together creatively to build on the best of what is available to help ensure that disadvantaged individuals and communities can indeed benefit from the changes that are currently taking place. The case study 'LifeLines India' (pp. 162–3) provides an interesting example of the creation of an apparently successful and sustainable business model that is providing information of real benefit to farmers in India.

### The regulatory environment

One way in which global organisations and governments have sought to balance these competing interests is through the creation of regulatory environments that seek to maximise both public interest and private profit (see pp. 150–9). In the contemporary hegemonic global context, competition is seen as the key means of driving prices down, so that less prosperous people can afford technologies that were once the preserve of the rich. Regulation is thus viewed primarily as a means of ensuring a well-functioning competitive market that will maximise benefits from private-sector participation in a liberalised marketplace. There has therefore been considerable pressure from both governments and the private sector for the opening up of the telecommunications sector globally, and for traditional, state-owned national telecommunication operators to be privatised. The complexity of telecommunications regulation and the very rapid changes that have taken place in ICTs themselves have nevertheless meant that not all such regulation has been successful. As Levy and Spiller (1994, p. 242) have noted, 'the success of a regulatory system depends on how well it fits with a country's prevailing institutions. If a country lacks the requisite institutions, or erects a regulatory system that is incompatible with its institutional endowment, efforts at privatization may end in disappointment, recrimination, and the resurgence of demands of renationalization'.

Underlying much of the changing pattern of regulation has been a coalescence of interests between the private sector, governments and international organisations, notably the ITU. Indeed, there is too little public debate as to whether telecommunication privatisation has been entirely beneficial, particularly for the poorest and most marginal groups. As the South African example cited above (p. 159) indicates, not all such initiatives have achieved their desired objectives. All too frequently, a lack of transparency and insufficiently rigorous legal systems have meant that a relatively small number of individuals and companies have gained most of the real benefits from such privatisations. The very rapid expansion of mobile telephony in much of Africa, for example, has indeed been encouraged by the introduction of competition into the sector, but it is crucially important that appropriate and effective regulatory mechanisms are put in place to ensure that such benefits are distributed as widely as possible, both spatially and socially. The market alone cannot provide appropriate services for all people, particularly those living in isolated areas. It is therefore of great importance that where universal *service* cannot be guaranteed, governments put in place mechanisms to permit universal *access* to telecommunications, and that they consider the introduction of special funds to support roll-out of services to rural areas. As Wellenius (1997) has illustrated, this was particularly successful in Chile, where just over $2 million of public funds was used to leverage $40 million of private investment for the installation of telephones in 1,000 locations at about one-tenth of the cost of direct public provision.

### *Balancing supply and demand in ICT4D programmes*
One of the main reasons why so many ICT4D programmes have tended to fail has been because they have paid insufficient attention to balancing supply and demand. The international community, governments and the private sector all have specific interests in providing ICT services to an ever-increasing number of people, but such initiatives will fail if such services are not developed in response to the needs of those for whom they are intended. Typical of such problematic initiatives has been the NEPAD e-Schools Project (Farrell *et al.*, 2007), which was led by private-sector consortia with insufficient understanding of or interest in the educational contexts within which their solutions were being supplied. Some of the private-sector companies involved are adamant that this initiative did indeed serve many of their needs, bringing them closer together with African governments and other private-sector partners, introducing them to many of the challenges involved in delivering educational solutions in Africa, and enabling them to gain a toehold in these markets. However, there is little evidence that the long-term educational needs of the countries in which these projects were implemented have as yet benefited substantially.

This highlights the potential structural imbalances that are to be found at the heart of many ICT4D programmes, and returns us to the discussions of different types of 'development' practice outlined in Chapters 2 and 3. While the private sector's core interests coincide closely with the dominant global economic growth agenda, the role of governments, civil society organisations and international agencies is in part to ensure that there is a balance in provision so that the needs of disadvantaged communities and individuals can also be met. It is therefore critically important that all those involved in delivering ICT4D initiatives seek to identify the most appropriate technologies that can be used to serve the information and communication needs of those with whom they are working. Chapter 4 outlined the potential of many such technologies, while this chapter has provided a broad overview of the policy and regulatory context within which such initiatives are being implemented. The remaining chapters build on these, by examining in detail the practical ways in which demand in particular sectors, such as health and education, can be matched with appropriate technologies.

### *Towards a framework for multi-stakeholder partnerships*

The above emphasis on balancing supply and demand highlights the importance of organisations working together collaboratively to deliver effective ICT4D policies, strategies and initiatives. Earlier sections of this chapter have also linked this emphasis on ICT4D partnerships with the emerging global consensus on the value of development partnerships more generally, reflected for example in the UN Global Compact (http://www.unglobalcompact.org) (see also Tennyson, 2003; Warner and Sullivan, 2004; Binder *et al.*, 2007; Cassidy with Paksima, 2007; Martens, 2007; Draxler, 2008).

There are many different approaches to the implementation of such partnerships, with a recent review commissioned by UNESCO and the World Economic Forum's *Partnership for Education* initiative suggesting that they can bring five main advantages in the education sector: they make education relevant for the economic needs of a country; they bring much-needed innovation into the education sector; they enable programmes to be targeted to specific groups; they provide financial and management techniques not usually found in government or the education sector; and they can improve the learning environment (Draxler, 2008). In concluding this review, Draxler (2008, pp. 17–18) also makes six valuable recommendations that apply across most development partnerships: that clear principles should underlie all such partnerships; that sound regulatory mechanisms need to be in place; that the relevance of the partnership should be made clear to all involved; that partnerships do not always reduce overall costs; that the benefits are potentially high and should be used in negotiating the creation of the partnership; and that all stakeholders should commit to transparent reporting.

Insufficient monitoring and evaluation of such partnerships has nevertheless hindered the development of a systematic understanding of the real value of 'development partnerships' (although see for example Warner and Sullivan, 2004). An exception to this has been Cassidy's review of the

World Economic Forum's Global Education Initiative activities in Jordan, Egypt and Rajasthan (Cassidy with Paksima, 2007). These initiatives all involved private-sector partners (both international and local) working with governments to introduce effective ICT-based activities into education systems, although in some cases the ICT element was also alongside other partnership activities. Cassidy's conclusions have relevance far beyond just the education sector and are therefore worth considering in some detail. Table 5.6 thus provides an overview of the main lessons learnt and promising practices identified from these three initiatives. A key finding from this is that partnerships do not just happen; they require a considerable amount of work in designing, implementing and maintaining them. Central to Cassidy's argument is the important point that many components need to be in place to ensure the effective operation of such partnerships, and this is a conclusion that resonates far beyond just the educational partnerships that he reviewed.

In seeking to pull together collective understandings of ICT4D partnerships, three fundamental issues are of especial relevance. First, we must replace simplistic models of 'public–private' partnerships with more sophisticated and complex conceptualisations of 'multi-stakeholder' partnerships if they are going to be truly effective (Unwin, 2005b). The failure of many ICT4D partnerships in the past has often been because they have concentrated only on the 'private' and the 'public' sectors, and have not sufficiently incorporated the resources and interests of other key stakeholders. In particular, the exclusion of civil society organisations from many such partnerships has meant that their crucial contributions have often been omitted. Increasingly, the term 'tri-sector partnerships' (see Warner and Sullivan, 2004) has come to be used to reflect the incorporation of civil society alongside the public and private sectors. The London School of Economics' Centre for Civil Society (LSE CCS) provides a useful definition of civil society as 'the arena of uncoerced collective action around shared interests, purposes and values. In theory, its institutional forms are distinct from those of the state, family and market, though in practice, the boundaries between state, civil society, family and market are often complex, blurred and negotiated' (http://www.lse.ac.uk/collections/CCS/what_is_civil_society.htm). There nevertheless remain some (see for example Draxler, 2008, with her emphasis on UN policy and the Global Compact) who persist in seeing civil society as a subset of the private sector, and wish therefore to retain the use of the term 'public–private partnerships' (see also USAID, 2006). This runs counter to recognition of the distinct identity of civil society as an important entity in development practice, both practically and conceptually. The DAC policy statement issued in 2001 and entitled *Rising to the Global Challenge: partnership for reducing world poverty* (DAC, 2001, p. 1; see also OECD, 2002) places particular prominence on the value of partnerships with civil society, with its preamble stating that 'Developing countries must assume leadership and formulate effective national strategies for reducing poverty.

**Table 5.6** *Promising practices and lessons learnt from the World Economic Forum Global Education Initiative*

| Promising practices | Lessons learnt |
|---|---|
| 1  High-level championing of the initiative from a senior figure or figures within each country or state has been an essential element of its success, ensuring that there is appropriate buy-in at all levels, and that the initiatives have been given the necessary publicity to contribute to their acceptance and success. | 1  Multi-stakeholder partnerships initiatives can be very effective in supporting ongoing education reforms and in adding value to the activities and public images of participating partners. |
| 2  An important feature of the GEI model is the role of the Project Management Office/Unit in managing and directing the initiatives. Although different in form in each of the initiatives, an effective management unit has been an essential ingredient of their success. | 2  To be successful, multi-partner initiatives must be very well and systematically managed. |
| 3  A state or national steering committee, working independently, but in concert with an international steering committee, has been seen to provide more timely decision support to the local initiative management team than might otherwise have been possible. | 3  To be successful, leadership and management teams must include a balanced representation of educators, ICT experts and representatives of all types of partners. |
| 4  The organisation of initiative activities into tracks, as is the case in all three initiatives, has proven to be a very effective way to organise the various activities involved in the delivery of the educational change programme. | 4  Changing what goes on in schools, and particularly changing teaching practices in classrooms, is a much more complex and challenging undertaking that is going to take more time than partners often believe. It is critically important to give such initiatives sufficient opportunity to achieve their results. |
| 5  A careful plan including an outline of the resources required successfully to implement it can contribute to effective identification, recruitment and participation of initiative partners. | 5  Teachers and principals are at the heart of the change process and must be involved actively in their design and implementation. |
| 6  The establishment of an initiative trust fund, giving management a degree of discretionary control over how some of the resources are allocated, is a valuable mechanism to ensure that timely interventions are possible. | 6  Sustained partner involvement, particularly of the many private-sector partners and some donor and lending agency partners, should not be taken for granted. There needs to be active management of the partnership arrangements if these initiatives are to be successful. |
| 7  Activities that provide public-sector employees with opportunities to work in private-sector settings can contribute to shifts in organisational culture, notably work ethics and habits. | 7  Monitoring and evaluation, and considerations of scaling-up and sustaining current initiatives, must be given much greater attention in all such initiatives. |

*Source:* Cassidy with Paksima (2007, p. 24)

These strategies should integrate economic, social, environmental and governance concerns within a comprehensive approach to development at the country level. We pledge to help them meet this challenge, in partnership with civil society, the private sector and multilateral institutions'. While the term 'tri-partite partnerships' goes some way to recognising the importance of civil society in ICT4D partnerships, it is increasingly being understood that effective partnerships need to be even more diverse than this. Hence, the notion of multi-stakeholder partnerships is being advocated as a more inclusive term that can also serve as a reminder of the importance of diversity in delivering effective change (Unwin, 2005b; see also Gerster and Zimmerman, 2003).

Second, it is of fundamental importance that such multi-stakeholder partnerships pay explicit attention to the balance between supply and demand in both their conceptualisation and their implementation. For effective development impact that will empower poor people and marginalised communities, their interests as end beneficiaries need to be paramount (see Unwin *et al.*, 2007), and they should therefore be seen as full partners in any such initiative. In school-based ICT4D initiatives, for example, it is essential to involve teachers, pupils and community leaders at an early stage in shaping and implementing the initiative. Moreover, there are many types of local entity, including for example private-sector companies, civil society organisations and local government officials, who should be important demand-side partners in any such initiative. A fundamental shift needs to take place in much ICT4D policy and practice towards the recognition that if such initiatives are to make a real impact on poverty, their prime emphasis needs to be on these demand-side interests. Typical supply-side partners that can help deliver such initiatives are equally diverse, and can include funding agencies, government departments, private-sector companies, research institutions and international agencies. In bringing together these supply and demand partners to deliver effective partnerships, it is crucially important to identify trusted and respected broker organisations who have the capacity to manage them. These organisations need to have a deep understanding of many aspects of ICT4D policy and practice, as well as practical experience of the complexity of delivering such initiatives on the ground, and the task can perhaps best be accomplished by experienced international agencies. Alternatively, it could be a role for bilateral donors, as exemplified by the Imfundo initiative based within DFID (http://imfundo.digitalbrain.com), which between 2001 and 2004 explicitly sought to match resources provided by its partners with the needs of educational providers in Africa.

A third crucial factor for effective multi-stakeholder partnerships is the importance of maintaining a transparent ethical framework through which they can be implemented. At the very least, such a framework should combine clear acknowledgement of both the benefits that partners expect to gain from their involvement and also the contributions that they are willing to make, as for example in the Imfundo model, and also in the World Economic Forum and UNESCO's Partnerships for Education initiative (http://www.pfore.org). Such information should be shared openly among the partners, and these agreements need to be updated regularly through the duration of an initiative, as expectations and implementation needs change over time. It is therefore also important for those managing ICT4D multi-stakeholder partnerships to maintain a detailed overview of their organisational complexity, so that the benefits offered and contributions made can be matched to the demand and supply dimensions of any particular initiative. In so doing it should be emphasised that those partners primarily designated as being on the demand side, such as community health workers, also have much to contribute, through for example their labour, local knowledge and insights into what practices might actually be most effective. Typically, partner contributions in ICT4D initiatives can be grouped under the headings of human resources, physical ICTs, social networks, infrastructure and finance, whereas the benefits of partnership are often seen as being in terms of an organisation's identity, networking opportunities, economic returns, and research and development potential.

## Delivering effective ICT4D partnerships

Many well-intentioned ICT4D partnerships have failed to be as successful as their proponents would have liked, or indeed anticipated. This does not mean that we should give up seeking to implement them, but rather it suggests that we need to develop much more sophisticated understandings of how these can best be effected. This chapter has sought to contribute to this debate through a review of the institutional history of ICT4D, a summary of some of the main ICT4D policy initiatives that have been attempted, and a reflection on key issues associated with the implementation of multi-stakeholder ICT4D partnerships.

In conclusion, three key messages need to be reiterated. First, there are many competing interests in implementing ICT4D initiatives, and not all of these are necessarily compatible. This in part reflects fundamental differences in the types of development practice that people have sought to implement through the use of ICT. It also, though, highlights the different institutional emphases of the various partners involved. The interests of the private sector, governments, and civil society organisations do not always coincide. However, as we approach the end of the first decade of the 21st century, there does now seem to be an increasing realisation by most parties involved that they need to work together if effective changes designed to reduce poverty are indeed to be implemented. This has, for example, been typified by the alliance brokered by the World Economic Forum in 2007 and 2008 to bring together bilateral donors, governments, the private sector and civil society organisations to support educational reform in parts of Africa. A challenge nevertheless remains in identifying the most appropriate mechanisms through which such partnerships can be implemented most effectively (Tennyson, 2003; Unwin, 2005b).

Second, it is of paramount importance that ICT4D programmes should explicitly focus on the information and communication needs of poor and previously disadvantaged people if they are indeed intended to enhance equity. They should therefore begin with the demand side of the equation, and only then seek to identify the optimal and most cost-effective ways of using ICTs to empower such communities. Far too many ICT4D programmes to date have been top-down, supply-led, and focused on the technologies rather than the information and communication needs of poor people. It is largely because of this that they have as yet failed to make a significant impact on poverty. Alternative schemes designed to use ICT to foster economic growth can indeed contribute to 'development' defined as economic growth, but this is something very different from the empowerment of the poor.

Finally, there is an important need for high-profile champions to become actively involved in advocating for the value of multi-stakeholder partnerships in delivering effective ICT4D initiatives. Evidence to date, be it in terms of national ICT strategies, the implementation of specific programmes such as Grameenphone (http://www.grameenphone.com), or local initiatives in individual schools and hospitals, suggests that these are most effective where they are championed by committed individuals at all levels. Effective partnerships do not just happen. They need to be led by people who have the skills to bring together disparate partners who can see mutual benefit in using ICTs to make a significant impact on the lives of poor people and marginalised communities.

## Key readings

Cassidy, T. with Paksima, S. (2007) *The Global Education Initiative (GEI) Model of Effective Partnership Initiatives for Education.* Geneva: World Economic Forum

Friedman, T.L. (2006) *The World is Flat: the globalized world in the twenty-first century.* London: Penguin; updated edition

Gilhooly, D. (ed.) (2005) *Creating an Enabling Environment: toward the Millennium Development Goals. Proceedings of the Berlin Global Forum of the United Nations ICT Task Force.* New York: UN ICT Task Force

GKP (Global Knowledge Partnership) (2003) *Multistakeholder Partnerships: issue paper.* Kuala Lumpur: GKP

ITU (2006) *E-Strategies – empowering development.* Geneva: ITU

Labelle, R. (2005) *ICT Policy Formulation and e-Strategy Development: a comprehensive guidebook.* New Delhi: Elsevier for UNDP-APDIP

Unwin, T. (2005b) *Partnerships in Development Practice: evidence from multi-stakeholder ICT4D partnership practice in Africa.* Paris: UNESCO Publications for the World Summit on the Information Society

# References

Annan, K. (2001) Launching Information and Communications Technology (ICT) Task Force, Secretary General appeals for support from private sector (http://www.unicttaskforce.org/welcome)

APC and ITeM (Association for Progressive Communications and Third World Institute) (2007) *Global Information Society Watch 2007*. Uruguay: Association for Progressive Communications and Third World Institute

Binder, A., Palenberg, M. and Witte, J.M. (2007) *Engaging Business in Development: results of an international benchmarking study*. Berlin: Global Public Policy Institute

Cassidy, J. (2003) *Dot-con: how America lost its mind and its money in the internet era*. New York: HarperCollins

Cassidy, T. with Paksima, S. (2007) *The Global Education Initiative (GEI) Model of Effective Partnership Initiatives for Education*. Geneva: World Economic Forum

Celik, A.P. (ed.) (2007) *Foundations of the Global Alliance for ICT and Development*. New York: United Nations

CTO (2002) *DOT Force: final report of the G8 DOT Force, and its legacy for ICT for development* (http://www.ictdevagenda.org/frame.php?dir = 07&sd = 10&id = 227)

DAC (2001) *Rising to the Global Challenge: partnership for reducing world poverty*. Paris: OECD

DAC (2003) *Donor ICT Strategies Matrix, 2003*. Paris: OECD DAC

DAC (2005) *Financing ICTs for Development – efforts of DAC members: report to the UN Task Force on financial mechanisms for ICT for development*. Paris: OECD DAC

Dandjinou, P. (2003) The status of e-strategies in Africa (revisiting e-strategies). Paper presented to Conference on e-Strategies for Development in Africa, held in Maputo, 1–4 September 2003

Development Cooperation Ireland (2003) *Report of the Task Force on ICT and Development*. Dublin: Development Cooperation Ireland, Ministry of Foreign Affairs (http://www.irishaid.gov.ie/Uploads/ICT%20TF%20Report.pdf)

Digital Opportunity Task Force (2002) *Report Card: digital opportunities for all*. Canada: DOT Force (http://www.g7.utoronto.ca/summit/2002kananaskis/dotforce_reportcard.pdf)

Drake, W.J. (ed.) (2005) *Reforming Internet Governance: perspectives from the Working Group on Internet Governance (WGIG)*. New York: UN ICT Task Force

Draxler, A. (2008) *New Partnerships for EFA: building on experience*. Paris: IIEP/UNESCO; Geneva: World Economic Forum

ECLAC (2005) *Public Policies for the Development of Information Societies in Latin America and the Caribbean*. Santiago de Chile: UN ECLAC and @LIS

Engelhard, R. (2000) Information and Communication Technologies: technical, political and institutional trends and their implication for national agricultural systems in ACP countries. Paper presented at CTA Seminar 2000, Paris (http://www.contactivity.com/contactivity/content/download/235/1429/file/ICT_trends_implications_NAS_CTA_2000%5B1%5D.pdf, accessed 6 August 2007)

Farrell, G., Isaacs, S. and Trucano, M. (2007) *The NEPAD e-Schools Demonstration Project: a work in progress*. Washington, DC: *info*Dev/The World Bank; Vancouver: Commonwealth of Learning (http://www.infodev.org/en/Publication.355.html)

Friedman, T.L. (2006) *The World is Flat: the globalized world in the twenty-first century*. London: Penguin; updated edition

G8 Information Centre (2001) Digital opportunities for all: meeting the challenge. Report of the Digital Opportunity Task Force (DOT Force) including a proposal for a Genoa Plan of Action (http://www.g7.utoronto.ca/summit/2001genoa/dot-force1.html)

Gerster, R. and Zimmermann, S. (2003) *Information and Communication Technologies (ICTs) for Poverty Reduction*. Berne: Swiss Agency for Development and Co-operation (SDC) (http://www.cefe.net/forum/ICTforPovertyReduction.pdf)

Gilhooly, D. (ed.) (2005) *Creating an Enabling Environment: toward the Millennium Development Goals. Proceedings of the Berlin Global Forum of the United Nations ICT Task Force*. New York: UN ICT Task Force

GKP (Global Knowledge Partnership) (2001) *Annual Report 2001*. Kuala Lumpur: GKP

GKP (Global Knowledge Partnership) (2003) *Multistakeholder Partnerships: issue paper*. Kuala Lumpur: GKP

Hanna, N.K. (2007) *From Envisioning to Designing e-Development: the experience of Sri Lanka*. Washington, DC: World Bank

Harris, R.W. (2004) *Information and Communication Technology for Poverty Alleviation*. Kuala Lumpur: United Nations Development Programme's Asia-Pacific Development Information Programme (UNDP-APDIP) (http://www.apdip.net/publications/iespprimers/eprimer-pov.pdf)

Hilbert, M. and Katz, J. (2003) *Building an Information Society: a Latin American and Caribbean perspective*. Santiago de Chile: UN CEPAL

Hilbert, M., Bustos, S. and Ferraz, J.C. (2005) *Estrategies Nacionales para la Sociedad de la Información en América Latina y el Caribe*. Santiago de Chile: UN CEPAL, @LIS

Horwitz, R.B. and Currie, W. (2007) Another instance where privatization trumped liberalization: the policies of telecommunications reform in South Africa – a ten year retrospective. *Telecommunications Policy*, 31, pp. 445–62 (Sept–Oct 2007) (http://web.si.umich.edu/tprc/papers/2007/778/SA%20Telecoms%20Horwitz Currie.pdf)

Hudson, H.E. (2005) *From Rural Village to Global Village: telecommunications and development in the information age*. Mahwah, NJ: Erlbaum

IICD (2006) *Making it Work: 10 years of people, ICT and development with IICD*. The Hague: IICD (http://www.ftpiicd.org/files/temp/IICD-anniversary-booklet.pdf)

International Freedom of Expression Exchange Tunisia Monitoring Group (2005) *Report on Tunisia* (http://www.ifex.org/en/content/view/full/64689)

ITU (2006) *E-Strategies – empowering development*. Geneva: ITU

ITU (2007) *Measuring the Information Society 2007: ICT Opportunity Index and world telecommunication/ICT indicators*. Geneva: ITU (http://www.itu.int/ITU-D/ict/publications/ict-oi/2007/index.html)

Kelly, T. (2004) World Summit on the Information Society (WSIS) and the Digital Divide. Presentation to KADO/APWINC Digital Opportunity Conference, Seoul, 24 November 2004 (http://www.itu.int/osg/spu/presentations/2005/kelly-wsis-digital-divide-24-nov-04.pdf)

Khan, S. (2007) Introduction. In Celik (ed.) (2007), pp. 1–4

Kothari, U. (ed.) (2006) *A Radical History of Development Studies: individuals, institutions and ideologies*. London: Zed Press

Labelle, R. (2005) *ICT Policy Formulation and e-Strategy Development: a comprehensive guidebook*. New Delhi: Elsevier for UNDP-APDIP

Lallana, E.C. (2004) *An Overview of ICT Policies and e-Strategies of Select Asian Economies*. New Delhi: Elsevier for UNDP-APDIP

Levy, B. and Spiller, P.T. (1994) The institutional foundations of regulatory commitment: a comparative analysis of telecommunications regulation. *The Journal of Law, Economics and Organization*, 10 (2), pp. 201–46

MacLean, D. (ed.) (2004a) *Internet Governance: a grand collaboration. An edited collection of papers contributed to the United Nations ICT Task Force Global Forum on Internet Governance, New York, March 25–26, 2004.* New York: UN ICT Task Force

MacLean, D. (2004b) Herding Schrödinger's cats: some conceptual tools for thinking about internet governance. In MacLean (ed.) (2004a), pp. 73–99

MacLean, D. (2005) A brief history of WGIG (http://www.wgig.org/docs/book/A_ Brief_history_of_WGIG.html)

Maitland, D. (1984) *The Missing Link.* Report of the Independent Commission for World Wide Telecommunications Development, December 1984. Geneva: ITU. (http://www.itu.int/osg/spu/sfo/missinglink/The_Missing_Link_A4-E.pdf)

Maitland, D. (2005) An interview with Sir Donald Maitland. In Milward-Oliver (ed.) (2005), pp. 229–36

Martens, J. (2007) *Multistakeholder Partnerships – future models of multilateralism?* Berlin: Friedrich Ebert Stiftung

Mercer, C. (2003) Performing partnership: civil society and the illusion of good governance in Tanzania. *Political Geography,* 22 (7), pp. 741–63

Milward-Oliver, G. (ed.) (2005) *Maitland + 20. Fixing the missing link.* Bradford on Avon: Anima

Nicol, C. (2003) *ICT Policy: a beginner's handbook.* Melville: Association for Progressive Communications

O'Brien, R. (2000) Enabling civil society participation in global policy making: the APC and the United Nations (http://www.apc.org/english/about/history/full_ story.shtml?x = 9955)

OECD (2002) *Harmonizing Donor Practices for Effective Aid Delivery.* Paris: OECD

Ó Riain, S. (2004) *The Politics of High-tech Growth: developmental network states in the global economy.* Cambridge: Cambridge University Press

Sachs, J. (2005) *The End of Poverty.* London: Penguin

Sayo, P., Chacko, J.G. and Pradham, G. (eds) (2004) *ICT Policies and e-Strategies in the Asia-Pacific: a critical assessment of the way forward.* New Delhi: Elsevier for UNDP-APDIP

Sen, K. (ed.) (2006) *Restructuring Health Services: changing contexts and comparative perspectives.* London: Zed Books

Seung-soo, H. (2001) United Nations General Assembly statements and messages from the President. Opening Remarks by Dr Han Seung-soo at the Forum of Small States (http://www.un.org/ga/president/56/speech/010910b.htm)

Souter, D. (2005) Then and now: what would be the remit of a modern-day Maitland Commission. In Milward-Oliver (ed.) (2005), pp. 3–20

Souter, D. with Jagun, A. (2007) *Whose Summit? Whose Information Society? Developing countries and civil society at the World Summit on the Information Society.* Melville, South Africa: Association for Progressive Communications (http://rights.apc. org/documents/whose-Summit-EN.pdf, accessed 17 September 2007)

Tegge, A. (1994) *Die Internationale Telekommunikations-Union: Organisation und Funktion einer Weltorganisation im Wandel.* Baden-Baden: Nomos Verlagsgesellschaft

Tennyson, R. (2003) *The Partnering Toolbook.* London: International Business Leaders Forum and Global Alliance for Improved Nutrition

Tipson, F.S. and Frittelli, C. (2003) *National Strategies of 'ICT for Development': global digital opportunities.* New York: Markle Foundation

Ulrich, P., Chacko, G. and Sayo, P. (2004) Overview of ICT policies and e-strategies in the Asia-Pacific region. In Sayo *et al.* (eds) (2004), pp. 1–55

UN ICT Task Force (2001) Plan of action of the ICT Task Force (http://www. unicttaskforce.org/about/planofaction.html)

UNDP (2001) *Human Development Report 2001: Making new technologies work for human development*. New York: Oxford University Press for the United Nations Development Programme

Universalia (2007) *Independent Evaluation of the Information for Development (infoDev) Global Trust Funded Program* (http://www.infodev.org/en/Publication.453.html)

Unwin, T. (2005a) Beyond budget support: pro-poor development agendas for Africa. *Third World Quarterly*, 25 (8), pp. 1501–23

Unwin, T. (2005b) *Partnerships in Development Practice: evidence from multi-stakeholder ICT4D partnership practice in Africa*. Paris: UNESCO Publications for the World Summit on the Information Society

Unwin, T. (2007) No end to poverty. *Journal of Development Studies*, 43 (5), pp. 929–53

Unwin, T., Tan, M. and Pauso, K. (2007) The potential of e-learning to address the needs of out-of-school youth in the Philippines. *Children's Geographies*, 5 (4), pp. 443–62

USAID (2006) *Public–Private Partnerships for Development: a handbook for business*. Washington, DC: USAID

Warner, M. and Sullivan, R. (2004) *Putting Partnerships to Work: strategic alliances for development between governments, the private sector and civil society*. Sheffield: Greenleaf

Webster, C. (2002) *The National Health Service: a political history*. Oxford: Oxford University Press

Weigel, G. and Waldburger, D. (eds) (2004) *ICT4D – connecting people for a better world*. Berne and Kuala Lumpur: Swiss Agency for Development and Cooperation and Global Knowledge Partnership

Wellenius, B. (1997) Extending telecommunications service to rural areas – the Chilean experience. Washington, DC: World Bank [Public Policy for the Private Sector, note no. 105]

World Bank (1999) *World Development Report 1998/99: knowledge for development*. Washington, DC: The World Bank, International Bank for Reconstruction and Development

World Bank Development Grant Facility (2002) Information for Development Program (http://wbln0018.worldbank.org/dgf/dgf.nsf/7e994d22ce39b56585256c 92005bc140/00b1fb20976745f285256d9b005d57b0?OpenDocument)

World Economic Forum (2001) *Annual Report 2000/2001*. Geneva: World Economic Forum (http://www.weforum.org/pdf/AnnualReport/annual_report_2000_2001. pdf)

World Economic Forum (2005) *Building on the Monterrey Consensus: the growing role of public–private partnerships in mobilizing resources for development*. Geneva: World Economic Forum in Partnership with Financing for Development and the Swiss Agency for Development and Cooperation

World Economic Forum (2006) *Building on the Monterrey Consensus: the untapped potential of development finance institutions to catalyse private investment*. Geneva: World Economic Forum in Partnership with Financing for Development and the Swiss Agency for Development and Cooperation

*Community radio station at Nabweru, Uganda, 2008 (source:* Tim Unwin).

6 | ICTs, enterprise and development
Michael L. Best and Charles Kenny

- Both macroeconomic and microeconomic approaches are important in understanding the roles of ICTs in broad economic development processes.
- Private, competitive and well-regulated ICT markets attract greater investment flows and see larger telecommunications revenues than those that are not liberalised.
- In order to enhance markets and economic development in poor countries, we need to reduce the information divide between them and richer countries.
- ICTs have helped firms become more efficient and profitable, and have helped consumers save money and receive better services. This notwithstanding, there is a significant failure rate in firm-level ICT interventions within the developing world.
- Mobile telephony may have a particularly large impact on productivity in developing countries while the internet and advanced computing also has great promise for the future.

## ICT industries and ICT use

It has long been understood that obstructions and imperfections in the flow of information and knowledge serve as an important determinant of persistent poverty (Stiglitz, 2002). In turn, the low use of modern information and communication infrastructures in the developing world – the *digital divide* – is one cause of poverty, because it limits this flow of information. Closing this divide will nurture enterprise and enhance economic development within the world's poorest nations.

This digital divide has indeed been closing. The spread of ICTs in developing markets, while a longstanding general phenomenon, has reached an unprecedented rate of diffusion in the last few years. It is common to find a television in a developing-country household that lacks piped water, networked electricity, a concrete floor or even a solid roof. For example, over half of Indonesian households living on two dollars per person per day have a television, while less than 20 per cent of the same households have a water tap (Banerjee and Duflo, 2006). Expenditures on ICTs rose twice as fast in low-income countries as in their high-income counterparts from 1993 to 2001 (Qiang et al., 2003), and the mobile phone revolution has only extended the lead of ICTs' penetration into poor households and rural areas over other infrastructure services. In Africa it is now estimated that more than 70 per cent of households make regular use of phones (McKemey et al., 2003). Access to telephony is now the norm worldwide, where only a decade ago it was limited to the global elite.

The rate of diffusion of the internet in low-income countries has been on the rise (Best and Wilson, 2007). Nonetheless, it has not reached the level of penetration enjoyed by the telephone nor certain broadcast media. Only 2 per cent of people living in low-income countries are estimated to be internet users, and this figure includes people who share internet subscriptions and use cybercafés (ITU, 2006). Given this differential in penetration levels between particular ICT media (Milward-Oliver, 2005), scholars have deftly emphasised a shift in the meanings of 'digital divide'. Twenty years ago the concern was simply how to get a communications network, generally conceived as the plain old telephone, within everyone's reach. Today the digital divide is not centred on simple telephone access but instead focuses on richer communication and information connectivity via the internet and beyond. As stated by Deane (2005), it is not a 'telecoms divide' or a technology-centred 'digital divide' but an 'information divide'.

It has recently been argued that the 'real digital divide' is between those who have access to mobile phones and those who lack them – rather than differential distribution of access to information as carried by various media including phones, the internet and computers (The Economist, 2005). In the sections below we offer some cases where the economic impact of mobile phones in low-income settings has been profound, so in that sense we agree that mobile phones are powerful engines for economic empowerment. One of us (Kenny, 2006) has argued elsewhere that internet-enabled computers are just one tool to close the information divide, and that in many cases telephones and broadcast radios work well and are more affordable. At the same time, a dialectic pitting mobiles against the internet is overly simple, because it does not account for the range of technologies on offer, the differences between them, nor the rapidly changing nature of the underlying technologies and the uses they are put to (Wilson et al., 2005). Indeed, the internet has already proven itself in many instances to be a powerful agent for entrepreneurship and income generation, as we demonstrate below. The convergence of data and voice as well as mobile and fixed networks ultimately renders much of this techno-focused debate moot.

In order to enhance markets, enterprise and economic development in poor countries, we need to reduce the information divide between them and the richer countries. Information technologies are useful tools in the service of this ambition, but sweeping generalisations are risky and we need to have much more evidence-driven assessment before conclusive assertions can be made. Picking one winner from a false dichotomy of technologies is similar to a fault among those who argue between the benefits of the

ICT industry itself (telecommunications firms, ISPs, media companies, ICT manufacturers) versus broadly considered ICT use (how the tools of the sector are applied to all sorts of markets and problems). Both the *ICT industry* and *ICT use* can have significant economic impacts, and the two are at least to some degree symbiotic. As a result, this chapter discusses the impact and potential of both the 'supply side' and 'demand side' of the ICT milieu.

## ICTs and economic development

The growth of ICT penetration reflects a strong demand among even the very poorest of the world's people to be entertained, to communicate and to learn. It also reflects the considerable power of ICTs as forces of economic and social development. This involves their role not only at the household level, but in improving firm competitiveness and the efficiency of government service delivery. Because of the multiple roles of ICTs, it is important to take both a microeconomic perspective – looking at individual ICT use in particular settings – as well as a macroeconomic perspective – trying to evaluate the role of ICT investment in overall economic growth. This chapter employs both approaches.

The rapid pace of change in the ICT sector means that robust economic evidence of impacts, especially regarding more recent technologies in developing-country settings, is sparse. As a result, the conclusions presented in the chapter are often preliminary. Because of the relative novelty of the new generation of ICTs, and because of the excitement surrounding the dramatic changes that we have all seen in the way we live and work as a result of this technological advance, a 'discourse of success stories' (Heeks, 2002) has dominated reports of internet use in low-income environments. Even the scholarly literature has all too often been atheoretical (Roman, 2003) and preliminary in its findings (Kenny, 2006). Thus, in our treatment here, we are careful to rely on studies that we feel are analytically well founded and rigorous.

The chapter focuses particularly on the use of mobile telephony for three main reasons: this is where some of the most rigorous research has been done; the nature of the technology (two-way, but simple to use) suggests that it may have a particularly large impact on productivity in developing countries; and the revolutionary spread of the mobile telephone is unprecedented even compared to previous communication technologies. At the same time, the chapter also discusses broadcast technologies and the internet, as well as the ICT production and ICT-enabled industries where a considerable part of the economic impact of these technologies is being felt.

### The role of information in markets

It has long been understood that improved information flows have an important part to play in extending and improving the operation of markets, and they can also improve governance, the delivery of services and education. John Stuart Mill suggested that improved communication was one of the main sources of progress, while the *Communist Manifesto* even suggested that improved communications was central to the coming proletarian revolution (Forestier *et al.*, 2002). Dating back to the 1980s, reports have claimed that modern communication systems are core infrastructures to ensure a country's economic growth.

More recent empirical analyses have backed these claims that modern communication systems are critical to development and can lead to better-functioning markets, increased earnings for poor people and the spread of ideas and information regarding health, education and politics. For instance, survey evidence from within developing countries suggests that areas that gain access to telephones see reduced prices for inputs, the growth of non-farm incomes, the expansion of small and medium enterprises (SMEs) and improved delivery of public services (Forestier *et al.*, 2002). Similarly, case studies have shown examples where internet access has helped to create new businesses and business opportunities within villages and communities (Best *et al.*, 2007).

While this chapter focuses on economic impact, there is significant evidence (discussed in other chapters of this book) of a broader social or political development impact. For instance, educational outcomes can be improved not only through the use of technologies such as interactive radio (Chapter 7), but also through improved governance fostered by information flows (Chapter 9). In a programme that created a three-fold increase in spending on primary schools in Uganda in the early 1990s, only one dollar in fifty of the increased funding actually reached schools (World Bank, 2004). The government then started publishing in newspapers and broadcasting over the radio the exact amounts transferred to each school and required them to maintain public notice boards, posting funds received. Funds reaching schools rose from 2 per cent in 1991, to 26 per cent in 1995, and more than 90 per cent in 1999. Another example is how media freedom and increased use of ICTs is positively correlated with measures of political and civil freedoms in a country. For example, enhanced citizen use of ICTs and new media are connected with significantly lower levels of corruption (Kaufmann *et al.*, 2003) and ultimately stronger democratic practices (Best and Wade, 2007).

### The ICT industry in the macroeconomy

ICT as an economic sector has been historically split into three separate entities: the producers and distributors/broadcasters of mass media products such as television stations, newspapers or film studios; the telecommunications sector responsible for fixed (and then wireless) voice telephony services; and the computer sector selling personal computers, computer network technologies, and so forth. The process of convergence – both among businesses but also around converged digital technologies – has blurred or removed these sector borders (Chapter 4). In this section we explore the economic impact of components of the ICT sector, as a domestic industry, in developing countries.

The European Union's mass media sector accounts for an estimated 5 per cent of GDP, suggesting that it is about the same size as the telecommunications and computer industries combined (http://cordis.europa.eu/econtent/studies/studies.htm). The exact proportions and divisions of these three components within the overall ICT industry are different in developing countries, especially as some countries are able to leap-frog to more converged and cutting-edge business approaches that integrate activities. However, the mass media sector is still likely to remain significant. The telecommunications industry is another major contributor to a developing country's GDP. Available ITU (2006) data for developing countries indicate that telecommunications revenues as a proportion of GDP may average 2.5 per cent and in some cases rise above 4 per cent. This suggests that telecoms may be a $300 billion industry in low- and middle-income countries. Similarly, investments may be above $70 billion each year, or around 1 per cent of GDP.

The ICT industry has, in particular, been a magnet for growing private (and foreign) investment. From almost complete state dominance of telecoms companies and investment in the 1980s, private-sector participation has increased phenomenally (Chapter 5). In the period 1990–2005, private investment in developing-country telecommunications operations totalled $472 billion, compared to $357 billion for energy and water projects combined (data from the World Bank PPI database). Some 132 developing countries have attracted private investment, thanks to the almost universal presence of private competitive mobile service provision around the world. Even countries in fragile post-conflict situations such as Afghanistan and Liberia (see the case study on pp. 182–3) have attracted large-scale investment in mobile companies, often as one of the first major private investments that they see.

ITU data suggest that direct employment by telephone companies in the developing world is likely to be above 5 million people. This direct impact is probably a small part of the total job creation brought on by a rapidly expanding sector. In Bangladesh the GrameenPhone network, which is putting mobile telephones in the hands of women villager operators who then sell on phone services, is generating net incomes of $624 per operator (Forestier *et al.*, 2002).

Examining the IT and telecommunications industry as a whole, the share of the hardware, software and communications industries increased from 2.7 to 4.2 per cent of GDP in the United States over the 1990s (US Department of Commerce, 1999). Computing power per dollar invested has risen by approximately 10,000 times over the last 25 years, and this has been reflected in the considerable increase in productivity in ICT industries. An improved performance in total factor productivity (TFP) growth in US IT and telecommunications industries accounted for a third of a percentage point of additional GDP growth a year in the US economy from 1995 to

(*continued on page 184*)

# Case study: Telecoms in post-conflict Afghanistan and Liberia

Michael Best

*Assistant Professor, Georgia Institute of Technology, USA*

Charles Kenny

*World Bank Sustainable Development Network*

## Afghanistan

At the end of Taliban rule, there were 20,000 working telephone lines in the country of Afghanistan, all fixed and largely concentrated in the city of Kabul. The great majority of Afghans had no access to telephone services, and the sector contributed almost nothing in terms of employment, output or tax revenues.

Between the start of 2002 and 2006, the sector underwent revolutionary growth. From one active telecoms provider in 2001, the country had four private mobile and one state-owned fixed operator offering services to 1.6 million subscribers in 2006 (an eighty-fold increase in the subscriber base, suggesting a teledensity of nearly 5 per cent). There is telephone service in every province and at least 60 per cent of people in the country live in areas with mobile signal coverage.

Beyond the impact of telephone access on the lives of Afghan citizens, the growth of the sector is significant for attracting foreign investment, leading private-sector growth. There has been approximately US$500 million in investment in the sector, the great majority of which is from overseas. The sector was the first to attract significant private foreign investment and remains the largest recipient to date. Investors were reassured by the passage of a state-of-the-art telecommunications law in 2005 that guaranteed regulatory independence and private competition.

At the start of 2006, the telecoms sector was employing 8,000 people directly and another 30,000 indirectly in activities such as phone-card sales and reselling time on mobiles to those without their own phone. Firms in the sector have also paid over US$40 million in taxes; in 2004, taxes paid by mobile companies accounted for 14 per cent of the government's domestic revenues.

## Liberia (adapted from Best et al., 2007)

Liberia, founded in 1847 by freed African slaves from the USA, is situated on the Atlantic coast of West Africa with Sierra Leone, Guinea and Côte d'Ivoire as bordering countries. A relatively small country with approximately 3.3 million inhabitants, it is attempting to right itself after decades of civil conflict. Unrest has been a staple within Liberia for more than 25 years, with two major civil wars during this time.

Currently, mobile phones are the only voice service provided in the country; the entire fixed-line network was destroyed during the civil conflicts and the copper infrastructure was looted. But prior to the recent wars there was a fixed-line operator, the Liberia Telecommunications Corporation (LTC), which offered a limited phone service. In 1985, LTC had an estimated revenue of US$36 million. By 2000, this number was down to US$8 million (Guermazi, 2005), and today it is near zero with an estimated US$150,000 coming from equipment leases to the mobile operators. The decline in fixed-line subscribers follows a similar trend – from over 9,300 in 1990 (0.36 per cent teledensity) to 6,900 in 2002 (0.21 per cent teledensity) to zero today.

Activity in the mobile sector began as early as 1998, but up until 2003 mobile density remained at 0.06 per cent, due to the ongoing conflict and an unorganised licensing regime. Spectrum management and allocation had been the province of the Ministry of Posts and Telecommunication until recently when the responsibility was passed to the newly established independent regulatory authority, the Liberia Telecommunications Authority. Spectrum management by the ministry has had a very poor record. At one point, there were 14 mobile operator licences issued with very little oversight of the spectrum allocation – several had overlapping frequencies or large gaps between spectrum allotments. In 2003, the spectrum plan was sanitised, redistributing the frequencies to the four current mobile providers.

By 2006, the market was very active, with the four operators collectively enjoying a customer base exceeding 400,000, giving a telephone penetration at 12–13 per cent. It is estimated that 60–70 per cent of the population centres receive signal from at least one of the mobile providers. And operators are actively extending both their networks and services. Competition has dramatically improved pricing, and all providers now offer per-second rounding, low entry fees (SIM cards for under US$5) and a growing array of services.

*Liberia: a phone-charging business run off an $80 Chinese generator*
(*source:* John Etherton).

2002 (Kenny, 2006). As a rule, the IT-telecom sector is smaller in developing countries than it is in wealthy countries – computer and telecommunications expenditures average 5.7 per cent of GDP in the developing world (Neto *et al.*, 2005). However, in some developing countries, the sector is considerably larger than this average expenditure level might suggest. In the Philippines, the IT and telecommunications sector accounted for around 11 per cent of the total private-sector formal workforce, and for as much as 20 per cent of the private sector's contribution to GDP (UNCTAD, 2006).

ICT production is particularly important for the East Asian region. Some 21 per cent of Malaysia's GDP is accounted for by production of ICTs, and information and communications equipment accounts for 28 per cent of the country's exports (Qiang *et al.*, 2003). In particular, 'outsourced' electronics manufacturing, where local companies build products for sale by transnational brand-name firms such as Nokia or Sony, has become a $200 billion global industry concentrated in the developing world and East Asia in particular. China alone accounts for about half of this production (Marsh, 2007). At the same time, the industry is largely concentrated in this particular part of the world; low-income countries as a whole are responsible for only 0.3 per cent of the world's high-technology exports (Kenny, 2006). Furthermore, the economic impact of productivity gains in ICT manufacturing is being felt largely by wealthy-country consumers, not developing-country producers, which may help to explain the weak link between the size of ICT exports and overall total factor productivity growth in East Asian countries (APEC, 2001).

Beyond equipment production, another important component of the ICT industry in developing regions has been the rise of offshoring of IT-enabled services, including such activities as communications, insurance and financial services, computer and information services, royalties and licence fees, accounting, consulting, advertising, engineering, educational and health services. Trade in such services was above $800 billion in 2003, of which about 17 per cent was accounted for by developing countries, which in turn equals approximately 2 per cent of developing-country gross national income (GNI) (UNCTAD, 2006; World Bank, 2005b).

Computer and information service exports (offshore call centres and transcription services as well as programming and other business process outsourcing) expanded at a rate six times faster than total ICT-enabled service exports from 1995 to 2003. By 2003 they accounted for a little over $70 billion of global exports, of which 20 per cent was accounted for by developing countries, which in turn equals approximately 0.2 per cent of developing-country GNI.

It is worth noting that this export activity was highly concentrated, with India alone accounting for approximately four fifths of the developing world's computer and information services exports. Employment in India's software industry is estimated to have increased from 242,000 in 2000 to 568,000 in 2004, while business process outsourcing employment increased from 70,000 to 246,000 over the same period. This level of concentration suggests that elsewhere in the developing world the sector is comparably small. Indeed, outside India, computer and information service exports equal approximately 0.04 per cent of developing-country GNI (UNCTAD, 2006; World Bank, 2005b).

## The scale of ICT use in the developing world

Before turning to the use of these technologies in enterprise development beyond the ICT sector itself, it is instructive to review the penetration of ICTs in the developing world from the vantage of households and businesses. These levels of diffusion and usage are paramount in determining their role in economic development.

### Mass media

Broadcast technologies have reached near ubiquity across most of the world. For example, 90 per cent of people in rural areas of Tanzania, Uganda, Mozambique and Gujarat in India regularly use broadcast technologies (Souter, 2005). In South Africa, over 98 per cent of the population has access to a radio and 65 per cent to television. In India as a whole, the same figures are 98 and 45 per cent respectively (Eltzroth and Kenny, 2003).

### Telecommunications

There has recently been a massive roll-out of voice telecommunications infrastructure. Half of the world's households have a fixed telephone connection, and the mobile footprint probably covers more than 77 per cent of the world's population (Kenny and Keremane, 2007). More than one half of the world's two billion mobile subscribers are in the developing world, and the number of subscribers in low- and middle-income countries tripled from 2001 to 2005 (UNCTAD, 2006). If we consider just India in 2004, there were an estimated 47 million mobile phone users, and this figure is likely to be 100 million in 2008 (ITU, 2006; Sharma, 2005). Low-income countries account for most of the current growth in mobile phone subscriptions.

The spread of mobiles has been accompanied by the spread of mobile applications. Around five hundred billion SMS text messages were sent worldwide in 2004 (http://www.cellular.co.za/stats/stats-main.htm, accessed 2 January 2006). Many developing countries are active participants in the use of SMS – the Philippines accounts for nearly 55 billion messages each year (http://www.givemeunlimited.com/main/aboutus.asp, accessed 2 January 2006). Usage has spread to fishermen in Kerela, India, and Lake Victoria in Africa as a cheap way to get information on landing prices for fish before arriving at a particular market. More advanced uses are also spreading – the Philippines already has over 3.5 million m-commerce users, and banking over mobile phones is available in South Africa and Kenya. M-commerce volumes in the Philippines may equal $52–105 million per day (infoDev, 2006).

Furthermore, convergence has led to the widespread adoption of internet-based communication applications, such as Skype, to carry voice traffic in the developing world. In many countries this can result in significant consumer savings due to the increased technical efficiencies of VoIP (voice over internet protocol) systems as well as frequent (unintended perhaps) regulatory benefits. Approximately 755 billion minutes of voice traffic were carried worldwide by VoIP in 2005 (estimated from http://www.ilocus.com/ui_dataFiles/voipminutes3q05.htm and http://www.infoworld.com/article/05/12/16/HNvoipcompetition_1.html, both accessed 2 January 2006). In 2004, VoIP accounted for about half of inbound international calling minutes to Mexico, Brazil and Bangladesh. Among customers of Peru's *cabinas publicas*, people from the poorest socioeconomic groups were more likely to use VoIP than richer groups (Proenza, 2005).

Other types of internet use have also expanded rapidly, and growth rates have been higher in the developing world than in the OECD since the mid-1990s. The number of users has tripled over the 2001–2005 period in the developing world, reaching over 440 million. Annual growth rates in the developing world averaged 34 per cent compared to 12 per cent in wealthy countries, suggesting very rapid diffusion and convergence (Figures 2.3 and 2.4, p.29). In Africa, there has been a fivefold increase in internet penetration from 2001 to 2005 (UNCTAD, 2006).

Nonetheless, internet usage is significantly lagging behind access, a result not seen with telephony. A survey (Souter, 2005) involving people from villages in Gujarat (India), Mozambique and Tanzania, all located near towns with internet access, found that less than 2 per cent of those surveyed had ever used the internet compared to 70 per cent having used a telephone and 90 per cent reporting use of broadcast technologies such as the radio. In urban India and South Africa in 2001 as many as one quarter of the population had access to the Web, but only 10 per cent were regular internet users (Pastore, 2001). In Indonesia in 2005, between 20 and 25 per cent of the population had access but only 5 per cent actually used the internet (Halewood and Kenny, 2005).

Examining enterprise use, a number of developing countries lead the way in internet access. In Brazil, 95 per cent of enterprises with ten or more employees use the internet, compared for example to 87 per cent in the UK (UNCTAD, 2006). The average for 52 developing countries surveyed between 2001 and 2003 was over 50 per cent of enterprises connected to the internet, with 78 per cent of Kenyan firms for example using e-mail (Qiang *et al.*, 2006). However, there remain major gaps in developing-country business usage. Secure servers use encryption technologies for internet transactions and are commonly used for e-commerce. Of 110,498 secure servers in the world in 2004, just 224 were in low-income countries (World Bank, 2005a). This reflects a common finding in the developing world that while firm access is approaching ubiquity, advanced use (such as for website development and e-commerce) remains highly concentrated. Figure 6.1

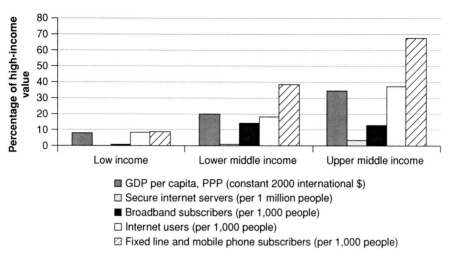

Figure 6.1 *Percentage of high-income value from ICTs in different types of economy* (*source:* World Bank, 2007 World Development Indicators).

suggests that there is a far larger 'digital divide' in terms of advance access and use – covering secure servers and broadband – than there is in basic ICTs such as fixed and mobile telephones.

A survey of e-commerce use by businesses in least-developed countries was only able to find a few examples of advanced use (online sales using Web-based technology, for example), largely serving niche markets, limited to sales between $2,000 and $30,000 per year and employing a maximum of 50 people (UNCTAD, 2001). Likewise, a 2003 survey of Vietnam's small-scale handicrafts enterprises in the Red River Delta found that while 100 per cent of enterprises had a phone and 75 per cent had e-mail access, only 25 per cent had a website (Konstadakopulos, 2006). Furthermore, many of these websites were not accessible and those that could be accessed were of basic design and poor content. None offered e-commerce facilities. Again, a survey of 74 garment and horticulture firms in Kenya, South Africa and Bangladesh found that 95 per cent were using e-mail for business, but only 44 per cent had a website and 7 per cent had made a sale via an e-marketplace (Humphrey *et al.*, 2003). Similar results emerge from surveys in Brazil, Chile, China, Malaysia, Mexico and South Africa (Molla, 2005). There are exceptions to this general performance, especially in India, but businesses in the developing world as a whole appear to be comparatively slow to adopt advanced internet applications even while they were incredibly rapid to adopt e-mail and voice telephony.

In summary, while the growth rates for telephony and the internet in developing areas are now the world's highest, low- and middle-income countries still do not enjoy pervasive levels of access. This is particularly true for the internet as compared to mobile telephony which has shown explosive recent growth. Obviously, access is not enough for transformative use and enterprise development. While in some ways the developing world has led the way in the use of ICTs, for instance in truly inventive m-commerce applications, in others they have a long way to come. Ultimately, two questions remain: Why do we see astounding growth of mobile telephony and considerable growth of the internet? How much does this growth contribute to enterprise development and wealth generation?

## The macroeconomic impact of use

There is a strong correlation between ICT penetration and use, on the one hand, and a country's economic growth on the other – richer countries have higher rates of ICT use. Researchers have attempted to probe this relationship more deeply, examining the precise relationships between, and the factors that cause, ICT growth and GDP growth (Forestier *et al.*, 2002; Waverman *et al.*, 2005).

Many studies have applied multivariate linear regressions to examine the relationship between voice telephony and macroeconomic growth. However, this approach is risky due to such problems as endogeneity or omitted variables, and the approach overall requires significant faith in the underlying models (Forestier *et al.*, 2002). Having said that, a large number of studies have found a statistically and economically significant impact of telecoms roll-out on growth (see for example Waverman *et al.*, 2005).

Turning from voice telephony to the internet, we maintain that this is probably too new a technology for penetration numbers to appear as a statistically and economically significant variable in cross-country growth regressions when models are cautiously constructed. Nonetheless, a few scholars have tried to find evidence of economic impact in the available data. Freund and Weinhold (2000), for instance, have argued that a 10 per cent increase in the number of internet host sites in a country is associated with a 1.7 percentage point boost in the country's exports to the United States. This is a compelling statistical result, but one that may require more data and analysis to establish robustly over time.

Examining ICT investment more broadly, it is likely that growth in investment in ICTs in the US from the levels of the period 1979–1995 to the levels of 1995–2000 was responsible for as much as 0.4 per cent additional annual growth in labour productivity (Kenny, 2006). At the same time, the evidence that investment in ICT by firms in the OECD produced particularly high returns (as measured by total factor productivity increases) is mixed. There are some firm-level studies that might suggest such a link (for example Lehr and Lichtenberg, 1999) but many regional and cross-country studies fail to find it (David, 2000; Schreyer, 2000; Gordon, 2002; Stiroh, 2002). This may reflect a wide dispersion of outcomes for IT investments, where some applications have considerable and immediate payoffs while others fail completely. After all, as many as 42 per cent of US corporate IT projects are abandoned before completion (Triplett, 1999).

Evidence regarding the productivity impact of ICT investment in developing countries is scarcer, but what is available reflects a similar pattern to OECD countries. Lal (1996) found no productivity impact of IT investment in Northern India, and Choudhury and Wolf (2002) found a similar result for SMEs in East Africa. At the country level, there appears to be no link yet established between IT investment and rates of economic growth in developing countries (Pohjola, 2001). Limited evidence of a growth impact of ICTs may reflect divergent returns to ICT investments, suggesting a considerable payoff to policy prescriptions that increase the proportion of successful ICT investments.

In summary, the macroeconomic evidence for the role of voice telephony in a country's economic growth rates seems fairly well established. In OECD countries, the evidence suggests that investments in computers and digital networks promotes growth at least as effectively as other types of investment. Current evidence in low-income countries remains scarce, but there is no compelling reason to imagine that this investment is considerably less effective than in high-income settings and one of us (Best) remains strongly optimistic.

## The microeconomic impact of use

While macroeconomic analysis focuses mostly on the effects of ICTs on country-level growth, microeconomic studies consider issues such as firm, labour and welfare productivity. Such studies seek to answer questions such as: How can ICTs assist a small company to make money, farmers to enhance their productivity, or consumers to ensure they are getting the best available price on goods purchased? In this section we consider the microeconomic impacts of modern ICTs, starting with mobile telephones and then turning to the internet.

### Telecommunications

In India, mobile telephones are still marketed as prestige items for elite urban dwellers and rich teenagers, but mobile phone growth, and its ultimate value to India, is not about prestige use. As Rama Bijapurkar (personal communication), a prominent market strategy consultant puts it, mobile phones are *productivity tools*, not prestige objects. The mobile phone users in Mumbai are the 'pimps and vegetable sellers' – small-scale entrepreneurs who need to connect with suppliers or search for work and customers. From a microeconomic perspective, the difference here, as considered within the *uses and gratifications* literature (Blumler and Katz, 1974), is between *instrumental* use that is task focused and *intrinsic* use that is social or emotionally related. The boom in mobile phone diffusion and penetration throughout the Global South will ultimately serve instrumental purposes that should have economic, social and political development impacts for a wide range of people.

For example, in Kerala in India, mobile phone service was introduced over the period 1997–2001, resulting in a dramatic improvement in the efficiency and profitability of the fishing industry. The spread of mobile phone service allowed fishermen to land their catches where there were wholesalers ready to purchase them. This reduced waste from between 5–8 per cent of total catch to close to zero and increased average profitability by around 8 per cent. At the same time, consumer prices fell by 4 per cent (Jensen, 2007). Numerous other studies from countries including Bangladesh, China, Mozambique and Peru have found a link between prices received for agricultural outputs and the local presence and ownership of a telephone (Bayes *et al.*, 1999; Jenson *et al.*, 2004).

Above we briefly mentioned the employment opportunities generated by village phone services, such as those offered by GrameenPhone in Bangladesh (see also Chapter 10). This programme has leased cell phones to poor rural women who set up local village pay-phone shops (Bornstein, 2005), and this service has been found to be of considerable benefit to both the provider and the users. Not least, the average operator was earning between 24 and 40 per cent of household income from providing phone services and the estimated consumer surplus from phone usage ranged as high as $2.70–$10 per call (Richardson *et al.*, 2000). In a related study, Bayes *et al.* (1999) interviewed over 400 users and operators across 50 villages. They found, in addition, that the village phone programme was particularly pro-poor and led to specific social development outcomes. For instance, the intensity of use among villagers living below the local poverty line was 50 per cent higher than non-poor persons and the majority of calls placed by poor users were related to economic matters. The poor community members enjoyed a much higher consumer surplus for each call as compared to non-poor users. These researchers also discovered that by placing the mobile phones in the hands of the women of the village, there was a noticeable empowerment of these women with reports of enhanced mobility, decision-making powers, knowledge and confidence among these village females – a powerful social development outcome.

Phone-based SMS services have been used to deliver agricultural information in Senegal, increasing farm profits by as much as 15 per cent, and a similar operation is in place in Kenya (Davis and Ochieng, 2006). A new agricultural trading system for mobile phones has also been deployed in Africa. Created at BusyLab, a small software development company in Accra, Ghana, founded by serial IT entrepreneur Mark Davies, TradeNet aims to link a wide range of African agricultural traders using mobile phone SMS capabilities. According to popular press reporting and Web contributions (http://topics.developmentgateway.org/trade/rc/ItemDetail.do ~ 1088956? itemId = 1088956), TradeNet has been piloted for the last twelve months in African markets, collecting price and supply-chain information. According to these online reports, Uganda Foodnet has conducted user satisfaction assessments concluding that 68 per cent of those farmers contacted had used TradeNet to access market information and 91 per cent reported these interactions having a positive impact on their business (*Balancing Act*, 2006).

In a study of mobile phone users in South Africa and Tanzania supported by Vodafone, mobile users identified considerable intrinsic uses of the
phone and, in particular, the ability to communicate with family and friends
(Samuel et al., 2005). Additionally, phones were being used to reduce travel
costs, to search for jobs, and for other instrumental purposes. Samuel et al.
(2005, p. 46) thus relate observing how 'mobile phones were essential for
searching for work, not only for getting information and making an application, but also as a means of being contacted by a prospective employer'.

Besides these mobile phone applications in livelihood development and
enhanced business efficiency, phones are increasingly being used to provide financial services targeted specifically at low-income individuals. The
Consultative Group to Assist the Poor (CGAP) has examined the WIZZIT
programme, a mobile banking service in South Africa explicitly aimed at
poor customers (Ivatury and Pickens, 2006). Mobile banking services could
prove to be particularly valuable and pro-poor because basic financial services including secure savings accounts, non-usurious credit opportunities,
currency management and fund transfers are critical to many low-income
communities. A major obstacle for commercial banks to serve low-income
communities is the high transaction costs associated with very modest-sized
accounts. Mobile banking technologies significantly lower the transaction
costs as compared to bricks-and-mortar banking, and this means that many
poor unbanked individuals can receive a service. According to the CGAP
study customers used WIZZIT 'because it is "cheaper" (70 per cent), "safe"
(69 per cent), "convenient" (68 per cent) and "fast" (68 per cent). By comparison, customers visiting a bricks-and-mortar bank report spending an
average of 32 minutes and US$2.27 to reach a bank branch by bus or other
transport' (Ivatury and Pickens, 2006, p. 3). In this case, mobile banking
enjoys both reduced transaction costs to the commercial bank and a consumer surplus for the users.

Q-sort methodology (Brown, 1993) has been used to probe why individuals in low-income African countries use mobile phones. This methodology
combines strengths from both qualitative and quantitative approaches, and
is effective in grouping users based upon how closely they identify with
specific claims around mobile phone use. Survey respondents are asked to
rank how closely they identify with statements such as: 'I use my mobile
phone to stay in touch with my customers', 'Having a mobile phone makes
me feel more important' and 'My mobile phone makes me feel more secure'. Donner (2004) used the Q-sort method to survey mobile phone use
in Kigali, Rwanda. He found that for many users mobile phones made their
lives more convenient, allowing them to be more productive and further
their business needs. His results suggest that doing business, and saving
money in business, represent a major motivation for most of the mobile
phone users in his sample. A smaller set of respondents focused more on
intrinsic values such as how the phone made them feel more important. A
related Q-sort study has been conducted in Monrovia, Liberia (Best et al.,

2007), where a common intrinsic response was that the phone was used to keep in touch with family members. Otherwise the most common responses from those surveyed were business related, and in open-ended questioning responses focused on the cost savings to their business and the ability to find work with the phone.

It appears, then, that mobile phones are seen as important to business productivity among small and micro entrepreneurs and agricultural-sector activities even in countries like Liberia and Rwanda. Both of these places have some of the world's lowest development indicators and both have emerged from relatively recent civil conflicts. This provides the demand side of the story in relation to the rapid roll-out of mobile phone services witnessed in post-conflict communities.

### *The internet*

We now turn from the microeconomic effects of mobile phones to similar studies of the internet, beginning with its role in firm-level productivity. One venture that has been documented by Richa Kumar (2004) and others is the e-Choupal project of ITC (http://www.itcportal.com/ruraldevp_philosophy/echoupal.htm; see also Chapter 9). In this project ITC, a major Indian agri-business conglomerate, used the internet to re-engineer the supply chain of their soybean business. Prior to the ICT intervention small-scale farmers (owning on average only one or two acres) would bring their soybean harvest to a local market (or *mandi*). A commissioning agent working with ITC evaluated the quality of the farmer's product and a price was set via a market auction. The produce was bagged and manually weighed and finally the farmer was paid (though sometimes not immediately). With the e-Choupal system, however, the farmer gets a fixed-price quote for the day from an internet-enabled agent (called a *sanchalak*) and is offered a printed sales slip. ITC pays for transport of the legume to a local processing plant or warehouse where it is weighed on large automated scales. The farmer then receives full payment. Analysis by Kumar (2004), Annamalai and Rao (2003) and others reveals the substantial return on investment for ITC in this venture as well as the benefits to the farmer. Since most of this product comes from small-scale growers, ITC is accustomed to a very large number of very small transactions. For each transaction, it is estimated that under the internet-enabled programme ITC saves roughly US$5 and the farmer saves a similar amount (Kumar, 2004). For the first year, ITC estimated a 2 per cent total savings in production costs associated with their soybean business and a similar boost in profit due to enhanced quality. Of course, this benefit does come, to some extent, through dis-intermediation of the market agents, some of whom ultimately launched protests against the programme.

The internet may also have a role in helping small-scale farmers branch out on their own and sell more directly to end consumers. One project designed to help rural growers in Rwanda has included an internet component. Over the past few years, USAID has been actively involved in providing management and technical support to coffee cooperatives in the Rwandan coffee sector (http://www.usaid.gov/stories/rwanda/ss_rwanda_coffee. html). This support has helped create relationships between the small-scale growers and US or European roasters, enhancing sales of specialty coffee that brings much higher prices than traditional coffee. These higher coffee prices mean more profits for coffee cooperatives and farmers that may lead to increased economic development in rural areas of Rwanda. However, for the success to continue, the coffee cooperatives and farmers must begin to manage their business relationships on their own. A critical part of managing these business relationships includes communicating between customers and suppliers which ultimately requires some forms of modern communication technologies.

One of us (Best) has spent over five years studying a rural internet access project in India, the Sustainable Access in Rural India (SARI) programme. This project suggests that, in the right circumstances, public internet access can carry significant economic benefits even in rural areas of a poor country. The project demonstrates both the potential for positive economic impacts of the internet in rural and under-resourced areas as well as the pitfalls. The SARI project was inaugurated in November 2001 and, at its peak, consisted of more than 80 rural internet kiosks situated in villages within the Madurai district of Tamil Nadu, India. These kiosks have deployed a range of services including basic internet and cybercafé functions; telemedicine, tele-agriculture, and tele-veterinary services; photography and video services; and training. In one study we followed the outcome and impacts of the provision of e-government services (Kumar and Best, 2006). A number of these services are directly targeting poverty elimination and economic stability. Indeed, on a per-capita basis, the most popular e-government service provided at these centres was income and community (caste) certifications. Income certification verifies that the individual is below the Indian poverty line while community certification confirms that they are members of a historically under-privileged community, such as the scheduled castes or *dalits*, and tribal groups. Receiving these government certifications allows an individual to avail of various government schemes and welfare programmes. In the study, when we control for village size, we find that those communities with internet kiosks had a per-capita income and community certification rate of 1.4 times and 1.7 times (respectively) those villages without kiosks. Furthermore, we found that citizens enjoyed savings in time and money by using the internet to obtain certification as compared to alternatives such as travelling to the local government office and attempting to obtain the materials in person. Reported user savings ranged from one to seven days of time, and 50 cents to nearly $10 in financial savings. These savings were the product of reduced travel times, reduction in graft, and opportunity costs. Our study confirmed that a significant consumer benefit was enjoyed by community members who made use of rural shared internet facilities. Regrettably, the e-government programme was not able to sustain operation after its first year due to the collapse of political and institutional support within the district.

While the e-government service, when in operation, was clearly pro-poor and of economic benefit to the least advantaged community members, given that the popular internet-enhanced services were for low-income certification and caste certification, we found in another study (Kumar and Best, 2007) that most services offered by the internet facility benefited relative elites of the community. Roughly 5 per cent of the population in the villages studied had used the internet kiosk, but this 5 per cent was clearly not selected 'at random' from the village population as a whole; some selection biases drove kiosk use. In particular, we found usage biases along the dimensions of gender (more males than females), age (users were usually younger than 30), caste (scheduled caste members were less likely to use the facilities save in those villages where the facility is located in an area mostly populated by members of those castes), religion (Muslims and Christians were under-represented as users in some villages), educational attainment (with few illiterate users) and income (users were relatively rich as measured by standard surrogate indicators). Rogers' (1983) theory of diffusion of innovation offers an explanatory framework for these diffusion biases, where early adopters to new technologies are usually drawn from relative elite, educated and wealthy populations.

The SARI project and other similar interventions raise the possibility that micro-entrepreneurs in under-resourced rural areas can enter the sector in potentially innovative ways. This suggests a democratisation of ICT *provision* and not just of ICT *use*. In further work, we studied the business case and financial self-sustainability of internet kiosks under the SARI project (Best and Kumar, forthcoming). Over the multi-year period of the study, a majority of the local entrepreneurially run kiosks had closed down, because of a lack of long-term financial viability and poor technical and operational support by the internet service provider. At the same time, some telecentres that had received comparatively better support from the service provider, were owned by individuals with prior training in computers, or had a separate trained operator, remained operational for a longer period (see also http://www.telecentre.org).

Small and medium enterprises (SMEs) are key elements for the economic growth of low-income countries. While our studies of the SARI experiment focused on the economic and social benefits of the internet to the individual community member, other studies have more explicitly examined the role of the internet in support of micro-, small and medium enterprises and livelihood development. Research Africa! (2006), in a survey of 280 SMEs across 14 African nations, found that over half of the respondents reported that the internet was either important or very important to their business. That notwithstanding, they found that only 18.7 per cent of responding enterprises had direct access to the internet while a full 40 per cent had direct access to a computer, and more than 80 per cent had access to a mobile phone.

Indeed 40 per cent of the SMEs that stated they did not have direct access to the internet nevertheless felt that the technology was important or very important to their business. Significantly, 70 per cent of SMEs that did not have a mobile phone also felt that it was important or very important. This dramatic access gap was closed in a majority of cases through the use of cybercafés and other shared access facilities. Some 72 per cent of respondents that did not have direct access to the internet were able to use cybercafés for some access. In summary, this report demonstrates significant awareness of the role of ICTs broadly, including the internet, in the efficient operations of SMEs. Many enterprises relied on cybercafés, however, for their access.

In a similar though more focused survey, Hinson *et al.* (2007) received survey responses from 106 Ghanaian SMEs engaged in 'non-traditional exporting' (NTE), that is exports other than from the traditional sectors of cocoa, gold, timber and energy. In Ghana, such exports are growing both as a percentage of all exports as well as absolutely, and under the government's development strategy should account for 20 per cent of all exports by 2020. This study examined the relationship between internet use and internationalisation of SME activities, finding that the internet helped businesses investigate potential new customers easily and cheaply and to receive client orders from abroad. Their study did not, though, find that SME NTE companies used the internet as a payment method or for public relations or marketing purposes.

The eCenter project, a USAID-supported initiative in Kyrgyzstan, is explicitly focused on developing SME support for low-income communities by providing training and access to community internet facilities. Our preliminary findings allow for only anecdotal comments, including the observation of farmers using the internet to purchase farm equipment and seeds at savings and honey traders using the internet to establish new business partners (Best *et al.*, 2007). Preliminary survey work finds that 15 per cent of the programme participants stated that their participation in the programme resulted in subsequent employment opportunities and 5 per cent stated that the programme led them to creating a new small business.

It is important to note that differences in the utility of the internet to businesses will drive differential rates of usage and that differences will exist across countries, regions and sectors. A 2003 multi-country business survey conducted by Qiang *et al.* (2006) found that 58 per cent of businesses in Tanzania used e-mail for interacting with clients and suppliers, while in Kenya that number reached 78 per cent. There are significant differences in usage rates between different industry types and between companies with heavy levels of export activity as opposed to those that focus on domestic markets. For example, a 50-country survey of the developing world found that internet access among micro-enterprises that served national markets was only 30 per cent, compared to 80 per cent among exporting micro-enterprises. The percentage of tourism firms with a computer in Uganda is five times and in Tanzania ten times the percentage of food firms with a computer, although the food firms are on average larger (Kenny, 2006).

These differences in utility will drive different returns to ICT use – and, in particular, advanced internet use. For example, a survey of 74 firms in the garment and horticulture industry in South Africa, Bangladesh and Kenya found that all had access to the internet, and 95 per cent of firms were using e-mail to place and accept orders. At the same time only 34 per cent had a website, only 23 per cent had registered with an e-marketplace, and only 7 per cent had actually made a sale on an e-marketplace (Humphrey *et al.*, 2003).

A plethora of anecdotal evidence suggests how the internet has enhanced SME profitability and efficiencies. At the same time it is difficult to find solid research results from developing-country settings that robustly demonstrate this effect sustained over time. The available survey results suggest that SME executives report a critical role for the internet in their business, and the widespread adoption of ICT use including internet applications suggests that the financial cost of ICT access is considerably outweighed by its benefit to business. Nonetheless, there is limited micro-evidence to date of a dramatic return to ICT use in developing-country business settings – and this is especially the case regarding advanced uses. Surveys of computer use in manufacturing firms in Northern India in 1996 and of IT use among SMEs in East Africa thus failed to find a labour productivity impact (Kenny, 2006).

Overall microeconomic analysis of ICTs in enterprise and economic development has shown some interesting results. Voice telephony has been shown to have considerable impacts on firm productivity and to offer consumer surpluses, enhanced market efficiency and reduced waste. Similar results have been documented with the internet – for instance enhancing efficiencies along an agriculture supply chain and providing consumer surpluses for fee-for-service e-government transactions. However, broad and sustained evidence has not yet been fully acquired. While the case for the internet is growing, as a newer technology with lower levels of penetration and higher costs to ownership, these outcomes will lag behind the telephone.

## Success factors for ICT use

We have shown evidence – but also argued that there is a need for fuller and more robust research – of the link between many forms of ICTs and economic development in low-income countries. One component of this link is the role of the ICT industry itself as an engine for growth and enterprise. Other components are the way that ICT investments may (or may not) impact national productivity or how a specific ICT intervention might enhance a firm's productivity or benefit a consumer. We conclude with some thoughts on what factors may (or may not) enhance the likelihood that ICTs will improve a nation's, firm's or consumer's economic success.

### *Building an ICT industry*

The last twenty years have shown that a private, competitive and well-regulated ICT market will attract considerably greater investment flows and see larger telecommunications revenues than those that remain unre-formed (World Bank, 2005a). One estimate suggests that low-income countries that had seen considerable reform towards competition saw a growth of 1,075 per cent in internet users over the 1998 to 2000 period, compared to 405 per cent growth in countries that were lagging on the basic reform agenda. The same study suggested that fixed and mobile teledensity was approximately 80 per cent higher in reformed low-income countries than in non-reformed countries (Kenny *et al.*, 2003).

There is also strong evidence that ICT firm 'cluster' can be an important success factor – examples include the highly concentrated regions for ICT innovation such as Silicon Valley in California and Bangalore in India. At the same time, the evidence suggests that 'cluster effects' are due to the uneven distribution of high-skilled labour, sources of venture capital, research capacity in local universities and an economic and political climate that allows for innovation (Kolko, 2002). Therefore, attempts to create clusters in the developing world have at best had a mixed impact. Most East Asian countries have followed interventionist policies including direct investments in human resources and technology development, as with Taiwan's Industrial Technology Research Institute, and they also provide incentives for private investment in the industry (Neto *et al.*, 2005). These appear to have played an important role, if at the cost in some cases of backing the wrong technology. At the same time, there have been some expensive failures, such as Malaysia's Multimedia Supercorridor, where ten-year tax breaks, $10 billion in public investments and numerous other incentives from 1996 to 2000 were matched by just $475 million of private investment and 7,300 related jobs. Reasons given by firms for not moving to the corridor included capital controls, red tape, slow visa approval, weak intellectual property and privacy rights and the absence of a suitable skills base (Kenny, 2006). This mixed history suggests the importance of the broader business environment for success in the ICT industry, a subject that we return to below.

### *Macroeconomic factors enhancing investment, diffusion and use*

Why the mixed picture regarding ICT investments in the developing world? Microeconomic evidence suggests that ICT investments can garner very high returns. But at the same time ICT investments appear to be very risky, with high failure rates, and returns (once again) dependent on the broader economic environment for success (Neto *et al.*, 2005).

Looking at business use, for example, it is not clear that limited access to advanced infrastructure (including broadband) is the key factor delaying the roll-out of e-commerce. For example, South Korea's broadband penetration, at 25 per cent in 2004, was one of the very highest in the world – nearly ten percentage points ahead of countries like the US and the UK. It leads the world in terms of enterprise connectivity to

*(continued on page 200)*

# Case study: Chilean ICT policies and micro-entrepreneurs

Dorothea Kleine

*Lecturer in Human Geography, Royal Holloway, University of London, UK*

Chile is a good example of a country that has adopted a national ICT strategy that includes explicit reference to the role of enterprises. Centre-left governments have followed a neo-liberal macroeconomic course while trying, in parallel, to reduce the country's immense social and regional inequalities. Chile's *Agenda Digital*, which focuses both on economic competitiveness and on universal access, reflects these goals. One of the seven priorities of the *Agenda Digital*, published in 2004, was to promote the use of digital technologies in enterprises (Grupo de Acción Digital, 2004), especially medium, small and micro-sized enterprises (MSMEs). In 2002, it was estimated that only 37 per cent of small enterprises and 10 per cent of micro-enterprises (micro-enterprises are defined in Chile as having a turnover of less than 2,400 UF or $82, 680, and small as those with less than 25,000 UF or $861, 250) owned a connection to the internet (Díaz and Rivas, 2005).

A conducive regulatory framework has helped bring down the cost for telephony and internet access, while a network of public *telecentros*, often based in local libraries, offers free access and free ICT training courses. E-government has increased significantly, so that by 2005 there were over 300 transactions available online (Díaz and Rivas, 2005), among the most significant of which were the filing of tax declarations and the public e-procurement system *Chilecompra*.

Ethnographic research (Kleine, 2007) among micro-entrepreneurs in Algún (name changed to protect privacy of respondents), a small town (13,000 inhabitants) in rural southern Chile, revealed the diffusion of ICTs and the impact of government ICT policies on livelihoods. This differed depending on firm size and sector. According to the last census in 2002, 43 per cent of households in Algún had their own telephone (19 per cent fixed-line and 24 per cent mobile), 5 per cent had a computer and 2 per cent had access to the internet at home, but there was a tradition of shared access, with six call centres and 28 public telephones (single or double phone boxes in the street or in shops and bars). Pre-paid mobile phones were becoming very popular, and at around $38 for the hand-set and $6.65 for the cheapest airtime voucher they were relatively affordable. However, one minute of airtime on a pre-paid mobile cost around 60 ¢ and so many micro-entrepreneurs only used them to receive calls. By 2006, apart from the local *telecentro* in the library, seven privately run cybercafés had set up, which offered internet access for $1 per hour. In a country where the minimum monthly wage was around $228 and many micro-entrepreneurs made less than that, shared access to ICTs was the norm and usage outside the state-subsidised *telecentro* was expensive.

The more affluent owners of small businesses were able to buy IT hardware for their enterprises to adapt particularly to the shift online in state procurement policy in 2005. They also paid for external IT training services or, often based on higher levels of formal education, trained autodidactically, rather than going to the public *telecentro* for free IT courses. Many of the poorer micro-entrepreneurs, of which over half operated informal businesses, had only basic or incomplete secondary education and some individuals were illiterate. Several micro-entrepreneurs took free ICT courses at the local *telecentro*, particularly since this was looked upon favourably by the state services who also decided on business grants. Only a fraction of those who had taken the course returned to use the internet, but those who did so used the internet for a variety of business and private purposes.

Accessing the e-procurement system was more burdensome for entrepreneurs without private internet access, but all enterprises felt the increased pressure on prices caused by the change to an e-procurement system. From mid-2005 onwards, public servants from the local authority were obliged to use e-procurement for every transaction over 3 UTM (the Chilean Monthly Tax Unit) or about $171. They expressed their satisfaction at the transparency of the system and cost-savings for the state as prices for goods and services had gone down by an estimated 20 per cent. Local small and micro-enterprises, however, found it hard to compete against larger companies from the regional and national capital online. Entrepreneurs producing goods felt that the importance of price over quality had increased, entrepreneurs involved in retailing found themselves competing with their own suppliers online, and those offering services experienced pressure on labour costs. A larger percentage of orders were placed with suppliers from outside the community, particularly with companies from larger cities and the capital.

*Telecentre in rural Chile (source:* Dorothea Kleine).

broadband, with 92 per cent of firms connected. Nonetheless, the percentage of firms with ten or more employees in the Republic of Korea that sell online, at 6.8 per cent, is a fraction of the level in Brazil, where 27 per cent of firms sell online, or China, where the number is above 9 per cent. The Republic of Korea's performance in this area puts it on a par with Thailand – a far poorer country with considerably more limited broadband roll-out (UNCTAD, 2006). Again, it is the broader environment that poses the challenge. For example, weak institutional capacity is correlated across countries with lower host site development (Kenny, 2003; Oxley and Yeung, 2000). To take the example of financial institutions, in Latin America only 28 per cent of online transactions use credit cards, compared to 54 per cent using cash (Hilbert, 2001).

Human resources are also important. ICTs are closely connected with 'skills upgrading' within firms. In the US, investment in IT by firms is followed by increased employment of graduates (Autor *et al.*, 1998), and in Indian manufacturing IT investments are correlated with a more skilled workforce (Lal, 1996). If those skills are scarce, ICT investments are likely to garner lower returns. They can be lacking even in some of the most developed of developing countries. An OECD study carried out in 2000, for example, found that while Chile had an official illiteracy rate of 5 per cent, only one in five of the population had the reading skills to integrate sources of information and learn new skills from online sources, for example (OECD, 2000). Against this context, the case study on pp. 198–9 provides a good example of the way in which Chilean micro-entrepreneurs have engaged with ICTs.

### Microeconomic factors affecting efficiencies and effectiveness

We have seen a number of cases where ICTs – from mobile phones to the internet – have helped firms become more efficient and profitable and helped consumers save money and receive better products and services. However, we are also aware of the significant failure rate in firm-level ICT intervention within the developing world and the risks involved.

A literature of sustainability failures (Best and Maclay, 2002; Heeks and Bhatnagar, 1999; Aichholzer, 2004) has done a good job underlining the range of success and failure factors for ICT projects. In particular, attention has been paid to the importance of sustained institutional and political support, attention to capacity and training, and financial issues. Indeed, we have studied numerous cases where the political and institutional changes have brought down otherwise highly successful programmes.

### ICTs and economic growth: the way forward

There is no doubting that ICTs have had a significant development impact. Micro- and macroeconomic approaches alike suggest that the roll-out of ICTs has improved livelihoods and increased the productivity of businesses. At the same time, the ICT industry itself has been a significant source of profitable investment and employment. This is not, however, to suggest that ICTs are a silver bullet to solve the problems of underdevelopment. Successful utilisation of communications technologies – and perhaps in particular the internet – takes a broader economic environment that is conducive to their exploitation. Similarly, ICT industries and ICT-enabled businesses need an investment climate that includes an educated workforce with appropriate technical skills, access to entrepreneurial finance and business talent, reliable infrastructure, a robust but reasonable regulatory environment, and so on. Sober, evidence-based analysis is required to reveal examples of success and reasons for failures. In this chapter we have attempted to offer just such a cautious and evidence-based treatment. In the end, ICTs have a role to play in the development process, but they are one player in a large ensemble cast.

## Key readings

Best, M.L. and Maclay, C.M. (2002) Community internet access in rural areas: solving the economic sustainability puzzle. In *The Global Information Technology Report 2001–2002*, ed. G. Kirkman, J. Sachs, K. Schwab and P. Cornelius. Oxford: Oxford University Press, pp. 76–88

Jensen, R. (2007) The digital provide: IT, market performance and welfare in the South Indian fisheries sector. *Quarterly Journal of Economics*, 122 (3), pp. 879–924

Kenny, C. (2006) *Overselling the Web: development and the internet*. Boulder, CO: Lynne Rienner

Schware, R. (ed.) (2005) *E-Development: from excitement to effectiveness*. Washington, DC: World Bank

UNCTAD (United Nations Conference on Trade and Development) (2006) *Information Economy Report, 2006*. Geneva: UNCTAD

## References

Aichholzer, G. (2004) Scenarios of e-government in 2010 and implications for strategy design. *Electronic Journal of e-Government,* 1 (1), pp. 1–10

Annamalai, K. and Rao, S. (2003) *What Works: ITC's e-Choupal and profitable rural transformation*. Washington, DC: World Resources Institute

APEC (Asia-Pacific Economic Cooperation) (2001) *The New Economy and APEC*. Singapore: APEC

Autor, D., Katz, L. and Kreuger, A. (1998) Computing inequality: have computers changed the labor market? *Quarterly Journal of Economics*, 113 (4), pp. 1169–214

*Balancing Act* (2006) TradeNet launches market Intel platform for buying and selling agricultural goods. *Balancing Act*, 341, unpaginated (http://www.balancingact-africa.com/news/back/balancing-act_341.html)

Banerjee, A. and Duflo, E. (2006) *The Economic Lives of the Poor*. MIT Department of Economics Working Paper 06-29

Bayes, A., Braun, J.V. and Akhter, R. (1999) *Village Pay Phones and Poverty Reduction: insights from a Grameen Bank initiative in Bangladesh.* Bonn: Center for Development Research

Best, M.L. and Kumar, R. (forthcoming) Sustainability failure of rural telecenters: the Sustainable Access in Rural India Project. *Information Technologies and International Development*

Best, M.L. and Maclay, C. M. (2002) Community internet access in rural areas: solving the economic sustainability puzzle. In *The Global Information Technology Report 2001–2002: readiness for the networked world,* ed. G. Kirkman, J. Sachs, K. Schwab and P. Cornelius. Oxford: Oxford University Press, pp. 76–88

Best, M.L. and Wade, K. (2007) Democratic and anti-democratic regulators of the internet: a framework. *The Information Society*, 23, pp. 405–11

Best, M. and Wilson, E.J., III (2007) The velocity of rebirth. *Information Technologies and International Development*, 3 (4), pp. iii–v

Best, M.L., Jones, K., Kondo, I., Thakur, D., Wornyo, E. and Yu, C. (2007) Post-conflict communications: the case of Liberia. *Communications of the ACM*, 50 (10), pp. 33–9

Blumler, J.G. and Katz, E. (1974) *The Uses of Mass Communication.* Newbury Park, CA: Sage

Bornstein, D. (2005) *The Price of a Dream: the story of the Grameen Bank.* Oxford: Oxford University Press

Brown, S.R. (1993) A primer on Q methodology. *Operant Subjectivity*, 16, pp. 91–138

Choudhury, S. and Wolf, S. (2002) Use of ICTs and economic performance of small and medium scale enterprises in East Africa. Paper presented at the WIDER conference on the New Economy in Development, 10–11 May 2002, Helsinki

David, P. (2000) Digital technology and the productivity paradox: after ten years, what has been learned. Mimeo, Stanford University, CA

Davis, K. and Ochieng, C. (2006) ICTs as appropriate technologies for African development. In *Business and Development: the private path to prosperity,* ed. IFC/Financial Times (http://www.ifc.org/ifcext/economics.nsf/AttachmentsByTitle/ict_africa.pdf/$FILE/ict_in_africa_bronze_essay.pdf)

Deane, J. (2005). Not a telecoms, nor a digital, but an information divide. In Milward-Oliver (ed.) (2005), pp. 51–63

Díaz, À. and Rivas, G. (2005) Innovación tecnológica y desarrollo digital: El aporte de los gobiernos de la Concertación. In *La Paradoja Aparente – Equidad y Eficiencia: Resolviendo el Dilema,* ed. P. Meller. Santiago de Chile: Aguilar Chilena de Ediciones, pp. 473–526

Donner, J. (2004) Microentrepreneurs and mobiles: an exploration of the uses of mobile phones by small business owners in Rwanda. *Information Technologies and International Development*, 2 (1), pp. 1–21

Eltzroth, C. and Kenny, C. (2003) *Broadcasting and Development.* Washington, DC: World Bank (World Bank Working Paper 11)

Forestier, E., Grace, J. and Kenny, C. (2002) Can information and communication technologies be pro-poor? *Telecommunications Policy*, 26 (11), pp. 623–46

Freund, C. and Weinhold, D. (2000) On the effect of the internet on international trade. *International Finance Discussion Paper* 693, Board of Governors of the Federal Reserve System (US) (http://ideas.repec.org/p/fip/fedgif/693.html)

Gordon, R. (2002) Technology and economic performance in the American economy. Cambridge, MA: NBER Working Paper No. 8771

Grupo de Acción Digital (2004) *Agenda Digital – Chile 2004–2006. Te Acerca el Futuro.* Santiago, Chile: Grupo de Acción Digital

Guermazi, B. (2005) *Liberia Telecommunications Sector, Overview of Issues and Road-map for Reform.* Global Information and Communications Technologies Department, Policy Division, The World Bank Group

Halewood, N. and Kenny, C. (2005) Young people and communications technologies. Background Paper for the 2007 World Development Report. Mimeo, Washington, DC: World Bank

Heeks, R. (2002) *Failure, Success and Improvisation of Information Systems Projects in Developing Countries.* Manchester: IDPM, University of Manchester

Heeks, R. and Bhatnagar, S. (1999) Understanding success and failure in information age reform. In *Reinventing Government in the Information Age: international practice in IT enabled public sector reform,* ed. R. Heeks. London: Routledge, pp. 49–74

Hilbert, M. (2001) *Latin America on Its Path Into the Digital Age: where are we?* Santiago, Chile: CEPAL/ECLAC

Hinson, R., Sorensen, O. and Buatsi, S. (2007) Internet use patterns amongst internationalizing Ghanaian exporters. *Electronic Journal on Information Systems in Developing Countries,* 29 (3), pp. 1–14

Humphrey, J., Mansell, R., Pare, D. and Schmitz, H. (2003) *The Reality of E-Commerce with Developing Countries.* Brighton: Institute of Development Studies

*info*Dev (2006) *Micro-Payment Systems and their Application to Mobile Networks.* Washington, DC: *info*Dev

ITU (2006) *World Telecommunication Indicators.* Geneva: ITU

Ivatury, G. and Pickens, M. (2006) *Mobile Phone Banking and Low-Income Customers: evidence from South Africa.* Washington, DC: Consultative Group to Assist the Poor; The World Bank and United Nations Foundation

Jensen, R. (2007) The digital provide: IT, market performance and welfare in the South Indian fisheries sector. *Quarterly Journal of Economics,* 122 (3), pp. 879–924

Jenson, M., Myers, M. and Southwood, R. (2004) The impact of ICT in Africa. Paper prepared for the Commission for Africa, London

Kaufmann, D., Kraay, A. and Mastruzzi, M. (2003) *Governance Matters III: governance indicators for 1996–2002.* Washington, DC: World Bank

Kenny, C. (2003) The internet and economic growth in developing countries: a case of managing expectations? *Oxford Development Studies,* 31 (1), pp. 99–113

Kenny, C. (2006) *Overselling the Web: development and the internet.* Boulder, CO: Lynne Rienner

Kenny, C. and Keremane, R. (2007) Toward universal telephone access: market progress and progress beyond the market. *Telecommunications Policy,* 31, pp. 155–63

Kenny, C., Lanvin, B. and Lewin, A. (2003) The access divide. In *ICT and Development: enabling the information society,* ed. World Bank. Washington, DC: World Bank, pp. 38–43

Kleine, D. (2007) Empowerment and the Limits of Choice: microentrepreneurs, information and communication technologies and state policies in Chile. Unpublished PhD thesis, London School of Economics and Political Science.

Kolko, J. (2002) Silicon mountains, silicon molehills: geographic concentration and convergence of internet industries in the US. *Information Economics and Policy,* 14, pp. 211–32

Konstadakopulos, D. (2006) From public loudspeakers to the internet: the adoption of information and communication technologies (ICTs) by small-enterprise clusters in Vietnam. *Information Technologies and International Development,* 2 (4), pp. 21–39

Kumar, R. (2004) e-Choupals: a study on the financial sustainability of village inter-net centers in rural Madhya Pradesh. *Information Technologies and International Development*, 2 (1), pp. 45–73

Kumar, R. and Best, M.L. (2006) Impact and sustainability of e-government services in developing countries: lessons learned from Tamil Nadu, India. *The Information Society*, 22 (1), pp. 1–12

Kumar, R. and Best, M.L. (2007) Social impact and diffusion of telecenter use: a study from the Sustainable Access in Rural India Project. *Community Informatics*, 2 (3), unpaginated

Lal, K. (1996) Information technology, international orientation and performance: a case study of electrical and electronic goods manufacturing firms in India. *Information Economics and Policy*, 8, pp. 269–80

Lehr, B. and Lichtenberg, F. (1999) Information technology and its impact on pro-ductivity: firm-level evidence from government and private data sources, 1977–1993. *Canadian Journal of Economics*, 32 (2), pp. 335–62

Marsh, P. (2007) India set to gain from outsourcing. *Financial Times*, 22 July 2007, p. 4

McKemey, K., Scott, N., Souter, D., Afullo, T., Kibombo, R. and Sakyi-Dawson, O. (2003). *Innovative Demand Models for Telecommunications Services*. London: Gamos

Milward-Oliver, G. (ed.) (2005) *Maitland + 20: fixing the missing link*. Bradford on Avon: Anima

Molla, A. (2005) Exploring the reality of e-commerce benefits among businesses in a developing country. Manchester: IDPM Manchester Development Informatics Working Paper Series No. 22, Manchester, UK

Neto, I., Kenny, C., Janakiram, S. and Watt, C. (2005) Look before you leap: the bumpy road to e-development. In *E-Development: from excitement to effectiveness*, ed. R. Schware. Washington, DC: World Bank, pp. 1–22

OECD (2000) *Literacy in the Information Age: final report of the international adult literacy survey*. Paris: OECD

Oxley, J. and Yeung, B. (2000) E-commerce readiness: institutional environment and international competitiveness. Mimeo, University of Michigan Business School

Pastore, M. (2001) Why the offline are offline (http://asia.internet.com/news/print. php/784691/Why + the + Offline + Are + Offline.htm)

Pohjola, M. (2001) Introduction. In *Information Technology, Productivity and Economic Growth*, ed. M. Pohjola. Oxford: Oxford University Press, pp. 1–32

Proenza, F. (2005) The road to broadband development in developing countries is through competition driven by wireless and VoIP. Paper prepared for the workshop Wireless Communication and Development: A Global Perspective, Annenberg Research Network on International Communication, 7–8 October 2005

Qiang, C., Pitt, A. and Ayers, S. (2003) *The Contribution of Information Communica-tion Technologies to Growth*. World Bank Working Paper 24

Qiang, C.Z.-W., Clarke, G.R. and Halewood, N. (2006) The role of ICT in doing busi-ness. In *Information and Communications for Development 2006*, ed. The World Bank. Washington, DC: The World Bank, pp. 57–86

Research Africa! (2006) *Towards an African e-Index: SME e-access and usage across 14 African countries* (http://www.researchictafrica.net/images/upload/SME_book-Web.pdf)

Richardson, D., Ramirez, R. and Haq, M. (2000) Grameen Telecom's village phone programme in rural Bangladesh: a multi-media case study. Mimeo, TeleCom-mons Development Group, Bangladesh

Rogers, E.M. (1983) *Diffusion of Innovations*, 3rd edn. New York: Free Press

Roman, R. (2003) Diffusion of innovations as a theoretical framework for telecenters. *Information Technologies and International Development*, 1 (2), pp. 53–66

Samuel, J., Shah, N. and Hadingham, W. (2005) Mobile communications in South Africa, Tanzania and Egypt: results from community and business surveys. In *Africa: the impact of mobile phones*, Newbury, UK: Vodafone Group Plc, pp. 44–52

Schreyer, P. (2000) The contribution of information and communications technology to output growth: a study of the G7 countries. Paris: OECD, STI Working Paper DSTI/DOC(2000)2

Sharma, C. (2005) *India is the Model for Next Wave of Global Wireless Growth*. St Louis, MO: DataComm Research

Souter, D. (2005) *The Economic Impact of Telecommunications on Rural Livelihoods and Poverty Reduction*. London: Commonwealth Telecommunications Organisation

Stiglitz, J.E. (2002) *Globalization and its Discontents*. New York: W.W. Norton

Stiroh, K. (2002) Are ICT spillovers driving the new economy? *Review of Income and Wealth*, 48 (1 March), pp. 33–57

*The Economist* (10 March 2005) *Special Issue on Technology and Development*. London: The Economist

Triplett, J. (1999) The Solow productivity paradox: what do computers do to productivity? *Canadian Journal of Economics*, 32 (2), pp. 309–34

UNCTAD (United Nations Conference on Trade and Development) (2001) *E-Commerce and Development Report*. Geneva: United Nations

UNCTAD (United Nations Conference on Trade and Development) (2006) *Information Economy Report, 2006*. Geneva: UNCTAD

US Department of Commerce (1999) *The Emerging Digital Economy II*. Washington, DC: Department of Commerce

Waverman, L., Meschi, M. and Fuss, M. (2005) The impact of telecoms on economic growth in developing countries. In *Africa: the impact of mobile phones*, ed. Vodafone, Vodaphone Policy Paper No. 2, pp. 10–23

Wilson, E.J., III, Best, M.L. and Kleine, D. (2005) Moving beyond 'the real digital divide'. *Information Technologies and International Development*, 2 (3), pp. iii–v

World Bank (2004) *World Development Report*. New York: Oxford University Press

World Bank (2005a) *Financing Information and Communication Infrastructure Needs in the Developing World: a World Bank contribution to the World Summit on the Information Society Working Group on Financing ICT*. Washington, DC: The World Bank

World Bank (2005b) *World Development Indicators*. New York: Oxford University Press

# 7 | ICT in education: catalyst for development

## Michelle Selinger

- ICTs can be used effectively to enhance both the quality and the quantity of educational delivery, but only if used appropriately.
- There remains too much duplication of effort in the delivery of ICT in education initiatives, and we urgently need to learn the lessons from previous initiatives to ensure that expensive mistakes are no longer replicated.
- The use of high-quality multimedia learning resources in whole-class and small-group teaching can transform student learning experiences.
- Focusing on digital literacy rather than enhancing teaching with multimedia resources in situations where there are limited ICT resources may lead to a poorer learning environment for students and limited use of expensive resources.
- Teachers must be involved in the design of ICT initiatives in education, and supported in the effective delivery thereof.

## Introduction

> Education is the most powerful tool which you can use to change the world.
> (Nelson Mandela, cited by HM Queen Elizabeth, 2005)

Nelson Mandela is one of many people who understand the power of education and agree that improving the quality of education is vital for economic and social development. This chapter examines whether ICTs can indeed hold the key to a step change towards improvement in the world's education systems. ICT is certainly not a panacea for education, but it is a powerful tool that when implemented appropriately can catalyse and accelerate education reform and development. ICTs play an increasingly important role in this development because we now live in an inter-connected world in which 'Globalisation and networking technologies will enable firms to use the world as their supply base for talent and materials. Processes, firms, customers and supply chains will fragment as companies expand overseas, as work flows to where it is best done and as information digitises' (Economist Intelligence Unit, 2006, p. 3). For developing countries to compete and grow, they will need to find their niche, develop their aspirations for participating in the global economy, and prepare their populations accordingly through appropriate and relevant education.

All countries need an education system with a strong focus on capacity development programmes to provide citizens with those skills necessary to make the most of their resources for economic prosperity. Education is important for social cohesion which, according to Delors' (1996) report to UNESCO, consists of the four pillars of learning: learning to know, learning to do, learning to live together and learning to be. According to the World Bank Fast Track Initiative (FTI), 'capacity development' in the education sector means 'developing skills, organizations and institutions at all levels right down to the classroom' (World Bank FTI, 2006, p. 2). For this reason this chapter, while focusing heavily on primary (or basic) education, acknowledges the continuum through to secondary, higher and vocational education as well as considering non-formal education for capacity building. It explores education specifically in the context of a country's wider development agenda. 'Insufficient capacity has several causes, among them the lack of the right knowledge, skill mix and experience at all levels and structural weaknesses in organizational and institutional arrangements' (World Bank FTI, 2006, p. 2). *Reform* is the term commonly used for the reorganisation and improvement of a system that is not reaching its desired economic and social goals. As such, governments often now refer to changes in their education systems as 'education reform'. Education reform will be more successful if it takes place in a climate that is already focused on improvements in other sectors of society; since improving the quality of education will raise aspirations and expectations, it is vital for economic development that school leavers and university graduates are provided with opportunities to obtain jobs and develop a worthwhile career in their own country. This implies a need for the development of commerce and industry so that new jobs are created that require a skilled, well-educated workforce.

One impact of globalisation is that countries are competing for human capital, and the movement of people, particularly those who are well qualified, is leading to a brain drain from developing countries which has high financial, institutional and societal costs (Tebeje, 2005; Solimano, 2005). Career prospects and rewards overseas are often higher, so there is little incentive to return or remain (Tebeje, 2005). Many developing countries get little return from their investment in higher education as too many graduates leave or fail to return home at the end of their studies. This leads to a dwindling professional sector that has a knock-on effect as institutions become increasingly dependent on foreign expertise. To fill the human resource gap created by the brain drain, Africa, for example, employs up to 150,000 expatriate professionals at a cost of US$4 billion a year (Dervis, 2007). To stop this clear diversion of resources from the indigenous population, developing countries have another reason and an immediate need not only to develop the quality of education, but also to increase job opportunities and career prospects for their people.

Education features very highly in the United Nation's Millennium Development Goals (MDGs). The explicitly education-related goals are to ensure that all boys and girls complete a full course of primary schooling (universal primary education) (MDG2) and to eliminate gender disparity in primary and secondary education by 2015 (MDG3). These themes are echoed in the UNESCO Education for All mission (EFA) outlined in the Dakar Framework for Action (UNESCO, 2000) and listed below:

The Education for All goals

1  Expanding and improving comprehensive early childhood care and education, especially for the most vulnerable and disadvantaged children
2  Ensuring that by 2015 all children, particularly girls, children in difficult circumstances and those belonging to ethnic minorities, have access to and complete free and compulsory primary education of good quality
3  Ensuring that the learning needs of all young people and adults are met through equitable access to appropriate learning and life skills programmes
4  Achieving a 50 per cent improvement in levels of adult literacy by 2015, especially for women, and equitable access to basic and continuing education for all adults
5  Eliminating gender disparities in primary and secondary education by 2005, and achieving gender equality in education by 2015, with a focus on ensuring girls' full and equal access to and achievement in basic education of good quality
6  Improving all aspects of the quality of education and ensuring excellence of all so that recognized and measurable learning outcomes are achieved by all, especially in literacy, numeracy and essential life skills.

(UNESCO, 2000, p. 8)

In fact most of the eight MDG goals can be addressed in some way by improved standards of, and access to, education. However, to be successful, other economic drivers need to be in place to provide the incentive for students to remain in country for work and to participate in further and higher education.

## Education in developing countries

According to the UN MDG report of 2007 (UN, 2007), net enrolment ratios in primary education had increased to 88 per cent in developing countries in the school year 2004/05. Progress is slowest in sub-Saharan Africa, and although this region has made significant progress since 1990/91, there are still seven countries in which fewer than half the children of primary-school age are enrolled in school. In a report for the World Bank, Bruns *et al.* (2003) discuss the variation in prospects for completion of universal primary

**Table 7.1** *Prospects for universal primary completion (UPC) by 2015*

| Progress rating | Low-income countries[a] | Middle-income countries[b] | All developing countries |
|---|---|---|---|
| On track | 22 | 47 | 69 |
| Achieved UPC | 11 | 26 | 37 |
| On track to achieve UPC by 2015 | 11 | 21 | 32 |
| Off track | 51 | 19 | 70 |
| Off track to achieve UPC by 2015 | 28 | 15 | 43 |
| Seriously off track | 23 | 4 | 27 |
| No data available | 9 | 7 | 16 |
| At risk, subtotal | 60 | 26 | 86 |
| Total | 82 | 73 | 155 |

[a]Countries eligible for lending from the International Development Association (IDA) and 'blend' countries eligible for IDA and IBRD lending, plus non-member low-income countries such as the Democratic People's Republic of Korea.
[b]Countries eligible for lending from the International Bank for Reconstruction and Development (IBRD), plus non-member middle-income developing countries.
*Source:* Bruns *et al.* (2003).

education (UPE) between developing countries (Table 7.1). Nearly a quarter of the poorest countries are seriously off track, compared to 8 per cent in middle-income countries.

However, attendance at school is insufficient for wider capacity development and economic growth unless the quality of education that students receive provides them with the knowledge, skills and understanding necessary for poverty reduction. A recent UNESCO (2005) report on literacy stated that 60 per cent of children passing through primary school are still failing to acquire basic literacy skills, and an evaluation of the World Bank's education support concluded that for universal primary education 'it will not suffice to ensure that children achieve the basic literacy and numeracy essential for poverty reduction. Primary education efforts need to focus on improving learning outcomes, particularly among the poor and other disadvantaged children' (World Bank Independent Evaluation Group, 2006, p. x). This evaluation also suggests that costs of improving learning outcomes would be higher than achieving UPE and that 'efforts are urgently needed to improve the performance of sector management in support of learning outcomes' (World Bank Independent Evaluation Group, 2006, p. x; see also the recent initiative by the Hewlett Foundation, 2006).

### Data sources and comparators

Many indicators purport to measure the effectiveness of a country's education system. Few are truly global, and many do not effectively report on measures of educational or learning outputs. OECD (2003) provides data

Average performance
(reading, mathematical and scientific literacy)

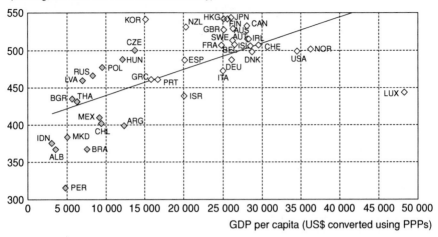

Figure 7.1 *Relationship between average performance and expenditure per child in basic education* (*source:* OECD PISA database 2003).

for 51 countries on a wide range of indicators. They have examined the percentage of GDP spent on education in 28 countries which they correlate with educational success in literacy in reading, mathematics and science. However, only one or two countries in this study are developing countries, and so it is difficult to make any real comparisons between developed and developing countries (OECD, 2003) (see Figure 7.1).

OECD's PISA study (http://www.pisa.oecd.org) administers tests to between 4,500 and 10,000 students per country in reading, mathematical and scientific literacy. These tests are internationally standardised assessments that have been developed jointly by participating countries for 15-year-olds in schools. Since 2003, they have included problem solving in an attempt to make them relevant for real-world contexts. How real these contexts are, though, depends very much on the country in which students live, and it is questionable as to how relevant all of the questions are for the lives of students in developing countries (Wallbank, 1934; Seeley Brown and Duguid, 2001; Mulder, 2007). All developing countries do significantly less well in the PISA tests, which explains why an emphasis on the quality of education is so crucial. Figure 7.2 illustrates the extent of the relatively poor performance of developing countries in mathematics from the 2003 PISA study. It should be noted that relatively few students stay in school beyond primary education in developing countries, so that those taking the tests are already the more privileged ones. These figures highlight the extent of the poor quality of education.

The index that has possibly the most global reach is the Human Development Index. Developed by UNDP, and covering 177 countries plus

*Two girls in ICT lab at Mukuru skills centre, Kenya (source:* Michelle Selinger).

another 17 UN member countries for which complete data are not available, it measures average achievements in three basic dimensions of human development: living a long and healthy life, measured by life expectancy; being educated, measured by adult literacy and enrolment at the primary, secondary and tertiary levels; and having a decent standard of living, measured by purchasing power parity and income. Figure 7.3 shows the gap increasing extensively between South Asia and sub-Saharan Africa, with South Asia overall making strides to close the gap with the rest of the world. The reasons for this growing differential are certainly not all educational, but enhancing education, and particularly health education, will be an important factor in improving the index for sub-Saharan Africa.

Finally in this account of indices, the UNESCO EFA Development Index covers 125 countries and incorporates the four most 'quantifiable' EFA goals: UPE, gender, adult literacy and education quality. It also reviews data on public expenditure on education as a percentage of GNP and reports on the dollar amount given in aid for education. On average only 4.8 per cent of total aid allocated to all developing countries is for basic education (UNESCO, 2006, p. 19), and of this Oxfam International (2006, p. 6) believes that 70 per cent is spent on technical consultancy from the West.

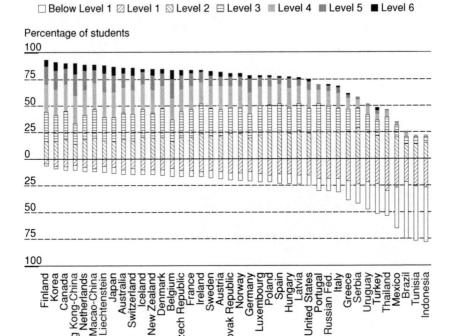

Figure 7.2 *Percentage of students at each level of proficiency on the PISA mathematics scale* (*source:* OECD PISA 2003 database, Table 2.5a).

*Schoolchildren in Malawi, 2002 (source:* Tim Unwin).

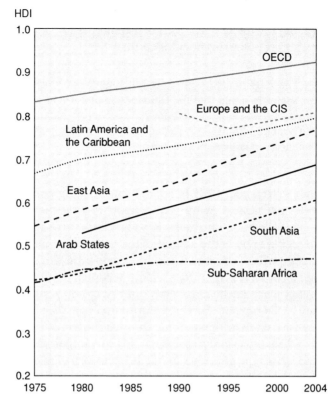

Figure 7.3 *The Human Development Index* (*source:* UNDP, 2006).

These data have limitations as comparators between countries because they reduce education to a culture-free set of indicators. Education is not just about making sure that the citizens of a country are able to compete on an equal footing with the rest of the world. It is also about helping new generations to understand the context of their own cultural and social traditions, and to identify and associate with what it is that makes them unique so they can specialise in providing a particular set of goods and services. Education policymakers need to take account of such indices, but only in the context of helping them to identify and prioritise their country's own needs for education for economic and social development. The needs of society should be focused not only on the particular forms of scientific and mathematical literacy that meet international standards, but also on the skills relevant to the economic focus of the country. This causes tensions in what to teach and how to teach it. Moreover, it must also be emphasised that education should be about providing people with the skills and understanding necessary for them to take full control of their lives, and that it therefore has important political and ideological implications.

### The roles of ICT in education

An *info*Dev (2005) review of what is known about the impact of ICT on education in developing countries concluded that:

> While impact on student achievement is still a matter of reasonable debate, a consensus seems to argue that the introduction and use of ICTs in education can be a useful tool to help promote and enable educational reform, and that ICTs are both important motivational tools for learning and can promote greater efficiencies in education systems and practices.
>
> (*info*Dev, 2005, p. 8)

The rationale for the use of ICT in educational development is also fuelled by the rhetoric that almost every government around the world believes that technology and education are the keys to competitive advantage. Many countries are racing to be at the advent of the technology transformation in their area, and groups of countries within a region are working together to become global leaders. It is therefore widely accepted that technology has a real and relevant place in the classroom not just to equip students with the digital literacy skills needed for the 'information age' (Castells, 2000), but also to improve access to understanding through the use of multi-modal representations of difficult-to-grasp concepts. It is also important to understand what level and what type of access to ICT is necessary to raise achievement to justify the expenditure on wiring up schools, connecting them to the internet and providing the necessary student–computer ratio. Furthermore, it is crucial to recognise that there is little value in simply training people in the use of ICT if there is no real reason to use it and if there is no access to ICTs on leaving school. However, if access to ICT resources raises the quality and relevance of learning then the expenditure can be made more justifiable. Above all, these newly acquired ICT skills must then be used to enhance the quality of the wider learning experiences encountered by those who utilise them.

ICT can be a catalyst by providing tools which teachers use to improve teaching and by giving learners access to electronic media that make concepts clearer and more accessible. It can also remove inequalities particularly between urban and rural communities. Sugata Mitra (2006), for example, suggests that ICT makes more difference in rural areas than it does in urban areas because the best teachers migrate towards the towns and therefore technology introduced in rural areas has a greater impact on learning outcomes where it can compensate for poorer-quality teaching. ICT can also be a catalyst to support and accelerate this education transformation and can reduce costs, but not until we change how we make effective and efficient use of this limited resource. Currently ICT is being used in many countries to teach what they already teach in the same way, and have taught for decades, instead of considering where teachers can specifically make use of the interactivity and multimedia capability to help make learning easier and more accessible for their students. The tasks given to students and the assessment strategies employed still focus on the 'what' rather than on the 'how' and the 'why', which does not necessarily prepare students for the needs of society or the modern workplace.

The argument is no longer about teachers being the transmitters of knowledge; teachers are now positioned within a constructivist notion of 'teacher as facilitator'. The foundation for constructivism in education is generally attributed to Jean Piaget (1954), who describes constructivism as a process of *accommodation* and *assimilation*, by which learners construct new knowledge from their experiences. Learners assimilate the new experiences into their existing framework while accommodation takes place through the re-framing of their current mental models of the world to fit new experiences. Constructivism is often associated with pedagogic approaches that promote learning by doing. Many educators focus on the importance of 'social constructivism' (Vygotsky, 1978) when attempting to reform education. Four main principles apply in a social constructivist classroom (Maddux *et al.*, 1997):

1  Learning and development is a social, collaborative activity.
2  The zone of proximal development (i.e. a more knowledgeable other supports the learner to reach the next stage in their learning) can serve as a guide for curricular and lesson planning.
3  School learning should occur in a meaningful context and not be separated from learning and knowledge children develop in the 'real world'.
4  Out-of-school experiences should be related to the learner's school experience.

As our understanding of cognition and meta-cognition grows, this view of teaching has taken hold almost globally. Yet the rhetoric is far from reality. In both the developed and the developing world many commentators perceive technology as an important catalyst that can change pedagogy (see for example Cornu, 1995; Joshi and Murthy, 2004; McLoughlin and Oliver, 1999). However, for technology to have that impact, the educational model that supports a constructivist view of pedagogy must be viewed as central to the process that is then supported, rather than dictated to, by the technology. There are three important areas that should be considered when implementing ICT solutions in developing countries: linguistic, pedagogical and technological.

*Linguistic considerations*
In developing countries in South America, the Middle East and Africa the language of instruction in post-primary education is usually a European language, yet cognitive reasoning skills are usually far more developed in the mother tongue. Learning in a second language therefore incurs greater difficulty. Collier (1995, p. 5) showed that to learn effectively through a second language, students need to have a high level of cognitive development

in their first language and then academic knowledge and conceptual development will transfer from the first language to the second language. In many developing countries the quality of primary education is often extremely poor, so learning through the medium of a second language can be highly problematic.

This has important implications for ICT because much more content is developed in European languages than in the indigenous languages of developing countries. This illustrates the importance of a blended learning approach. To be effective, teachers need to familiarise themselves with electronic resources written in a second language and make themselves aware of the difficult concepts that are being taught. They can then ensure that students receive some prior instruction on this content in their first language before interacting with the content in the e-learning materials. Teachers can also identify key concepts that are deemed essential for students' progress in the course or concepts that are difficult to grasp, and prepare lessons, presentations and other resources in the student's first language to help their understanding. They can also adapt these local language resources to suit their own teaching styles and their students' learning preferences (Selinger, 2004a).

*Pedagogical considerations*

On the surface, teaching styles across the world appear to vary very little. However, cultural beliefs about teaching and learning, and 'lack of experience and knowledge of how traditional instruction interfaces with web-based teaching materials' (Selinger, 2004b, p. 215), have a significant influence on the way in which programmes are taught. The role of culture is important (Vygotsky, 1978; Bruner, 1996). Bruner (1996, p. 20), for example, argues that 'education must be conceived as aiding humans in learning to use the tools of meaning making and reality construction, to better adapt to the world in which they find themselves and to help in the process of changing it as required', while Vygotsky (1978) asserts that culture is the prime determinant of individual development.

In many developing countries, where there is a distinct lack of resources – digital or otherwise – the transmission model of education is still very much in evidence and students are still learning by rote. Technology has enormous potential to address the challenge of education transformation and some governments are very aware of the development of new teaching models that will ensure greater knowledge retention and conceptual understanding. In Jordan, for example, the World Bank-funded Education Reform for the Knowledge Economy (ERfKE) has teacher development programmes aligned to the educational reform process which introduces teachers to new teaching and learning paradigms (USAID, 2006). The World Economic Forum initiated the Jordan Education Initiative (JEI) in 2003 as a parallel initiative designed to involve the private sector in the education reform process, and to accelerate ERfKE through the provision of ICT-based solutions that complemented the ERfKE process (World Economic Forum, 2007). A major component of the JEI is the development of e-curricula resources authored in Arabic which are designed to incorporate professional development elements to help to develop teachers' understanding of the constructivist pedagogy identified by the government as the way forward (see Selinger, 2005).

*Technological considerations*

Assumptions are too often made that there is cheap and easy access to computers and the internet across the globe (Gibson and Selinger, 2005). Internet access across Africa, for example, is far more expensive than in many Western countries, especially when compared with the average per-capita income (ITU, 2003). For example, in more than half of Africa's countries, annual internet access costs range from more than 500 per cent of average annual income to just over 100 per cent of annual income. In Sierra Leone annual costs were 857 per cent of annual income compared to the US where internet access costs just 0.5 per cent of annual income. However, cost is only one factor, because in most developing countries very few people have access to the internet at home and the internet bandwidth available to many universities and schools, where it is provided, is usually far less than the bandwidth going into the average home in the North. When sharing resources and teaching ideas internationally, it is important to avoid creating a 'technology dissonance' (Selinger and Gibson, 2004). This goes beyond just the availability of different technology solutions, and includes teaching and learning situations in which the availability and nature of technology vary dramatically, and where culturally relevant learning models are fundamentally different, thus making a technology-based learning solution in one country difficult, if not impossible, to replicate. The host country needs help from the recipient country in understanding the difficulties faced, and by valuing what each party brings to the table, together they can then explore ways to ensure that the recipient country finds an acceptable solution to adapting the resources sufficiently so students can gain additional benefits.

## Developing and implementing new educational models

### Basic enablers for education success

ICT is not the panacea for education's ills. Before ICT can even be considered as an accelerator of education reform or change, other factors need to be taken into account. Figure 7.4 is a simple version of a model for education reform in which the introduction of ICT is seen as one part of a holistic solution.

This diagram shows that basic enablers and the social-economic framework need to be considered before determining an educational model to which a country aspires. These basic enablers include such things as access to clean water, the availability of basic shelter, personal safety, health

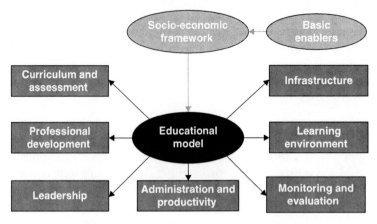

Figure 7.4 *The key elements in educational reform* (*source:* Michelle Selinger).

of students, free or affordable costs of schooling, and sufficient and well-trained teachers. This does not mean that ICT should not be introduced if some of these factors are not in place; but if ICT is going to have any meaningful impact and the expenditure justified, then it has to be located in an environment that will support learning.

An example from Mukuru in Nairobi, Kenya, indicates what can be done to introduce ICT when the basic enablers are in place. Living conditions are harsh yet attendance at four of the local schools is almost 100 per cent. The schools are part of a wider project run by the Sisters of Mercy and

*School building at one of the Mukuru schools, Nairobi, Kenya*
(*source:* Michelle Selinger).

they sit in very close proximity to the students' houses. Inside the grounds the younger children are given breakfast and all children receive lunch. There are toilets and running water and the grounds are kept immaculately clean. There is a clinic providing healthcare serving all four schools. A small technology centre in the skills centre of one of the schools is being well used, and both teachers and students are learning quickly. The headteachers are fully involved and are planning for labs to be introduced in the other three schools. Four laptops per school have also been made available by British Airways for the headteachers and other staff to use and to communicate with one another. Two key teachers from each school have been identified to champion the use of ICT and to help train and support the staff, and a set of lessons has been planned for year 6 students to use the facilities for subject-focused projects but especially health education. A teacher portfolio is planned which will be assessed towards a professional qualification. Internet access, currently provided free by the ISP, is available on all of the computers donated by Microsoft in the skills centre and made available by a donation of wireless cards and a wireless access point from Cisco. The basic enablers have given both donors and staff the confidence to invest time and resources in developing the use of ICT.

The headteachers' confidence has grown so that they are now determining the direction the initiative takes and they are taking control of the development of both the ICT facilities and how ICT is deployed in their schools. Their buy-in took time to develop, but now they own the initiative and this will help in sustainability and further developments. This shows what can be achieved, and is in marked contrast to experiences in some other parts of the world, where a lack of basic facilities in schools combined with low pay among teachers contribute to situations where donors are reluctant to implement technology solutions because the risks of failure are so large. Non-formal education through ICT is also being supported in Mukuru. Because of the proximity of the ICT facilities, the hairdressing school is benefiting. Colemar (Revlon) provides a free six-month course in hairdressing in the Mukuru skills centre for local youth, most of whom are females from the slums. At the end of their training each successful student is provided with a hair salon kit by Babyliss so they can make a living as a hairdresser and giving them a real opportunity to provide for their families. Colemar were limited in their ability to provide the necessary level of theoretical training by the prohibitive costs of the theory books and also found that the content was not always relevant to the care of black hair. The availability of the ICT lab meant that the theory of hairdressing can be provided in an electronic format. The materials are being developed by a South African-based educational software company with Cisco's and Colemar's support, and will focus on the particular treatments most requested for African hair. The text-based materials will be in English and there will be voiceovers in both English and Swahili, recognising that literacy and English skills may be problematic.

### Socio-economic framework

There needs to be the political will for education reform with clearly articulated visions, goals and directions for education that are matched to the needs of society and to aspirations and directions for economic growth. Sufficient funding also needs to have been identified and earmarked so that current initiatives and new programmes can be built on, or integrated into, existing developments. Funding requests to donors and aid agencies will be more successful if potential costs and time savings are identified. Moreover, a defined organisational change strategy with strong governance processes needs to be in place with a framework, the roadmap and priorities outlined. Singapore and Jordan are examples of two countries that are attempting to do this. Jordan has ERfKE under way funded by the World Bank, and the Jordan Education Initiative, now established as a Jordanian-led NGO, will continue to work with the government on developing and piloting innovative solutions that support and accelerate the reform process in line with the existing roadmap and priorities (JEI, 2007; http://www.jei.org.jo). Singapore's Intelligent Nation 2015 (iN2015) is a 10-year master plan to help realise the potential of ICTs over the next decade. iN2015 is a multi-agency effort that is the result of private, public and people sector co-creation, and education reform is one part of iN2015 that will help provide the skills to ensure iN2015 is successful.

Well-defined sustainable and replicable business models will help pilot initiatives to be successfully scaled. Replicability, sustainability and scalability have proved to be the most difficult achievements for most development projects in education. Even in the developed world, countries like the UK which piloted many projects and used the findings to inform policy (Scrimshaw, 1998; Somekh et al., 2005, 2006) have found that in implementing a country-wide deployment of ICT infrastructure, content and teacher training, ICT use is improving but not embedded in the curriculum universally despite the level of funding (Becta, 2006). Furthermore this level of government funding for ICT is unsustainable (Lucey, quoted in Sirius, 2006). In a developing country, sustainability and replicability will require the full engagement and involvement of all relevant stakeholders. This will include NGOs as well as national and local business support and sponsorship to identify innovative ways of using resources in schools effectively and to the full.

### The education model

Clear roles and beliefs about education in the context of both local and national needs are essential in developing an educational model for development and in which ICT requirements can be located. There is international consensus that for education to be successful, learning should be an active process that involves collaboration, problem solving and critical thinking with mentor support from teachers. This is in preference to the behaviourist model of learning that is believed to persist in so many countries in which teachers are transmitters of knowledge and students are passive recipients (UNESCO, 2005; James, 2002; O'Sullivan, 2003).

Whatever the assumptions or realities, the overall direction many governments want to pursue is towards a constructivist model of learning that places learners at the centre and acknowledges student autonomy as an essential component in the development of any society – knowledge or otherwise. Learning to learn is a vital component of any learner-centric model, but to be successful the role of teachers in facilitating such a learning environment has to move from a transmission approach, where the teacher is perceived as the font of all knowledge, to one where learners acquire knowledge through interaction with a wide range of resources. Teachers are usually more expert in the subjects that students study, and so if they are well trained and prepared they are able to provide the learner with the scaffolding that is necessary to take them on to the next stage in their learning. For ICT in education to be successful and embedded into teaching and learning, it is therefore important for it to be included in pre- and in-service teacher training.

For transformation strategies towards a more effective education model, there needs to be a holistic approach in which the seven critical elements identified in Figure 7.4 are in place. The educational model takes a central role in which connectivity, technology, content, leadership development and teacher training are then focused and aligned to support the realisation of the model. This implies that:

- the curriculum is relevant and up to date, with assessment structures that measure the skills and knowledge needed for the social and cultural context and for the workplace;

- professional development of teachers is provided to facilitate adoption of teaching methods that meet the demands of a new educational model as well as ensuring that ICT and other skills are sufficient to improve the quality of student learning;

- leadership development and change management strategies are in place;

- administrative processes for efficiency and transparency and for improved productivity are implemented;

- infrastructure such as buildings, ICT, security and maintenance is available and in good repair;

- a learning environment exists that supports the educational model, including involvement and engagement of the community and the family, and school and classroom organisation;

- monitoring and evaluation of implementations are in place, so that effectiveness can be measured and interventions made where necessary.

International experience confirms that training teachers or altering the curriculum on their own are not sufficient to improve learning outcomes (Fullan, 2000; Goodlad, 1990). This suggests that offers of support to contribute to one of the elements outlined in the model in Figure 7.4 should be considered only if there are offers of support for the other elements for system-wide implementation, or if the government has developed a strategy and has the funding for holistic change that includes all elements, including the implementation of ICT.

### Professional development of teachers

Teacher development is the most important aspect of education reform, but on its own is insufficient for systemic change. It has to fit into the larger education reform context, as countries design and redevelop their educational systems to produce the 21st-century skills required for a competitive workforce and to promote social cohesion (DfES, 2003; ILO, 2000). If EFA goals are to be met then there is an estimated teacher shortage in developing countries of between 2.4 and 4 million (UNESCO, 2006, p. 3). This means that not only is recruiting and training new teachers a priority, but also that sufficient emphasis is placed on teacher retention. It is critically important that the quality of their initial and in-service training is such that teachers are able to deal with large classes yet still produce the best learning outcomes for their students with limited resources. This requires a professional development programme that is targeted and focused on each teacher's individual needs while recognising the difficulties that might exist in doing so.

There are also considerations about the level of resources committed to in-service in relation to pre-service teacher education. Unwin (2004) provides an analysis of the benefits of each, referring to the high costs of maintaining initial teacher training establishments and the drawbacks of school-based teacher training. He argues that ICT should be introduced first in pre-service teacher training and that the facilities in these institutions should be made available to in-service teachers to develop and enhance their skills. What is important is that teachers receive continued support in developing pedagogy and integrating ICTs in their teaching.

To help plan the development of teachers' ICT knowledge and skills, UNESCO (2008) launched an ICT competency framework for teachers in January 2008 aimed at supporting governments to design ways in which to improve teachers' practice, particularly in developing countries. These standards do not merely focus on ICT skills but aim to combine them with innovations in pedagogy, curriculum, and school organisation. The framework is designed for the professional development of teachers to improve their skills and to embed ICT resources to improve their teaching, collaborate with colleagues, and perhaps ultimately become leaders of innovation in their institutions. While the UNESCO project specifies the competences needed to realise these goals and objectives, it will be up to approved governmental, non-governmental and private providers to deliver appropriate training for these competences. The intention of the standards is to guide these providers in constructing or revising their learning materials in support of these goals. The standards will also enable teacher development decision-makers to assess how these course offerings map onto required competences in their country, and thereby help to drive the development of specific skills for the teaching workforce that are appropriate to the profession and to national economic and social development goals.

The standards also recognise that each country's education system is at a different level and each teacher, depending on their role in the school and the subjects they teach, will have differing needs. The standards are therefore set across three levels defined as technology literacy, knowledge deepening and knowledge creation:

- *technology literacy approach*: increase the technological uptake of the workforce by incorporating technology skills in the curriculum;
- *knowledge deepening approach*: increase the ability of the workforce to use knowledge to add value to economic output by applying it to solve complex, real-world problems;
- *knowledge creation approach*: increase the ability of the workforce to innovate and produce new knowledge and the ability of citizens to benefit from this new knowledge.

Moving across the approaches, students acquire increasingly sophisticated skills needed to support economic growth and an improved standard of living. Each approach has different implications for education reform and improvement and how that affects the other five components of the education system: pedagogy, teacher practice and professional development, curriculum and assessment, and school organisation and administration. ICT plays a different role in each of these approaches. Figure 7.5 sets out the component under each approach and the details of each component are developed into a set of competency statements by which training programmes can be matched as well supporting policy formulation.

Many countries devolve teacher professional development to the school or local education authority. While this may produce targeted and focused training relevant to local needs, the quality of that training is often variable. When professional development is designated centrally, teachers can feel overwhelmed, over-trained and in receipt of training in areas that are irrelevant to them. In such cases where educational reform is being instigated and, especially in the pilot stage, teachers may find themselves called at a moment's notice to attend a professional development course, they are unaware of the nature and purpose of the training they are attending and are not given adequate notice to make suitable arrangements so they can attend (Selinger, 2006).

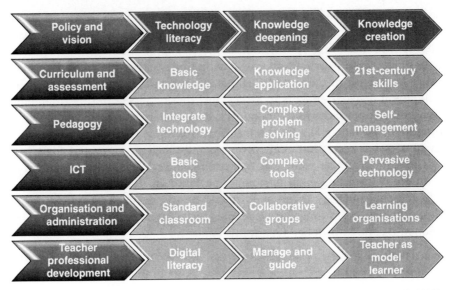

Figure 7.5 *UNESCO ICT competency framework for teachers* (*source:* UNESCO, 2008).

Sequencing and timing of training can also be a problem because lack of coordination often means that teachers do not get access to a computer to develop and consolidate the skills they have learnt until some time after they have received training, by which time they have forgotten much of what they were taught. Additionally, there is often no follow-up support after teachers have tried to implement new skills and try out novel teaching methods, which means that there is less motivation to continue to do so. When training primary teachers in Namibia, O'Sullivan (2002) found that follow-up was an essential contributory factor to teachers implementing new practices and improving their teaching. In her study of a three-year professional development programme for unqualified and under-qualified primary teachers in Namibia, her strategies for follow-up included grading, classroom observation, and trainer's use of pressure and/or support in follow-up. However, she found that teachers' impoverished educational and professional background made it difficult for them to reflect, in the Western sense, on their lessons and that the shortage of teachers limited the intensity of follow-up support that could be provided to make a real difference.

In evaluating the Jordan Education Initiative, the importance of teacher-to-teacher support in the process of teacher change was recognised, and as a result the Ministry of Education endorsed the development of a group of Jordanian 'master' teachers trained by CADER (Changeagent for Arab Development and Education Reform, http://www.caderco.com), a collaborative venture between Dutch and Jordanian teacher educators. These master teachers work alongside classroom teachers, advising and supporting them in changing their pedagogical approach with the support of ICT-based solutions. This model also accords with Larry Cuban's (2003) view that in-classroom support is paramount to teacher success in changing their practice. The master teachers model good practice alongside classroom teachers, and because they have taught in the Jordanian school system, they are aware of the challenges that teachers there face.

Location of training is also a contributory factor as teachers are not always able to travel the distances required because of economic as well as social reasons. Sometimes teachers who attend training are not those who have been targeted and the attendance at training sessions is generally very low (Selinger et al., 2006). Sometimes this is due to the fact that designated teachers are no longer available because they are moved to other schools, and this reflects a lack of coordination that can occur when new processes are being set up. Issues such as this indicate the importance of the need for greater coordination and planning with all stakeholders.

Additionally, if no quality-control procedures are in place, there will be variation in the quality of training. Overall coordination for teacher training needs to be both taken up by the Ministry of Education and devolved to professional development centres, where they exist; otherwise teachers will not have a coherent training programme. School principals also need to be consulted to ensure that training is relevant to the school, and each teacher needs to be in a position to understand their own professional development needs and work with their principal and their training centre to define their own training plan and progression (see for example O'Sullivan, 2003).

Teacher training is expensive. Consideration has been given to cheaper alternatives by using ICT to provide online or CD-based courses in professional development as well as video case studies of best practice, radio programmes about teaching or supported teaching as in the Open Learning Systems Education Trust (OLSET) model (UNESCO, 2001, pp. 21–2). Teachers in one school can undertake professional development together, thus helping to reduce costs, but there still needs to be some face-to-face support and 'clinics' are necessary in which teachers are able to voice concerns, share resources and teaching ideas, as well as seek technical support or be introduced to new resources. Where possible and where internet connectivity is available, online mentor and peer support and collaboration fora can also be made available.

### School leadership and change management

If teacher training is going to be effective and teachers put their new-found skills into practice, then recognition of the role that school principals play is vital. In many professional development programmes the focus is often only on training teachers and not on training school leaders. There is considerable international research that demonstrates the importance of school principals' vision and leadership if they are to provide the environment to support their staff (Fullan, 2001; Leithwood et al., 1999; Selinger et al., 2006).

Fostering a school climate in which the introduction of technology brings excitement and enthusiasm is important in ensuring the success of any initiative, and it is only by getting principals' buy-in and support that this will happen. Before training teachers, it is therefore prudent to conduct training programmes for school principals that address: the introduction of technology into their schools; what their role as a principal is in technology integration in their school; how they can support and encourage staff to undergo training and to integrate e-curricula in the classroom, as well as using technology as a catalyst to improve teaching and learning.

However, even this is not enough. Change management has come to be recognised as a crucial element in educational development. This is not just at the school level but also within Ministries of Education. Administrators and government education officials are often omitted from any professional development programmes. The Minister of Education may buy into education reform and see the role that ICT can play in helping the country achieve a better-quality education, improve the management and administration of schools, and supplement outdated textbooks with electronic resources, but the people who have to implement the reform initiatives do not always share or understand the vision, nor do they always have the capabilities to work with the schools and other stakeholders to ensure the implementations take place in a timely and effective manner. Training for administrators is therefore a critical component of education reform that perhaps should come before teacher development and at the same time as school principal development.

Follow-up training is important for teachers to refresh their skills and to bring up any concerns and questions about integration of technology. If possible this training can be made more accessible and relevant if it is conducted on-site in selected schools for teachers and principals in an area. Finally teachers need to feel valued and rewarded for their efforts to improve. This involves accrediting them for any training they have undertaken and financial rewards for successful implementation of new pedagogies or content. In many developing countries the financial incentives offered to teachers are usually very low which leads many to focus their energies on other jobs or out-of-school tutoring to provide for their families. If tutoring is lucrative relative to their teacher salary, then any incentive to improve their teaching in school without financial reward is going to be unsuccessful.

The case study on pages 228–9 describes how ICT is being introduced into mathematics and science teaching in schools in Rwanda as part of EdQual, a five-country initiative led by Bristol University in the UK. The programme in Rwanda recognises that ICT resources are in short supply, so they have chosen to focus on two subjects in negotiation with the government. The researchers also understand the low level of teachers' ICT skills, so have chosen to focus on one application for each subject: spreadsheets in mathematics and science simulations. This strategy protects teachers from cognitive overload yet introduces them, through well-selected applications, to the power of ICT in helping to bring concepts alive for their students and consequently improve learning and retention.

Distance education for teacher training has long been considered appropriate for developing countries where the shortage of teachers makes it difficult to bring them out of school for training and where teachers' skills need to be updated. ICT can facilitate this through online resources, CD-ROMs, television and audio (Perraton et al., 2002; Mattson, 2006). Indeed, with an increasing move to decentralisation of teacher education, ICT has an increasingly important role to play in linking professional development centres through centralised support, by providing access to remote resources and through the sharing of good practices.

Distance learning is also being used for initial teacher training for new and serving teachers with few or no qualifications. These untrained teachers are often in countries in post-conflict situations or in refugee camps (Imfundo, 2001; Mattson, 2006). Some are receiving very little or no support as these teachers are based in countries where, for various reasons, education is under-funded by donors (Save the Children, 2007). ICT can improve distance learning by providing remote access to tutors and supporting school-based teacher training. In the case study on pages 230–1 Bernadette Robinson describes the China Gansu Basic Education Project in which ICT was used to support school-based teachers' learning resources centres.

ICT is also critically important in initial teacher training (Unwin, 2004). Implementing ICT in schools may well be easier in situations where teachers have undertaken a course in their initial training that includes the use of ICT for teaching and learning, so that they come to their first posts with some knowledge, awareness and understanding of the role of ICT in education. These new teachers are able to support the ICT developments and work alongside their colleagues as mentors and coaches in the use of ICT for both professional and personal use. A study in the UK (Selinger, 1996) found that beginning teachers who had been taught how to use ICT for teaching and learning became the champions for ICT use when they entered their first teaching posts. Their ICT skills made them valuable colleagues which both gave them confidence in their abilities and increased their value to the school. In Asia, UNESCO has also recognised the value of prepared beginning teachers and has launched an initiative across initial teacher training institutions for post-primary teachers in ten countries entitled 'Preparing the next generation of teachers through ICT' (http://www.unescobkk.org/index.php?id = 3430).

### Curriculum and assessment

The curriculum debate was discussed earlier, focusing on what to teach for international competitiveness and comparison. Curricula relevance is not

(continued on page 232)

# Case study: ICT and education in Rwanda

Alphonse Uworwabayeho, Jolly Rubagiza and Edmond Were

*Lecturer and Senior Lecturers at the Kigali Institute of Education, Rwanda*

Rosamund Sutherland

*Professor of Education, University of Bristol, UK*

ICT is often viewed as being an important tool for building Rwanda's prosperity, reducing poverty and improving the quality of life for all people, with a particular focus on disadvantaged groups. Part of this ambitious programme lies in the extension of basic education to children up to the age of 15 or 16, and provision of computers to schools, with a particular emphasis on improving science and mathematics education. Within this context, we are working on a DFID-funded project (led by a Rwandan team and including partners from Chile, the UK and South Africa) which aims to develop and evaluate strategies for effective introduction and use of ICT to support teaching and learning of mathematics and science in basic education. A particular focus is to build teacher capacity on how to exploit the available technology for teaching and learning. Additionally the team is working with policy makers to support the implementation of ICT in education policy. The project centres around an interactive and iterative model of teacher development in which groups of teachers, teacher educators and researchers work together to design and evaluate learning initiatives (see Figure 7.6). This builds on both the InterActive Education project (Sutherland *et al.*, 2004) and research and development work in Chile (The Atenea Project, Moënne *et al.*, 2004).

In order to understand what might be possible in Rwandan schools the team visited a sample of rural and urban primary and secondary schools in May 2006. At this time we found that in many cases computers available in schools were relatively old, with the majority of computers running Windows 98. Often the only software available was Microsoft Office and some games, with CD-ROMs and internet access often not working. However, a small number of schools visited were very well resourced by international standards. In the urban areas young people and teachers often had the opportunity to use internet cafés outside school. Despite the relative lack of resources we found in some schools that teachers were working to exploit the potential of the available technology. For example, in Gahini Primary School (a francophone school with a population of 868 students) three computers located in the principal's office were being used to introduce students to using computers, with the teachers working after school and in the holidays to try things out and learn for themselves. From these visits six schools were chosen to be involved in the first phase of

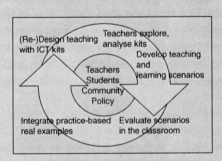

Figure 7.6 *Iterative model for teacher development.*

the project, with four of these schools being in disadvantaged areas with minimum levels of technology and electricity available, and two of these being well equipped with technology. Three of the chosen schools are in rural areas and three are in urban areas.

Exploiting available resources: computers in the principal's office at Gahini Primary School.

Teachers engage with and evaluate a science simulation.

The interactive and iterative model of teacher development involves a partnership of teachers, teacher educators and researchers working together to evaluate and develop ICT-based scenarios for learning science and mathematics. As a starting point, at the first workshop with teachers in November 2006 the team were offered a set of mathematics and science scenarios that had been used successfully in Chile and England. These included work with spreadsheets for learning mathematics and work with simulations for learning science. The scenarios incorporated guidelines for ways of working with the ICT resources in the classroom. Within the workshop the participating teachers developed and critically evaluated the scenarios from the perspective of using them with their own students and presented their ideas to other members of the workshop for feedback. Following the workshop, teachers have been developing these scenarios by using them in their own classrooms. The overall aim is that at a second workshop teachers will be offered new scenarios that have been explicitly developed in and for the Rwandan context. These learning scenarios are being evaluated using video recordings of classroom teaching and learning processes, together with the use of more standard assessment tools.

It is clear that the potential success of the project relates to the support that teachers are given by members of the research and development team, as explained by a teacher at the first workshop: 'I am of the view that you need to keep consistent communication with teachers. You have to take into account that teachers have a lot of work. Even when someone does something in a workshop, he or she may not put this into practice. You have to keep in touch. We say that we shall do things, and we may give you many excuses. So much as the headteachers are supportive please be in touch with us.'

(*Source:* Rosamund Sutherland, for all figures and photographs in this case study.)

# Case study: EU-China GBEP – an ICT-supported system for school-based professional development

Bernadette Robinson

*Special Professor, UNESCO Centre for Comparative Education Research, University of Nottingham, UK*

ICT resource centres for teachers have been growing as a means of supporting teacher development, but sometimes fail, because they are provided either as an add-on or as an inessential or isolated element of in-service provision. This is a threat to their sustainability. In the EU-China Gansu Basic Education Project (EU-China GBEP) (2002–2006), a systems approach was taken in establishing teachers' learning resource centres (TLRCs) in rural schools. The project's purpose was to help improve the quality of basic education in the poorest 41 of all 86 counties in Gansu (a poor province in north-west China). It aimed to assist teachers to prepare for a new national curriculum and to improve their teaching methods (moving to active learning, student-centred learning, problem solving and creativity from more teacher-centred, rote-learning methods). However, most of the teachers and headteachers lived in rural areas, some in remote and mountainous villages. The usual way of providing in-service training (through out-of-service residential courses of varying length at county and provincial level) was infrequent, costly and slow to reach all teachers. In the rural schools, teachers had few or no resources for their professional learning – often the school textbooks were the only resource for teachers.

To solve the problem of lack of access to in-service education and a scarcity of local learning resources, the EU-China GBEP set up a school-based system of ICT-supported TLRCs, providing more than 90,000 teachers and headteachers with opportunities for professional development. Altogether, 686 TLRCs were set up at primary and junior-secondary schools. Each district typically contained 12–20 large and small village schools and each TLRC served as an in-service centre or hub for them. Each TLRC was provided with a set of equipment (television, satellite dish, satellite software, two computers, laser printer, portable hard disk, VCD-player, CD-rewriter, modem, digital camera) and 232 items of learning resources (print, CD-ROM and VCD). The equipment enabled teachers to access, download and store information, view and record satellite television and video programmes, and use computers and the digital camera to create teaching materials and individual teacher portfolios.

Provision of the equipment alone would not have achieved the intended purpose for the TLRCs, and so the EU-China GBEP developed human and organisational systems to create a positive dynamic for TLRC activity (Figure 7.7). This integrated the TLRCs within the administrative structures for education at different levels (provincial, county, district and school) as well as within the structures for teacher management and in-service education. Each TLRC had a core team whose role was to manage the centre and mobilise teachers, under the supervision of a TLRC management committee. The core team consisted of the headteacher (as director), a teacher responsible for technical support, and one or two 'backbone' teachers responsible for learning support to other teachers. The TLRCs were supported by county-level officers and by mobile training teams from provincial and county levels. These teams travelled to TLRCs on

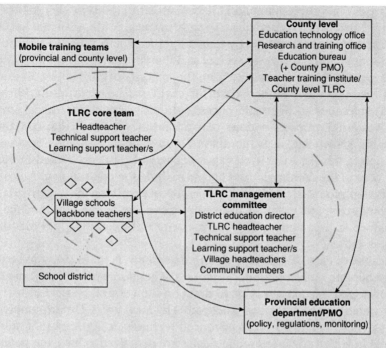

Figure 7.7 *System for the management and support of TLRCs, Gansu* (*source:* Bernadette Robinson).

an occasional basis and held workshops there, provided demonstration lessons or gave feedback on local teachers' lessons, gave coaching in the use of ICT and its integration into teaching, and solved problems. Teachers' participation in TLRC activities was officially recognised as part of their fulfilment of continuing education requirements each year and, in some counties, participation in TLRC activities for teachers and headteachers was a condition of promotion. This helped to ensure that the TLRCs were active with good rates of participation.

In developing the TLRCs, training was given a strong emphasis. It was provided mainly on three aspects: the use and management of ICT at the TLRCs and its integration into teaching; the new curriculum and teaching methods; and school-based training. Training was provided for all involved in establishing and running the TLRC system: technical support teachers and learning support teachers at the TLRC; headteachers in their roles of TLRC manager and school manager; county-level administrators on the management and support of TLRCs; teacher trainers at provincial and county-level institutions, mobile training teams, county-level units within the County Education Department and materials developers at the provincial level. Reporting and record-keeping systems were set up at county and TLRC level, and workshops and conferences were organised for sharing experience and materials developed by teachers.

Through the TLRC system, a platform for rural teacher in-service education has been developed for nearly half of Gansu's counties. This is now being further extended by other counties joining in this approach. It has the potential to be a province-wide system and, as connectivity improves, to include more online services for rural teachers.

just an ICT-based phenomenon. Jeevanantham (1998, p. 217) argues, for example, that because curricula currently in use at South African schools are still Eurocentric in nature, 'they reflect the life experiences and culture of a small segment of our diverse society and thereby announce as insignificant those experiences that emanate from the majority of our people'. To explain what he means by 'Eurocentrism of curricula' he cites Muthukrishna's (1995) reference to linguistic codes, cultural assumptions, social images and Western/European notions that underpin what it is that constitutes desirable knowledge. Jeevanantham (1998, p. 218) also adds another dimension to this list – the irrelevance of curricula that 'are rooted in the experiences of the dominant class and so exclude the cultural practices of the dominated group'. He forcefully adds, 'By maintaining such curricula, we are reinforcing and creating anew, repressive conditions that produce and reproduce silence among the vast majority of humanity' (Jeevanantham, 1998, p. 218).

Because of ease of delivery, electronic content is more likely to be used across borders than traditional resources. Therefore such content needs to be developed in such a way as to draw on the cultural context of learners and teachers, or be sufficiently adaptable by local users. Unfortunately this is rare; those countries more advanced technologically impose a cultural context in which advanced technologies are perceived to have the potential to improve the learning context for those whose educational systems are yet to develop, and are failing to look behind to ensure that all partners derive benefits. From the perspective of the less advanced countries these developments are often considered to be culturally imperialistic and technology determinist (Gibson and Selinger, 2005).

### Why digitise?

There is a danger in thinking that putting all resources into electronic format will solve the problems of outdated and irrelevant textbooks and teaching. The language issues referred to earlier are just one consideration, but thought also needs to be given to the relevance of much of the electronically available content and why it should be in an electronic format. There are concepts that are too fast or too small to be seen with the naked eye, and the opportunity to model these or to rotate objects and see through them is obviously not possible in conventional textbooks. The development of graphic animation through computer modelling has meant that young children can see food being swallowed and digested; the passing of electrical current can be modelled by some animation to illustrate how electricity is not 'used up' when it passes through a light bulb. However, publishers and donors are unable to develop content that is relevant to every context, and not all teachers will have time or motivation to develop their own resources even when they are given a bank of resources tailored to their needs and an electronic environment in which to do so. If teachers can work together in collaborative virtual environments like the Teachers without Borders toolkit (http://www.twblive.org/site) which enables teachers (and their students) to collaborate on developing lesson plans and customising resources for their classes, then it is more likely they will be motivated to develop and contextualise resources. As this environment is available both online and offline, it can ensure operability at affordable costs, since users do not need to be online to access resources once they have been developed.

A blended model of teaching is often the best scenario. This was the option selected for the Jordan Education Initiative (http://www.jei.org. jo), where expertise from the West was brought in early in the process to work with Jordanian content developers and teachers and supervisors from the Ministry of Education. Teachers of the six subjects digitised were given a laptop and data projector with wireless connectivity, and curriculum development included media that teachers could use in a whole-class situation as well as in the lab by students working on their own or in a small group, with embedded teaching ideas and professional development that would continuously support the teachers to develop their practice and help them to engage learners more productively in classroom discourse and activity (Cisco, 2007). The Jordanian e-curricula for years K–12 (kindergarten through 12th grade) was developed in line with a set of standards and guidelines that had been developed based on research on effective practice in the West, but the actual e-curricula development was undertaken in country by local media developers and teachers from Jordanian schools.

*Web-based resources*
It is often argued that considerable work and intermediation is required before digital resources found on the Web are ready for classroom consumption (Baluteau and Godinet, 2005; Gibson and Selinger, 2005). However, Sugata Mitra (2004) reports that in whatever environment he placed his 'hole in the wall' PCs, the results were the same: students soon moved from games to communication with others, to searching for information on the internet. The resources the students find come from numerous sources that are neither necessarily 'sanitised' nor tailor-made for them, and yet they are compelling enough for students to want to learn from them. Mitra's research also demonstrates that the focus on teaching digital literacy skills may be unnecessary (see Mitra's case study in Chapter 10, pp. 340–1). The children using the hole-in-the-wall kiosks teach each other the skills they need to retrieve the information they want from the internet and to communicate with others through the technology. Access to information, to people and to learning resources is what is most important in schools where there are limited ICT resources. Digital literacy skills have a place, but only on a need-to-know basis. Focusing on digital literacy in situations where there are limited ICT resources rather than focusing on access to multimedia learning resources in whole-class or small-group situations will lead

to a poorer learning environment for students and limited or inappropriate use of an expensive resource.

*Learning from the community*

Not all curricula or content need to be created electronically and put online. Much can be learnt from the community and links between communities can also be facilitated through ICT. The Gardens for Life Project (http://www.edenproject.com/education/2217.html) is one such example: initiated by the UK's Eden Project, the project aims to develop a new international learning strategy which integrates the global dimension with gardening, science teaching and school partnerships. This project brings together young people and teachers in the UK, Kenya and India to share their experience of gardening and classroom learning, integrating the global dimension into core curriculum learning. The pilot schools have all established gardens to grow food crops. Teachers have been encouraged to use the designing, development and management of gardens for teaching curriculum subjects and the global issues around food. This also means that the students have a common basis of experience and a reason to communicate with the other schools across the world.

There are additional benefits too: with so many parents in Africa dying of HIV/AIDS and related illnesses, much traditional local knowledge is fast being lost. For example, child-headed households do not learn the skills of growing their own food from their parents who were unable to pass on their knowledge before they became sick and died, and so their children could be in danger of starvation if the knowledge and wisdom of crop production is lost. The project goes well beyond the realms of a simple e-twinning project; it engages the communities to help in supporting the school garden so that skills are transferred while health and nutrition issues are addressed at the same time. The collaboration element helps promote greater global understanding especially in knowledge of the food chain, the difference in the variety of food and the ease of availability of food in different parts of the world. New skills are also shared and learnt, such as discussion around appropriate growing environments for different crops (Eden Project, 2005, para. 4).

In Kenya, the schools are reaping further benefits including the teaching of relevant curriculum; science learning is improved as students learn about how to grow plants; and students are cooking and eating their produce so nutrition is also improving. Students are also learning commerce skills as they sell surplus produce to the community. The project coordinator for Gardens for Life sums up the essence of this project: 'Plants and food, while providing for common human needs, are also fundamental to cultural diversity. Any initiative which attempts to be truly global needs to celebrate difference while emphasising commonality' (Potterton, 2005, p. 39).

Other initiatives such as the Global Gateway (http://www.global-gateway.org.uk), the Global Virtual Classroom Clubhouse (http://www.

virtualclassroom.org/clubhouse/3A.html), the Global Schoolhouse (http://www.globalschoolnet.org) and IEARN (http://www.iearn.org) are all fora where students and teachers from all over the world can collaborate on-line, finding out first hand from each other about their lives or working together on projects of mutual interest. Cultural understanding can also come through communities working together on resources that can be viewed from different perspectives. Speaking at a conference in December 2005, Professor Menachem Magidor, President of the Hebrew University of Jerusalem, said that no university was value free and that 'ethnic, religious and political views all had a part to play' (Magidor, 2005). Together, Al Quds University and the Hebrew University have created a website exploring the history of Jerusalem not just from the Arab and Jewish Israeli cultural perspectives, but also from the religious perspectives of Buddhists, Christians, Jews and Muslims. The atmosphere they created was one in which everyone was perceived as having a legitimate story to tell and as a consequence the site is all the richer for collaboration (see http://www.jerusalem-library.org). Learning from each culture and each religion together has the potential to promote the path to peace and helps avoid the violence that prevents economic development and social cohesion.

### Infrastructure
ICT solutions for schools are most effective when they are aligned with the education model the government is trying to implement. Across the developing world, country policies for technology integration in schools are reminiscent of the efforts of the western world in the 1980s. The wheel is being reinvented time and time again. The education ministry works closely with the ministries of telecommunications and of information and communication technology, yet rarely takes the lead in decision making about what ICTs go into schools and how they are deployed to achieve maximum effectiveness in improving teaching and learning.

This was well exemplified during a visit in 2005 to a North African country, where the decision to place computers in labs in primary and secondary schools had almost been taken. The thinking was that students in primary schools would have access for one hour a week and students in secondary schools would have two hours. It was thought that this would provide them with enough time to become digitally literate. There was little consideration about to what use the new digital literacy would be put and how curriculum subjects could also be taught in this time, although the decision makers anticipated that this would somehow happen as all teachers were to be trained in the use of the technology. A two-day workshop was held with experts and officials from the various ministries (few were from education) to discuss alternative solutions, but despite the overwhelming evidence presented from countries with similar cultures, the decision-making process was too far advanced to be reversed and the investment decision was taken to implement this lab-based solution.

In this scenario, there appeared to have been little or no consultation with other governments and little cognisance taken of international research into the effectiveness of different models of technology deployment in schools. It was acknowledged that the government's budget was limited and the Ministry of Education wanted to achieve equity by making sure the computer–student ratio was the same across every school in the country, so the computer lab seemed the most effective solution. For the other ministries this was also the easiest solution technically so the technology case overruled any educational rationale. What was not considered in initial deliberations within the Ministry of Education, and what the workshop urged them to think about, was to replace the labs with 'computers on wheels' (COWs) – wireless carts containing twenty or so laptop computers. The versatility of such solutions coupled with a limited number of data projectors means that not all computers are in one location with classes allowed in one at a time. Teachers are able to use a laptop for lesson preparation and personal productivity or to enhance whole-class teaching when connected to a data projector; or the laptops can be distributed over a number of classes for use by selected groups of students during the school day. The security issues around storage of laptops also offer cheaper solutions as securing a computer room is far more costly than securing a cupboard.

In contrast to the scenario above, the Jordan Education Initiative developed a model based on the research and experience of other countries. Most schools already had a computer lab and broadband over fibre was in the process of being installed in every school, so it was decided that if teaching was to change and was to provide students with the skills required for the knowledge economy, the technology needed to be in the hands of the teachers. E-curricula and training would then be provided that would support the development of this pedagogy, in addition to the 'CADER' model described above. Other technology solutions for student computer access are also being tried in Jordan: labs are being compared to COWs, which have been introduced to be used with a whole class or to be deployed across a number of classes for students to work on individual or small-group tasks.

This debate as to whether labs or laptops are the best solution for education may soon be obsolete as the computer lab is being overtaken by the flexibility and falling prices of laptops, while mobile technology is moving even faster. The advent of low-cost laptops, such as the Intel Classmate (http://www.intel.com/intel/worldahead/pdf/cmpcbrochure.pdf) and the OLPC (http://www.laptop.org) – as well as other solutions such as thin client technology which provides low-cost computing by connecting computers without hard disk, CD drive and expansion slots to a central server which holds all applications and individuals' data – have changed the options available to those planning to introduce computers into schools. Increasingly sophisticated internet-enabled PDAs have also encouraged those in developed and developing countries alike to start to re-think the optimal technology solutions and products for their schools. How-ever, if this is to happen in a productive and effective way in order to enable education transformation, then countries need to have access to the latest information about what is possible and how it can have a positive impact on learning. This will enable a government to undertake a comparative evalu-ation of the merits of each solution, given its unique cultural context and existing technology infrastructure base. One way improvements in educa-tion can be accelerated is through increased information and experience sharing between governments.

None of this negates the value of mobile phone technology, or the value of radio and TV which have been the mainstay of technology in education for many years (Trucano, 2005; OLSET, http://www.olset.org.za) (see the case study on pp. 102–3). What has happened in Jordan was premised on a reasonable level of internet access so the technology dissonance that could have been met along the way was minor. However, in other countries like Ethiopia, internet access in schools is still under development. Here the government wanted to do something to improve the quality of education in secondary schools. Older technologies such as broadcast television, video and radio all have a part to play in supporting learning, and the Ethiopian government has purchased 7,000 plasma screens for 450 secondary schools and are broadcasting over the TV network specially commissioned televi-sion enhanced by graphics and animation alongside live footage. A South African company has been involved in the production of the content (Frith, 2005; see also Hussein, 2006). This move is a far cry from the interactivity that newer technology brings, but nevertheless it is claimed by those in-volved that it has made a real impact on students' motivation, interest and achievement in schools (an evaluation of the impact is currently under way). The next stage is to use the plasma screens for internet-streamed digital video, including instructional films and quizzes, as soon as the planned broadband network is rolled out (Frith, 2005). In countries where textbooks are limited, teacher quality is variable and there is a wide-scale shortage of qualified teachers, any resources that can enhance knowledge are welcome and capacity-building tools are even more in demand.

### Monitoring and evaluation
The lack of sound evidence about teaching styles has already been high-lighted. In fact monitoring and evaluation of education reform initiatives in many developing countries is piecemeal and often poorly conducted (Wagner et al., 2005). There are few baseline studies, and high costs of ro-bust monitoring and rigorous evaluations and timeframes that are too short mean a loss of valuable learning that can provide evidence of good, as well as ineffective, ICT-focused interventions (Farrell and Isaacs, 2007). Wagner

(2005, p. 5–9) thus comments that 'there is also a well-known ignorance of the consequences or impact of ICTs on education goals and targets' and that 'A relevant and credible knowledge base is an essential part in helping policy makers make effective decisions in ICT4E'. Unwin (2005, p. 45) likewise suggests that well-managed monitoring and evaluation is essential for effective implementation and that 'monitoring and evaluation activities themselves also have a significant influence on educational management and enhanced capacity building in poor countries'. Wagner *et al.* (2005, p. 9) provide a valuable conceptual framework for monitoring and evaluation (Figure 7.8). James and Miller (2005, p. 57) suggest further that the monitoring and evaluation process should be factored into the planning of an education programme; that 'appropriate, realistic and measurable indicators' are selected for monitoring; that monitoring and evaluation decisions should be made jointly between all the stakeholders and that approximately 10 per cent of total project costs should be allocated for monitoring and evaluation.

A final important point to note about monitoring and evaluation is that it can play a valuable role in ensuring transparency and accountability in the delivery of any ICT-based initiatives. Further, there is some evidence that ICT-based Education Management Information Systems (EMIS) can also help to improve the efficiency of delivery of education systems as well as increasing teacher productivity (Imfundo, 2001).

## External involvement in enhancing educational delivery
The private sector has been very important in initiating ICT activities in education, and this final section addresses some of the complexities of the processes involved (see also Chapter 5). It also briefly seeks to emphasise the importance of ICTs in supporting people with special educational needs, as well as learning for those outside formal primary and secondary education.

### *The role of the private sector*
In an increasingly globalised world of multinational corporations, the private sector has begun to play a significant role in educational development from curricula to teacher training. The JEI is a prime example of the private sector partnering with governments. The technology industry has played a significant role in curriculum development in both developed and developing countries, with companies such as Microsoft (http://www.microsoftitacademy.com) and Cisco (http://cisco.netacad.net) offering IT curricula to schools and colleges that provide vendor qualifications and immediate job opportunities on leaving formal education. Additionally, Intel offers a teacher training programme and electronic content for mathematics and science (http://www.intel.com/education/K12Education/index.htm); IBM has recently launched a change management programme for education (http://www.reinventingeducation.org/RE3Web), while Oracle

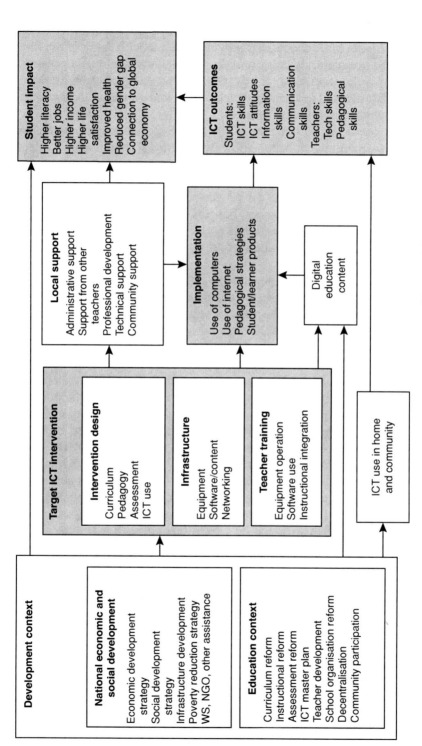

Figure 7.8 *Conceptual framework for ICT monitoring and evaluation in education* (*source*: Wagner *et al.*, 2005).

has a collaboration tool for use across education (http://www.think.com). For some, this may look like the commodification and takeover of education by global corporations, whereas others see it as an opportunity to put relevant curricula into schools that provide students with some of the 21st-century skills not currently being provided by the formal education system. In many cases the international private sector working with the local private sector has also led to capacity development and growth of local companies, and created employment opportunities.

However, there can be tensions in such multi-stakeholder partnerships. Business investment in education will only continue if shareholders can see quick results for the social investments made, whereas education moves at a much slower pace and results often take more time to come to fruition. What is needed is a 'quick win' for private-sector donors in order to maintain their interest and involvement, but it is also important for the private sector to realise that an intervention in education reform will affect a child's life chances and that caution and careful research is needed before an intervention is made.

The NEPAD (http://www.nepad.org) e-Schools demonstration initiative is an example of private-sector engagement in developing countries. Here African governments, the private sector, foundations, development agencies and civil society organisations have come together for a common technology project developed and driven by Africans for Africa. Five industry-led consortia were selected to set up between them year-10 classes in six schools in each of 16 African countries with all the necessary technology, content, training and infrastructure to enable teachers and students to acquire digital literacy and for teachers to use technology to enhance teaching and learning in health education, mathematics, science, business studies and a second language. The process is being evaluated by the Commonwealth of Learning, and it is intended that the most effective solutions will form the basis for the potential roll-out to 600,000 schools across the continent. The private-sector consortia are led by industry giants but they have encouraged local partners to join their consortia so both can learn from each other and provide the best solutions for each country's social, economic and geographical context. An interim evaluation of the NEPAD e-Schools initiative (Farrell et al., 2007) has suggested that while there have been some successes, salutary lessons have also been learnt, most notably that such initiatives take longer to deliver than expected, that there needs to be effective management and leadership, that many assumptions about ICT and education in Africa have been proved to be invalid, that civil society needs to be involved in such initiatives if they are to be successful, and that not all countries were equally prepared to take on a project of this nature (for a wider review of ICT and education in Africa, see also Farrell and Isaacs, 2007).

Bilateral and multilateral donors are very important in the context of these partnerships. The international private sector is not always willing or able to donate products beyond a certain value. They will offer expertise in business processes as well as technical and educational consultancy and training and development programmes. For continuous development and implementation of an education reform strategy, funds are also needed and therefore donors have to be engaged and their policies and the government policies aligned.

### *Beyond basic education*

In a review of good practice in the education of children with special needs, Casely-Hayford and Lynch (2003) highlight the plight of children in developing countries who have disabilities or special educational needs, and note that fewer than 2 per cent of children with disabilities are in school. In the developed world ICT has brought education to children with special needs in unprecedented ways and this impact needs to be highlighted so that special needs are included in education reform policies. There are low-cost ways of helping children with disabilities in developing countries, whether their impairment is mental, physical or sensory, but this requires greater awareness on the part of donors of their availability and the need to include this sector in aid programmes.

MDG 2 focuses on primary or basic education, which is necessary yet insufficient for real economic growth and development. The UNESCO EFA monitoring report for 2007 (UNESCO, 2006) noted an increasing pressure on the need to expand secondary schooling, but despite this gross enrolment rates are still low. They argue that 'Low numbers of secondary places slow the achievement of universal primary education because they reduce the incentive to complete primary school' (UNESCO, 2006, p. 3). The number of children of primary age not in school has fallen from 84 million in 1994 to 77 million in 2004, but this improvement is not uniform, and it is in sub-Saharan Africa where the increase in number attending primary school has risen the least (UNESCO, 2006, p. 11).

In a report published on skills development in sub-Saharan Africa by the World Bank (Johanson and Adams, 2004, p. xv) it was recognised that:

> In no region other than Africa is the trade-off drawn more sharply between the achievement of skills development with TVET and the provision of universal basic education. Both are important to economic growth and poverty reduction, but the fiscal and administrative capacity of the state to meet both goals is limited.

Skills development for youth who are unable for financial, economic or social reasons to attend secondary education provides them with opportunities for jobs only as long as the skills they learn are needed in the community.

Higher education in many African countries is in disarray. A recent report (Polgreen, 2007) highlighted the overcrowding and the lack of resources that has occurred as funding has been diverted to achieve UPE. Add to this the brain drain, then the demise of universities will continue. The Open Education Resources initiative funded predominantly by the Hewlett Foundation (2007) is seeking to help address this problem, but commentators have noted that the cultural imperialism of the English-speaking West will predominate unless more developing countries are involved in co-production. Currently less than 10 per cent of the $68 million of Hewlett funding goes to projects involving developing nations (Mulder, 2007). Coupled with this, the lack of internet access and power supply will exclude so many potential learners. Mobile phone technologies may hold the key.

## Conclusions

According to research by UNESCO (2003), globalisation tends to push governments away from equity-driven reforms, because it increases the pay-off to high-level skills relative to lower-level skills. This reduces the complementarity between equity and competitiveness-driven reforms, and in most developing countries finance-driven reforms dominate educational change in the new globalised economic environment. Such reforms tend to increase inequity in the delivery of educational services. The demand for and prioritisation of UPE as a result of the UN Millennium Summit in September 2000 has meant that equity, to some extent, has had to be balanced against the need for global competitiveness.

Lady Murrugurra from Peru (2005, para. 7) in a discussion on the impact of technology suggests that the 'internet and other ICT resources will play a contributing role in linking youth, the future leaders and prompting new youth activism'. She believes ICT has the potential for 'leapfrogging' in developing countries to accelerate the development of both the young and adult generations, 'to empower them to access and to use information, which was for long a barrier, to learn faster and eventually to stimulate local entrepreneurship for the benefit of their local communities' (Murrugurra, 2005, para. 8). If ICT in education is to have such a real and measurable impact, then realistic time-scales need to be set for results to be achieved. Evidence of the time taken and the impact of implementation of ICT in education in the developed world demonstrates this very well. However, unless the evaluation results of initiatives across the world are taken into account, few lessons will be learnt and the developing world will make expensive mistakes they simply cannot afford to make.

Transparency and coordination of efforts are also essential, and the work of coordinating efforts in developing countries, bringing partners to the table and involving local and international NGOs, is vital. Initiatives such as the Partnerships for Education programme led by the World Economic Forum and UNESCO (http://www.pfore.org) may well be one of the ways forward. They can help avoid isolated, unsustainable and overlapping projects that are difficult to replicate, and lead to the appropriate support of sector-wide approaches to education reform. Here again ICT can play a vital role in connecting all the stakeholders and will avoid duplication of effort. ICT tools too can help in prioritising and mapping various initiatives, ensuring that ICT and related infrastructure is implemented, teachers are trained and electronic resources are available at the appropriate time and in the best sequence, so that the integration of ICT into teaching and learning is as seamless as possible, brings about the desired and culturally relevant change in pedagogy and, above all, ensures that local ownership is embraced as early as possible.

## Key readings

Brown, A. and Davis, N. (eds) (2004) *World Yearbook of Education 2004: digital technologies, communities and education.* London: Kogan Page

Cuban, L. (2003) *Oversold and Underused: computers in classrooms.* Cambridge, MA: Harvard University Press

Farrell, G., Isaacs, S. and Trucano, M. (2007) *The NEPAD e-Schools Demonstration Project: a work in progress.* Washington, DC: infoDev

Maddux, C.D., Johnson, D.L. and Willis, J.W. (1997) *Educational Computing: learning with tomorrow's technologies* (2nd edn). Needham Heights, MA: Allyn and Bacon

Mattson, E. (2006) *Field-Based Models of Primary Teacher Training. Case studies of student support systems from sub-Saharan Africa.* London: Department for International Development

Perraton, H., Robinson, B. and Creed, C. (2002) *Teacher Education Through Distance Learning: technology, curriculum, cost, evaluation.* Paris: UNESCO

UNESCO (2005) *Education for All: the quality imperative. EFA Global Monitoring Report 2005.* Paris: UNESCO

## References

Baluteau, F. and Godinet, H. (2005) Netlearning: from formal curriculum to connected curriculum. *Proceedings of WCCE 2005*, University of Stellenbosch, Cape Town, South Africa, 4–7 July 2005

Becta (2006) *The Becta Review 2006. Evidence on the Progress of ICT in Education.* Coventry: Becta (http://publications.becta.org.uk/download.cfm?resID=25948)

Bruner, J. (1996) *The Culture of Education.* Cambridge, MA: Harvard University Press

Bruns, B., Mingat, A. and Rakotomala, R. (2003) *Achieving Universal Primary Education by 2015: a chance for every child.* Washington, DC: The World Bank

Casely-Hayford, L. and Lynch, P. (2003) *A Review of Good Practice in ICT and Special Educational Needs in Africa.* An Imfundo KnowledgeBank Initiative. London: DFID (http://imfundo.digitalbrain.com/imfundo/web/papers/SEN/SENPHASE1FINAL.pdf, accessed 16 June 2007)

Castells, M. (2000) *The Rise of the Network Society (The Information Age: economy, society and culture,* vol. 1, 2nd edn). Oxford: Blackwell

Cisco (2007) *The Jordan Education Initiative Overview.* White Paper. London: Cisco

Collier, V.P. (1995) Acquiring a second language for school. *Directions in Language and Education*, 1 (4). National Clearinghouse for Bilingual Education (http://forbin.qc.edu/ECP/bilingualcenter/Newsletters/Acquiring2ndLangV3-1.pdf)

Cornu, B. (1995) New technologies: integration into education. In *Integrating Information Technology into Education*, ed. D. Watson and D. Tinsley. London: Chapman and Hall, pp. 3–11

Cuban, L. (2003) *Oversold and Underused: computers in classrooms*. Cambridge, MA: Harvard University Press

Delors, J. (1996) *Learning: the treasure within*. Report to UNESCO of the International Commission on Education for the Twenty-first Century. Paris: UNESCO

Dervis, K. (2007) Keynote address at the International Labour Organization 11th African Regional Meeting Addis Ababa, 25 April 2007 (http://content.undp.org/go/newsroom/2007/april/dervis-ilo-african-meeting-20070425.en;jsessionid = ax bWzt8vXD9)

DfES (2003) *21st Century Skills: realising our potential. Individuals, employers, nation*. London: Department for Education and Skills

Economist Intelligence Unit (2006) *Foresight 2020: economic, industry and corporate trends*. London: EIU

Eden Project (2005) *Gardens for Life* (http://www.edenproject.com/3701_5874.htm, accessed 29 January 2006)

Farrell, G. and Isaacs, S. (2007) *Survey of ICT and Education in Africa*. Washington, DC: *infoDev* (http://www.infodev.org/en/Publication.353.html)

Farrell, G., Isaacs, S. and Trucano, M. (2007) *The NEPAD e-Schools Demonstration Project: a Work in Progress*. Washington, DC: *infoDev* (http://www.infodev.org/en/Publication.355.html)

Frith, H. (2005) Ethiopia leaps into the information age. *Times Online*, 12 August 2005

Fullan, M. (2000) The three stories of education reform. *Phi Delta Kappan International*, 17 April 2000 (http://www.pdkintl.org/kappan/kful0004.htm)

Fullan, M. (2001) Whole school reform: problems and promises. Ontario Institute for Studies in Education. University of Toronto (http://www.michaelfullan.ca/Articles_01/06_01.pdf)

Gibson, I. and Selinger, M. (2005) Technology dissonance: climbing the mountain of global learning and cultural relevance. *Proceedings of WCCE 2005*, Cape Town, South Africa, 4–7 July 2005

Goodlad, J.I. (1990) *Teachers For Our Nation's Schools*. San Francisco, CA: Jossey-Bass

Hewlett Foundation (2007) *Quality Education in the Developing World*. Hewlett Foundation (http://www.hewlett.org/Programs/GlobalAffairs/QualEd)

HM Queen Elizabeth (2005) *Education, creating opportunity, realising potential*. A Message from Her Majesty the Queen, Head of the Commonwealth, Commonwealth Day, 2005 (http://www.thecommonwealth.org/shared_asp_files/uploadedfiles/498D59CA-D557-491A-BEA4-2AF24D6EE32B_Message.pdf)

Hussein, J.W. (2006) Locating the value conflicts between the rhetoric and practices of the public and teacher education in Ethiopia within the hegemony of the global neo-liberalism and seeking the alternative in critical pedagogy. *Journal for Critical Education Policy Studies*, 4 (2), unpaginated (16 pp.) (http://www.jceps.com/print.php?articleID = 80)

ILO (2000) *Lifelong Learning in the Twenty-first Century: the changing roles of educational personnel*. Report for discussion at the Joint Meeting on Lifelong Learning in the Twenty-first Century: The Changing Roles of Educational Personnel. Part 1. Geneva: International Labour Office

Imfundo (2001) *Imfundo: partnership for IT in education. Inception Report.* London: DFID

infoDev (2005) *Knowledge Maps: ICT in education. What do we know about using technology effectively in education in developing countries?* Washington, DC: World Bank

ITU (2003) *World Telecommunication Development Report 2003.* Geneva: ITU

James, M. (2002) But what do you mean successful? The role evaluatory activities play in creating and maintaining teacher quality. A case study of the Indian District Primary Education programme. Paper presented at the British Association of International and Comparative Education Conference, Nottingham University, UK

James, T. and Miller, J. (2005) Developing a monitoring and evaluation plan for ICT in education. In Wagner *et al.* (2005), pp. 57–76

Jeevanantham, L.S. (1998) Curriculum content: a quest for relevance. *Curriculum Studies*, 6 (2), pp. 217–30

JEI (2007) The Jordan Education Initiative (http://www.jei.org.jo)

Johanson, R.K. and Adams, A.V. (2004) *Skills Development in Sub-Saharan Africa.* Washington, DC: World Bank

Joshi, I. and Murthy, T. (2004) Paradigm change: effect of ICTs on modern education. *i4d* (http://www.i4donline.net/issue/march04/education.htm)

Leithwood, K., Jantzi, D. and Steinbach, R. (1999) *Changing Leadership for Changing Times.* Philadelphia: Open University Press

Maddux, C.D., Johnson, D.L. and Willis, J.W. (1997) *Educational Computing: learning with tomorrow's technologies*, 2nd edn. Needham Heights, MA: Allyn and Bacon

Magidor, M. (2005) Multicultural communities: the university role in a multi-ethnic, multicultural environment. Cisco Public Services Summit 2005, Stockholm, 9–10 December 2005

Mattson, E. (2006) *Field-Based Models of Primary Teacher Training. Case studies of student support systems from sub-Saharan Africa.* London: Department for International Development

McLoughlin, C. and Oliver, R. (1999) Pedagogic roles and dynamics in telematics environments. In *Telematics in Education: trends and issues*, ed. M. Selinger and J. Pearson. Oxford: Elsevier Science, pp. 32–50

Mitra, S. (2004) The hole in the wall. *Dataquest*, 23 September 2004 (http://www.dqindia.com/content/industrymarket/2004/104092301.asp#interact)

Mitra, S. (2006) Outdoctrination. The first Cisco-ICT4D Collective Lecture at Royal Holloway, University of London, 23 November 2006

Moënne, G., Verdi, M. and Sepúlveda, E. (2004) Enseñanza de las ciencias con uso de TIC en escuelas urbano marginales de bajo rendimiento escolar. *In Proceedings of Taller Internacional de Software Educativo TISE'2004*, Santiago-Chile, pp. 95–101

Mulder, J. (2007) Knowledge dissemination in sub-Saharan Africa: what role for open educational resources (OER). Unpublished Master's thesis in international relations, International School for Humanities and Social Sciences, University of Amsterdam

Murrugarra, L. (2005) Learning without frontiers. *i4d*, 3 (12), pp. 16–17 (http://www.i4donline.net/dec05/youth_awareness.asp)

Muthukrishna, N. (1995) Redefining the teaching of literature in the primary school as meaning construction. *Alternation*, 2, pp. 108–16

OECD (2003) *PISA 2003 Database* (http://pisaweb.acer.edu.au/oecd_2003/oecd_pisa_data.html)

O'Sullivan, M. (2002) Effective follow-up strategies for professional development for primary teachers in Namibia. *Teacher Development*, 6 (2), pp. 181–203

O'Sullivan, M. (2003) Needs assessment and the critical implications of a rigid textbook/syllabus for in-service education and training for primary English teachers in the United Arab Emirates. *Teacher Development*, 7 (3), pp. 437–56

Oxfam International (2006) *In the Public Interest: health, education, water and sanitation for all. Summary.* Oxford: Oxfam International (http://www.oxfam.org.uk/what_we_do/issues/debt_aid/downloads/public_interest_summary.pdf)

Perraton, H., Robinson, B. and Creed, C. (2002) *Teacher Education Through Distance Learning: technology, curriculum, cost, evaluation.* Paris: UNESCO

Piaget, J. (1954) *The Construction of Reality in the Child.* New York: Basic Books

Polgreen, L. (2007) Africa's storied colleges, jammed and crumbling. *New York Times*, 19 May 2007 (http://www.nytimes.com/2007/05/20/world/africa/20senegal.html)

Potterton, T. (2005) Partnerships: Gardens for Life. *Eden Project Friends Magazine*, 20, p. 39

Save the Children (2007) *Last in Line, Last in School. How donors are failing children in conflict-affected fragile states.* London: Save the Children

Scrimshaw, P. (1998) *Preparing for the Information Age: synoptic report of the Education Departments' Superhighways Initiative.* London: DfEE

Seeley Brown, J. and Duguid, P. (2001) *The Social Life of Information.* Boston, MA: Harvard Business School

Selinger, M. (1996) Beginning teachers using IT: The Open University model. *Journal for IT in Teacher Education*, 5 (3), pp. 253–70

Selinger, M. (2004a) The role of local instructors in making global e-learning programmes culturally and pedagogically relevant. In *World Yearbook of Education 2004 'Digital Technologies, Communities and Education'*, ed. A. Brown and N. Davis. London, Kogan Page, pp. 211–24

Selinger, M. (2004b) The cultural and pedagogical implications of a global elearning programme. *Cambridge Journal of Education*, 34 (2), pp. 213–29

Selinger, M. (2005) What is content? *Proceedings of WCCE 2005*, Cape Town, South Africa, 4–7 July 2005

Selinger, M. (2006) I teach you, you teach me. *Proceedings of SITE 2006*, Orlando FL, US

Selinger, M. and Gibson, I. (2004) Cultural relevance and technology use: ensuring the transformational power of learning technologies in culturally defined learning environments. In *Proceedings of EdMedia 2004*, ed. L. Cantoni and C. McLoughlin, 21–26 June 2004; Lugano, Switzerland

Selinger, M., Cassidy, T., Salameh, W. and Al-Majali, M. (2006) Jordan Education Initiative Report of Academic Advisory Board Visit, 5–7 March 2006. Unpublished Report to Ministry of Education, Jordan

Sirius (2006) *ICT Support in Schools: executive summary.* Weybridge: Sirius Corporation (http://www.siriusit.co.uk/index.php?page = ict-support-in-schools)

Solimano, A. (2005) The international mobility of talent and its impact on global development: an overview. Paper prepared for the project 'International Mobility of Talent' organised by UNU-WIDER with the cooperation of UN-ECLAC

Somekh, B., Underwood, J., Convery, A., Dillion, G., Lewin, C., Mavers, D., Saxon, D. and Woodrow, D. (2005) *Evaluation of the DfES ICT Test Bed Project Annual Report 2004.* Coventry: Becta (http://www.evaluation.icttestbed.org.uk/reports)

Somekh, B., Underwood, J., Convery, A., Dillion, G., Harber Stuart, T., Jarvis, J., Lewin, C., Mavers, D., Saxon, D., Twining, P. and Woodrow, D. (2006) *Evaluation of the DfES ICT Test Bed Project Annual Report 2005.* Coventry: Becta (http://www.evaluation.icttestbed.org.uk/reports)

Sutherland, R., Armstrong, V., Barnes, S., Brawn, R., Gall, M., Matthewman, S., Olivero, F., Taylor, A., Triggs, P., Wishart, J. and John, P. (2004) Transforming teaching and learning: embedding ICT into every-day classroom practices. *Journal of Computer Assisted Learning* Special Issue, 20 (6), pp. 413–25

Tebeje, A. (2005) *Brain Drain and Capacity Building in Africa.* Ottawa: IDRC (http://www.idrc.ca/en/ev-26269-201-1-DO_TOPIC.html)

Trucano, M. (2005) *Knowledge Maps: ICTs in education.* Washington, DC: infoDev/World Bank

UN (2005) *UN Millennium Development Goals* (http://www.un.org/millenniumgoals)

UN (2007) *The Millennium Development Goals Report 2007* (http://mdgs.un.org/unsd/mdg/Resources/Static/Products/Progress2007/UNSD_MDG_Report_2007e.pdf)

UNDP (2006) *Human Development Report 2006. Beyond scarcity: power, poverty and the global water crisis.* New York: UNDP

UNESCO (2000) *Dakar Framework for Action Education For All: meeting our collective commitments.* Text adopted by the World Education Forum, Dakar, Senegal, 26–28 April 2000 (http://www.unesco.org/education/efa/ed_for_all/dakfram_eng.shtm)

UNESCO (2001) *Teacher Education Through Distance Learning: technology, curriculum, evaluation, cost.* Paris: UNESCO (http://unesdoc.unesco.org/images/0012/001242/124208e.pdf)

UNESCO (2003) *Key Indicators 2003: Part 1 Education for global participation* (http://www.adb.org/Docments/Books/Key_Indicators/2003/pdf/theme_paper.pdf)

UNESCO (2005) *Education for All: the quality imperative. EFA Global Monitoring Report 2005.* Paris: UNESCO

UNESCO (2006) *Strong Foundations: early childhood care and education – summary.* EFA Monitoring Report 2007. Paris: UNESCO

UNESCO (2008) *ICT Competency Standards for Teachers.* Paris: UNESCO (http://www.unesco.org/en/competency-standards-teachers)

Unwin, T. (2004) Towards a framework for the use of ICT in teacher training in Africa. *Open Learning: The Journal of Open and Distance Learning,* 20 (2), pp. 113–29

Unwin, T. (2005) Capacity building and management in ICT for education. In Wagner *et al.* (2005), pp. 45–52

USAID (2006) *USAID in Jordan: education* (http://jordan.usaid.gov/sectors.cfm?inSector=17)

Vygotsky, L. (1978) *Mind In Society: The development of higher psychological processes.* Cambridge, MA: Harvard University Press

Wagner, D.A. (2005) Monitoring and evaluation of ICT for education: an introduction. In Wagner *et al.* (2005), pp. 5–9

Wagner, D.A., Day, B., James, T., Kozma, R.B., Miller, J. and Unwin, T. (2005) *Monitoring and Evaluation of ICT in Education Projects. A handbook for developing countries.* Washington, DC: infoDev/World Bank

Wallbank, T.W. (1934) The educational renaissance in British Tropical Africa. *The Journal of Negro Education,* 3 (1), p. 109

World Bank FTI (2006) The role of capacity development in the Education for All – Fast Track Initiative. Concept Note. *Capacity Development Task Team.* Education For All: Fast Track Initiative, Washington, DC: World Bank (http://www1.worldbank.org/education/efafti/documents/CD_TT_Concept_Note.pdf)

World Bank Independent Evaluation Group (2006) *From Schooling Access to Learning Outcomes: an unfinished agenda. An evaluation of World Bank support to primary education.* Washington, DC: The World Bank

World Economic Forum (2007) *Jordan Education Initiative* (http://www.weforum.org/en/initiatives/gei/Jordan%20Education%20Initiative/index.htm)

Wroe, M. and Doney, M. (2004) *The Rough Guide to a Better World and How You Can Make a Difference.* London: DFID/Rough Guides

*Ghana Society for the Blind's Computer Learning Centre, 2002 (source: Tim Unwin).*

## 8 | E-health: information and communication technologies for health

### S. Yunkap Kwankam, Ariel Pablos-Mendez and Misha Kay

- ICTs have transformed health delivery, especially through mechanisms such as electronic health records, computer-assisted prescription systems and clinical databases.
- The 'know–do' gap is the foremost challenge for public health in the 21st century; we need to identify how better knowledge management can foster health equity.
- More work is needed to design and deliver effective e-health processes that will truly benefit marginalised groups in poor countries.
- This chapter pays particular attention to the leading role of the World Health Organization in promoting the appropriate use of ICTs for health.

## Introduction

A nurse in a remote rural hospital – who has not had access to continuing professional education since he graduated from nursing school – completes an internet-based self-study course on the latest treatment protocols for drug-resistant tuberculosis, using the facility's newly installed computer system.

A psychiatrist, stumped by a patient's atypical presentation, confers with a colleague based at a university hospital on another continent as the two interview and observe the patient together via a video satellite connection. Together, they agree on a diagnosis and the best medication regimen.

A man in a comatose state is delivered to an emergency room by paramedics who have no information about what prompted his loss of consciousness but have found his identity papers. The attending physician accesses his medical history from a nationwide electronic health records system available through the hospital's computer network. On discovering the man has diabetes she is able to start prompt and life-saving treatment.

These examples show how around the world people make improvements in health as a direct benefit of information and communication technologies (ICTs). Every day, the lives of many people lie in the hands of health systems. From the safe delivery of a healthy baby to the care, with dignity, of the elderly, health systems have a vital and continuing responsibility to people throughout their lifespan. But what makes for a good health system? How do we ensure an optimal balance in countries in terms of human and physical resources, technology and pharmaceuticals? How do we provide equitable access to health services and coverage of target populations with effective interventions, in an environment of decreasing numbers of certain categories of health workers and increasing demands for quality healthcare by populations? How can ICTs best contribute to the resolution of these and similar challenges?

ICTs and the internet in particular have ushered in an era of profound opportunity and potential for worldwide advancement in public health and clinical care, and e-health systems today constitute a third major pillar on which the health sector is built. The first was based on chemistry and led to the development of pharmaceuticals in the 19th century. The second, in the 20th century, was built on physics and provided imaging systems and diagnostic and therapeutic equipment. Recognising the value of ICTs, the World Health Organization (WHO) has carried out three key actions that aim to bring the power of ICTs to bear positively on health challenges at national, regional and global levels: the development of an organisation-wide e-health strategy; the passage by the World Health Assembly (the highest organ of WHO) of a resolution on e-health in May 2005; and the endorsement by the

*Satellite connection in Pakistan near a rural healthcare centre (source: WHO, 2007).*

WHO Executive Board, in January 2006, of a set of priority action areas in e-health.

Four of the five main directions of the strategy are: strengthening health systems in countries; fostering public–private partnerships in ICT research and development for health; supporting capacity building for e-health application in member states; and developing and using norms and standards. Success in these areas is predicated on the fifth strategic direction: promoting better understanding of ICTs in health through investigating, documenting and analysing the diffusion into, and impact of, e-health in countries. The report entitled *Building Foundations for e-Health* (WHO, 2007) represents the first attempt at gleaning some of that understanding from a global perspective. It shows how e-health innovations like electronic health records, computer-assisted prescription systems and clinical databases are transforming health today, and that they hold even greater promise for the future. ICTs support clinical care, and provide health information to the general public and scientific information to professionals. They provide a platform for publishing, disseminating health alerts, and supporting administrative functions.

## Definitions of e-health

Mitchell (1999) describes e-health as an all-encompassing term for the combined use in the health sector of electronic information and communication technology for clinical, educational and administrative purposes, both at the local site and at a distance. This, however, is not a universally accepted description. There is no single formal definition of e-health, nor is there consensus on the precise meaning of the term. In a recent systematic review of published materials, Oh *et al.* (2005) identified 51 unique definitions, ranging from broad and all-embracing statements to concise descriptions (see also WHO, 2007; Eysenbach, 2001).

Despite this disparity in definitions, there is agreement that two core principles underlie e-health: the improvement of health, and the use of ICTs to do so. Such health improvement can stem from: increasing use of the internet as a source of health information by both professionals and lay persons; greater productivity of health professionals through access to patient information at the point of care; enabling attending clinicians to consult in a timely manner with other clinicians on difficult cases; access to published materials thus enabling health professionals to stay abreast of developments in their fields; better-informed policy based on successful mining of databases for new epidemiological knowledge; and a host of other pathways through which ICT can influence health. This is well captured in the claim by Eysenbach (2001, p. e20) that in a broader sense e-health characterises 'a commitment for networked, global thinking, to improve health care locally, regionally, and worldwide by using information and communication technology'. Extend that to health (as opposed to healthcare) and we have a broad definition, such as that used in WHO

*Health workers in Malawi using ICTs to record sample information and treatment results at the central hospital (source: WHO, 2007).*

documents, which covers a wide spectrum of current and potential applications of ICTs in health, including areas such as geographical information systems (GIS) for disaster management, e-learning and pattern recognition. The definition thus spans public health and the notion of patient-centred individualised care, which has dominated thinking in the promotion of e-health. ICTs are important tools for supporting health system functions and for achieving intermediary and final goals of the health system.

## Historical development of e-health

Four paths can be identified as having particularly contributed to the development of e-health: the trajectories for telemedicine or telehealth; the internet; decision-support systems; and health records. The oldest by far is telehealth; 'tele', from the Greek meaning 'at a distance'. The term 'telemedicine' was first coined in 1967 to describe the work of providing medical advice to clients at Boston's Logan airport in the USA, from Harvard University medical school, through a radio link. But its origins go back much further. The earliest form of telemedicine consisted of someone going to a healer, describing the symptoms of a patient too sick to travel to the healer, and then taking the recommended therapy back to the sick person (http://www.idshealthcare.com/hospital_management/global/UK_EHealth_Association/EHealth_History_Telephony_Videoconferencing/5_0/g_supplier_5.html). This age-old approach to telemedicine is still in use today in some remote areas.

Improvements in messaging and other communication technologies did not fundamentally modify the concept; they simply changed the modality. Thus messages could be delivered remotely – by semaphore, Morse code, telex and, today, fax or e-mail. Among the most important factors in changing the character of telemedicine, though, has been the internet (see also Chapters 3 and 4), which has enabled entirely new types of telemedicine to emerge.

One of the earliest ideas of a decision-support system in health is illustrated by the cover of the April 1924 issue of *Radio News*. It shows a patient interacting with a doctor through a device that incorporates diagnostic sensors, presumably laboratory testing as well, and interactive video, under the headline 'The radio doctor – maybe!' (Radio News, 1924). More than eighty years later, we are not quite there. Decision-support systems for diagnostic purposes have evolved through expert systems such as MYCIN in the 1970s, which, like all expert systems, held the promise of capturing and preserving for posterity the knowledge of an expert, thus endowing such knowledge with a life of its own beyond that of the expert. Today, such systems use the collective wisdom garnered from a body of scientific evidence to support the diagnosis of diseases or identification of potentially harmful associations of medications even before there are reported cases.

The idea of the electronic health record (EHR) system dates back to the 1960s, and received great encouragement from the Institute of Medicine (IOM) report on computer-based patient records in 1991. A major constraint to implementation has been the need for standards for full interoperability of the complex systems involved in supporting the set of eight core care delivery functions identified by the IOM: health information and data; result management; order management; decision support; electronic communication and connectivity; patient support; administrative processes and reporting; and reporting and population health. In addition, in order to make these function effectively, there would need to be a patient identifier system at national level.

A more recent development in this area has been the continuity of care record (CCR), which holds the most essential facts about a patient's condition, including information on the patient, provider, insurance, in addition to the patient's health status (such as allergies, medications, vital signs, diagnoses, recent procedures), recent care provided, recommendations for future care (a care plan) and the reason for referral or transfer (Waegemann, 2004). Such systems are not without their problems, and can be very expensive to install, as evidenced by the cost and complexity of implementing a new National Health Service computerised record scheme in the UK in the mid-2000s.

The 1999 IOM report on patient safety rekindled interest in information technology in the healthcare community, as prescription and medication errors are seen as amenable to computerised prescriber order entry (CPOE) systems. A combination of driving forces, standards developments and technological progress has resulted in substantial progress in the use of EHRs (Waegemann, 2004). Today EHRs not only provide a comprehensive longitudinal record of patients, but also automate and streamline the clinicians' workflows.

Two landmark events stand out in the development of e-health. One is the integration of various media into a single system around a computer – computers with telecommunication, videoconferencing and real-time data transfer. It occurred on 23 May 1993, when 'a cult movie entitled *Wax: Or the Discovery of Television Among the Bees* was broadcast over the internet to a small worldwide audience who watched and listened to it live on their computers. The video was fuzzy and in black and white, and the audio sputtered in and out, but this digital moonwalk marked another small, yet significant, step towards the much-heralded convergence of audio, video, and data' (Gore, 1994). This event demonstrated the use of the computer as an all-purpose communications device combining the functions of a telephone, television, e-mail, text, video clips, still images and audio.

A second seminal event occurred in April 1995. An SOS e-mail message was sent through the internet requesting international help for a young female Chinese university student, suffering from an unknown but severe disease. This led to the first recorded internet diagnosis – of Zhu Lingling, with Guillian-Barre syndrome (http://www.acep.org/NR/rdonlyres/BA992307-A653-43EA-8331-0CBD0964B7D2/0/telemedicine.pdf). Today, we can routinely send imaging studies through the internet, and carry out live demonstrations and remote consultations through videoconferencing.

## The contemporary e-health landscape

Telehealth, electronic health records, computer-assisted prescription systems, accessing clinical databases and other aspects of e-health are transforming health today and hold even greater promise for the future. In addition to supporting clinical care, ICTs are used for providing health information to the general public, electronic publishing, disseminating health alerts, and supporting administrative functions. They have made significant contributions to public health, as amply demonstrated by the role of telemetry data in the successful fight to control onchocerciasis in West Africa since the 1980s (http://www.who.int/blindness/partnerships/onchocerciasis_OCP/en) and, more recently, the use of the internet in the control of the SARS outbreak (see also Turkle, 1995; Herzlinger, 1997; Bauer and Ringel, 1999; Kilbridge, 2000).

### The potential of health telematics

There is increasing qualitative, and in some instances quantitative, evidence that telemedicine positively impacts the health system's attainment of its objectives in general and the delivery of health services in particular.

Available evidence points to beneficial use of telemedicine, from simple call centres that provide health information and advice demonstrating the demand for such services (Wootton, 2001) to more elaborate systems such as in Ethiopia, where radiologists are able to extend their expertise to patients throughout the country through teleradiology. Heartbeat Jordan, a telemedicine project carried out in Jordan, demonstrated a drastic reduction in unnecessary referrals of chest-pain patients to the Coronary Care Unit of the Nadim Hospital. Among other accomplishments, the project eliminated at least 50 per cent of unnecessary referrals reported, representing a cost saving of $167,500 in one district of the Jordanian health ministry in just three months. By comparison, annual per-capita spending on health in Jordan in 1997 was $119 using commercial exchange rates, or $285 when a purchasing power parity rate is used (WHO, 2000; see also Roine et al., 2001).

The telemedicine programme of the South African Department of Health had 28 sites up and running in 2001, providing services in six provinces. Preliminary evaluation pointed to availability of services where none existed before, improvements in the skills of young clinicians in diagnosing and managing difficult conditions, and reductions in the number of referrals to distant facilities, especially in the area of trauma (Strachan, 2001; see also Dansky et al., 2001).

In developing countries, where collection and delivery of health data is problematic, health telematics can be used for timely transfer to central services for planning and management purposes (Kwankam and Ningo, 1997). It is crucial that decision-makers are provided with accurate and appropriate information upon which to develop health policies. The use of demographic surveillance systems alongside geographical information systems can enable more effective monitoring, thus providing the necessary context for understanding the effectiveness of different kinds of intervention.

Greater application of ICTs also has the potential for dramatic reduction in medical errors, more knowledgeable workers, greater worker retention, improved patient care at the point of care, improved health system management, and evidence-based care through best practices (US President's Information Technology Advisory Committee, 2001). The movement to wireless and mobile internet applications will lead to migration from desktop platforms to wireless and mobile configurations, with a significant impact on future healthcare delivery systems (Laxminarayan and Istepanian, 2000).

### A global survey of e-health

In 2005, the WHO Global Observatory for e-health undertook the first worldwide survey to determine the progress at regional and global levels in the building of the necessary foundations to support the growth of this field. The results presented in the report *Building Foundations for e-Health* (WHO,

2007) enable governments to compare their progress against other countries as well as to apply regional and global statistical means as benchmarks from which to gauge their own development. The report also provides a collection of 112 e-health country profiles that are country-by-country summaries of actions taken to support the development of e-health, their perceived effectiveness, the successes and challenges, and future plans (country profiles are available online at http://www.who.int/goe/data/country_report/en/index.html).

The global survey for e-health was based on the premise that the optimal approach to the implementation of e-health at the national level is to have a framework of strategic plans and policies that lay the foundations for development. These strategies are best developed within the context of an overall national e-strategy which addresses all sectors (Figure 8.1). This generally ensures a more consistent and collaborative approach among sectors and an increased chance of adoption by governments. Furthermore, enabling actions need to take place that ensure that the services provided are accessible to all citizens, regardless of culture, language or geographical location, while protecting their privacy and confidentiality. Moreover, the delivery of e-health systems and services is more likely to be successful if supported by solid foundation actions as well as appropriate enabling policies (World Bank, 2005).

National foundation actions form the basis of e-health in countries. These include the creation of an appropriate governing body (a multi-stakeholder national-level e-health authority to provide leadership and direction), the development or adoption of e-health policy to define the vision and action

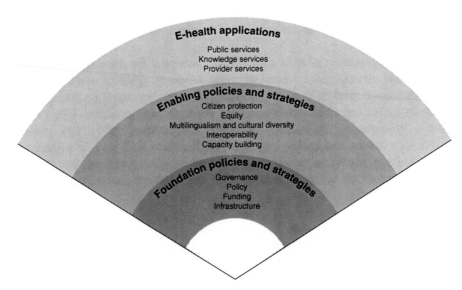

Figure 8.1 *E-health development model* (*source:* WHO, 2007).

required (or broader information or e-policies), the development of a funding framework to support the vision, and mechanisms to develop ICT infrastructure for the provision of e-health services.

The second layer consists of enabling actions, which broadly act as a bridge between foundation actions and the planned outcome of providing e-health services for all. They protect the citizen, promote access and equity, and are established to respect the need for multiculturalism in cyberspace. They include e-health interoperability policies, and strategies to ensure that systems can communicate with each other. Finally, they include a component to build the ICT capacity of health professionals and students.

The last layer, e-health applications, is made up of e-health systems and services provided for the citizen. The success of these applications is largely dependent on the actions leading up to them; that is, services in this layer will be more effective if the actions in the first two layers have been executed well. Solid foundational layers lead to more effective e-health systems and services.

### Foundation and enabling actions for e-health

Governance, policy formulation and infrastructure development are the most important foundation actions required for effective e-health delivery.

Overall, solid advances in building the foundation policies and strategies for e-health were reported along with positive growth projections for 2008. One area requiring particular attention due to its strategic significance is *e-health governance*. Almost half of the responding countries have no governance mechanisms in place for e-health. Establishing such mechanisms will ensure that national e-health planning and implementation can be more effectively and transparently managed based on inter-sectoral collaboration as well as participation of all key stakeholders (e-Health Insider, 2007).

The development of *e-health policies* will be the focus of attention of many governments in the coming years, particularly those of developing countries. Good practices as well as lessons learned from failures will be documented and published by WHO to help streamline the process in countries and to ensure the creation of robust and visionary policies.

*Public–private partnerships* are increasingly being utilised in moving forward – to build infrastructure and to advance specific e-health programmes. This approach is gaining acceptance as a way in which to attract funding or in-kind support for e-health development. It is a positive sign as funding e-health initiatives was reported as being a major challenge for many member states (Nishtar, 2004).

The level of *infrastructure development* varies substantially across countries and the need for its systematic and coordinated implementation has become increasingly clear. There is a growing tendency to use 'technology roadmaps' or blueprints to assist with the planning process. These are national plans for the development of ICTs in health, and are central to facilitating the systematic design and implementation of national infrastructure. Fortunately, the trend in this area is positive, with more responding countries developing such plans (Chetley, 2006).

The WHO survey found that the layer of *enabling policies and strategies*, which can help citizens to benefit from e-health, was not well developed. Almost all of the actions under this rubric need increased attention. Although growth is anticipated, the responses for both citizen protection and equity of access show that only one in two countries have adopted policies. Concerted action by governments, with the support of WHO, will seek to give citizens the assurance they need that their personal electronic health data is secure from potential misuse, as well as extend access of e-health services to all societal groups.

### Primary impact areas: WHO priorities

In 2005, WHO's e-health activities at the global level fell into two broad categories, namely: access to reliable, high-quality health information for professionals and for the general public; and use of ICTs to strengthen various aspects of country health systems, such as e-learning for development of human resources and support for delivery of care services. WHO launched the Health InterNetwork Access to Research Initiative (HINARI) in 2002 in partnership with leading biomedical publishers, academic institutions, and organisations of the United Nations system. It provides free or very low-cost online access to 2,900 major journals in biomedical and related social sciences to local, non-profit institutions in developing countries, and is one of the world's largest collections of biomedical and health literature. In 2007, 2,400 institutions in 113 countries were participating in the network, and during 2006 users downloaded over 3,000,000 articles.

To cater to the needs of the general public, WHO started the Health Academy in December 2003. This innovative approach to improving health provides the general public with health knowledge through e-learning, designed to help people make the right decisions for preventing disease and leading healthier lives. The initiative draws on the organisation's information resources and expertise in health and its access to health information worldwide.

Regional language-specific e-health networks have been developed to support the creation and operation of regional knowledge communities: Arabic in the Eastern Mediterranean region, and Spanish in the region of the Americas. An inter-regional Portuguese-language network (ePORTU-GUESe) has also been created for WHO's Portuguese-speaking member states (WHO, 2005). ePORTUGUESe aims to improve access to health-relevant information available in Portuguese, building on the work of the Latin American and Caribbean Center on Health Sciences information and, in particular, its Virtual Health Library (BIREME, 2000).

*Pupils of the Gamal Abdel Nasser school in Cairo, Egypt, following the Health Academy e-learning course (source: WHO, 2007).*

Besides these global/inter-regional programmes, WHO's regional offices are engaged in key e-health activities, such as the e-health 'road map' for the regional office for Africa. E-health is also a central activity of the knowledge management and sharing strategy of the regional office for the Americas, with programmes at various stages of conceptualisation or implementation, including the Virtual Health Library. E-health applications are being used for prevention and for patient management in the South-East Asia region, and innovative approaches are supporting countries with healthcare delivery, public health and research in the regional office for Europe, in partnerships with ITU, the European Commission, and the European Space Agency.

WHO has also identified other priority areas, including the following:

- *WHO e-health legal and ethics committee.* Increased use of e-health services requires a legal and ethical environment that ensures data privacy, security and confidentiality.
- *Global observatory for e-health.* The aim is to improve the evidence base in order to guide policy and practice through analysis of country indicators, reporting on best practices for integration of e-health into national health systems, evaluation of impact, and formulation of standards.
- *Public–private partnerships in e-health.* Principles and frameworks will be drawn up for governance of e-health partnerships, which will facilitate national cooperation and international exchange in e-health services, promote research and development in information technology for public health, and encourage donation of equipment and software.

- *ICTs in support of human resources for health.* In all countries, there is a need for continuing professional development and measures to prevent brain drain. ICTs can significantly improve the way healthcare professionals are trained through targeted e-learning programmes, and can improve the efficiency of health services, especially in areas with a small health workforce.

- *ICTs for health education and promotion.* The spread of ICTs, including the internet and mobile telephones, provides an opportunity to reach the public at home, school and in the workplace. These technologies can be used to provide health education and promotion, monitor chronic conditions, and deliver information on demand.

- *E-health for healthcare services.* E-health can contribute to improving quality of, safety of and access to health care. The WHO Secretariat will develop and promote 'e-health essentials', a set of minimum requirements for responsible use of e-health within health systems, including the technical, human and financial resources required at the operational, managerial and political levels of the health system. Model e-health solutions will be identified or developed which, with appropriate modification, could be established in national centres and networks of excellence for e-health.

The establishment of the e-Health Standardisation Coordination Group (eHSCG) was proposed by the workshop organised by ITU-T Study Group 16 on standardisation in e-health held in Geneva in May 2003 (see http://www.who.int/ehscg/en for more details). The overall objective of the group is to promote stronger coordination among the key players in the e-health standardisation area. Its purpose is to oversee the development and coverage of ICT standardisation activities in the health sector. The eHSCG is therefore a platform to promote stronger coordination among the key players in all technical areas of e-health standardisation. The group is a place for exchange of information and works towards the creation of cooperation mechanisms to:

- identify areas where further standardisation is required and try to identify responsibilities for such activities;

- provide guidance for implementations and case studies;

- consider the requirements for appropriate development paths for health profiles of existing standards from different sources in order to provide functional sets for key health applications;

- support activities to increase user awareness of the existing standards and case studies.

In addition to its work in the area of standardisation in e-health, the ITU has study groups in each of its three sectors. Study group 2, of the Telecommunications Development sector, focuses on development and management of telecommunication services and networks and ICT applications. It examines:

- methods, techniques and approaches that are the most suitable and successful for service provision in planning, developing, implementing, operating, maintaining and sustaining telecommunication services which optimise their value to users;
- the implementation and technical application of ICTs, using studies by the other sectors, taking into account the special requirements of the developing countries.

In particular, one of the subsections of the study group addressing question 14-2 deals with e-health, and more specifically with telemedicine. The study question is concerned with:

- guidelines on telemedicine policy and strategy highlighting the role of telecommunications in the introduction of telemedicine services;
- guidelines on how to assist medical universities/medical schools in developing countries with the introduction of telemedicine in their training programme;
- a database on pilot projects and experience in developing countries (financing mechanisms, technologies used, services provided, results, lessons learned).

### E-health in the knowledge economy

*Emergence of knowledge management in health*
While the fundamentals of sharing and applying knowledge are not new and occur broadly in health, important contextual factors are making knowledge management more important now than in the past. The most important of these factors are:

- the value of knowledge in health;
- the growing know–do gap and the prospects for achieving the Millennium Development Goals (MDGs);
- increasing complexity of health systems;
- new technological and managerial solutions;
- growing investment in health;
- the ICT revolution;
- democratisation of knowledge.

The *value of knowledge in health* and the economy are increasingly recognised. Gains in life expectancy in the 20th century alone surpassed all gains throughout recorded history before then, and knowledge has been a key driver of these health gains. A UK White Paper (DTI, 1998) proposed that a knowledge economy (including the health sector) is 'one in which the generation and exploitation of knowledge has come to play a predominant part in the creation of wealth. It is not simply about pushing back the frontiers of knowledge; it is also about the more effective use and exploitation of all types of knowledge'.

A knowledge economy is characterised by:

- an economic and institutional regime that provides incentives for the efficient use of existing and new knowledge and the flourishing of entrepreneurship;
- an educated and skilled population that can create, share and use knowledge well;
- a dynamic information infrastructure that can facilitate the effective communication, dissemination and processing of information.

While knowledge has helped the world make major gains in life expectancy, inequalities remain among countries and within countries. The situation is particularly difficult in Africa, where HIV/AIDS has pushed the clock back to the 1960s, with regression of life expectancies in some countries posing a tremendous challenge to the achievement of the MDGs in the region.

Ezzati *et al.* (2003) suggest that most of today's premature deaths, especially among poor children and women, are due to problems which are either preventable or for which there is a known solution. This is echoed by Grol and Grimshaw (2003) and Pfeffer and Sutton (2004), who claim that the chasm between innovative research and effective practice, often referred to as the *'know–do gap'*, contributes to missed opportunities in public health. Moreover, according to Davis *et al.* (2003) and Geiger (1993), the knowledge accrued during the 20th century is now ripe for strategic development ('translation') and application (see also Berwick, 2002).

Plsek and Greenhalgh (2001) believe that the *increasing complexity of health systems* is driven by historical, political and economic developments. The end of European colonialism changed the landscape of the field, and with it the label from 'tropical medicine' to 'international health'. The end of the cold war saw a further revamping of the context for health (including decentralisation and non-state actors) and the emergence of a new label of 'global health'. The explosion of public–private partnerships of the 1990s may not have been possible in the 1970s, and the Alma Ata health declaration in 1978 may not have occurred 20 years later. Understanding these waves of history is crucial to setting the future strategic direction of any organisation in the health field.

*Investment in health is growing steadily* and now accounts for over 10 per cent of global GDP. Compelled by the Millennium Declaration, the world for the first time has the resources – financial, technical and political – to eliminate poverty and related diseases within a century. This offers an unprecedented challenge and opportunity for both the public health and the development communities. However, as emphasised in the

Crisp (2007) review, these two communities need to work more closely together.

In addition to new science, *new technological and managerial solutions* offer new paradigms for health. A hundred years ago new scientific paradigms were developed in germ theory, natural evolution, genetics and new physics which propelled a century of unprecedented scientific discovery, all the way to the recent sequencing of the human genome. Without endorsing the end of science (see Horgan, 1997), the paradigm emerging with the 21st century is more technological and managerial.

*The ICT revolution* is one of the most visible drivers of knowledge management. ICT has transformed itself into a powerful professional tool, and connectivity and access to information are transforming the roles and possibilities of health systems. It is a visible driver of the knowledge management movement, and is enabling new social networks and triggering an explosion in the amount of, and access to, health information. It is also highlighting the digital divide (Smith, 2003), the importance of multilingualism (more than geographical borders), the need for interactive search-and-retrieval systems (far more valuable than average information *per se*), and the importance of experiential knowledge (which cannot be digitalised). Open-access and open-source agendas will soon take over the intellectual property (IP) debates currently focused on patents and access to medicines.

Driven by ICTs after the cold war, there is an abundance of information, annihilation of distance and some hierarchies, de-territorialisation of the state and shrinking government, with growing importance of local knowledge, human capital and social networks (Granovetter, 1973). This is transforming the roles and relations of people and institutions from vertically integrated systems (Stern, 1998) to new, open and powerful networks which could well add to the state and markets as means of organising economic production. The resulting networks of people and technology offer new opportunities for learning communities working toward health equity and require innovative knowledge management systems for their effective delivery (see also Prusak, 1997; Guthrie, 2001; Shou and Fink, 2003). The Chinese symbol for learning is made up of two components: study, the traditional learning from explicit worded messages; and practice, emphasising that this is an important source of innovation and learning. Knowledge management therefore acknowledges and seeks to legitimise and harness the tacit dimension of knowledge gained through practice and experience.

Before formal knowledge management was invented, it had been foreseen in health in the WHO constitution, which states, in part, 'The extension to all peoples of the benefits of medical, psychological and related knowledge is essential to the fullest attainment of health' (http://www.who.int/entity/governance/eb/who_constitution_en.pdf). The 'know–do' gap is the foremost challenge for public health in the 21st century, as better knowledge management can foster health equity. Bridging the know–do gap is about organisational effectiveness: changing the behaviours of people and institutions. It is a dialectic process involving action and learning, as knowledge is not just the latest research publication but several other sources, often contextual. To bridge the know–do gap three things are essential. First, motivation and accountability must be aligned with the solution of a problem. Second, the strategic process of 'knowledge translation' and diffusion of innovation must be well understood and planned for – it is much more complex than 'knowledge' transfer. Finally, you just have to do it – and that takes leadership and good management. Work can occur at individual behaviour level, the health system (clinical services or management) and in the social sphere (policy making). Success and scale-up require learning before, during and after. ICTs and strategic management are key in bridging the know–do gap.

In 2000, the then United Nations secretary-general, Kofi Annan, launched the Health InterNetwork in the Millennium Action Plan 'as a concrete demonstration of how we can build bridges over digital divides'. The Health InterNetwork (Kuruvilla et al., 2004) initiative focused on four main components: connectivity (facilitating information access and use through ICTs); content (providing timely, relevant and high-quality information); capacity building (developing skills in ICT management and use); and policy (lowering the barriers to ICT integration into public health practice). The HINARI programme discussed above is the most significant practical response to this.

*Knowledge mining*
Use of available knowledge is key to the capacity of human resources to solve health problems, and thereby improve the performance of a health-care system. One mechanism for knowledge production is through knowledge discovery in databases, or knowledge mining, the statistical process of discovering previously unknown knowledge from databases. It is applied to very large databases because its success relies heavily on the quantity of quality and detailed data (Gale, 1997). Telemedicine infrastructure can be used to close the feedback loop on data and information both vertically and horizontally, to create the requisite databases. The potential for learning is significant, as the data when properly processed with the right algorithms could yield new knowledge about certain health conditions for clinical and promotional use, and especially epidemiological information for health system planning and reforms. In resource-poor environments, such as developing countries, where experts are not as plentiful, knowledge sharing through expert systems is a viable alternative to locally available know-how (Boyom et al., 1997). Knowledge-based systems provide a means of leveraging available human capabilities to create additional decision-making capacity. A few well-trained individuals, supported by adequate decision support system tools and linked to complete and accurate information sources, can

produce the decision-making equivalent of significantly more persons without adequate tools and with limited access to information. Furthermore, interventions from a distance, using live experts or through disembodied knowledge bases, offer a new perspective on, and possible solution to, the problem of local skill mix. Expert systems can also help leverage the specialised knowledge of individuals. Such systems endow the knowledge of an expert with a life of its own, independent of the expert, by capturing and preserving this knowledge. They also permit simultaneous use, in several places, of this disembodied expertise. They can thus be used to preserve health system 'corporate' know-how for posterity (see also Rockefeller Foundation's Equity Initiative for the development of support information and knowledge sharing in the health sector, http://www.rockfound.org).

*Strengthening health systems through e-health*
E-health can strengthen health systems by focusing on the interactions between ICTs and health systems – the development, deployment and use of these technologies to support health system goals and functions. This interaction is concerned with the policy and practice environment within which the ICTs are operated to support capacity building and to provide services that improve health outcomes – an environment defined by socio-economic, financial and institutional policy; human and material resources; and organisational and managerial models. This approach to e-health aims at providing policy and implementation options and tools to maximise the capacity of countries, as well as technical programmes, effectively and efficiently to deploy ICT to strengthen health systems in countries and improve service delivery, whether targeted at specific groups or entire populations.

In the generation and effective use of knowledge, medical practice would appear to need an information infrastructure efficiently to connect those who produce and archive medical knowledge to those who apply the knowledge. In addition, Weed (1997) suggests that knowledge should preferably be stored in reservoirs that are easy to update and to use as opposed to storage in human brains that are expensive to load. In the knowledge economy, the role of ICTs can be cast in the form of a knowledge paradigm for e-health. Decision-making in health systems is supported by the availability of the right knowledge, at the right place, at the right time and in the right format, through an ICT-based knowledge-coupling system (illustrated in Figure 8.2) that ensures that:

- all relevant options are readily available for consideration;
- unique features of the situation at hand that bear on the discrimination among these options are appropriately evaluated;
- appropriate associations are made between the unique features of the situation and the options;
- the right technology is deployed and local capacity is developed, to facilitate access to the knowledge and its translation into action.

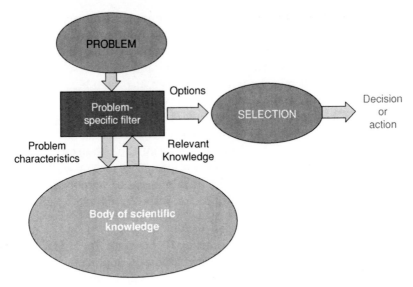

Figure 8.2 *ICT-enabled knowledge-coupling system* (*source:* S. Yunkap Kwankam).

The knowledge paradigm for e-health would promote collaborative work with a view to:

- helping us know what we need to know;
- ensuring that we all know what others know; and
- making what we know contribute effectively to improving health in countries.

An often-cited example of the successful use of ICTs and knowledge management to resolve health problems on the ground is the Tanzania Essential Health Interventions Project (TEHIP) in districts in Tanzania (see Figure 8.3) (Masanja *et al.*, 2008). It is one of many instances that show that solutions to local problems can indeed take place involving the necessary knowledge translation, social entrepreneurship and scaling-up of successful programmes. In this case, basic information systems generated enough evidence to have a more rational allocation of resources, which coupled with sound management and a modest investment translated in halving children mortality within five years.

### Trade in health services

Singh *et al.* (2002) have extensively discussed the implications for trade in health due to developments in e-health. The material in this section is taken from their work. International trade in health services and, by extension, e-commerce in health services are both an opportunity and a challenge for e-health. Limitations to trade in health services affect the development of e-health.

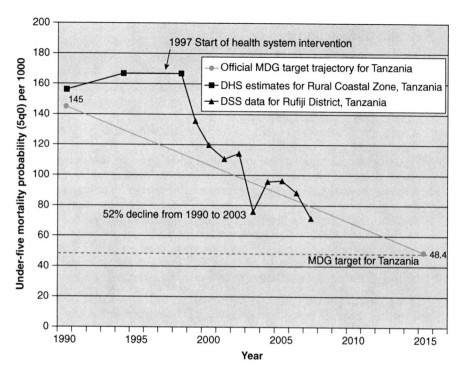

Figure 8.3 *Reversing the trend in child mortality: impact of District Health Interventions in Rufiji District, Tanzania (source:* The TEHIP Project, Ifakara Health Institute, Masanja, H. and de Savigny, D.).

Complex issues arise vis-à-vis health transactions as e-commerce. The boxed example on page 268 illustrates some of the complexities in the types of transaction that are now possible with e-health in relation to, say, an ordinary health-fitness programme. These scenarios have implications not just for existing international trade agreements but also for future negotiations and positions to be taken by countries including the developing world.

Some argue that the majority of trade in health services online can be characterised as mode 1 trade in services as defined by GATS (General Agreement on Trade in Services) (see the box on page 269). Will they then be limited to the country commitments here? In order to understand the implication of this it is important to outline how GATS will impact on e-health.

GATS does not prescribe legal obligations on the number, level or sectoral pattern of a country's commitments. The opposing ends of the spectrum of the level of commitments are guaranteed market access and/or national treatment without limitations (full commitments) and the denial of such guarantees (no bindings).

The levels of commitments in GATS in the health and education sectors are a reflection of the countries' resistance to, or acceptance of, trade

## E-health transaction and its complexities

1  A consumer could just buy it at a nearby store, packaged in a video or CD. (This could be an imported product.)
2  The manufacturer could send it over the internet to local or cross-border distributors who then copy the programme on to CDs and sell them at their store to local consumers.
3  A consumer could order it over the internet from a domestic or cross-border manufacturer and it would be mailed to him.
4  A consumer could order it over the internet and it could be sent in digitised format directly to the computer of the consumer (i.e. supplied online).
5  A consumer while ordering the programme could choose an option whereby the programme is regularly updated through the internet by the supplier.
6  Another option could be that it would be updated or modified based on interactive and customised requirements of the buyer.
7  A further possibility could be that the consumer makes an illegal copy of the programme and just passes it on to a friend or in fact sells it, either in the form of a CD or as an attachment to an e-mail, for example.

Of the seven different variations on the transaction (there could be more) only the first conforms to traditional processes of buying and selling and is fully covered by existing trade agreements. The rest are internet- or e-commerce-enabled transactions. Even in the first, a consumer may have checked out prices or store locations via the internet before going to a regular store to purchase the fitness programme.

Some of the complexities are the following.

- First, there is a question of tariff. This becomes an issue in all cases where goods have not passed through a recognised customs or domestic tax point (when they do, the existing tariff structure would be applicable). In all the other cases, it would depend on the supplier, distributor or consumer to declare the transaction and pay the relevant duty or tax. For governments the issue is not just enforcement but also valuation.
- Second, this raises the question of whether the trade transaction was for goods (a CD: variants 1, 2 and 3 above) or services (advisory fitness programme: 4 and 5). And if it is a service was it non-standardised and customised (no. 6)?
- Third, the issue of intellectual property protection arises in the last case (no. 7).

liberalisation. They thus serve as a possible indicator or response to the commercial success of cross-border applications in e-health for the country. That said, it is important to note that, globally, the commitments made in the health and education sectors have been the fewest.

While 70 per cent of WTO members committed at various levels of commitment on financial or telecommunication services in the Uruguay round, less than 40 per cent committed on education and health. Among the different types of commitments on health services, there is a high percentage

## Background note on GATS

GATS aims to reduce or eliminate measures that prevent or discriminate against trade in services. All services are covered in the GATS except services 'supplied in the exercise of governmental authority'. In this context, it should be noted that in most countries, with the notable exception of the USA, health services are generally supplied by the government.

GATS defines four modes of supply of services.
- Mode 1 is cross-border trade in services (e.g. cross-border provision of telehealth).
- Mode 2 is residents of one country consuming services in foreign markets (e.g. a patient seeks medical treatment abroad).
- Mode 3 is when the supplier establishes a branch in the consumer's territory (e.g. a foreign company invests in domestic medical facilities).
- Mode 4 involves foreign natural persons moving into a country for the purpose of providing a service (e.g. foreign physicians move to a country to provide services).

Commercial applications of e-health fall primarily into the mode 1 of trade in services. (For more information see http://www.wto.org/english/tratop_e/serv_e/gats_factfiction4_e.htm.)

of non-bindings for mode 1, possibly reflecting the perception, at that time, that cross-border provision of these services was not technically feasible, when in fact e-health has been made possible with (subsequent) advances in telecommunication infrastructure.

However, the non-commitment from a country does not necessarily imply that there is no trade in health services, especially in those conducted over the internet. By its very nature and the difficulty in monitoring traffic and transactions online, the internet provides enough scope for unmonitored transactions. The commitment levels therefore can at best be interpreted as governments' current strategies and readiness toward trade liberalisation in health services. It is important to note that growth in e-health applications and demand for e-health services can be influenced by other trade issues such as availability of services locally, comparative quality of services provided by local sources, competitive price structures, and availability or lack of special facilities and human resources. All these vary from country to country and will influence the potential of providing cross-border e-health services.

### Gender and e-health
The relationships between gender and health are both policy and strategy issues. What impact does e-health have on women who are often underserved by traditional health services? Surveys in the USA, Canada and Europe in 2000 indicate that women seek health information on the internet much

more than men do (Intel Corporation, 2000). Women's use of the Web to find health information can be seen as an extension of their predominance as health information seekers and users of consumer health collections. It is also related to their role as family caregivers: women look for health information to address not only their own health concerns, but also those of loved ones. Many websites are being developed to cater to the special requirements of women (see for example http://www.who.int/gender/en, http://www.forwarduk.org.uk; Wootton, 1997). However, there are differences between countries and regions in terms of ethno-racial demographics, official languages, and in the way their healthcare systems operate. In order to get the maximum benefit from e-health, women require specialised health sites and services that are relevant to their areas of interest and concern. For developing countries this is all the more important as in many cultures women have restricted physical public access due to a wide range of factors.

### Other e-health activities

Important national initiatives include: Canada's Health Infoway; the national health information system of South Africa (NHISSA) and its telemedicine network, with 32 sites in six provinces; Malaysia's vision 2020 and the strong role envisaged for ICTs in health; the NHS IT project in the UK; electronic health records systems, with attendant health cards in Germany, Slovenia and other countries. Interestingly, the health card concept has been shown to work in a developing-country environment – a project on prevention of mother-to-child transmission (PMTCT) in Eldoret, Kenya (Siika et al., 2004).

Professional societies are championing the cause of e-health. By far the largest such body is the American Telemedicine Association, with its various special interest groups, including one on international developments (http://www.atmeda.org). Internationally, there are: the International Medical Informatics Association (IMIA) with affiliate groups in various continents (http://www.imia.org); the International Society for Telemedicine and e-Health (ISfTeH), a federation of national telemedicine and e-health societies (http://www.isft.net), and its partners such as the European Health Telematics associations (EHTEL) (http://www.ehtel.org). A recent North American addition, the Health Information Management Systems Society (HIMSS), is poised to make its influence felt around the globe. The three main journals in this space – Telemedicine and e-Health Journal, Journal of Telemedicine and Telecare, Journal of Internet Medical Research – are also drivers of change in e-health. The level of readership of these journals in developing countries remains a challenge to improving access to e-health knowledge, and may be seen as another component of the digital divide.

International agencies are championing e-health through provision of enabling environments for the economic viability of programmes. They include: the ITU through its e-Strategies Unit; the World Bank's *infoDev* programme; UNESCO – e-learning activities including virtual universities; and the Commonwealth's Open and Distance Learning (ODL) programmes run by the Commonwealth of Learning (COL).

### Spending on e-health

Global investment in health research and development (R&D) has more than tripled in the last 20 years. An estimated $105.9 billion was spent globally on health research in 2001; significantly, this represents 3.5 per cent of all health expenditures worldwide, up from 2.6 per cent in 1998. The Global Fund to Fight AIDS, Tuberculosis and Malaria, and private philanthropy, especially the Bill and Melinda Gates Foundation, have been important contributors to this increase in funding for health research. Yet the 'know–do' gap, the gulf between what is known and what is done in policy and practice, remains and paradoxically is growing.

In 2001, public spending on health research was an estimated $46.6 billion: $44.1 billion in high-income countries and $2.5 billion in low- and middle-income countries. Private-sector spending was $59.3 billion, of which $51.2 billion came from for-profit companies and, significantly, $8.1 billion from not-for-profit organisations. Overall, R&D expenditure grew 24 per cent in high-income countries and 23 per cent in low- and middle-income countries between 1998 and 2001. The private for-profit sector is the largest investor globally, accounting for 49 per cent of funds for health research in high-income countries and 32 per cent in low- and middle-income countries. The private not-for-profit sector (private universities, foundations and charities) supplies less than 10 per cent of funding.

Official development assistance (ODA) reached an all-time low in 1997 at just 0.22 per cent of the combined national income of donor countries. In 2001–02, the trend reversed, resulting in a 7.2 per cent real increase in ODA. Health ODA rose from $1.6 billion in 1998 to $2.7 billion in 2001 of which an estimated $400.0 million (15 per cent) went to health R&D. As to the future, predictions are that expenditures in nanotechnology will soon outstrip investments to date in genomics and biotechnology. In 1999 the healthcare industry in the USA spent approximately $12 billion to $14 billion a year on IT in general (Raghupathi and Tan, 1999). This was approximately 1 per cent of all health expenditure. Elsewhere, the market for ICTs in health appears to be just as strong. In Europe the ICT systems and services share of health expenditure is expected to rise from about 1 per cent in 2002 to 5 per cent by 2010.

## Assessing the impact of e-health

### Goals and functions of the health systems

To assess the impact of e-health, it is important to examine its influence on the broader goals of the health system. A health system is defined in the

*World Health Report 2000* to include all actions whose primary purpose is to promote, restore or maintain health (WHO, 2000). This report identifies three specific goals for a health system:

- improve the health of the population served (health – level and distribution);
- respond to people's legitimate expectations (responsiveness – level and distribution);
- provide financial protection against the cost of ill-health (fair financing).

Health systems attain their goals by carrying out four main functions: stewardship, financing, resource generation and service provision. Resource generation involves developing the human resources, knowledge, technology and commodities needed for planning and provision of health services, while provision of personal and non-personal services is aimed at delivering the right mix of interventions, to the appropriate people, at the best quality possible for the resources available. For the effective provision of health services it is necessary for there to be a combination of inputs into a production process that takes place in a particular organisational setting and that leads to the delivery of a series of interventions.

Despite the impressive examples of the use of ICTs in health, given at the beginning of this chapter, and the great potential of e-health, much of the evidence of its impact is inconclusive and taken as a whole precludes definitive statements. To appreciate this better, it is instructive to look at the case of telemedicine, one of the oldest techniques by which the health sector takes advantage of developments in ICTs.

### Making a stronger case for telemedicine

While the use of computers as an integral part of and support tool for health has been demonstrated, that of telemedicine in particular is yet to be conclusively and definitively made for all but a small number of modalities, such as teleradiology, telecardiology, telepsychiatry and teledermatology (Working Party on Telemedicine, Ministry of Health and Social Affairs, Norway, 1999). Available studies often suffer from methodological deficiencies, such as small sample sizes, context and study design (Mair and Whitten, 2000), weak study methodologies (Hailey and Crowe, 2000), application in niche areas for which telemedicine is the only alternative (Wootton, 1996), so that generalisability of results is not obvious (Hailey and Crowe, 2000), and sustainability of projects and programmes is doubtful (Wright, 1998). The US Agency for Healthcare Research and Quality (AHRQ) has undertaken a review of 455 studies relating to telemedicine programmes for the medicare population, 93 from outside the US, and representing 30 medical specialties. Overall, AHRQ (2001a) concluded that telemedicine is a growth technology that can be used beneficially from clinical and economic standpoints. However, the report also states that definitive statements cannot be made beyond this (see also AHRQ, 2001b). Low- and middle-income countries present a particular challenge. These countries account for 84 per cent of the world's population and 93 per cent of the disease burden, yet they spend only 11 per cent of world expenditure on health ($250 billion, or 4 per cent of GDP in the countries) (WHO, 2000). They are also characterised by paucity of data.

If telemedicine is to be adopted by more countries, taken up by providers, and become integrated into routine clinical care, there must be evidence that it contributes to the improvement of performance of health systems. At the provider level, this translates to evidence that it increases access to interventions, improves quality of care and outcomes, leads to cost reductions, and provides access to knowledge for decision-making (Telehealth Think Tank, 2000a, 2000b). Despite the growth of telemedicine equipment and ICT tools in health, their impact depends largely on whether or not they are used, and how, when and where they are used, which in turn is greatly influenced by the organisation of provider systems and the behaviour of care givers. Experience has shown that it is much harder to change attitudes and organisations than to provide ICT equipment (Whitten and Collins, 1997).

Even now, it seems clear that for the foreseeable future many developing and transitional countries will continue to be plagued by problems of insufficiency and/or poor distribution of skilled professionals in their national health systems. The need for proper coverage of target populations and equitable access to health services means that experts will need to provide services beyond the areas of their immediate physical reach. The question then is not *if* telemedicine services should be adopted, but *when* (Telehealth Think Tank, 2000a, 2000b).

### *Appropriate assessment frameworks and tools*
To facilitate assessment of the impact of telemedicine programmes on health system goals and functions, an appropriate framework is needed. This is a daunting task. First, direct contributions to health system goals by ICTs are remote, as the causal pathway from telemedicine activities to health system goals is not fully charted. Ideally, indicators need to be developed which trace clear influence pathways from telemedicine interventions to the objectives of the health system. The difficulty here is two-fold. As with other contributors to service provision, it is difficult to isolate the impact of telemedicine from that of other components of the service delivery system. The hospital or other facility in which care is provided, and the service providers who intervene, are essential elements of the telehealth value chain and clearly affect how successful the telemedicine exercise is in meeting health objectives. The complexities of health systems are such that direct links between telemedicine activities and health outcomes are not easy to establish. The problem is further complicated by the proliferation of indicators currently in use for assessing attainment of health systems goals, which seek to measure various attributes of the

system, such as efficiency, equity, health outcomes and responsiveness (Hrst and Jee-Hughes, 2000). There is a dearth of literature on telemedicine's effect on utilisation of health services. This is understandable, as increased utilisation of telemedicine is itself an outstanding issue. There is also a lack of adequate assessment tools and methodologies. Economic benefit is one of the key areas of assessment for which new methodologies will need to be developed in order to overcome the limitations of current assessment modalities (Readon, 2001).

In other areas of health, the accepted way of circumventing the problem of direct influence pathways to final outcomes is to examine contributions to intermediate goals. Sisk and Sanders (1998) have noted that intermediate outcomes may be acceptable measures of health-related effects (see also Irvine, 2005). The pathway is shorter and more traceable. Moreover, results of measurements can more readily be used by programme managers to make decisions or take corrective action. Two intermediate health system goals are effective coverage and provider performance. The degree to which the health system carries out critical activities that have an impact on people's health can be assessed by examining how effectively populations are covered by health interventions. A framework could be developed to assess telemedicine in terms of contributions to coverage and to provider performance (Field, 1996). The challenge of assessing telemedicine and other e-health modalities has been taken up by IMIA, which in 2006 devoted its annual yearbook, the IMIA *Yearbook of Medical Informatics*, to the subject (IMIA, 2006).

## Limitations of e-health

While industrialised countries have raced forward in developing e-health, many developing countries remain at the starting gate. E-health is far from being a panacea for all that ails health systems around the world. As with any technology, it is important to recognise its limitations, even as we work to overcome them. Current e-health efforts have focused heavily on contributing to improved health through supporting healthcare interventions. This is understandable, given the added value of ICTs in healthcare delivery processes and the large share of the health system dollar spent on care. However, this narrow focus ignores the other significant pathways to improved health. A constant refrain in the arguments against investing in e-health in developing countries is the fact that basic needs – water and sanitation, housing and shelter, food and nutrition, basic education – are not met in many resource-challenged health systems. The e-health community needs to examine how ICTs can contribute to these other determinants of health. The ecology of medical care shows that in a given month, as many as 25 per cent of those served by the healthcare system show no signs of illness. Investments in prevention would reap significant benefit in heading off greater expenses in providing care to the sick. Recent evidence points to preventive health as the primary domain of improvement from the use of information technology in health, and decreased utilisation of care as the major efficiency benefit realised (Chaudhry *et al.*, 2006).

There is a need to broaden the influence pathways through which ICTs can contribute to improved health. The e-health community needs to examine how ICTs can be used to improve efficiencies in the delivery of basic health services. E-learning has tremendous potential in the developing world. Seeking to tap that potential, WHO has created the Health Academy, which provides internet- or CD-based access to reliable and current knowledge and information on health using text, audiovisual aids, illustrations, photos and animations. However, many hurdles beyond those of technical knowledge, economic viability and resistance to change will have to be overcome if the full potential of e-health is to be realised.

## The future of e-health

The future of e-health lies in mobile and ubiquitous computing. Personal digital assistants (PDAs) and handheld computers have already been used successfully for data collection and in clinical practice in resource-challenged health systems such as in Uganda. The European Commission has invested significant resources in funding the development of wearable computing devices. In the not-so-distant future, ubiquitous computing, which will embed computation into the environment and everyday objects, will permit people to move around and interact at any moment with information and the internet (see the case study 'The internet of things' in Chapter 4). These advances will open new vistas for e-health. For example, short-range mobile transceivers embedded into devices with increasing processing capability will permit communication between people and medical devices, and between devices themselves (ITU, 2005), thus bringing the dream of healthcare for everyone, *wherever they may be* (mobile health or m-health), a little closer.

Electronic health records (EHR) will provide lifelong information on individuals, from birth to death. At the level of the individual, personal risk factors for contracting any disease could be determined and appropriate interventions developed. The electronic health record holds the promise of expanding our understanding of human biology and disease phenomena, if EHR databases that cross-link with information on genomics and proteomics become available to researchers. Such visions nevertheless raise difficult questions about information security and the purposes for which individual health information may be used, and cannot move forward until ethical, legal and confidentiality issues are satisfactorily addressed.

The increasing use of ICTs in health is driven by strategic forces from both health and technology (Telehealth Think Tank, 2000a). Health factors include actual and latent demands:

- expanding diagnosis and treatment options;
- prospects for substantially reducing the cost of providing care, especially home care;

- market forces, deriving from the perception in industry that the health sector is a major market sector for generic information and communications technology products;
- consumer demand;
- urbanisation and globalisation.

On the technology side, developments in aspects of telecommunications, such as wireless communications, satellite systems, fibre optics and cables, increasing convenience of services, digital processing power and storage capacity, and the trend toward the networked household, have all led to new e-health applications and increased demand for the services they provide (Telehealth Think Tank, 2000b).

Although e-health is riding global trends and taking advantage of these developments, it should be directed by health needs and not driven by technology (WHO, 1997). While advances in areas such as bioinformatics, artificial intelligence, miniaturisation and nanotechnology, the quest for wider telecommunications coverage and universal access help shape health systems and health service delivery, health sector needs such as health promotion, disease prevention, diagnosis, treatment, rehabilitative care and health system performance improvement could play a more significant role in driving future developments in ICT.

## Conclusions

ICTs are transforming not just health and other systems but the way people live and work. Four main challenges need to be overcome if we are to realise the full potential of e-health: *organisational barriers* – technical knowledge, economic viability, organisational support and behaviour modification; perennial issues of *security, privacy and confidentiality*; *legal and ethical challenges* dealing with accountability and liability – determining where transactions occur, which laws apply and which courts have jurisdiction; and, above all, generating evidence that the *technology contributes to performance improvement in health systems*, can help build human capital for health, and at the provider level, improves access to knowledge, supports decision-making, and leads to better outcomes for patients.

In the absence of clear evidence of its value, e-health is likely to be driven by 'technology push' and not needs-based and evidence-led 'technology pull'. Poorer countries are likely to invest their limited resources in dazzling and sophisticated equipment, perhaps to the detriment of more productive approaches for development of human capital, providing quality services, and generally enhancing performance of the health system. An important role that WHO can play is therefore to monitor developments in relevant fields and advise member states accordingly. This chapter is an attempt to address this issue from a truly global perspective, and is thus a key component to helping countries realise the full potential of ICTs in health.

E-health extends beyond healthcare to a larger concept of public health that embraces support of all health system functions. Consequently it is meant to include such applications as geographical information systems (GIS) for disaster management and studying the spread of vector-borne diseases by analysing the habitat of the vectors, and use of grid technology to make resources available for resolution of computation-intensive problems in health such as analysis of disease outbreak patterns and modelling of disease phenomena.

Despite the great potential of e-health, many countries, especially in the developing world, are unable to derive benefit from it because they lack the capacity systematically to evaluate developments in ICT and make informed decisions about potential applications, country readiness for their adoption and adaptation to country-specific needs, circumstances and resources. They look to WHO and other development partners to provide guidance and technical assistance on how to use e-health to strengthen their health systems. As custodians of international health, WHO has nine main responsibilities, consistent with its core functions, in relation to the use of ICT in health development:

1 articulating consistent, ethical and evidence-based policy and advocacy positions with regard to the use of ICT in health;

2 carrying out assessments and aggregation of knowledge and best practices in e-health, and sharing the results throughout WHO and in countries;

3 monitoring trends in the field of ICT, identifying new areas of ICT application in health, and promoting ICT research and development to meet identified health needs;

4 building capacities, creating synergies, and facilitating the development of networks of expertise, for ICT-based knowledge management in countries;

5 knowledge mapping – contextualising health information and knowledge in both space and time;

6 developing and maintaining partnerships for improved development and application of ICTs in health;

7 promoting the development and application of e-health norms and standards, including information exchange standards, protocols, methods and policies for improving data and information quality and interoperability in countries;

8 facilitating the development of frameworks, guidelines, methods and tools for improving policy development and enhancing practice in e-health in member states;

9 serving as convener, among development partners, on issues of ICT and health development.

In this way, WHO can continuously monitor developments in relevant fields and country readiness for e-health, and advise member states as to when it is most opportune to introduce such services. In order to offer advice to developing countries, particularly in view of the strong driving forces associated with ICTs in health, it is important to strengthen the evidence base on the impact of e-health on, and identify best practices in its use for, improving resource generation and service provision, increasing coverage of populations in need and supporting assessment of provider performance. This is a prerequisite to designing e-health policies and programmes to improve service delivery and system performance.

## Key readings

IMIA (2006) *Yearbook of Medical Informatics: assessing information technologies for health.* Stuttgart: Schattauer

Oh, H., Rizo, C., Enkin, M. and Jadad, A. (2005) What is e-health (3): a systematic review of published definitions. *Journal of Medical Internet Research*, 7 (1), p. e1 (http://www.jmir.org/2005/1/e1)

Roine, R., Ohinmaa, A. and Hailey, D. (2001) Assessing telemedicine: a systematic review of the literature. *Canadian Medical Association Journal*, 165 (6), pp. 765–71

WHO (2007) *Building Foundations for e-Health*. Geneva: WHO, Global Observatory for eHealth

## References

Agency for Healthcare Research and Quality (AHRQ) (2001a) *Telemedicine for the Medicare Population*. Evidence Report/Technology Assessment no. 24, Rockville, MD: Agency for Healthcare Research and Quality

Agency for Healthcare Research and Quality (AHRQ) (2001b) Supplement to *Telemedicine for the Medicare Population*. Evidence Report/Technology Assessment: Number 24, Rockville, MD: Agency for Healthcare Research and Quality

Bauer, J. and Ringel, M. (1999) *Telemedicine and the Reinvention of Healthcare: The Seventh Revolution in Medicine*. New York: McGraw Hill

Berwick, D. (2002) A learning world for the Global Fund. *British Medical Journal*, 325, pp. 55–6

BIREME (2000) (http://www.virtualhealthlibrary.org/php/index.php?lang=en, accessed 15 June 2007)

Boyom, S.F., Kwankam, S.Y. and Asoh, D.A. (1997) Health 2000: an integrated large-scale expert system for the hospital of the future. *Methods of Information in Medicine*, 36, pp. 92–4

Chaudhry, B., Wang, J., Wu, S., Maglione, M., Mojica, W., Roth, E., Morton, S.C. and Shekelle, P.G. (2006) Systematic review: impact of health information technology on quality, efficiency, and costs of medical care. *Annals of Internal Medicine*, 144 (10), pp. 742–52

Chetley, A. (ed.) (2006) Improving health, connecting people: the role of ICTs in the health sector of developing countries. A framework paper. Washington, DC: *info*Dev

Crisp, N. (2007) *Global Health Partnerships: the UK contribution to health in developing countries.* London: COI

Dansky, K.H., Palmer, L., Dhea, D. and Bowles, K.H. (2001) Cost analysis of Telehomecare. *Telemedicine Journal and e-Health*, 7 (3), pp. 225–32

Davis, D., Evans, M. and Jadad, A. (2003) The case for knowledge translation: shortening the journey from evidence to effect. *British Medical Journal*, 327, pp. 33–5

DTI (Department of Trade and Industry) (1998) *White Paper: Our Competitive Future – building the knowledge-driven economy.* London: HMSO

e-Health Insider (2007) Information governance will be ongoing challenge (http://www.e-health-insider.com/news/item.cfm?ID=2654)

Eysenbach, G. (2001) What is e-health? *Journal of Medical Internet Research*, 3 (2), p. e20 (http://www.jmir.org/2001/2/e20)

Ezzati, M., Vander Hoorn, S., Rodgers, A., Lopez, A.D., Mathers, C.D., Murray, C.J. and the Comparative Risk Assessment Collaborating Group (2003) Estimates of global and regional potential health gains from reducing major risk factors. *The Lancet*, 362, pp. 271–80

Field, M.J. (ed.) (1996) *Telemedicine: a guide to assessing telecommunications in health care.* Washington, DC: National Academy Press, Institute of Medicine

Gale, M. (1997) Healthcare knowledge mining in a decentralized, web-based environment. MCC Technical Report (http://citeseer.ist.psu.edu/55789.html)

Geiger, R.L. (1993) *Research and Relevant Knowledge: American research universities since World War II.* Oxford: Oxford University Press

Gore, A. (1994) Speech given by then Vice President Al Gore on January 11, 1994, at Royce Hall, UCLA, Los Angeles, California (http://archives.obs-us.com/obs/english/books/editinc/satel.htm, accessed 15 June 2007)

Granovetter, M. (1973) The strength of weak ties. *American Journal of Sociology*, 78, pp. 1360–80

Grol, R. and Grimshaw, J. (2003) From best evidence to best practice: effective implementation of change in patients' care. *The Lancet*, 362, pp. 1225–30

Guthrie, J. (2001) The management, measurement and the reporting of intellectual capital. *Journal of Intellectual Capital*, 2 (1), pp. 27–41

Hailey, D.M. and Crowe, B.L. (2000) Assessing the economic impact of telemedicine. *Disease Management and Health Outcomes*, 7 (4), pp. 187–92

Herzlinger, R. (1997) *Market-driven Health Care: who wins, who loses in the transformation of America's largest service industry.* Cambridge, MA: Perseus Books

Horgan, J. (1997) *The End of Science: facing the limits of knowledge in the twilight of the scientific age.* New York: Broadway Books

Hrst, J. and Jee-Hughes, M. (2000) Performance measurement and performance management in OECD health systems, labour markets and social policy. Paris: OECD, Occasional Papers no. 47

IMIA (2006) *Yearbook of Medical Informatics: assessing information technologies for health.* Stuttgart: Schattauer

Intel Corporation (2000) Women's health on the internet. Internet Health Initiative (http://www.intel.fr/intel/e-health/women_overview.htm, accessed 2 May 2002)

Irvine, R. (2005) Mediating telemedicine: ethics at a distance. *International Medicine Journal*, 35 (1), pp. 56–8

ITU (2005) *Internet Reports 2005: the internet of things – executive summary.* Geneva: ITU

Kilbridge, P. (2000) E-healthcare: urging providers to embrace the Web. *MD Computing*, 17 (1), p. 36

Kuruvilla, S., Dzenowagis, J., Pleasant, A., Dwivedi, R., Murthy, N., Samuel, R. and Scholtz, M. (2004) Digital bridges need concrete foundations: lessons from the Health InterNetwork India. *British Medical Journal*, 328, pp. 1193–6

Kwankam, S.Y. and Ningo, N.N. (1997) Information technology in Africa: a proactive approach and the prospects of leapfrogging decades in the development process. *Proceedings. INET 97* (http://www.isoc.org/inet97/proceedings)

Laxminarayan, S. and Istepanian, R.S. (2000) Unwired E-Med: the next generation of wireless and internet telemedicine systems. *IEEE Transactions on Information Technology in Biomedicine*, 4 (3), pp. 189–93

Mair, F. and Whitten, P. (2000) Systematic review of patient satisfaction with telemedicine. *British Medical Journal*, 320, pp. 1517–20

Masanja, H., de Savigny, D., Smithson, P., Schellenberg, J., John, T., Mbuya, C., Upunda, G., Boerma, T., Victora, C., Tom Smith, T. and Mshinda, H. (2008) Child survival gains in Tanzania: analysis of data from demographic and health surveys. *The Lancet*, 371, pp. 1276–83

Mitchell, J. (1999) From telehealth to e-health: the unstoppable rise of e-health. A report prepared for NOIE. Canberra: Commonwealth Department of Communications, Information Technology and the Arts (DOCITA)

Nishtar, S. (2004) Public–private 'partnerships' in health – a global call to action. *Health Research Policy and Systems*, 2 (5), unpaginated (http://www.health-policy-systems.com/content/2/1/5)

Oh, H., Rizo, C., Enkin, M. and Jadad, A. (2005) What is e-health (3): a systematic review of published definitions. *Journal of Medical Internet Research*, 7 (1), p. e1 (http://www.jmir.org/2005/1/e1)

Pfeffer, J. and Sutton, R.I. (2004) *The Knowing–Doing Gap: how smart companies turn knowledge into action*. Boston, MA: Harvard Business School Press

Plsek, P.E. and Greenhalgh, T. (2001) The challenge of complexity in health care. *British Medical Journal*, 323, pp. 625–8

Prusak, L. (1997) *Knowledge in Organizations*. Boston, MA: Butterworth-Heinemann

Radio News (1924) The radio doctor – maybe!, *Radio News*, April 1924, p. 1406

Raghupathi, W. and Tan, J. (1999) Strategic uses of information technology in health care: state-of-the-art survey. *Topics in Health Information Management*, 20 (1), pp. 1–15

Readon, T. (2001) Expanding the framework for economic analysis of telemedicine. Telemedicine Symposium, Ann Arbor MI, August 2001

Roine, R., Ohinmaa, A. and Hailey, D. (2001) Assessing telemedicine: a systematic review of the literature. *Canadian Medical Association Journal*, 165 (6), pp. 765–71

Shou, A.Z. and Fink, D. (2003) The intellectual capital web: a systematic linking of intellectual capital and knowledge management. *Journal of Intellectual Capital*, 4 (1), pp. 34–48

Siika, A.M., Mamlin, J.J., Einterz, R.M., Rotich, D., Smith, F. and Tierney, W.M. (2004) The Moi Medical Records System: an electronic medical record for Ambulatory HIV Care in Eldoret, Kenya. *International Conference on AIDS*.

2004 Jul 11-16; 15: abstract no. ThPeE8027 (http://gateway.nlm.nih.gov/MeetingAbstracts/102281788.html)

Singh, A.D., Drager, N. and Kwankam, Y. (2002) Trade and health related services and GATS: eHealth: potential and challenge for healthcare. Unpublished draft, July 2002

Sisk, J.E. and Sanders, J.H. (1998) A proposed framework for economic evaluation of telemedicine. *Telemedicine Journal*, 4 (1), pp. 31–7

Smith, R. (2003) Closing the digital divide. *British Medical Journal*, 326, p. 238

Stern, C.W. (1998) The deconstruction of value chains perspectives, September 1998. The Boston Consulting Group (http://www.blowntobits.com/reading/372_Deconstruction_of_Value_Chains_Sep98.pdf, accessed 25 May 2004)

Strachan, K. (2001) Update: telemedicine in South Africa. *Health Systems Trust Newsletter*, 59 (ftp://ftp.hst.org.za/pubs/update/update59.pdf)

Telehealth Think Tank (2000a) Fact sheet 6, proceedings of Telehealth Think Tank Melbourne, 2000. Melbourne: Telehealth Think Tank

Telehealth Think Tank (2000b) Fact sheet 7, proceedings of Telehealth Think Tank Melbourne, 2000. Melbourne: Telehealth Think Tank

Turkle, S. (1995) *Life on the Screen: identity in the age of the internet*. New York: Simon & Schuster

US President's Information Technology Advisory Committee (2001) *Report to the President: Transforming Health Care Through Information Technology* (http://www.internet2.edu/health/files/pitac-hc-9feb01.pdf)

Waegemann, C.P. (2004) The year of the EHR? (http://www.providersedge.com/ehdocs/ehr_articles/The_Year_of_the_EHR.pdf)

Weed, L.L. (1997) New connections between medical knowledge and patient care. *British Medical Journal*, 315, pp. 231–5

Whitten, P. and Collins, B. (1997) The diffusion of telemedicine. *Science Communication*, 19, pp. 21–40

WHO (1997) WHO/DGO/98.1. A Health Telematics Policy in support of WHO's Health-for-All Strategy for Global Health. Development Report of the WHO Group Consultation on Health Telematics, 11–16 December 1997, Geneva (unpublished document)

WHO (2000) *World Health Report 2000: Health Systems – improving performance.* Geneva: World Health Organization

WHO (2005) (http://www.who.int/eportuguese/en)

WHO (2006) *eHealth: proposed tools and services – report by the Secretariat.* Geneva: WHO

WHO (2007) *Building Foundations for e-Health: progress of member states.* Geneva: WHO, Global Observatory for eHealth (http://www.who.int/entity/goe/publications/bf_FINAL.pdf)

Wootton, J.C. (1997) The quality of information on women's health on the internet. *Journal of Women's Health*, 6 (5), pp. 575–81

Wootton, R. (1996) Telemedicine: a cautious welcome. *British Medical Journal*, 313, pp. 1375–7

Wootton, R. (2001) Recent advances in telemedicine. *British Medical Journal*, 323 (8), pp. 557–60

Working Party on Telemedicine, Ministry of Health and Social Affairs, Norway (1999) Telemedicine in Norway: status and the road ahead, final report (translation from Norwegian) (http://www.regjeringen.no/nb/dep/hod/dok/ rapporter_planer/rapporter/1998/Telemedicine-in-Norway-.html?id = 420022)

World Bank (2005) *E-Strategies Monitoring and Evaluation Toolkit*. Washington, DC: World Bank (INF/GICT V6.1B, 3 January 2005)

Wright, D. (1998) Telemedicine and developing countries. A report of study group 2 of the ITU Development Sector. *Journal of Telemedicine and Telecare*, 4 (2), pp. 1–85

*Complexe Sanitaire et Educatif des Insuffisants Moteurs – Nabeul (Medical and Educational Centre for People with Motor Disabilities – Nabeul), Tunisia 2007 (source:* Tim Unwin).

# 9 | E-government and e-governance
## James Guida and Martin Crow

- From a practitioner's perspective, the most challenging issues in the implementation of technology-dependent government services derive from the governance aspects of the initiatives.
- For governments in the developing world, the most important benefits of adopting a standards-based architecture lie in the area of procurement of applications and application services.
- Mobile phones, in providing affordable broadband network access, can offer a valuable means of delivering e-government services.
- There is high risk associated with e-government investments, and though the rewards are potentially substantial they may be hard to quantify.
- Capacity building and formal change management strategies are essential if e-government programmes are to be effective.

## Introduction

The terms *e-government* and *e-governance* are frequently used as interchangeable phrases to describe government agencies' use of information and communication technologies (ICTs) more efficiently to deliver services and transform relations with citizens, businesses and other arms of government. To begin to understand how ICTs can best be used in the government sector to further development agendas, we first need to provide some definitional scope to the suffixes *-ment* and *-ance*.

The term *e-government* is generally used to describe the delivery of services via network technologies to citizens, businesses and government agencies such as customs clearance, tax payments or licence processing. It encompasses both the 'front-office' and 'back-office' use of ICTs to support the business processes that a government performs, typically the provision of information and services (see Anttiroiko and Malkia, 2006; Cordella, 2007; Department of Economic and Social Affairs, 2007).

The term *e-governance*, in contrast, is here used to differentiate two sets of issues (Heeks, 2001; Backus, 2001; Finger and Pécoud, 2003). First, e-governance is used in the sense of issues in the management of technology initiatives in the government sector, and describes the issues and policies (e.g. information privacy and standardisation) and the institutional culture problems (e.g. change management and human resources capacity building) necessary for e-government projects to be implemented successfully. Second, e-governance is also used to refer to the transformation of the relationship between government and citizens in an information society, and describes the goals and potential, however elusive, of utilising the transformational nature of technology to create a more open, fair and empowered society which is actively engaged in the process of being governed (Sheridan and Riley, 2006).

In addition to the terminological confusion noted above, there are many conflicting viewpoints as to the efficacy of ICTs as a tool to reform governance processes. According to Pippa Norris (2002, Chapter 6, p. 1), there are two camps:

> Cyber-optimists are hopeful that the development of interactive services, new channels of communication, and efficiency gains from digital technologies will contribute towards the revitalisation of the role of government executives in representative democracies, facilitating communications between citizen and the state. In contrast, cyber-pessimists express doubts about the capacity of governments to adapt to the new environment, stressing that it is naïve to expect technology to transform government departments as organisations that are inherently conservative, hierarchical and bureaucratic.

From a practitioner's perspective, neither optimism nor pessimism are useful perspectives for viewing the job at hand, but this debate does touch on some of the key issues involved with designing an effective e-government strategy. If practitioners bear in mind the factors of inclusiveness, equity, democratic accountability, transparency, civic engagement and other values embedded in the notion of 'good governance' to provide a substantial ethical grounding for e-government, it is possible to devise and implement a series of interventions involving ICTs that help address two key challenges facing governments in developing nations today: how to develop a public sector that is more effective and responsive in addressing persistent development challenges; and simultaneously how to help prepare the nation generally, and its public sector in particular, to participate in the global information and communication revolution.

## E-government: its evolution and its challenges

A significant body of knowledge has accumulated over the past two decades regarding ICTs and the means for targeting specific service improvements utilising the various available tools (Anttiroiko and Malkia, 2006). As the technologies further evolve and analytical tools such as business process re-engineering (BPR) software become commonly used, commercial-off-the-shelf (COTS) software products are made increasingly available to serve a wider range of common government functional processes, and reference tools such as IT Infrastructure Library (ITIL) are more readily available for assessing and managing technologies, the guesswork and attendant risk in identifying the appropriate networking and software options are steadily being reduced.

E-government, therefore, is becoming a well-defined and well-documented field of endeavour (Finger and Pécoud, 2003; Anttiroiko and Malkia, 2006; Hanna, 2008). Improvements in service efficiency which were considered speculative as recently as a decade ago are increasingly evidence-based, and a consensus has developed among practitioners regarding the potential for technology greatly to improve the ability of government to serve its citizens (see ECOTEC, 2007) (Figure 9.1).

Concurrent with growing acceptance of the potential of technology has come the realisation that the human side of technology-based government initiatives – the social engineering issues associated with changing how civil servants approach their jobs, how citizens view their roles in the governing process, and how and when partnerships to deliver government services involving business or not-for-profit organisations should be utilised – is where the most vexing challenges lie. This is particularly true in many developing nations. One might initially assume, for example, that the challenges posed by widely variable and generally inadequate network infrastructures in developing nations, or the complexities involved in programming foreign languages and writing systems, would pose the greatest hurdles to overcome in instituting an electronic service initiative. While these are indeed challenges that are often inherent in assessing which technologies are appropriate for implementation in developing-nation contexts, practitioner-developed analytical tools such as readiness assessments and new technologies such as robust programming languages and low-cost, hybrid VSAT/wireless networks have rendered these problems manageable.

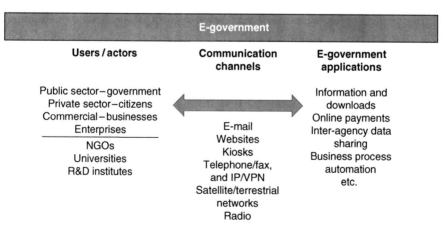

Figure 9.1 *E-government constituents, media and applications* (*source:* James Guida and Martin Crow).

Nonetheless, as an OECD (2001) study found, most governments have encountered problems in delivering large-scale ICT projects. Richard Heeks (2003) has likewise shown that most e-government projects in developing nations are generally considered to have failed. Many factors are at play in this disappointing record, including the application of inappropriate technologies, a field-level disconnect between multilateral banks and donors and other project sponsors and the client governments they serve, and an excessive reliance on top-down government approaches which do not account for user needs or citizen demand. For the most part, these failures can be attributed to the governance side of the equation: lack of transparency and citizen involvement, resistance by an entrenched bureaucracy, corruption, regressive policy and regulatory environments, and unskilled human resources all add considerably to the complexity of identifying workable e-government solutions (ECOTEC, 2007).

For the practitioner, interpreting the theoreticians' 'cyber-optimism' and 'cyber-cynicism' debate in terms of the '-ment/-ance' paradigm is probably the most useful approach. While e-government, or the application of technological tools to improve specific service delivery methods and improve government efficiency, shows increasing promise, e-governance, or the managing of human interactions in a technological environment to improve government, on the other hand, is the area in which the most formidable problems occur, as well as being the area which holds the most valuable potential returns.

### Forces driving the demand for e-government

Forces that drive the demand for e-government are either top-down and supply-driven, characterised by interventions initiated by the bureaucracy itself, or bottom-up and demand-driven, characterised by initiatives undertaken in response to growing demand for better services from citizens. Supply-side drivers are perceived as the need to improve cost and service efficiencies, whereas demand-side drivers are perceived as the need for anytime interaction and improved access to services with government (e-Government, New Zealand, 2004).

In the developing world, probably the key factor driving e-government is that many countries have gone through a process of economic liberalisation and economic growth under advice from multilateral lending agencies. Having completed the first phase of economic policy reform, such countries are now under compulsion to move to the next phase of reform, namely governance reform. Since e-government has demonstrated a positive impact in advanced economies in the delivery of services, provision of information and internal administration of the public sector (see for example Anttiroiko and Malkia, 2006), the parties involved often see e-government as a tool with the potential to have a similar effect on issues of concern in developing countries such as corruption, transparency, and reductions in cost and improvements in quality of service (Harris, 2004, p. 16). Another key driver is the shared commitment reflected in the United Nations' Millennium Development Goals, where good governance is included as one of the elements of MDG 8.

### The potential benefits of e-government in a development context

E-government can provide tangible benefits to citizens of developing nations in three main ways: by reducing costs and delays attendant to utilising government services by consolidating multiple services under one roof; by reducing the need for visits to government offices by making interaction possible via the internet in homes, offices and public access centres; and by increasing transparency and curtailing corruption. Corollary benefits of e-government can include reducing the costs of doing business by removing administrative roadblocks and red tape, streamlining licensing and regulation procedures across various agencies, and improving government procurement processes.

E-government implementations generally target a combination of the following high-level goals (World Bank, INF/GICT, 2005):

- *efficiency* – greater efficiency in delivering government services to citizens and businesses as well as improved intra-government services;
- *provision* – development and delivery of new services to the population, or provision of services to populations previously underserved, especially in rural or less densely populated areas;
- *responsiveness* – increased responsiveness of governments to the needs of their citizens, including new possibilities for citizens and governments to interact with each other;
- *accountability* – greater transparency and accountability of governments and administrations, including in the area of public procurement;
- *participation* – higher levels of citizen participation in public decisions and management, hence strengthening democracy.

In the same way that e-commerce allows businesses to transact with each other more efficiently (B2B) and gives customers better access to businesses (B2C), e-government aims to make the interaction between government and citizens (G2C), government and business enterprises (G2B) and inter-agency relationships (G2G) more convenient, transparent and inexpensive (see Table 9.1). E-government is therefore potentially much more than just a tool for improving cost–quality ratios in public services. It holds the potential to be an instrument of reform and a tool to transform government.

### Phases of e-government

Practitioners generally refer to e-government as following a common evolutionary path (Seifert, 2003) as depicted in Figure 9.2.

The first three phases are largely about using ICTs to provide citizens with another service channel in addition to over-the-counter, mail and telephone

**Table 9.1** *E-government: target users, applications and benefits*

| Target users | Applications | Benefits |
|---|---|---|
| Citizens | Information<br>Education<br>Healthcare<br>Benefits transactions<br>Tax payments | More convenient channels, lower transaction costs, increased transparency and reduced corruption, greater democratic participation |
| Businesses | Information and guidance<br>Licensing and regulation<br>Tax payments | Faster interactions that reduce transaction costs, reduced regulatory burden, reduced corruption |
| Suppliers | E-procurement | Improved access to government marketplace, reduced transaction costs, greater transparency and reduced corruption |
| Other agencies of government | Information sharing<br>Data transfer and back-office process automation | Greater accuracy and efficiency, reduced transaction costs, better information sharing |

*Source:* James Guida and Martin Crow.

services that already exist. Phases 1 to 3 represent a fundamental move from the absence of ICTs to employing ICTs for the first time, whether for service delivery or other purposes. This shift requires foundational work to be undertaken, such as construction of an internal and external infrastructure.

As governments move through phases 4 and 5, they are no longer thinking about the introduction of technology or the use of technology for specific projects. Rather, not unlike the telephone, ICTs become an integrated and assumed enabler of all that government does – from consultation and policy creation through to programme design and delivery. In this light, e-government is not viewed as an end state such as a government portal, but as government – enabled by technology – that is continuously adapting to the challenges of the future.

### The e-government context
Successful e-government implementations depend on many supporting, or enabling, factors. Factors that must be carefully assessed include the 'digital divide' issues that impact user demand and capacity, including skills, access, trust and demographics. Other contextual factors are those that constrain or enable the supply of e-government, such as technical infrastructure and enabling legislation/regulation.

There are four main demand factors that must be considered in any e-government programme:

- *user demand* – who wants e-government, and how do they want it delivered?
- *user capacity* – are citizens ready to interact online?

| Phase 1 | Phase 2 | Phase 3 | Phase 4 | Phase 5 |
|---------|---------|---------|---------|---------|
| **INFORM** | **INTERACT** | **TRANSACT** | **INTEGRATE** | **INNOVATE** |
| Making government information available on the internet | Allowing citizens to provide comments and questions electronically, and receive replies | Enabling citizens and businesses to carry out service transactions and payments with government online | Bringing services together in new ways – e.g. clustering via life events processes such as birth, marriage and death, and making services available in a single location such as a 'one-stop shop' portal or telecentre | Using technology to transform all operations of government, and thereby leverage new models of government and governance |

Figure 9.2 *Phases of e-government* (*source:* James Guida and Martin Crow).

- *trust* – do users trust the technology and the government's use of it?
- *technological accessibility* – can users access and afford the services?

Likewise, three important supply factors should be considered:

- *technological infrastructure* – is the appropriate network technology available?
- *institutional capacity* – is the organisation ready to serve citizens in the knowledge age?
- *legality* – does the legislative and regulatory environment support e-government?

## The technologies

The exponential growth of the use of IT in the private sector that began in the early 1980s had, by the mid-1990s, resulted in a business environment in which IT procurement was essentially out of control. IT procurement – largely focused on maintenance and integration of existing systems rather than the development of new services – was consuming an ever larger share of budgets. The lack of a coherent governance structure meant that purchasing decisions devolved to the smallest work unit and there was little attention to organisation-wide business continuity. This situation was mirrored in the government sector as well.

In response to this situation, termed the 'IT abyss' by McKinsey & Company in a 1997 study commissioned by Microsoft (Murray, 2006), companies began to explore strategies for making explicit the causal relationships between technologies, procurement and governance. Out of this process emerged concepts such as standardisation, interoperability frameworks and many current industry buzzwords such as ITIL (Information Technology

Infrastructure Library) and IT Service Management (ITSM). Governments on the other hand, due to their bureaucratic 'stove-pipe' nature and rigid procurement practices, have been slower to adopt these integrated, best-practice frameworks. Driven by lenders such as the World Bank and other donors, over the past few years momentum has nevertheless built in developing countries for adopting the approaches successfully utilised by the private sector to rein in the anarchic situation vis-à-vis technology choices.

The first step in bringing order to the chaos that is frequently evident in government technology procurement is to decide on an overall, 'enterprise-wide' architecture for the delivery of services. In this section we will first look at the current thinking as regards architecture, and then discuss the network technologies and applications that are commonly utilised.

### Architecture

Architecture is the set of standards and technologies that provide the foundation for the delivery of ICT-based solutions. Good architecture underpins cost-effective, reliable and secure delivery of e-government solutions and maximises flexibility by ensuring that, as the needs of the government change over time, they can be serviced as quickly and effectively as possible. Service-oriented architecture (SOA) is one such set of standards, in which software components can be exposed as services on the network, and so can be re-used over and over again for different applications and purposes. In theory, developing new applications in a SOA environment can be a simple matter of mix-and-match: decide on the application that you need, find out the existing components that can help build that application, and then knit them together to produce the intended functionality. In practice, things are not that simple, but SOA represents the evolution of the concept of interoperability that had its beginning in the mid-1980s with attempts to build standard middleware or application programming interfaces, such as the distributed computing environment (DCE) and common object request broker architecture (CORBA). Implementing an architecture such as SOA cuts development time and costs, and allows governments to create new applications almost on an as-needed basis.

The benefits from implementing a SOA are compelling. While most leading private-sector companies are already well advanced in their plans for implementing a SOA approach, governments, particularly in developing nations, are just beginning this transformation. The move to standards-based architectures such as SOA will increasingly open up opportunities to ensure more flexible and effective procurement practices. Open-standards-based architectures are vendor-neutral and facilitate integration of new services and systems, eliminating the need to replicate infrastructure and enabling the integration of new systems through the well-defined SOA interfaces. Adopting SOA by governments offers many potential benefits, both in terms of reducing the complexities involved in choosing the right technologies as well as in bringing clarity to the procurement and governance processes.

## Networks

E-government relies on a readily available supply of connectivity infrastructure if it is to be useful on any scale. A fast, reliable ICT backbone is a critical part of any e-government strategy, and there are at least as many options in backbone technologies as consumers have for last-mile connections. The vast majority of developing countries' internet users currently access the internet via traditional dial-up subscriptions. However, sophisticated e-commerce or e-government sites incorporate images, video, audio and transaction mechanisms, and require higher-speed, 'broadband' networks.

Given the low market mass and high cost of deployment of fixed-line telephone services in rural areas, network providers are rapidly moving away from the common urban fixed-line broadband (ADSL) model, particularly in Asia, to code-division multiple access (CDMA) and other mobile or fixed wireless technologies. In contrast to computers, which are generally beyond the purchasing power of an individual or family in developing countries, mobile telephones offer an affordable broadband network access device. Though early handheld devices were limited by somewhat awkward interfaces such as wireless application protocol (WAP) and limited content, so-called 3G (third-generation) mobile technologies hold great promise.

## Applications

E-government software applications are the function-specific tools that are supported by the networks and architecture. Applications are loosely grouped into 'front-office' and 'back-office' categories depending on whether they serve to enable citizens and businesses to transact government business online (front), or enable government agencies to coordinate inter-agency information flows and achieve process efficiencies (back) (Municipal Web Services, 2007). Table 9.2 lists a few examples of common public service applications.

In a context where decentralisation is becoming widespread worldwide, e-government applications at the local level are also becoming critical in enhancing the efficiency and transparency of local governments (DOT COMments e-Newsletter, 2005). At the local government level, 'life event' applications are a way of organising services based on a person's needs. For example, they pull together from all government levels all information associated with what happens when a person moves house, under a heading called 'moving home'. This would include advice on selecting a school, registering to vote, finding out about local taxes, how to find a job locally and so on (Windley, 2006).

E-government applications often require a combination of several component software systems from the same or different organisations into

**Table 9.2** *Examples of e-government services*

| Public services for citizens | Public services for business |
|---|---|
| Marriage, birth, death certificates | New business registration and licensing |
| Citizen 'how to' directory | Business income tax payments |
| Employment applications | Permit applications |
| Utility bill payments | Inspection records |
| Personal income tax payments | Customs declarations |
| Automated online social security/insurance | Employee licence creation/renewal |
| Driving licences database/creation/renewal | Employee background checks |
| Fishing/hunting licences | Employee benefits/workers' comp. database |
| News and information | E-marketplace |
| Land registration and property value reports | E-auctions |
| Civic and community calendars | E-bids |
| Public hearings calendar | Corporate and multinational registration |
| Fora, complaint and petition management | Insurance licensee roster |
| Police accident reports | Economic development data |
| Traffic incident reports | Housing development reporting |
| Civil court information | Agricultural marketing information centre |
| Online government directory/catalogues | |

*Source:* James Guida and Martin Crow.

one distributed software system. Network-enabled or 'integrated' data processing applications (e.g. management information systems, customer care systems, knowledge and document management systems) link the various agency information silos via the internet, intranets and extranets, often secured through the use of virtual private network (VPN) technology. To the end user, the various back-office systems appear as a single unified system. Interoperability is a key issue in enabling all of this to happen. For data to be exchanged between systems while allowing each system to process information independently, an agreed set of standards for sharing information must be utilised. These common data standards and protocols make up an 'interoperability framework' which allows disparate systems to be linked and robust applications such as those listed in Table 9.3.

### The technology system

Network access without content can result in unproductive uses of time – for example by government employees who surf the internet at the expense of more mundane work-related tasks they should be performing – as well as an unnecessary burden on state budgets in the form of procurement of mere potential rather than actual benefit. In 2004, Ethiopia brought *WoredaNet* – a VSAT-based network linking over 500 district offices to Addis Ababa – online to great fanfare (Kinde, 2007). In addition to providing video conferencing capability, the system was intended to enable timely data transfer from the regions to improve decision-making capability, and enable integrated

**Table 9.3** *Integrated e-government applications*

| External service systems | Internal office systems |
|---|---|
| *Oriented to citizens* | *Oriented to government officials and agencies* |
| Information kiosks | DMBS: Stores and manages data, maintains internal |
| Licensing | records, presents data and records to citizens and to |
| Permits | government through the Web. Can support concurrent |
| Registrations | access to data having controls to access |
| Utility payments | CRM: Creates confidence in citizens by aligning |
| | government business processes with citizen needs to |
| | manage and ensure they are served in a logical manner |
| | and decrease costs of providing services |
| *Oriented to enterprises* | ERP: Establishes interactive relationships between public |
| Auctions | sector organisation. Supports information flow across |
| E-marketplace | all functions of organisation to automate business |
| E-procurement | processes |
| Online catalogues | EAI: Integrates both intra- and inter-organisational |
| | systems by securely incorporating functionality from |
| | disparate applications in government organisations |
| | Data warehousing: Gathers and integrates data |
| | from disparate sources extracted from multiple, |
| | heterogeneous, autonomous, and distributed |
| | information systems. Can be used for decision support |
| | systems |
| | Knowledge management: Systemic approach to capturing |
| | information and knowledge about an organisation, |
| | its processes, products, services, customers, |
| | used to conduct planning and evaluations from |
| | capital formation to forecasting and performance |
| | measurements |
| | Document management: Stores and manages multimedia |
| | format records that are associated with automated |
| | workflow and electronic document repositories |

*Source:* James Guida and Martin Crow.

service applications to function between the central and regional governments (Spintrack, 2004). Three years later, the system is still used only for video conferencing as no automated data reporting or service applications have been implemented. Further, many of the ground stations have fallen into disrepair due to lack of qualified technicians to provide maintenance (Selam Development Consultants, 2007). While video conferencing certainly offers benefits, it is doubtful that the limited benefits of such a system justify the considerable costs.

Likewise, content with insufficient access also fails to achieve the full impact desired from e-government initiatives. While the causes for insufficient access may include an inhibitive regulatory environment, market factors such as low population density in rural areas or lack of affordability in urban areas, and technical factors such as difficult terrain or

(*continued on page 296*)

# Case study: Local e-government services: Takalar, Indonesia

Martin Crow

*Consultant to World Bank on the Kabupaten Governance Reform Initiatives Project (KGRIP) April 2003*

In early 2000, Takalar District in Sulawesi inaugurated the first local e-government services system in Indonesia. Called SIMTAP (*Sistem Informasi Manajemen Satu Atap* – Information Management System Under One Roof), the goals of this initiative included improving the delivery of government services to citizens, increasing the transparency of government decision-making, and boosting economic growth of the district and local business through reduction in red tape, internet promotion and wider access to markets.

A Web-enabled modular software system was designed to deliver a total of 12 life event and business permitting services. In its first phase of deployment SIMTAP linked departments responsible for issuing identity cards, permits, licences and similar documents, to a centralised service centre in a building adjacent to the office of the district head. The second phase of deployment was planned to extend services to over 14 sub-district offices, some as far as 30 kilometres from the district capital.

When visited three years after its inception, the Takalar SIMTAP system was processing an average of 30+ transactions per day. Citizens generally displayed a high level of satisfaction with the simplicity and clarity of the system, particularly the 'one-stop' aspect and the speed of service. Identity cards that previously took 3 weeks to process were now finished in less than 5 minutes. According to the project coordinator, the approximately US$50,000 implementation cost was recouped in the first two years through labour and materials savings accruing from electronic data processing. Fees and tariffs were posted on the wall inside the service centre, and the system proved very effective in reducing corruption of the 'incidental service fee' variety.

However, despite the Takalar government website being put online and made ready for integration with SIMTAP for remote service delivery, the system continued to operate solely on the district office LAN because the only connectivity option was dial-up service from the incumbent monopoly, Telkom. The high price of this service rendered internet-based service delivery fiscally unsupportable. All services had to be delivered face-to-face, requiring citizens from throughout the district to travel to the centre to obtain services – in some cases a full day of travel via public transport. Potential transparency benefits were reduced by lack of citizen access via the internet, and lack of affordable connectivity also adversely impacted the district's ability effectively to promote local business, as most local businesses still could not afford e-mail capability and few had websites.

Other problems included sourcing human resources in the local area – generally there was no difficulty in finding qualified, locally educated data-entry or counter personnel, but adequately trained programmers and maintenance personnel were much more difficult to locate.

Culturally predicated minor difficulties frequently arose, including citizens unwilling to queue, often crowding or shoving at the counter to be the first served. Citizens also frequently lacked proper documentation, and tried to bribe staff or leverage connections of relatives or friends. Counter staff cited the need for additional in-house training, particularly in service and communication skills, as well as better informational materials for the public such as printed brochures and wall displays.

There were some lingering problems as well with technical implementation of the system, including perforated paper forms that did not correctly fit the printers used, and the need for each sub-district head to hand-sign 5,000 copies of the identity card form at a time.

Among the lessons learned from this case study were the following.

- Local government service delivery processes can be vastly improved and costs significantly reduced through the use of e-government technology.
- Such applications have the potential significantly to promote good governance at the local level through reduction of corruption, increased transparency and improved administrative oversight.
- Improved services are valued by citizens and, with some attention to socialisation and education, use of the services is within reach of the average citizen.
- The positive potential of such initiatives will remain limited if infrastructure and bandwidth costs and human resources issues related to internet connectivity and public access are not satisfactorily addressed in programme design, as lack of connectivity and access will significantly curtail the project's impact among the general population, and reduce the effectiveness of efforts to promote local business and economic development.
- The need for extensive user and operator training should be addressed in programme design if the new business processes that accompany the system are to run smoothly and efficiently.

*The use of radio and television for democracy, Uganda, 2008 (source: Tim Unwin).*

ageing infrastructure, the effect is always to reduce the reach and therefore the impact of the initiative to be run. Networks, applications and the architecture that supports them all require careful needs assessment, sequencing in time, and proficiency in deployment and operation and maintenance in order to achieve full benefit from an e-government implementation. The technical variables, as well as human and environmental variables, must be effectively harmonised to realise the full potential presented by technology. This harmonisation of the purely technical with the vastly more fluid and complex human and environmental factors is the realm of e-governance. The issues in e-governance range from practical issues such as sequencing deployment and training users, to philosophical issues touching on concepts of good governance. The case study on pages 294–5 illustrates some of the complexities involved and indicates the manner in which failure to account for any of these variables can reduce the impact of an e-government initiative.

## E-governance as management of IT implementations in government

Eventual achievement of larger, 'optimistic' goals for e-government in any given country is dependent on factors including ubiquitous infrastructure, affordability of access, the availability of basic knowledge and e-literacy across society – all of which are interlinked with achievement of other ICT4D goals and wider national development. From an e-government practitioner's perspective, the immediate prerequisites for successful planning and implementation must begin with ensuring the political will of government authorities to reform and improve government processes through effective ICT acquisition and management, and generating the support and engagement that such efforts will require from the civil service.

### The management of IT implementations in government

Most e-government projects that fail do so due to the human factor, not as a result of problems with the technology. The most common e-governance project risk factors include:

- lack of institutional capacity (including human resources);
- lack of government commitment;
- too many project components (coordination problems);
- vested interest of various stakeholders;
- low utilisation of newly developed system;
- unclear responsibilities of project sponsors;
- failure to provide sufficient counterpart funding;
- change of government priorities;
- coordination failure between central and local governments;

- lack of or weak legal framework;
- government employees' unwillingness to share information with practitioners.

Against this background, it is interesting to note that Ethiopia has declared its intention to roll out broadband connectivity to all rural communities by the year 2011. Yet the national telecommunications provider, ETC, holds an absolute monopoly and has resisted all attempts to liberalise the regulatory regime and allow increased competition. Under these conditions it is highly unlikely the stated goal will be achieved.

*Tools for planning and implementing successful e-government projects*
The primary challenge that developing countries face in implementing e-government projects is that most still do not have the advanced technology industry, the financial capacity or the supportive regulatory environment necessary to duplicate what governments are achieving in more developed countries. Increasingly, developing countries are identifying their ICT options for e-government through 'benchmarking' (Freedman, 2001; UN, 2005; World Economic Forum, 2007). By observing what others have accomplished and from comparison with local readiness characteristics, it is possible to pick and choose what is best in the particular circumstances for each government (Heeks, 2003).

The most effective technique for avoiding the pitfalls of previous projects is by tracking the lessons learned in other countries through seeking and applying 'best practices'. This term refers to the most effective documented ways to perform processes or sub-processes that have been identified for a particular context (Davenport, 2000). Many examples of best practice have been published for the benefit of new projects in e-government, and are easily accessible online through the many available 'e-government toolkits' (see for example Wimmer, 2004; UNESCO, 2005). These e-government toolkits help policy makers and practitioners determine how ICTs can be put to use to advance specific public reform agendas within varied contexts, obtain guidance related to key environmental, organisational and crosscutting issues, learn from case studies and stories of similar initiatives, and provide downloadable planning aids, organisational aids and other resources.

For some e-government business processes and services 'turnkey' packages are available that will provide total systems for specialised functionality. In other cases consultants can analyse and design a customised solution that includes such elements as new equipment, software upgrades and ongoing user training. Direct technology transfer (DeLong, 2004), facilitated by multilateral banks, donor agencies and NGOs, can also facilitate solutions in response to the needs of developing nation governments. Another tool for effective planning is IT Infrastructure Library. ITIL is a resource for IT organisations seeking to define and evolve their processes from a best-practice perspective in support of what ITIL calls 'IT Service Management' (ITSM). ITIL provides libraries that can help organisations collaborate more efficiently across administrative and data silos, address user requirements more effectively, and align technology more closely with the business processes IT supports. ITIL and ITSM support the implementation of enterprise-wide architectures such as SOA.

*Keys to success*

The goals, policies, human resource needs and other environmental factors surrounding planned initiatives predispose them to success or failure at least as much as choice of appropriate technologies. Successful interventions share a combination of the following characteristics.

- *They address priority development needs that require government involvement.* E-government applications are best embedded in areas that are perceived as being closely related to the priority development needs of the society. This brings broad support and makes it easier to overcome inherent difficulties and sustain attention, commitment and funding.

- *Efficiency and effectiveness are set as the key success criteria of government involvement.* It is best if the role that the government plays in such areas is judged partly or predominantly by factors that ICT can influence. The link between ICT applications, optimisation of government operations and achievement of important social development goals is a very convincing argument for continued development of e-government.

- *There is availability of (initial) funding.* Even initial pilot e-government operations should start with a good understanding of costs involved and assured funding that follows careful analysis of opportunity cost. Whenever advisable and feasible, funding should be treated as a business investment and carry expectation of returns.

- *There is support from the civil service.* Civil servants must be able (through ICT, change- and project-management and partnership-building skills) and willing to support e-government, or, at a minimum, must be eager to learn and change. The culture prevailing in the civil service determines the assessment of expected loss that e-government application can bring to individual civil servants and the resultant strength and effectiveness of the anti-change lobby.

- *There is an effective mechanism/structure for project coordination.* Needed 'backroom' coordination and effort – within and between government agencies – must be ironed out before any e-government application goes on line to avoid duplication, assure interoperability and meet the expectations of users.

- *There is an adequate policy, legal and regulatory framework.* E-government introduces unique legal requirements and these should be addressed early on.

- *ICT infrastructure needs have been accurately identified and costed.* Infrastructure needs should be assessed against the background of requirements and desired results of planned e-government development. Anything short of this limits both. Anything that goes beyond this carries the danger that ICT infrastructure will be converted into expensive and idle office equipment.

- *There is strong political leadership and long-term political commitment to the initiative.* The chief executive officer of the public sector must be committed to e-government, lead and build broad support for it, and be eager to learn. This generates the all-important positive signals that the civil service needs to receive from its top leadership.

- *There is a provision for public engagement.* The public should have a personal stake in e-government development. This should be reinforced by actively, genuinely and continuously soliciting people to participate in the development of e-government applications so that these are custom-crafted to the way people live and work.

- *There are effective plans in place for development of human capital and technical infrastructure.* There should be a vision and plans for closing the existing divides in skills and access. Otherwise, neither the public administration nor the society can hope to become ICT literate and capable – important ingredients for e-government success.

- *Partnerships have been explored and are utilised where practical and beneficial.* The government should see business firms and civil society organisations as potential partners in securing financial resources, skills improvement, better access and adequate capacity to service the ICT network, but partnerships should not be forged at the cost of transparency, accountability or economic soundness of investments.

- *An effective monitoring and evaluation plan is put in place.* Setting clear responsibilities and realistic benchmarks for e-government development, as well as for transparent monitoring, is an important ingredient for eventual success and builds up the overall transparency and accountability framework in the public sector.

- *The project provides added value.* Any design of e-government development must incorporate a calculation of the added value that the application intends to bring to individual users. It is best if this calculation proves to be congruent with the views of the users.

- *There is a provision for user access and ease of use.* It should be made easy in terms of time, cost and effort for the potential users of e-government services actually to employ them. Imaginative solutions for increasing the level of this 'ease of use' must be part of any e-government development plan. They should include, but also transcend, individual access and skills.

- *Privacy and security are adequately addressed.* Security and privacy concerns must be addressed early on, openly and with demonstrated professional aptitude. Public trust will be adversely affected by any breakdown in this area.

Successfully planning for the e-governance aspect of e-government projects should follow a path beginning with needs assessment, followed by development of a vision and strategy to serve that need, then creation of an organisation to support and catalyse the strategy, build human capacity and enact policies that will attract private investment in infrastructure, and prioritise application development.

### Assessing user demand and capacity

It is important to assess user (citizen, business or government) demand for specific types of service before taking action. Understanding user demand is important to ensure that users receive what they want as opposed to simply what government thinks they want, as these are often not the same thing. Frequently the initial focus has been top-down and services do not cater effectively to users' needs. In the past, governments have often undertaken e-government initiatives without having a clear understanding of what potential users want. The resulting early failures have led to an understanding of the importance of organising e-government from the users' perspective, not from the perspective of government organisations, or of private-sector companies seeking to profit from e-government initiatives.

In order to exploit the benefits of e-government, citizens must first have the capacity to use it. This capacity requires a mixture of at least three elements: literacy, knowing how to use ICTs, and being aware of the benefits they can provide. The most accurate predictors of internet use include age, education level and income. As the most common form of interaction on the internet is written language (as opposed to video or audio interaction), more literate individuals are likely to gain more benefit from its use. Capacity also requires accessibility, as well as convenience, culturally and locally appropriate content, and affordable cost. Simply having an ICT backbone to carry information does not mean that the 'last mile' solutions will be available, affordable or valuable.

Trust is another key factor of user capacity. Whereas a high level of trust in government and technology can facilitate the use of e-government, a lack of trust can be a barrier. Many citizens already have low levels of trust in government, and thus may be apprehensive to engage it. Perceived high levels of corruption also undermine levels of trust. To engage citizens online in a meaningful, mature fashion (beyond simply providing information) governments must address two fundamental dimensions of trust: do citizens trust government; and do citizens trust technology?

Fortunately, the provision of e-government services and information may in fact boost interest in the internet, as long as services are provided in local languages and reflect local issues. From this perspective, the relationship between e-government and ICT4D is reciprocal; the investment in technology and skills necessary to make e-government relevant also builds the foundation for a networked world, and e-government services themselves can be a draw to entice citizens to participate on the internet.

### Readiness assessment and strategy formulation

E-government strategies vary considerably in terms of their focus and the degree of change they aspire to undertake. However, most e-government strategies include the following elements:

- a precise identification of the prerequisites for success (and indications on how to meet these prerequisites if necessary); and
- a clear definition of the objectives being pursued (output and outcome), ways of measuring success, and a time horizon within which such success is expected.

A prerequisite to developing an effective strategy is accurately assessing the readiness of government organisations to undertake the technology-related change. There are several dimensions to e-government readiness. One aspect of readiness is the maturity of technical infrastructure and back-office use in various departments. For example, extensive use of e-mail across government departments would be indicative of readiness. Readiness also depends on the attitudinal make-up of the civil service. Willingness to re-engineer, share more information and treat the citizen as a customer indicates high readiness (UN, 2005). Good tools for assessing e-readiness include those developed by the Information Technology Group at the Center for International Development at Harvard University (http://www.readinessguide.org/index.html), by GeoSINC International (http://www.apdip.net/documents/evaluation/e-readiness/geosinc01042002.pdf) and The UN Global E-Government Readiness Report 2005 (http://unpan1.un.org/intradoc/groups/public/documents/un/unpan021888.pdf).

### E-leadership

The term *e-leader* or *e-champion* applies to individuals or organisations within government responsible for taking the lead in improving the delivery and efficiency of services through the implementation of ICT. The role of e-leaders is to provide the vision and subsequently the leadership, to establish environments that are conducive to embracing change and innovation. The e-leader's vision must be supported with strong political will and linked to mechanisms that manage the occurrence of change. The e-leader must utilise an approach that is multi-stakeholder in nature to be able to achieve the necessary buy-in to attain the targets and results that are desired. Effective e-leadership is a prerequisite for project success. Projects with ineffective or disinterested leadership face difficulty in any organisational environment, and in change-resistant, bureaucratic government the hurdles are insurmountable.

### *Establishing a governance structure*

Coordinating IT governance across many diverse and distinct divisional and functional areas of government is not an easy undertaking. The optimal governance structure will depend on the objectives, lines of authority and accountability, and culture of a given government. The key is to ensure that governance structures are aligned with these factors. The most important factor to consider when developing a governance structure is the degree of change required. When a government seeks to integrate services it cuts across the traditional silo-based interests and authorities of organisations, and requires a greater degree of political leadership and coordination, as well as more sophisticated risk-management and partnership skills. The challenge of coordination is to find the right balance between autonomy for persons responsible for organisational results on the one hand, and government-wide needs for interoperable systems and information sharing on the other.

In basic terms, there are two approaches to coordination: centralised and decentralised. Centralised approaches usually involve a single point of control that oversees the development of e-government. Many governance structures are relatively centralised, for example where it is the responsibility of a national ministry to oversee the e-government strategy, report directly to the head of government, and liaise with officials from other ministries. Another commonly used model that provides somewhat more flexible levels of centralisation is based on the corporate Chief Information Officer. This position is invested with some degree of institution-wide authority and accountability, and facilitates e-government strategies. For this role to be effective, there must be a culture and acceptance of centralised approaches, and the centre must be able to wield some degree of authority in order to induce action and enforce standards. Decentralised approaches depend much more on collegiality, shared interests, negotiation and persuasion. While decentralisation might seem to encourage initiative and perhaps better spur development of a local software programming industry, it can also introduce many difficulties down the road, including interoperability, interface and alignment problems.

How far along the government is in its e-government journey is also an important factor in choosing a governance structure. An informal structure may be the best way to go at the idea and research stage, but once a decision has been made and implementation begins, a more formal structure is needed. If the government is committed to developing portals and service integration, for example, a greater degree of coordination will be necessary to ensure interoperability, information management, and a common look and feel. Likewise, if departments are simply intending to put up stand-alone websites, then limited coordination is needed.

When considering levels of coordination, it is important to understand the forms of coordination necessary for the government to achieve its e-objectives, and especially coordination within the organisation, across the organisation, across governments and across sectors. While the degree of coordination needed will be different for each country, there are some characteristics common to all forms of good coordination (Sørgaard, 2002). They tend to:

- provide sufficient incentives for organisational innovation;
- avoid the creation or maintenance of duplicative systems;
- provide fora for decision makers to come together to discuss, learn, make decisions and build interpersonal trust;
- create a culture that helps officials move beyond territory-related issues and focus on a common purpose.

It is also important that operational and regional departments be involved in the setting of objectives. Both have unique perspectives and strengths to bring to the issue. Whereas central agencies may be most concerned with issues such as privacy, secrecy, sharing information, learning and structures, experience shows that in the region issues such as a culture of risk aversion, different concepts of client, and the need to have regional sensitivities reflected in national approaches may be of greater concern. Both sets of issues are important, and both deserve attention when developing e-government objectives and strategies.

Depending on the objectives sought, there are at least two areas where coordination and standards should be considered: sharing data (interoperability), and website appearance and navigation. Whether or not these standards should take the form of policies (must do), guidelines (should do) or good practices (a good idea to do) will depend on the purposes and culture of each government. With respect to data, coordination is important once organisations begin to work together (as in the case of single-window services) because information must be searchable and shared across organisations. If standard approaches and coordination are not enforced, significant work may be necessary later. Common website appearance and navigation has also proven necessary for success, given that most governments deliver hundreds of programmes and thus have hundreds of websites. Standards that place emphasis on a common look and feel allow users to distinguish government programmes and services from other websites, and help them to navigate successfully from one government site to another and find information relevant to their needs.

### Capacity building and change management

Capacity building within the government is an important step in preparation for e-government so that its implementation can be managed effectively. Capacity building covers the scope of sustainable human development and encompasses an organisation's core skills and capabilities to achieve goals.

Resistance from civil servants is probably the biggest challenge to successful e-government implementations. For example, a World Bank evaluation of four projects in India hailed as successes indicates that two are actually moving towards failure (Bhatnagar and Deane, 2004). In its first year a computerised system tripled the revenue from fines imposed on overloaded trucks in Gujarat, India, but as soon as the project champion was transferred, disgruntled inspectors disabled the system.

Change management issues must be addressed as new work practices and new ways of processing and performing tasks are introduced. Change management programmes for encouraging adoption of changes from e-government projects need to be introduced sensitively. These can include introduction of incentives for employees to learn and change, and the establishment of well-structured plans that embrace employee participation throughout all stages of a change process. Similar programmes also need to be put in place to encourage citizen interactions and engagements with the government.

### Costing and financing

From a financial point of view, governments' experiences with the introduction of ICT to their operations are akin to a venture capitalist experience. There is high risk associated with investments for this purpose, and though the rewards are potentially substantial, they may be hard to quantify. Project feasibility analysis should start with an assessment of the size of the public sector's financial exposure due to e-government development. However, making an authoritative pronouncement on the financial cost of e-government is not easy.

Different funding strategies for longer-term e-government projects come with different accounting practices. Bond financing, for example, might consolidate anticipated costs of a project over its life cycle as capital investment in one fiscal year, whereas leasing is likely to spread related expenditures as operative costs over several fiscal years. Comprehensive data about the cost involved in back-office restructuring needed for e-government development are also not readily available. Comparisons of ICT spending for e-government across countries are further exacerbated by different ICT investment histories and thus differing installed bases, capital replacement costs and spending requirements for ancillary infrastructures for e-government readiness (Bertucci and Szeremeta, 2003). One particularly noteworthy problem is that budgets of e-government projects tend to shift during the life of the project, caused by political changes that can cut off the funding. But even if political support is maintained, the very nature of ICT investments puts a complex budget management problem in front of public-sector managers (Harvard Policy Group on Networked-Enabled Services and Government, 2001).

There is much anecdotal evidence about ICT procurement processes that have gone wrong. The causes range from officials who lack the expertise to decide what they really need, to local procurement processes that are so complex and time consuming that they all but ensure that the technology will be out of date by the time it finally comes online. The behaviour of some vendors, especially in countries less experienced in such complex technical contracts, is also known to leave a lot to be desired. Financially, large investments that are risky but may bring public value can be defended. It is much more difficult to defend a big, risky investment when one does not know how much the investment eventually will be or exactly what it is that will be purchased.

Funding mechanisms for e-government vary throughout the world. Forms of private financing for public–private e-development resemble those of conventional private-sector investment and run the gamut from direct domestic investments to foreign direct investments as well as domestic and foreign portfolio investments in publicly listed entities. Financial mechanisms that are in common use include:

- government initiatives for ICT for development;
- public–private partnerships;
- bilateral assistance funding;
- foreign direct investments;
- universal service obligations;
- direct ICT budget allocations.

In terms of geographic prevalence, national-scale ICT investment is most concentrated in Asia and South-east Asia, in part because of long-term strategies of transnational corporations for locating hardware production in emerging markets, as well as efforts by regional developing nations to nurture local ICT production capacities (Xengpei, 2005). A key role for practitioners is to foster an enabling environment through the adoption of national e-government funding mechanisms. Public–private partnerships (PPP) are often used for complex or high-cost projects in which knowledge and expertise from both public and private sectors need to be combined, or in which the government needs assistance in financing the project infrastructure. The potential of leveraging private pools of capital investment is attractive to government, just as government has frequently looked to industry for managerial techniques and governance practices. Accordingly, the concept of a public–private partnership typically denotes private-sector involvement in the construction and/or maintenance of a new capital asset. As ICT infrastructure becomes more strategic and technologically sophisticated, questions pertaining to financing become more central. Within government, then, this partnership logic extends from the creation of new, tangible infrastructure assets to the maintenance and upgrading of organisational and often less physically tangible forms of infrastructure. The choice of e-government project partners can vary from multinational management consultants to information technology vendors to local software companies. There are usually three main options for partners: to build a project; to build, own and operate it; or to build, operate and transfer. Regardless of the specific agreement, partnerships should build local capacity. If private partners are involved, contracts should be fair for both parties – so that the private sector earns reasonable profits and the public sector achieves its goals for efficiency and service delivery.

### *The enabling environment: legal, regulatory, privacy, security and information policy*

A nation's legal and regulatory policies have a profound influence on ICT investment and use. Legal rules create a complex web of incentives and disincentives for private-sector action – some of which will impact a society's desire and ability to develop or utilise ICTs. When a nation's public policy framework offers strong incentives for people to develop and acquire ICTs, governments will have greater ability to leverage the power of ICTs and drive economic growth more broadly. Although many of the prerequisites relevant to e-government also happen to be necessary conditions for the development and successful implementation of e-strategies as a whole, one cannot over-emphasise the importance of adequate legal, regulatory and institutional environments as necessary conditions for success in e-government. Whether such frameworks are designed and enforced at central or local (sub-national) levels, they have proven to be the single most important precondition for the successful and society-broad use of information technologies, mainly because they have allowed cost and prices to diminish. In areas in which public entities (that is to say governments, administrative departments, or state-owned enterprises) remain major players (as in e-government), the creation of such environments becomes particularly critical (and visible) because government is both on the supply side (for online services to citizens) and on the demand side (for e-procurement) of the equation.

## E-governance as transformation of the relationship of government to citizens in an information society

One of the most common themes evident in the above account of different strategies for e-government is the paradigmatic shift in perspective that it implies for government and its constituents. The new paradigm places citizens foremost, with the government providing services in ways that make sense from the citizens' point of view. This shift is fundamental to achieving the goals set out by the 'cyber-optimist' camp of e-government visionaries, who see in ICTs a medium capable of producing a change of this magnitude. Borrowing from private-sector customer relationship management terminology, this fundamental change in perspective is called 'citizen-centric' government (Digital Gateway: e-government, http://topics. developmentgateway.org/egovernment/index.do).

Governments are not traditionally organised from such a perspective but rather from a bureaucratically centred perspective of the various agencies that constitute the public sector as a whole. Frequently referred to as 'silos', these agencies typically do not communicate or coordinate with each other. Services have been distributed among different agencies, who 'own' the service. To access that service, citizens physically go there, after finding out which agency owns it, and the process is repeated for every necessary service (see Mayer-Schönberger and Lazer, 2007). The 'cyber-pessimists' are doubtful regarding the capacity of governments to change to meet the requirements of a paradigm shift of this magnitude, arguing that ICTs alone will be insufficient to overcome the entrenched, hierarchical and bureaucratic culture. They argue that the application of ICTs amounts to mere window dressing rather than meaningful transformation. As the pessimists caution, simply putting present practices and services online (automation) would not significantly affect what and how work is done within government. As a result, it risks replication of present service shortcomings. For example, where citizens have had to go to numerous government service counters to fulfil a particular service need, by simply putting those services online citizens would no longer go to counters, but would still need to go to numerous websites, and need to know which website to go to for which service. So the channel of delivery has changed, but the shortcomings remain. In fact, it could further confuse users and reduce their satisfaction with government service delivery.

The new paradigm is often referred to as 'integrated' services, in which ICTs enable a range of services to be virtually accessible via a 'single window', or 'one-stop shop', via a portal anywhere an internet connection is available. From the citizen's viewpoint, this is called 'seamless' government. Enabled by ICTs, the silos within the hierarchical and rules-bound institutions of the state are interacting, and are thereby transformed (see Table 9.4). The transformative potential of e-governance clearly lies not only in putting new practices and services online, but in improving the full range of what the public service does and how it does it. Instead of going to the websites of numerous organisations to get a number of related services, they could be obtained through one site or portal. This way, citizens would not need to know what department they are dealing with in order to get the service they need. This approach is about innovating, not just automating.

What is at issue is the effectiveness of ICTs as a tool for realising the values embedded in the notion of 'good governance'. Practitioners on the whole recognise that truly seamless government represents only the final stage of e-governance, which in practical terms is still far in the future. Current progress is achieved via identification of the good governance related

**Table 9.4** *Automation vs innovation in e-governance*

|  | Automation | Innovation |
|---|---|---|
| Services | • Put information about existing organisation services online<br>• Provide transactional services online<br>• Services only available on website of agency responsible for delivering them | • Provide a portal for all government services<br>• Cluster services by 'life events', organised according to citizen's perspective<br>• Integrate services across organisations |
| Transition to knowledge society | • Make existing publicly available information accessible electronically | • Manage knowledge better to improve public management<br>• Use information and knowledge management better to create, collect and integrate information for public use |
| Extend democracy | • Make existing publicly available information accessible electronically<br>• Make policies available online<br>• Make budgets, planning documents and performance reviews available online | • Create transparency and free flow of information<br>• Involve citizens in development planning and policy making<br>• Make public procurement information available online |

*Source:* James Guida and Martin Crow.

reform goals and correspondent applications and service delivery mechanisms (see Table 9.5).

### E-strategy

Making incremental progress towards a solution obviously implies the need for a well-considered plan which links specific reform goals with service efficiency gains available from the range of process automation applications and new communication media, while innovating to improve service delivery. A well-designed e-governance component of a developing nation's e-strategy will focus on these achievable, incremental results, tailoring the approach to implementation to the country's specific readiness characteristics and need, while bearing in mind the long-term goals of transformation of the governance process and the relationship between government and the governed.

The challenges inherent in crafting an effective e-governance strategy include (see for example Sachdeva, 2002; Kluver, 2005):

• a need for vision and leadership;

• consistency with other national development goals;

• coordination within governments;

• consultation for consensus building on objectives and approaches;

**Table 9.5** *Governance reform objectives and e-solutions*

| Reform objectives | E-solutions |
|---|---|
| Reforming public-sector institutions and civil service management | Major BPR, information-sharing solutions across agencies, HR management systems, payroll, etc. |
| Improving public resource mobilisation, expenditure management and financial management | Tax policy analysis and administration modernisation, integrated financial management systems, etc. |
| Strengthening governance, accountability and transparency | Local budget monitoring by citizens, performance rating of public services/agencies, grievance systems, etc. |
| Improving public services and making services work for the poor | E-citizen services and portals to provide information and transactions |
| Promoting effective decentralisation, improving efficiency, effectiveness and transparency of local governments | Systems in support of fiscal and administrative decentralisation, incl. local services online; GIS for urban planning, municipal management systems |
| Facilitating international trade, customs and logistics | Customs and ports modernisation, new applications to facilitate secure trade, trade nets |
| Improving the business environment and regulation of the private sector | Reforming G2B transactions; portals for investors, FDI, business licensing, etc. |
| Enhancing SME competitiveness through e-government services | Portals for SMEs, applications for microfinance, etc. |
| Reforming the public procurement, project implementation and focus on results, functions | E-procurement, national M&E systems, performance indicators |
| Improving knowledge management and learning systems | Support to communities of practice, etc. |
| Improving policy formulation and macroeconomic management | Modernising national statistical systems, cabinet-level decision support systems (e-cabinet) |
| Strengthening social participation, democracy and rule of law | E-democracy applications, e-justice applications, etc. |

*Source:* Hanna (forthcoming 2009).

- implementation of articulated and realistic plans of action;
- resources prioritisation and not based on mere wishful thinking;
- supportive legal framework to enable ICT policies;
- supportive policy frameworks to facilitate implementation; and
- objectives against which to monitor progress and produce defined results.

Coming to terms with these challenges requires the active involvement of all sectors of society, not just government. Key questions are who the stakeholders are and to what extent, in which areas and at what points of time in the development process should governments interact or engage with them.

*Stakeholders*

The e-governance vision belongs to society, not only to public-sector leaders, and it should be constructed accordingly to reflect the concerns and contributions of key stakeholders and provide broad social ownership and legitimacy. Government ministries, national private sector, regulatory bodies, NGOs, ICT personnel, and academic institutions should all play a role. Only the people affected can give effective depth to plans for e-government development. They can help in defining what constitutes the public value, and inform the political process of selecting the appropriate e-government applications, which would create a solid foundation for future e-government-related investments.

## Key issues in formulating a development- and reform-based e-governance strategy

A theoretical framework to guide the selection of appropriate e-government initiatives should focus on the opportunities to link the common challenges facing public-sector management practitioners to the potential use of ICT. Principles of 'good governance' (democratic, responsive, efficient, participatory, inclusive and transparent) are typically included in e-government visions. These principles provide added value to e-government, imbuing it with ethical imperatives as well as with a means for assessment (International Conference on e-Government for Development, 2002). The motivations of adopting such a framework are to:

- bridge the gap between development practitioners in the field of public-sector management and governance on the one hand, and the specialists in ICT and e-government, on the other, thus mainstreaming ICT for development;
- ensure that ICT applications are development- and demand-driven, not technology- or supply-driven, thus ensuring cost-effective investment in ICT for maximum development impact; and
- identify and assess the strategic options and issues involved in providing more systematic and effective development assistance, as a tool for improving governance as well as developing a competitive domestic market for ICT services.

To bridge the gap, it is important to start from the language of the business of development or governance. This perspective enables both development practitioners (public-sector management specialists) and ICT specialists to use ICT in an integral way to transform institutions, public services and overall public-sector management, and provides strategic opportunities to solve public-sector management-related development challenges. The remainder of this chapter explores a framework for identifying electronic service initiatives to support development based on ten widely agreed public-sector management reform goals.

## Improving public services and making services work for the poor

Putting services online or adding new electronic service delivery channels can improve service to citizens by improving accessibility and standard-ising and/or reducing costs. However, improving the delivery of public social services to promote development depends less on the skilful util-isation of ICT by government than it does on answers to questions such as: Does a society recognise the right of its members to equal access to services and the ability to participate in a knowledge society? What is the politically accepted role that a government is supposed to play in provid-ing such opportunities? Depending on these answers and given their pro-developmental thrust, a culturally grounded host of suitable ICT solutions can be leveraged upon. E-government in the area of delivery of social ser-vices can occupy a well-deserved place in poorer countries by, for exam-ple, delivering workforce, land use, agriculture, export/import, telemedi-cine, health and immigration systems through rural kiosks or telecentres (Szeremeta, 2005).

## Reforming public-sector institutions and civil service management

E-government programmes are most effective when they are accompa-nied by organisational change initiatives that align services with customer needs. Practitioners must set new expectations for investment in employ-ee training, business process re-engineering, and in systems that provide accurate and integrated information for decision making. Key strategies include:

- including employees in decisions regarding policies, procedures and performance standards in an e-government environment;
- investing in training and re-training for employees, particularly for those whose jobs are changed by e-government;
- holding employees accountable for results and outcomes, not regulatory compliance or inputs;
- planning for change management as part of e-government imple-mentation.

## Improving public resource mobilisation and expenditure management

'Efficiency' is a relative assessment that takes into account the rela-tionship between the level of performance of the government and the amount of resources used, under given conditions. E-government can have a wide impact on government efficiency and effectiveness, mak-ing services more convenient and cutting service delivery time by providing automated means for faster access to government services. Response time reduction and convenient service offerings through process automation can strengthen relationships with citizens, other government agencies and vendors, and lead to goals such as lower cost of operations and higher productivity. Significant cost savings can also result from a reduction in personnel requirements, but many governments are unwilling or unable to cut down the number of employees after the introduction of electronic delivery (Bhatnagar, 2003). Perhaps the maximal cost reduction takes place in storing paper files and moving to a paperless environment in which electronic documents flow from workstation to workstation for approval and action, which thereby lowers the administrative burden on decision-makers, releasing time for important issues of policy and decision-making. In reality, though, this can often actually increase the burden on the decision-makers, who find that the ease of digital communication means that they now get sent many more documents for consideration, thereby reducing the amount of time that they have for other activities.

### Strengthening governance, accountability and transparency

Strengthening governance, accountability and transparency means the use of ICTs to make public-sector decisions and actions more open to scrutiny. It runs from just providing basic information about government up to enabling public control over civil servants. There are process benefits (such as reducing costs for transparency), and also governance benefits (such as making public servants behave less corruptly, and empowering citizens). ICTs are an effective tool because of the way they can cut costs, open up access to information, automate corruptible processes and reduce problems associated with corrupt staff. For the poor, there can be particular benefits of e-transparency: saving money in dealings with government, improving the equality of treatment and participation of all members of the community, and improving the planning and implementation of relevant development projects (Heeks, 2004).

The increased ease of access to government information and services translates into increased transparency and consistency of service delivery. For example, if both citizens and officials have access to the same permitting processes, it is difficult for any official to act in a capricious or arbitrary manner. Nevertheless, while the potential of ICT in curbing corruption has been demonstrated in practice, ICT-augmented transparency cannot succeed as the main anti-corruption measure. Even in fighting corruption, ICTs need an enabling context: a culture that does not tolerate or reward corruption with high social status; a strong civil society and strong democratic institutions; multiparty democracy; a free press; and legal protection of whistle-blowers. Moreover, looking at transparency in this context alone is too narrow. Much more importantly, transparency – understood as an open, accessible public sphere that gives voice to every citizen – helps the government make correct decisions. It thus lowers the cost and increases the quality of democracy as well as enriches the pool of available, politically useful information on which citizens can creatively reflect in the process of creating the knowledge to maintain the drive towards developmental goals (Szeremeta, 2005).

## Reforming public procurement and project implementation functions

The transparency introduced by using e-procurement technology can sharply reduce the opportunity for fraud, put all bidders on an equal footing in terms of informing them of contract opportunities, and allow the public to view winning company bids. Transparent procurement procedures contribute to a more efficient allocation of resources through increased competition, higher-quality procurement and budgetary savings for governments and thus for taxpayers. They can also help attract more investment by lowering risk, and help enhance the efficiency of local suppliers as they compete for public contracts, thereby improving trade prospects by making these suppliers more competitive exporters (OECD, 2003). With public procurement accounting for up to 20 per cent of a country's GDP, e-procurement has the capacity significantly to impact the efficient use of national budgets. For example, after introducing transparent procurement procedures in the energy sector, Bangladesh was able to reduce electricity prices to less than US$0.03 a kilowatt-hour, roughly half the price of directly negotiated deals in Indonesia (Transparency International, 2002).

## Managing effective decentralisation

ICT-based e-government transformation can support more localised levels of public-sector management decision making and decentralisation by creating improved information flows to decision makers and process implementers in new locations, reducing the costs and increasing the speed of the decision-making process. Decentralisation can contribute to better governance, increased system efficiency and more efficient use of resources. Decentralisation usually involves a large group of stakeholders, which influences the flow of all major inputs to and from an automated system. For decentralisation to succeed, adequate time must be allowed for people to learn the lessons of pilots and to obtain the views and incorporate the plans of stakeholders at lower levels before a reform initiative is amalgamated into a nationwide initiative and expansion. A long-term view by stakeholders is therefore necessary in relation to the implementation of supporting e-government initiatives and achievement of the policy and reform objectives.

## Improving institutional knowledge management and learning systems

Just as in the corporate world, e-government systems for internal knowledge management (bringing people and information assets together) and institutional learning have a significant impact on institutional performance (Szeremeta, 2005; Misra, 2007). For practitioners, a vision and a strategy for developing a knowledge-based organisation is a must. It should address issues such as high-level knowledge management policies and procedures, overall infrastructure, staff/policy alignment, budget allocation, content management, tools and technologies, and networks to support the development of the knowledge-based organisations. The mindset needs to be changed from managing information traditionally to doing so in a modern way supported by IT systems.

### Improving the policy formulation process

ICTs can connect the arms, agencies, levels and data stores of government to strengthen capacity to investigate, develop and implement the strategy and policy that guides government processes. Examples of such connections are central-to-local, ministry-to-ministry, executive-to-legislature and decision maker-to-data store. Automation of information delivery supports this by digitising existing information channels and by creating new digital channels. The rationale is to provide clearer direction for public-sector and state processes and to provide for a more evidence-based approach to policy and process.

### Enhancing SME competitiveness and improving the overall business environment

Online government services for business theoretically pay dividends in time saved, reduced complexity and improved access to information. Developing nations fare particularly poorly in the amount of time required to complete the necessary procedures to start a new business. Automating and streamlining these procedures reduce the amount of time invested by prospective businesses dealing with regulation. This in turn helps boost competitiveness. E-government technology can thus also serve as an engine for economic development, and governments can maximise the economic competitiveness of their constituency by promoting the development of online government-to-business services. This can be accomplished through:

- use of the internet to establish a brand identity and provide useful information to attract businesses;
- driving the development of online business services to ease the burden of compliance, taxation and filing requirements for private-sector business;
- implementing the use of geographic information systems (GIS) to make geographic information available for business location and siting decisions;
- enhancing economic competitiveness through provision of market information quickly and accurately.

In many countries, notably India, the development of the software industry has been largely influenced by developments in governmental structures. Legislation has created a favourable environment and government departments have also been active in procuring innovative solutions from local companies. When local companies have been contracted to provide customised solutions, positive spillovers have emerged.

### Strengthening social participation and democracy

E-government can provide new avenues for citizens to contribute to the policy-creation process, thus enhancing citizen consultation, engagement and debate prior to decisions being made (ECOTEC, 2007). Active, involved citizens enhance the legitimacy of governments by articulating their preferences and holding governments accountable for the production of public value. The level of well-informed, popular participation is a good measure to evaluate a governance system.

ICTs can bring speed, precision, outreach and networking capacity to the governance process. As communication-enhancing technologies, the potentially positive impact that ICTs can have on governance – predominantly a communication process – cannot be underestimated. However, for ICTs to play this role, the citizens must be sure of their civic rights and freedoms, of accessibility and openness of the public sphere. If economics, politics, ideology or private interests shift the functions of a public administration away from what the people want, ICTs cannot fill this gap. It is pointless to hope that a positive impact can be achieved by simply introducing ICTs into situations where governance institutions do not allow for involvement of citizens of different social status, as for example where the public sphere is not open and accessible for all, or where groups of citizens are denied their voice.

The development of socially inclusive policies should aim to provide access to ICT-related services to the largest possible number of people and communities in order to improve their participation in a knowledge-based society and economy. The process should be facilitated, either directly or through intermediaries, by taking proactive measures to minimise the influence of socio-economic differences such as education, location, employment, disability, age or gender. To achieve this objective, alternative devices could be considered as viable means for promoting e-government and e-participation, through multi-channel strategies and solutions, such as mobile phones and community computing. By its very nature inclusive, e-government implies that proactive measures should be taken by governments to ensure that public services are available and accessible to all and that digital exclusion through e-government is avoided at all costs. Mobile phones, speech technology and wireless networking, for example, could all make e-participation more accessible to those with little or no educational attainment, as well as hard-to-reach and marginalised groups in society.

To promote e-participation, practitioners should focus on a combination of the following strategies:

- *target specific groups* such as the underprivileged, women, youth, the marginalised, and those living in remote areas;

- *target specific issues* of concern to the majority of the citizens, such as social benefits, job creation, maternal and child healthcare;
- *select a small number of priorities* that require meaningful dialogue among stakeholders and have a high policy impact.

Policy and strategy discussions should focus on addressing the above issues before determining any other requirements, such as technology, access and connectivity issues. A rush to embrace ICTs for use in government could backfire unless e-government strategies are designed and developed within the socio-cultural, economic and political context of the country, and adequate time is allocated for adoption and implementation.

## Conclusions

Visions of future government based on the innovation and transformation potential inherent in e-governance lie at the heart of all e-government initiatives. Because e-government success is a function of a combination of technological and cultural issues, working to achieve that potential requires that sufficient resources be allocated to solving the key issues on the human 'governance' side of the equation as well as on the technical 'government' issues.

Important factors in e-government initiatives range from political and economic models to inequities of financial, human and technical capital. Since e-government development reflects countries' willingness to share information and knowledge with their people, to a great extent political ideologies and the bureaucratic, insular institutional culture of government predetermine the effectiveness of e-government strategies. At present, e-government initiatives are mushrooming around the globe in a somewhat haphazard manner, leading to wide variations among countries in the provision of online information and basic public services. Citizen participation remains uneven, and in many developing countries information and services reach only a privileged few in urban areas. The primary technological factors impeding the reach of e-government in developing countries are the lack of infrastructure and trained human resources. Consequently there is an ongoing risk of the digital divide widening in terms of e-government.

Given these many challenges, the practitioner's role in shepherding the prudent and effective application of ICTs in government is a task that carries great responsibility. There is no 'one-size-fits-all' model for e-government development. Each country needs to devise its own e-government strategy and programme, taking into consideration its political, economic and social priorities and its financial, human and technological capacities. The practitioner's role also offers enormous potential for reward in terms of reforming the public sector to achieve greater efficiency and efficacy, reduce costs, increase and improve services to society, and create an inclusive, participatory governance structure which empowers all citizens. The key to effective e-government implementation is a multi-pronged approach based on technology as well as human development.

## Key readings
Anttiroiko, A.-V. and Malkia, M. (2006) *Encyclopedia of Digital Government.* Hershey, PA: Information Science Reference

Backus, M. (2001) *E-Governance and Developing Countries: introduction and examples.* The Hague: IICD (IICD Research Brief)

Department of Economic and Social Affairs, UN (2007) *E-Participation and E-Government: understanding the present and creating the future: report of the Ad Hoc Expert Group Meeting, Budapest, Hungary, 27–28 July 2006.* New York: United Nations, Department of Economic and Social Affairs, Division for Public Administration and Development Management

Finger, M. and Pécoud, G. (2003) From e-Government to e-Governance? Towards a model of e-Governance. *Electronic Journal of e-Government*, 1 (1), pp. 1–10

Hanna, N.K. (2008) *Transforming Government and Empowering Communities: the Sri Lankan experience with e-development.* Washington, DC: World Bank

Heeks, R. (2001) *Understanding e-Governance for Development.* Manchester: IDPM

Heeks, R. (2003) *Most eGovernment-for-Development Projects Fail: how can risks be reduced?* Manchester: IDPM Working Papers

MacLean, D. (ed.) (2004) *Internet Governance: a grand collaboration.* New York: UN ICT Task Force

## References
Anttiroiko, A.-V. and Malkia, M. (2006) *Encyclopedia of Digital Government.* Hershey, PA: Information Science Reference

Backus, M. (2001) *E-Governance and Developing Countries: introduction and examples.* The Hague: IICD (IICD Research Brief) (http://www.ftpiicd.org/files/research/reports/report3.doc)

Bertucci, G. and Szeremeta, J. (2003) *E-Government at the Crossroads.* World Public Sector Report for the United Nations Department of Economic and Social Affairs (http://unpan1.un.org/intradoc/groups/public/documents/UN/UNPAN012733.pdf)

Bhatnagar, S. (2003) Role of government: as an enabler, regulator, and provider of ICT based services. Indian Institute of Management, Asian Forum on ICT Policies and e-Strategies, UNDP-APDIP (http://www.apdip.net/projects/2003/asian-forum/docs/papers/session3.pdf)

Bhatnagar, S. and Deane, A. (2004) Building blocks of e-government. In *Lessons From Developing Countries.* Washington, DC: World Bank Poverty Reduction and Economic Management Network, PREMnote No. 91 (http://www1.worldbank.org/prem/PREMNotes/premnote91.pdf)

Cordella, A. (2007) E-government: towards the e-bureaucratic form? *Journal of Information Technology*, 22, pp. 265–74

Davenport, T. (2000) *Working Knowledge*. Boston, MA: Harvard Business School Press

DeLong, D. (2004) *Lost Knowledge*. Oxford: Oxford University Press, Babson College

Department of Economic and Social Affairs, UN (2007) *E-Participation and E-Government: understanding the present and creating the future: report of the Ad Hoc Expert Group Meeting, Budapest, Hungary, 27–28 July 2006*. New York: United Nations, Department of Economic and Social Affairs, Division for Public Administration and Development Management (ST/ESA/PAD/SER.E.99) (http://unpan1.un.org/intradoc/groups/public/documents/UN/UNPAN026527.pdf)

DOT-COMments e-Newsletter (2005) Local e-Government Applications – an example from Romania (http://www.dot-com-alliance.org/newsletter/print_article.php?article_id=135)

ECOTEC (2007) *A Handbook for Citizen-centric eGovernment*. Brussels: eGovernment Unit, DG Information Society and Media, European Commission (http://www.ccegov.eu/downloads/Handbook_Final_031207.pdf)

E-government, New Zealand (2004) *Networking in New Zealand E-government Supply and Demand* (http://www.e.govt.nz/archive/resources/conferences/gartner/al-meeting-20040428/chapter7.html)

Finger, M. and Pécoud, G. (2003) From e-Government to e-Governance? Towards a model of e-Governance. *Electronic Journal of e-Government*, 1 (1), pp. 1–10 (http://ictd.undp.org/egov/papers/issue1-art1-finger-pecoud.pdf)

Freedman, A. (2001) *The Computer Glossary*, 9th edn. Toronto: AMACOM

Hanna, N.K. (2008) *Transforming Government and Empowering Communities: the Sri Lankan experience with e-development*. Washington, DC: World Bank

Hanna, N.K. (forthcoming 2009) *Advanced Strategies for Development: ICT-enabled Economics*. New Delhi, India: Sage Publications

Harris, R. (2004) *Information and Communication Technologies for Poverty Alleviation*. Bangkok: UNDP-APDIP (http://www.apdip.net/publications/iespprimers/eprimer-pov.pdf)

Harvard Policy Group on Networked-Enabled Services and Government (2001) Imperative 4: Improve budgeting and financing for promising IT initiatives. *Eight Imperatives for Leaders in a Networked World*. Boston, MA: Harvard University, Kennedy School of Government

Heeks, R. (2001) *Understanding e-Governance for Development*. Manchester: IDPM (http://unpan1.un.org/intradoc/groups/public/documents/NISPAcee/UNPAN015484.pdf)

Heeks, R. (2003) *Most eGovernment-for-Development Projects Fail: how can risks be reduced?* Manchester: IDPM Working Papers (http://unpan1.un.org/intradoc/groups/public/documents/NISPAcee/UNPAN015488.pdf)

Heeks, R. (2004) *eGovernment for Development: using ICTs for government transparency*. Manchester: University of Manchester (http://www.egov4dev.org/topic2smry.htm)

Heeks, R. (2006) *Understanding and Measuring eGovernment: international benchmarking studies*. UNDESA (http://unpan1.un.org/intradoc/groups/public/documents/UN/UNPAN023686.pdf)

International Conference on e-Government for Development (2002) International Conference on e-Government for Development, Palermo, Italy, 10 April 2002, by UNDESA and Ministry of Innovation and Technology, Government of Italy

Kinde, S. (2007) *Internet in Ethiopia – is Ethiopia off-line or wired to the rim?* (http://www.ethiopians.com/Engineering/Internet_in_Ethiopia_November2007.htm)

Kluver, R. (2005) The architecture of control: a Chinese strategy for e-governance. *Journal of Public Policy*, 25, pp. 75–97

Mayer-Schönberger, V. and Lazer, D. (2007) *Governance and Information Technology: from electronic government to information government*. Cambridge, MA: MIT Press

Misra, D.C. (2007) Ten guiding principles for knowledge management in e-government. First International Conference on Knowledge Management for Productivity and Competitiveness (http://unpan1.un.org/intradoc/groups/public/documents/UNPAN/UNPAN025338.pdf)

Murray, J. (2006) *The GAP Principles: supporting IT projects and e-government through improved governance, architecture and procurement*. Microsoft (http://unpan1.un.org/intradoc/groups/public/documents/UNPAN/UNPAN025936.pdf)

Norris, P. (2002) *Digital Divide: civic engagement, information poverty, and the internet worldwide*. Cambridge: Cambridge University Press (http://ksghome.harvard.edu/~pnorris/acrobat/digitalch6.pdf)

OECD (2001) *The Hidden Threat to e-Government: avoiding large government IT failures*. Paris: OECD, Policy Brief no. 8

OECD (2003) *Transparency in Government Procurement: the benefits of efficient governance and orientations for achieving IT* (http://www.olis.oecd.org/olis/2002doc.nsf/LinkTo/NT00000D2A/$FILE/JT00143801.PDF)

Sachdeva, S. (2002) White Paper on e-Governance Strategy in India (http://unpan1.un.org/intradoc/groups/public/documents/APCITY/UNPAN014672.pdf)

Seifert, J. (2003) *A Primer on e-Government: sectors, stages, opportunities and challenges of online governance*. Washington, DC: Congressional Research Service, The Library of Congress. Report for US Congress (http://www.fas.org/sgp/crs/RL31057.pdf)

Selam Development Consultants (2007) *ICT Assisted Development Project M&E System Baseline ICT Laws Enacted and ICT Business Status in Major Towns of Ethiopia* (http://web.worldbank.org/external/projects/main?pagePK=64283627&piPK=73230&theSitePK=40941&menuPK=228424&Projectid=P078458)

Sheridan, W. and Riley, T. (2006) *Comparing e-Government vs. e-Governance* (http://www.egovmonitor.com/node/6556)

Sørgaard, P. (2002) *Implementing e-Government Leadership and Co-ordination*. OECD/PUM (http://webdomino1.oecd.org/COMNET/PUM/egovproweb.nsf/22afaebba539ba74c1256a3b004d5175/b3b8d25f219f4ae3c1256bd5004874f1/$FILE/Sorgaard.PDF)

Spintrack (2004) *ICT Diagnostic Study – Ethiopia*. Stockholm: Spintrack for the Centre for the Development of Enterprise

Szeremeta, J. (2005) ICT as a tool for good governance and good government. In *Access, Empowerment and Governance. Creating a world of equal opportunities with ICT*, ed. R. Abdul Rahim, D. Waldburger and G.S. Muinde. Kuala Lumpur: Global Knowledge Partnership, pp. 83–92

Transparency International (2002) *Transparency International Corruption Perceptions Index 2002*. Berlin: Transparency International

UN (2005) *UN Global e-Government Readiness Report 2005: from e-government to e-inclusion*. New York: UN

UNESCO (2005) *E-government Tool-kit for Developing Countries*. New Delhi: National Informatics Centre and UNESCO. CD-ROM (http://portal.unesco.org/ci/en/ev.php-URL_ID=19432&URL_DO=DO_TOPIC&URL_SECTION=201.html, accessed 28 January 2008)

Wimmer, M.A. (ed.) (2004) *Knowledge Management in Electronic Government: 5th IFIP International Working Conference, KMGov 2004, Krems, Austria, May 2004, Proceedings*. Berlin: Springer

Windley, P. (2006) Building good e-government websites, *ZDnet* (http://blogs.zdnet.com/BTL/?p = 3693)

World Bank, INF/GICT (2005) *E-Strategies Monitoring and Evaluation Toolkit*. Washington, DC: World Bank

World Economic Forum (2007) *The Global Information Technology Report 2006–2007*. Geneva: World Economic Forum

Xengpei, X. (2005) Financial mechanisms for ICT for development, South-East and East Asia Conference on Follow up to WSIS, Bali, Indonesia, 1–3 February 2005 (http://www.unescap.org/icstd/events/WSIS_2nd_Phase/docs/Bali/FM/ESCAP_FMx.ppt)

# 10 | Information and communication technologies for rural development

## Bob Day and Peter Greenwood

- The international development community has not yet articulated a shared, compelling vision for rural development. Though important, the MDGs are visionary targets, not a shared vision.
- Despite the consistently high hopes of proponents over the past 15 years, ICT-based initiatives continue to underperform, particularly in the highly diverse arenas of rural development.
- Much of the technical and social learning that has occurred over this period is still not being incorporated into current ICT4RD initiatives.
- Most policy analysts and decision makers do not consider the role or potential of ICTs as being central to their rural development policies, strategies or initiatives.
- The greatest impacts of climate change are being experienced by the world's poorest rural communities. Mitigation requires a coherent set of interdependent, long-term global programmes that will include vast investments in rural areas.
- It is important to develop a globally shared and integrated vision for rural development that addresses both mitigation strategies for climate change, and the eradication of rural poverty.
- ICTs and knowledge management can play a core role in the creation, dissemination and implementation of this vision for rural development.

## Introduction

The fundamental purpose of rural development should be to improve the quality of life of the 900 million people worldwide living in rural poverty, while improving the environmental sustainability of their existence and of the biosphere in general. As the global economy expands, with the elite becoming ever more wealthy, the fact that so many people continue to live in intransigent poverty and hunger is a major ethical, economic, health and security challenge to us all. It is important to recognise that such disparities between urban and rural life are not sustainable in the long term (Lipton, 1977).

How should we characterise rural development and rural poverty? First, we need to recognise that the term 'rural' is used widely and ambiguously because there is no agreed definition (Wiggins and Proctor, 2001; Maxwell and Heber-Percy, 2001). The core features of rural areas are pastures, fields, bush, woods and forests, streams and lakes, deserts and mountains, with only sparse human settlements such as smallholdings or villages. However, national distinctions between rural and urban areas are 'arbitrary and varied' (IFAD, 2001, p. 18). The issue of proximity to the socio-economic systems afforded by towns creates a further subcategorisation between rural areas that are peri-urban, middle countryside or remote (Wiggins and Proctor, 2001). Second, the majority of poor rural people live in areas that are resource poor, highly heterogeneous and risk prone (Conway, 1997). Third, the dynamics of rural demographic change and urban migration are crucial. During 2007, the balance of the global population shifted from being predominantly rural to being predominantly urban. Indications are that even in developing countries urban populations will exceed rural populations by 2020 (Cour and Snrech, 1998).

Generalising about rural poverty is often counter-productive. However, the following observations help to contextualise rural poverty as a significant global phenomenon:

- the vast majority of people in higher leadership positions (public and private sectors) are urban;
- three quarters of the 2.1 billion people living on less than $2 a day live and work in rural areas, but only 4 per cent of official development assistance goes to agriculture in developing countries (World Bank, 2007);
- 86 per cent of people living in rural areas depend, at least in part, on agriculture for their livelihoods (World Bank, 2007) – most of these are poor and live in Africa and South-East Asia;
- women in sub-Saharan Africa are responsible for producing up to 80 per cent of the basic food consumed there (http://www.fao.org/Gender/en/agrib4-e.ht);
- some 1.1 billion people in developing countries have inadequate access to water, and 2.6 billion lack basic sanitation (UNDP, 2006);
- 67 per cent of rural people are without electricity (IFC, 2007);
- in the developing world, one in four children under the age of 5 is still underweight, and one in three is stunted. These figures almost double in rural areas (UNICEF, 2005).

If the diversity of rural life today makes it hard to define precisely what we mean by it, what of its future? Maxwell and Heber-Percy (2001) argue that the rate of change in rural life has been high, and will continue to increase. They make a range of predictions, including the following:

- the great majority of rural people will be functionally landless, either without land altogether, or with only a small homestead plot;

- most rural income in most places will be non-agricultural in origin (though with linkages to agriculture in many cases);
- most farms will be predominantly commercial, that is to say buying most inputs and selling most of their output;
- farms (other than part-time subsistence or homestead plots) will be larger than at present, and getting larger;
- for those farmers able to engage in the commercial economy, their input and output marketing systems will be integrated, industrialised and sophisticated;
- as a result of all the above, disparities between rural areas will increase;
- agriculture's contribution to GDP will be no more than 10 per cent;
- agriculture will contribute no more than 10 per cent to exports (perhaps more in Latin America and sub-Saharan Africa).

The urban–rural system worldwide is far from being at an equilibrium point (Potter and Unwin, 1989). Decision makers (almost all of whom share an urban perspective) cannot continue to view issues of rural poverty in the face of urban wealth as being peripheral to the long-term sustainability of urban life (Lipton, 1977). Business as usual, based on the old industrial economy models, is no longer an option. A fundamental, far-reaching and globally shared vision for rural development is urgently needed. As we will argue, it is the lack of this shared vision that has resulted in a rash of un-coordinated ICT for rural development (ICT4RD) initiatives that have had little impact over the past couple of decades.

## Stakeholder issues
This section briefly reviews the historical and current thinking of the global development community, and then examines their implications from a rural perspective.

### Global development processes
Currently, the loosely knit components of the international aid 'system' consist of more than 150 multilateral agencies (http://www.oecd.org/dataoecd/8/60/2089808.pdf), 33 bilateral agencies that are members of the OECD Development Assistance Committee (DAC), at least 10 non-DAC governments providing significant funds for assistance, and an increasing number of vertical global funds. Many stakeholders observe that the aid system has reached an unnecessary level of complexity (Action Aid, 2005). Globally, there are now estimated to be more than 1,000 financing mechanisms, with as many new mechanisms emerging in the past decade as were created in the previous 50 years (Kaul and Conceicão, 2006). Adding to this complexity is a high proportion of bilateral aid and technical assistance, along with significant flows of private funding, and activities by non-government organisations (NGOs). The existence and evolution of the complex

variety of aid agencies is in part a response to the lack of trust and account-ability or even open information sharing between the various stakeholders (Martens, 2005). Some experts believe that the current international aid delivery system is 'not "fit for purpose"' (Burall *et al.*, 2006, p. 2).

As outlined in Chapter 2, the system is now undergoing some significant reforms, including the Paris Declaration on Aid Effectiveness and recent moves to reform the United Nations (UN), but even if these are implement-ed in full they do not provide a united vision for the global development system nor a strategy for its transformation (Burall *et al.*, 2006). It is clear, for example, that Poverty Reduction Strategy Papers (PRSPs) have not lived up to expectations, in part because the underlying theory that participation alone can generate accountability and an orientation to results has proved inadequate. Three interventions by the international donor community have been suggested to fill the gaps (Booth, 2005):

• more serious understanding of country contexts by donor staffs;

• a willingness to go public about issues that donors currently discuss behind closed doors;

• a more serious effort to construct regional 'neighbourhoods' and a global climate of opinion that would do what PRSPs have been unable to do – really incentivise the construction of developmental states in poor countries.

The latter two are especially relevant to the potential future of ICT4D, and particularly their incorporation within new knowledge systems for rural development.

### Status of the global rural development processes
No matter how unsatisfactory the situation is for development in general, it is even worse for rural development, as is evident from the following:

• the substantial lack of progress in reducing levels of rural poverty;

• the declining funding to the agricultural sector, where the real value of net aid in the late 1990s was only 35 per cent of the level ten years earlier (IFAD, 2001);

• after several decades, the continued rehashing of rural development policy by both international funding agencies and developing-country governments.

The lack of a shared vision for development in general is reflected in the diverse history of rural development policies, starting with the 'green revolution' some 50 years ago. In the 1980s, budgets were cut, expertise lost and institutions downsized as 'structural adjustment' pushed short-term thinking to extremes. In the 1990s, an upsurge of interest in poverty reduction and sustainable development brought some degree of balance to the market-oriented economic models. This view has been identified as a

Washington Consensus on food, agriculture and rural development (Maxwell and Heber-Percy, 2001), and is made up of the following components:

- the private sector will provide the main engine of development via growth;
- government will provide strategic policy and investment support for infrastructure, service delivery and marketing;
- participation will be encouraged (perhaps more in some models than others);
- safety nets will be provided.

A key question is whether there are any reasons to believe that this latest consensus will be any more effective than previous approaches.

*Focus on agriculture*
In the absence of a globally shared vision for rural development, it makes sense that development practitioners direct their energies towards those aspects of rural reality that appear to be best understood. Hence the rural development literature is dominated by the longstanding theory that agriculture is the best (and natural) way to reduce rural poverty. Indeed, agricultural growth (alone) has often been promoted as the means by which to reduce poverty, not only at a farm level and in the rural economy, but also nationally.

The predictions of various economic models and analyses have been used to show that agricultural growth can lead to reduced rural poverty, primarily by producing extra farm jobs and higher wages, followed by the impact of increased spending in the rural economy (Ashley and Maxwell, 2001). Added to this is the value of the reduced costs of locally produced foods to the national economy and to social welfare.

However, until recently, the consistent and long-term global fall in agricultural commodity prices coupled with worsening trade parameters has reduced confidence in these models, and has also resulted in shrinking agricultural profitability. In response, development practitioners have commonly presented two solutions. The first is the reduction of agricultural subsidies in the North (amounting to an estimated $360 billion a year in 2001), to create new markets and allow prices to rise. However, this may have less impact than is generally believed. For example, a 30 per cent reduction in protection (more than was achieved in the Uruguay Round) is estimated to raise wheat prices by only 6 per cent (Stevens, 2001).

A second solution deals with the ways in which the governments of developing countries might invest more broadly in public goods for agriculture. This goes beyond the current Washington Consensus on Agriculture (WCA), which limits the scope of investment in the sector to the development or application of new and improved technology aimed solely at increasing farm productivity (Kydd and Dorward, 2001). The WCA appears to reinforce the ideas behind the green revolution of the 1960s, hoping for similar dramatic growth in global food production. However, significant concerns regarding the implementation and longer-term impacts of the green revolution have been raised. Burch (2007) thus suggests that it will disrupt rural processes, will lead to an abandonment of indigenous knowledge, will exacerbate the loss of genetic diversity, will not reduce hunger, and will lead to the increased economic and technological dependency of smallholders (see also Desfilhes and Dufour, 2005; Duch Guillot, 2006).

Opinion is growing that the export-oriented industrial production model of agriculture based on monocultures and homogenous seeds, and utilising chemical fertilisers and pesticides, is unsustainable, both because it exhausts the soil and because an increasing number of farmers cannot afford the costs (Burch, 2007). The difficulty has been in devising locally contextualised mechanisms that ensure local food security as the first priority, without excluding sustainable agricultural production for local or export trade. A much more systemic approach is needed which goes beyond the traditional focus on the microeconomics of production. A wider range of issues needs to be taken into account, including the institutional arrangements, the transaction costs, as well as the many risks associated with output markets, input delivery and seasonal finance, particularly in the context of rising food prices in the last quarter of the first decade of the 21st century (Kydd and Dorward, 2001).

*The role of smallholder farmers*
Rural development via agricultural growth based on increasing the efficiency and productivity of the existing small farms rather than developing less labour-intensive farming models has been a dominant strategic concept in rural development thinking throughout the last half-century (Ellis and Biggs, 2001). The production of staples is key, usually in the form of semi-tradable cereals (Rahman and Westley, 2001).

Although the term 'small farm' has significantly different meanings in various parts of the world, the small-farm model has maintained its prominence for both theoretical and empirical reasons. In the historically positive view, small-farm agriculture is seen to address needs related to both food security and quality of life, as well as providing a platform for economic growth. It has empirical support going back to Schultz's (1964) pioneering work, as well as more recent evidence (IFAD, 2001). But, in the light of the fast-changing rural dynamic characterised by much greater income diversity, stronger rural–urban links and greater integration into the world economy, there are growing concerns regarding the ability of small farms to retain their financial and social value, with or without additional investments in rural public goods (Ashley and Maxwell, 2001). These concerns include doubts about the long-term ability of many smallholder farmers worldwide to respond adequately to population pressures (Killick, 2001), the difficulties faced by smallholders in competing in an increasingly globalised world (Kydd and Dorward, 2001), and the need for customised technological packages and appropriate research to support them (Tripp, 2001).

*The rural non-farm economy*

Since diversification out of agriculture appears to be an important factor in the growing dynamism of many rural economies, the future of the rural non-farm economy (RNFE) should be recognised as a core issue (Ashley and Maxwell, 2001). The need better to understand diversification by households can be facilitated by analysing the livelihood strategies of what are often described as 'multi-functional' households (Ellis and Biggs, 2001). Non-farm sources of income are estimated at 40–45 per cent of average rural household income in sub-Saharan Africa and Latin America, and 30–40 per cent in South Asia, with the major portion coming from local rural sources rather than urban migration (Start, 2001). Although some of this RNFE income is agriculture-related to varying degrees, much can be independent of agriculture (Canagarajah *et al.*, 2001). Stimulating the RNFE is a complex issue. Each component of the RNFE is likely to develop at a different rate, and its development may not be consistent in different rural locations. Different kinds of rural area may lend comparative advantages to different kinds of activity (Wiggins and Proctor, 2001).

Although an effective rural poverty reduction strategy must aim to harness the potential of the non-farm sector, stimulation of the RNFE will not automatically include the poorest rural people. Existing patterns of inequality tend to reproduce themselves with the relatively high-return new opportunities in the RNFE usually being accessible only to those with capital or skills, while the low-return coping strategies are left to the poor (Start, 2001). Interventions are needed which enable the poor to overcome entry barriers (Barrett *et al.*, 2001) and participate in the more productive aspects of the RNFE.

## ICTs for rural development: beginnings

Against this background, this section explores how ICT4D has contributed to rural development issues, focusing especially on the needs of the rural poor, and attempts to provide a vision for effective rural development (see also Torero and von Braun, 2006).

### Hope and hype

In the 1990s, with the rapid development of innovative ICTs that were transforming developed societies in ways that had hardly been anticipated just a few years previously, there was great expectation that ICTs could play a similar transformative role in developing societies, including in their rural sectors. The assumption made was that the deployment of 'information infrastructure' such as networks and computers in developing countries would, by itself, act as a catalyst to the widespread use of such technologies, resulting in economic and social benefit (Pyati, 2005). Some of these initiatives to deploy information infrastructure were launched with great fanfare, but then proved to be technically or commercially infeasible. Much effort was expended in, for example, setting up PC laboratories in schools, creating PC-based learning materials, linking PCs to the internet through dial-up access via the telephone network, and building telecentres that provided shared access to information services (bridges.org, 2001). However, this top-down and 'technology push' approach has not achieved what was anticipated (Mansell and Wehn, 1998).

It is digital technologies that have revolutionised the capabilities and therefore the opportunities for the use of ICTs over the past couple of decades. Digital technologies allow a wide range of information media, such as text, pictures, diagrams, photographs, video, speech and music, to be captured, stored, transmitted and manipulated in a uniform fashion (see Chapter 4). Despite the enormous power and benefit that digital ICTs have to offer, in a rural context it is also important not to lose sight of what non-digital ICTs can contribute, such as radio, TV, magazines and books (Winrock International, 2003; Ilboudo, 2003). These older technologies are often more widely accessible, and they are easy to use.

### Lessons learned?

It is now clear that information infrastructure *per se* is insufficient to trigger the transformative use of such infrastructure; that 'technology push' is largely ineffective in catalysing the extensive adoption and adaptation of technology-based solutions to the problems of social and economic life in developing countries. Nevertheless, valuable experience has been gained during the past two decades concerning the role of ICTs in development in general, and lessons have been learned.

Although the promise of ICTs for development has not been met during the past couple of decades, there has nevertheless been much opportunity to learn about how best to employ ICTs for enabling and enhancing development in general. Several compilations of recommended practices from various perspectives are readily available (Talyarkhan, 2004; IICD, 2006; http://www.bridges.org/12_habits; Burch, 2007). However, the focus of learning should not be on determining what is the *best* practice, since what is optimal in one set of circumstances may not be in another. Instead, what is a *good* practice, as identified through more than one initiative, might be a worthwhile candidate for adapting for use in a new project or initiative. Three common themes in these recommended approaches include the following:

- first, understand what has worked before, and what has not, and why – build on that;
- a local champion is essential; and
- use open technologies that comply with standards as far as possible.

### Multipurpose telecentres

During some ten or more years of experimentation and piloting, an approach to providing access to information services to impoverished communities based on multipurpose telecentres (MPTCs) has seen some maturation and success (UNDP, 2007). Sharing facilities is an obvious strategy in the face of high cost and few resources to cover that cost, and forms the basis for the MPTC approach. A MPTC may be defined as an organisation that offers a range of developmental services, including information, to a specific community and with a large degree of community involvement (NITF, 1998). A MPTC may be thought of as an example of a multipurpose community centre in which significant use is made of ICTs to facilitate a variety of support services.

A typical MPTC may include several PCs, some with internet connectivity, situated in a community where individuals and families are unable to afford to own a PC. Unlike a cybercafé, a MPTC has as a primary goal the improvement of the well-being of members of the community, as opposed to making a profit. Its staff will assist community members to use the PCs, focusing on areas such as education, health, other public services and business opportunities. While MPTCs have demonstrated their value in poor urban and peri-urban areas (NITF, 1998), they can have even greater impact in poor rural areas because of the paucity of alternative means of information access. In this setting a shared approach is essential for overcoming the general lack of available infrastructure and the high costs associated with building and linking infrastructure in remote areas. Their function is not only to be a vehicle for bringing knowledge into the community, but also to serve as a place of interaction where knowledge can be shared and even captured for use by others. In the absence of other facilities, a MPTC in a rural area can act as a platform for addressing a range of community needs, including information access, training and knowledge sharing, but important issues relating to location and long-term financial sustainability remain to be addressed (see also SAIDE, 2003; Jensen and Esterhuysen, 2001; Proenza, 2001; http://www.telecentre.org).

*Monitoring, evaluation and learning*
The selection above gives a flavour of the learning that is now distilled and being disseminated. However, we have nowhere near the insight that we could have had if effective monitoring and evaluation with a view to learning had been systematically applied across the board. It is all too tempting to skimp on the monitoring and evaluation aspects of a project, by focusing on assessment for administrative purposes, without creating a body of learning that may be disseminated among and built upon by others (see for example Farrell *et al.*, 2007). There are, of course, exceptions to this gloomy picture. One such example is the wireless village project currently being implemented in the Dwesa region in the Eastern Cape province of South Africa (see the box on p. 330), which involves implementing ICT-based applications for use by rural communities.

## The Dwesa wireless village project

The Dwesa e-commerce project involves the development and deployment of an e-commerce platform in Dwesa, a rural area in the Eastern Cape province in south-eastern South Africa.

The primary objective of this project is to develop and field-test the prototype of a simple, cost-effective and robust, integrated e-business/telecommunication platform, to deploy in marginalised and semi-marginalised communities in South Africa where a large percentage of the population live. These communities, by sheer size and because of current political dynamics, represent a strategic emergent market. A second objective is to build technically skilled human resources in the field of e-commerce, particularly in the context of supporting e-commerce activities in marginalised and semi-marginalised communities. The project is a joint collaboration between the University of Fort Hare and Rhodes University.

The e-commerce platform is designed to promote tourism and advertise local arts, crafts and music, and it entails several related projects. Deployment of infrastructure, technical support, promotion of the initiative and teaching of computer literacy take place during monthly visits of approximately one week, and involve young researchers from the two universities (one previously disadvantaged, the other historically privileged). This ensures a synergy between technical expertise and understanding of the local context (Dalvit *et al.*, 2007).

The lessons being learned as part of the Dwesa project reinforce and supplement those that have been referred to already. Some of the most important are the following:

- Building trust between the community and the external project team is an essential prerequisite for any form of practical ICT development initiative.

- Acquiring ICT skills is often sought after as a ticket out of a rural environment, particularly by younger members of the community. So the continuous loss of skills must be anticipated and accommodated.

- Having preconceived ideas as an outsider of what might be helpful to the community is not always a good approach. It is important to try as far as possible to engage with people from the community in the development of services that might be truly useful to them in the short term (Clayton, pers. comm., 2007).

The Dwesa project was initiated by two universities, but now involves several other role-players. Integral to the project is a monitoring and evaluation function, along with a commitment to publish on the activities and results of the project (Thinyane *et al.*, 2006; Dalvit *et al.*, 2007).

An important message for those involved in rural development using ICTs is that there is learning that should be hunted for, digested and applied when embarking on new initiatives. However, there is also much knowhow that is not readily available because it remains confined to the heads of current practitioners who tend to be action-oriented and often do not document and make available their considerable learning. Thus an equally important message for rural development practitioners and funders is that the time and energy required to record their experience and reflections must be spent in a disciplined manner, and must be funded, so that the whole field may benefit.

### Challenges related to ICTs for rural development

Although there are many challenges to face when attempting to harness ICTs for development as a whole, most of these challenges are increased when the context is rural, and additional challenges are also present. These hurdles are not peculiar to the use of ICTs; they are encountered in general in the context of any rural development initiative. When discussing the use of ICTs for rural development, there is a danger that by focusing on addressing the challenges, the use of the ICTs subtly becomes the goal, instead of remaining as an enabling tool towards achieving the goal which is development. Most if not all of the challenges correlate directly with the development that is sought. In this sense, addressing the challenges is the main goal. With this caveat in mind, some of these challenges are now highlighted.

#### The need for energy

ICT systems require electrical power to operate. For poor people living in urban areas, relatively inexpensive electrical power is often available, at least potentially, from the electric grid. However, more than 1.5 billion people who live in rural areas in developing countries lack electric power, and to extend the electric grid to reach them is usually very costly (Winrock International, 2003). Thus, the essential prerequisite of electric power for ICT systems to operate represents a formidable challenge to the widespread deployment of ICTs in rural areas in developing countries. Power-generation systems using renewable energy sources, such as photovoltaics and wind-electric turbines, or even hybrid systems which make use of a combination of diesel and renewable energy, can be very suitable for powering ICT systems, because the power requirements are fairly modest. Although the initial capital cost of renewable energy technologies is usually much higher than for the equivalent fossil-fuel-powered generator, their operating costs and environmental impact are much lower, and they are more reliable (Weingart and Giovannucci, no date). From the perspective of the total cost of ownership, renewable energy technologies can often represent the lowest-cost option for powering ICT equipment over the long term. When deploying ICT systems that will rely on off-grid power, careful attention should also be paid to the power requirements of the equipment. A traditional desktop PC and CRT monitor can consume up to five times more power than the equivalent energy-efficient desktop along with an LCD monitor, or a laptop computer.

*Literacy*

Rural areas of the developing world are characterised by extremely poor literacy rates (http://www.fao.org/newsroom/en/news/2004/51557/index.html), and this can represent a major challenge to harnessing ICTs in such areas. This challenge can appear to be particularly daunting to those who limit their interaction with ICTs to text-based interfaces. However, technological developments over the past several years mean that graphics-based and aural interfacing with ICTs have become not only feasible but increasingly ubiquitous. There are many successful pilot projects using multimedia interfaces (pictures, sound and video) that allow those with little or no literacy to use ICTs in rural areas (Day, 2003). Young people especially will rapidly assimilate the aural and visual cues and metaphors in a well-designed computer interface, even if they lack traditionally defined literacy skills (Buckingham, 2006). Thus there is considerable scope for overcoming limitations due to illiteracy by the careful use of the multimedia capabilities of ICTs (Wagner and Kozma, 2003).

*Gender*

Women dominate the rural agriculture sector, with more than 70 per cent of Africa's domestic food production being ascribed to women (Winrock International, 2003). Yet many of the most well-intentioned rural development initiatives fail to focus on this strategic point of leverage for raising agricultural productivity. The needs of rural women are overlooked because those responsible for policy and planning lack the relevant information and methodologies to address those needs. Another significant reason for this blind spot is that by far the majority of those involved in research, extension and technology transfer are men. Cultural norms often circumscribe information exchange between men and women, thus limiting the effectiveness of extension officers, who are almost exclusively male, among female farmers. A contributory factor is that extension services usually target commercial farming, while women farmers are primarily involved in subsistence agriculture.

*Other challenges related to the use of ICTs in rural development*

*Rights, privacy and soft issues.* For several years now the developed world has wrestled with some of the consequences for the private social domain of citizens in an age of electronic information services. Issues that range from the protection of privacy to appropriate use, or 'netiquette', are the subject of discussion, debate and sometimes legislation. They are also relevant in a developing rural context, and often in ways that differ from those in the developed world (Maassen, 2005).

*Information as a public good.* Inasmuch as information is understood to be essential to enable those caught in poverty to escape their impoverished circumstances, there is a strong case to be made that such information should be viewed as a public good and thus be accessible at no charge. It is hard to argue that such information should be provided on a purely commercial basis. There is a strong case for charging on an affordable basis rather than on a cost-recovery basis (Chapman *et al.*, no date).

*The cost–benefit equation of ICTs.* Bearing in mind the typical income of an impoverished rural community, the costs associated with deploying and maintaining ICT infrastructure are so high that investments in ICTs, and in particular in their long-term maintenance, appear proscriptive. But the longer-term benefits must not be overlooked. ICTs can support and enhance the communications, learning and knowledge components of almost any undertaking or enterprise, provided focus is kept on the information application or service rather than the technology. The capabilities of ICTs have continued to grow exponentially over the past several decades, and new applications continue to emerge that were not even thought of until very recently. Thus a focus on the cost–benefit ratio of ICTs in the context of rural development can be misleading. In the context of assessing the cost of ICTs, the phenomenon of Free and Open Source Software (FOSS) has an important claim to be considered, not least because its use does not incur the high licensing costs associated with proprietary software (Wong and Sayo, 2004). However, this limited focus on financial metrics is potentially dangerous since the wider social and economic implications tend to be ignored, even though this longer-term arena is where the greatest benefits of FOSS mostly lie, particularly for the developing world.

### ICTs for agricultural development
While rural development must by no means be equated with agricultural development, it is true that the agricultural sector remains the dominant player in the rural context. The quality of life in most rural areas will not improve without significant development of agriculture.

It was the discovery of agriculture some 10,000 years ago that enabled small groups of hunter-gatherers to settle down together and develop community life in one place. This transition led to the first use of symbolic information, or early forms of writing, as farmers kept records of commercial transactions involving the products of their agricultural efforts. In recent decades, agriculture is perceived to be a latecomer to the information age, but we should recognise that in one way it is agriculture that initiated our journey towards the information and knowledge-rich economy. Information has therefore always played an important role in agricultural activities. Farmers have always made key decisions, such as what and when to plant, how and when to harvest, how and where to sell, on the basis of information that was exchanged and transmitted using whatever means and technologies were available to them in their communities and cultures (Burch, 2007). Thus ICTs, broadly speaking, have always been important to agricultural enterprise, and continue to be so. The present challenge arises from the development of new ICTs that open up possibilities of enabling and enhancing the use of information and knowledge in ways that even two decades ago were not dreamed of. Access to information, not only where but also when it is potentially useful, becomes a viable possibility, even for communities that have thus far been marginalised, provided that the modes of access are not constrained by rigid approaches.

In the developed world, ICTs have spawned a dramatic transformation in many sectors, including agriculture (Winrock International, 2003). This transformation raises the question as to what might be the transforming effects of ICTs on agricultural activities in the developing world. The absence in impoverished rural areas of much of the infrastructure that exists in the developed world should prompt an assessment of how ICTs may add value in the context of a specific rural area. The alternative assumption, that ICTs cannot be effective without the basic infrastructure that is found in urban settings, should not be adopted as it leads to a scenario where rural agriculture in the developing world becomes ever more isolated and alienated from its potential markets, both local and global, thus exacerbating the divide between the rich and the poor.

When considering the deployment of ICTs in the agricultural sector the wide diversity of the sector must be taken into account (IICD, 2006). The sector includes multiple role-players and stakeholders including the farmers themselves, whether individual or corporate, cooperatives and other farmer organisations, traders and other private firms, multinational organisations, government organisations, research agencies and NGOs. For the sector to work productively, an effective flow and exchange of information is needed between the role-players, raising many opportunities for the use of ICTs. However, the different information needs of the various players, their socio-economic circumstances, the degree of technology literacy, among other factors, must play a key role in determining the specifics of ICT solutions employed.

A fundamental question to address when contemplating the use of ICTs to enhance agricultural production is whether increased export-oriented production should be the sole goal, or whether the nutritional needs of the farmers' families and the local markets should be satisfied first. Some argue that over the medium and long term the negative side-effects of export-orientation far outweigh any gains (Burch, 2007). While ICTs can aid agricultural stakeholders to become individually more productive through the provision of information about optimal production methods, the opportunity for ICTs in agriculture extends far beyond such a limited scope. For any system of innovation, the efficacy of the system depends on the interaction of the stakeholders in the system. The agricultural sector, viewed as a system, is no different, and it is through innovation that improved agricultural performance will be achieved, bringing with it the associated socio-economic benefits to rural areas. ICTs, therefore, have an as yet under-utilised potential in enabling information and knowledge exchange between the players in the innovation system, thus allowing innovations to be developed, refined and adopted collectively (World Bank Institute, 2007).

## Emerging possibilities

We have looked back at the beginnings of the application of ICTs to the problems of rural development. We now turn to look forward at what seem to be emerging as likely components of a more holistic approach to rural development that ICTs might enable and enhance, along the dimensions of access strategies, content creation, knowledge systems, and a systemic approach.

### *Access strategies*

The dramatic growth in use of mobile phones in developing countries demonstrates that, at least for some new ICTs, the barriers to assimilation and extensive use are low, even among the poor and marginalised. Mobile phone usage in Africa has exceeded initial expectations, and this is due primarily to usage by those with very low incomes (Scott *et al.*, 2004). On the other hand, the high expectations that PCs would become increasingly ubiquitous in developing countries due to the wide-ranging benefits they appeared to offer have seldom been fulfilled.

In a rural context, the obstacles to access are particularly high, even for mobile-phone-based access, let alone PC-based access. The low density of rural populations, together with their relative inability to pay for services, often makes deploying network infrastructure too much of a financial risk to network operators. Low literacy rates mean that traditional PC interfaces that rely significantly on textual cues become unintelligible to large portions of the rural population. This is aggravated by the fact that very often using the local language is a prerequisite for any effective communication.

The challenges for access to ICTs in rural areas, while formidable, may also be viewed as opportunities for innovative approaches that gel with their local contexts. Several approaches, summarised below, are emerging.

### *Synchronous and asynchronous access*

In light of the above constraints, efforts to introduce ICT access to a rural community might focus on asynchronous rather than synchronous access. Synchronous access refers to the access of information services in real time, without any appreciable delay between the request for information being sent, and the desired information being received. A well-known example of an information service used asynchronously is dial-up e-mail. E-mails can be read and written in offline mode. The user periodically connects to the network by dial-up at which time the e-mails that have been written are uploaded and transmitted to their recipients, while new incoming e-mails are downloaded and stored for reading once offline. Other information services lend themselves to asynchronous usage, such as RSS feeds, document downloads and even website access.

### *Direct and indirect access*

Almost all ICT users in the developed world interact directly with the ICT environment, whatever its specific modality (be it PC, mobile phone or kiosk).

In contrast, indirect access involves someone acting as an intermediary, who handles the information request on behalf of the end user. The use of intermediaries, coupled with asynchronous information services, holds much promise for breaking the pattern of exclusion from access, particularly in distant rural areas. A person acting as an information services intermediary might be equipped with portable ICT equipment such as one or more PCs or laptops, and would move from community to community, using appropriate transport (truck or motorbike), to provide the community with regular but intermittent access to ICT-based information services. If wireless connectivity is available then a level of synchronous service could be provided while the intermediary is in the community, but at the very least end users would be able to access information services asynchronously via the intermediary who has regular connectivity elsewhere on their rounds (http://other90.cooperhewitt.org/Design/internet-village-motoman-network). In addition, the role of intermediary opens up the opportunity for community-based entrepreneurs to set up as information service providers. The combination of direct versus indirect access, and synchronous versus asynchronous access, can be depicted as in Figure 10.1. The initial form of indirect asynchronous access is represented by the lower left block of the diagram. Once access has been provided, and demand begins to grow,

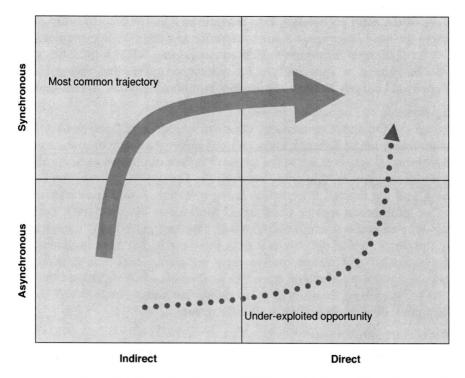

Figure 10.1 *Stages of rural access to ICTs* (source: Bob Day and Peter Greenwood).

improvement can follow one of two different trajectories to reach a state of direct and synchronous access.

The more commonly used trajectory in a rural context is to improve access by providing synchronous services via intermediaries (a MPTC often functions in this mode). While this approach clearly has value, it should not be used exclusively. The benefits of providing direct access, even if asynchronous, need to be explored more extensively. It is particularly important to recognise that, unlike indirect access, direct access to ICTs provides end users, even those living in the most remote areas, with the opportunity to develop familiarity with ICTs, thus setting them on the path to digital literacy, or even to become rural 'computer geeks'. In addition, this approach represents a business opportunity for entrepreneurs to act as asynchronous information services intermediaries (as mentioned above).

*Low-cost computers*

Low-cost computers provide another possible approach for people living in rural areas. Initiatives such as the XO-1 computer produced by the One Laptop Per Child foundation (http://www.laptop.org; Financial Times, 2008), the Indian-based Simputer (http://www.simputer.org), the Chinese Longmeng computer (http://en.wikipedia.org/wiki/Longmeng) and the Taiwanese Asus all seek to provide low-cost computer access. In education, it would be easy to assume that the teachers should be the conduit through which the benefits of computers should be channelled to the learners. However, such an approach would falter on the incorrect assumption, particularly in rural areas, that school teachers in general are proficient users of ICTs, and in turn are skilful educators of ICT expertise and skills. Instead, the opportunity for self-learning by the children themselves should be exploited to the greatest degree possible (Buckingham, 2006). This is the aim of the OLPC initiative – another advantage of which is that it uses FOSS, with its operating system being a version of Linux; it therefore does not place any limits on the technical depth at which a child may interact with the machine.

*Mesh networking*

Mesh networking is a promising technology for providing connectivity in rural areas (http://wirelessafrica.meraka.org.za/wiki/index.php/Wireless_Africa_Home_Page). In a mesh network, multiple nodes are connected together (often by wireless), either directly or through other nodes. When transmitting data from one node to another, a mesh network will reconfigure around a broken node or link by directing network traffic to hop from node to node until the destination is reached. Thus mesh networks are self-healing. The nominal range of most off-the-shelf wireless equipment, using the Wi-Fi standard, is 50 metres, but by using low-cost directional antennas, the range can be boosted to 20 kilometres or more (http://www.oreillynet.com/pub/a/wireless/2001/05/03/longshot.html). In a rural context the initial motivation for deploying a mesh network is often to provide telephony services. A side benefit, however, can be broadband access to the internet. The distributed nature of a mesh network means that management of the network is not centralised, but becomes the responsibility of individual nodes. Thus a wide range of business models can be accommodated, which means that local communities have the opportunity of a range of ownership options which should lead to both innovation and entrepreneurship.

*USB memory sticks*
Another technology that has major potential in a rural context is the simple and relatively cheap USB memory stick, which plugs into a standard USB port. Despite its extremely compact size, it can hold up to several gigabytes of data or software applications, and it can be kept in a pocket or even worn around the neck. Thus a rural ICT user may carry around a full, customised configuration of software and data. When desired, and a computer is available (through, for example, a mobile information services intermediary), the memory stick can be plugged in to provide immediate access to customised and personalised information services (see for example Floppy Office, http://www.xtort.net/office-and-productivity/floppy-office).

*Sharing resources*
In a rural context with extremely sparse infrastructure it is imperative that the little infrastructure that is available is shared to as great a degree as possible. Thus MPTCs are an obvious means of providing some level of access to information resources (see p. 329). However, the emphasis must rest on sharing, not only in terms of providing access to ICT-based facilities, but also in terms of ensuring that the infrastructure supports a range of services required by communities. For example, a MPTC could be the focal point for science and technology extension services into the community (MCT, 2006), a health clinic and a vocational training centre. Such an approach also helps to ensure that the ICTs do not become the focus themselves, but instead serve to support and enable services that address a range of well-established needs in the community. In turn, this approach creates the opportunity for local innovation and entrepreneurship.

The 'hole-in-the-wall' project, started in India in 1999, demonstrated that children can learn without outside assistance through mere access to computing facilities (http://www.hole-in-the-wall.com; see the case study on pp. 340–1). This concept has been built upon in another approach to providing access to shared resources, represented by the Digital Doorway project in South Africa. The Digital Doorway project seeks to provide people in rural and disadvantaged areas with free access to a multimedia-based computer environment, running open source software, and enabling them to experiment with and master the use of the equipment and software, without any formal training and with the minimum of external assistance (http://www. digitaldoorway.org.za/index_main.php). Results have exceeded expectations: children have proved most adept at teaching themselves the use of the computer system without outside intervention (Thinyane *et al.*, 2006).

A further innovative approach is the 'BingBee' kiosk, designed to improve literacy and numeracy skills in children through entertainment. It is a fully self-contained kiosk that can be installed behind a window. The primary innovation of this approach is the cheap and robust touchpad system that is installed on the window, allowing operation from outside a secure building. This makes it deployable in areas that are susceptible to vandalism (Slay *et al.*, 2006). Unlike school computer labs, a BingBee site can be completely unattended, it can remain available at all hours, it automatically turns on or off on a programmable schedule, and is centrally manageable via the internet. The BingBee approach creates an excellent opportunity to make the facilities of an MPTC or computer lab available to all community members overnight and during weekends without supervision.

*Radio*

Especially in a rural context, radio has a strong track record as a means of communication. Information can easily be conveyed in local languages through radio, and distance and terrain do not offer impediments. Community values, history and culture can be diffused and strengthened. Combined with mobile telephony, an effective two-way platform can be established for discussion and debate – the ubiquitous chat-show. Radio can also be used in creative (and, to the urban-dweller, unconventional) ways (Ramos and Díez, 2003). Now with the convergence of radio and other ICTs, further innovations should be expected and encouraged to harness the additional value and quality that digital ICTs have to offer.

### Open standards and open technology

The use of open standards is crucial, particularly in the rural context. By implementing technologies that adhere to open standards, the maximum amount of flexibility and choice for the future is assured, and this can be important to maintain a low cost of technology, especially appropriate in rural areas. Initial technology choices that pose high barriers to making other technology choices in the future place an inordinate amount of leverage in the hands of the incumbent technology supplier. Very often, technology choices are made by those who do not understand the longer-term impacts, and there is therefore considerable potential for technology lock-in. Some large ICT suppliers will engage with the highest levels of government leadership of developing countries (ministerial, even presidential) and secure agreements for the wide-scale deployment of proprietary ICTs, based on very attractive but usually short-term incentives. In doing so, and without realising it, these leaders in effect indirectly give away the freedom of their citizens to make future technology choices with ease, and the potential of some to innovate based on detailed knowledge of the software technologies on the desktop.

*(continued on page 342)*

# Case study: The hole in the wall, or minimally invasive education

Sugata Mitra

*Professor of Educational Technology, Newcastle University, UK*

*1999, January 26. My friend, Vivek, built a computer sunk into a wall near my office at that time, in Kalkaji, New Delhi. The screen was visible from the other side of the wall. A touch pad was built into the wall as well. Children came running out of the nearest slum and were at the wall, as though pasted with glue. A few hours later, a visibly surprised Vivek said the children were surfing.*

But how does this magical computer literacy happen? It took five years, a lot of travel and a lot of money to find out. There were great surprises and great disappointments on the way. But, in the end, Nature's lessons were simple, direct and, in retrospect, obvious. Further experiments in Madhya Pradesh and Uttar Pradesh showed the same results as in Kalkaji. The children seemed to learn to use the computer without any assistance. Language did not seem to matter. Neither did education. Had we stumbled on to something universal about children and computers?

The research design was simple. We would install computers in 22 locations across India, chosen for their diversity of human and climatic conditions. We would then choose 15 random children as a focus group and measure their progress over 9 months. We would then compare them with other children who do not have exposure to computers and see if we can get to an explanation for the 'hole in the wall' effect. But there were many problems to solve, not least a suitable process for measuring such progress and designing the technology that would enable them to access computers in the diverse physical environments of India.

We eventually began testing. An estimated 40,000 children used these computers. They have all made themselves computer literate. The average test scores of those using the computers rose. We have our proof of self-regulated learning. And this time we know that it will happen anywhere in the world, to any child, in any climate. I decided to call this method 'minimally invasive education' (MIE). The rest of the world continues to call it 'the hole in the wall' – alas (Mitra, 2003; Mitra *et al.*, 2005).

### What did we find?
Groups of 6- to 13-year-old children do not need to be 'taught' how to use computers. They can learn by themselves. Their ability to do so seems to be independent of variables such as educational background, literacy levels, gender or socio-economic level.

### What do they learn?
An estimated 300 children can learn to do most or all of the following tasks in approximately three months, using the 'hole-in-wall' arrangement with a single PC: use all Windows operational functions, draw and paint pictures on the computer, play games, surf the internet, set up e-mail accounts, chat online, download files, run educational games and many other things besides.

In addition to the above task achievement, local teachers and field observers often note that the children demonstrate improvements in:

- enrolment, attendance and school examinations, particularly in subjects that deal with computing skills;
- English vocabulary and usage;
- concentration, attention span and problem solving;
- working together and self-regulation.

We can generalise the findings from these last eight years (1999–2007) as follows:

1 Groups of children can self-regulate and self-organise their own learning, if given the appropriate resources.
2 While constructivism has been accepted as an effective educational method for a long time, we could re-define it with the statement 'learning is a self-organising system'.
3 Collaborative learning from public computers is a process of acquisition – the learning is not imposed, hence the children accept it easily. Since value systems are also acquired and cannot be imposed (unlike doctrine or dogma, which are imposed and cannot be acquired), such collaborative digital environments are capable of altering the acquisition of values.
4 The quality of education is related inversely to the remoteness of schools.

Minimally invasive education through public internet kiosks for children should, no matter who or where they are, form an integral part of primary education in the 21st century. It has the potential not only to close the 'digital divide' rapidly, but also to unlock the creative potential for self-development of children that eminent educationists have sought to do for over a century. In 2008, there are over 500 remote places in India, Africa and Cambodia where an estimated one million children use 'hole in the wall' – children who would otherwise not have had any access to computers.

*Kalkaji 1999: the original 'hole in the wall' (source: Sugata Mitra).*

When considering technology options in rural areas, careful attention should be given to technologies based on FOSS. These have several advantages, beyond the most superficial one of there being no acquisition cost of the software itself: their use ensures a high degree of standards compliance, thus preserving freedom of choice for the future; some FOSS software such as the Ubuntu operating system and the Thunderbird e-mail client is recognised for its reliability and robustness; FOSS software may be modified by users to be adapted to specific local requirements; and FOSS tends to encourage the emergence of computer 'geeks' in any society, especially among the young, thus promoting innovation, which can be especially important in sustaining rural communities (Castells and Himanen, 2002).

### Content creation

The sustainable development of poor and remote communities will not happen unless and until it is actively driven by individuals and groups from within these communities. Currently, however, the dominant mindset is to make content available to rural people that has been produced by others. If we examine the wide range of needs of the broad spectrum of people in rural areas, not just the elites, it becomes obvious that most imported content is of little use to the many millions of excluded people for reasons of literacy, language and/or culture, let alone their livelihood-sustaining needs. It has not been reconfigured for their culture and context. Instead of importing the dominantly text-based materials from the 'developed' world, materials can be developed locally that specifically address the needs of the majority. Content can be produced where text is replaced by the much more natural voice, and in local languages. These materials can use visualisation techniques rather than text to describe places, people and events more accurately. Moreover, they can use interactive animation and simulation to allow learners and users actively to investigate how things dynamically happen and work. Art, music and dance are readily captured using today's ICTs. Easily accessible digital multimedia tools exist to satisfy all these needs, many in the FOSS stable (http://www.osalt.com/multimedia-and-audio).

Providing the tools and developing the capability to support the local development and distribution of such relevant content in rural areas could initiate a positive spiral of continuous development and use of new knowledge and innovation to benefit the rural economy and society. The benefit lies not only in preserving cultural knowledge for subsequent generations, but also in the learning that is involved in the very process of capturing knowledge, and the ownership that this encourages. There is also a role for some community members to reconfigure external content for local consumption, making it relevant to and comprehensible by local people. When considering who should be involved with content creation in a rural context, the contribution that young people can make should be at the forefront.

### Knowledge systems

During the past few years, knowledge systems have started to emerge as the dominant way forward in harnessing ICTs in the service of development goals. One of their key aspects is that the knowledge in view is not confined to that which is explicitly captured in some form in databases or by other means. The knowledge that is implicitly held in the minds of the people in the system is as much a part of the system as any other. Thus the focus lies not on the technologies and gadgets that facilitate the functioning of the system, but on the participation of the people, as individuals and as groups, in the generation, exchange and utilisation of knowledge, by whatever means are convenient and effective. Given their importance and dramatic rate of development, it is likely that any definition of a knowledge system is soon doomed to be outdated (Gruber, 2008).

Examples of knowledge systems in an agricultural context include those that enable the sharing of market information such as price levels and information about logistics. Most of these systems appear to have been based on the assumption that through the operation of market forces alone, economic activity will be stimulated and increased, leading to significant reduction in poverty levels. Although this model is too simplistic (Kydd and Dorward, 2001), two examples of such knowledge systems are worthy of discussion here:

- *B2Bpricenow.com* was established to function as an e-marketplace in the Philippines, enabling farmers, fishermen and other small and medium enterprises directly to access market prices and to trade in their produce via a website or a cell phone. It was designed to empower farmers to respond more effectively to market requirements and changes, and thereby to command the best prices, instead of relying on traders who acted as intermediaries. Although B2Bpricenow.com received many accolades in 2002 and 2003 (http://web.worldbank.org/WBSITE/EXTERNAL/OPPORTUNITIES/GRANTS/DEVMARKETPLACE/0, contentMDK:21193438 ~ pagePK:180691 ~ piPK:174492 ~ theSitePK:205098,00. html; http://www.kiwanja.net/database/project/project_B2Bpricenow. pdf; Batchelor *et al.*, 2003), by 2007 its marketplace website showed no sign of life (http://www.b2bpricenow.com). The demise of B2Bpricenow. com illustrates how fragile the sustainability of an intervention can be, even if it appears to measure up well against a range of external assessment criteria.

- The e-Choupal initiative is designed to address the many challenges experienced by small farmers in India (http://www.itcportal.com/rural-devp_philosophy/echoupal.htm; Bhatnagar *et al.*, no date). The Indian Tobacco Company (ITC), which initiated the project, is a large agricultural processing company with annual revenues of US$2 billion. The main purpose of e-Choupal was to improve the efficiency of ITC's procurement process for agriculture and aquaculture products. Previously, companies like ITC would procure these commodities through agricultural market centres, known as *mandis*. A long chain of intermediaries was involved in moving the product from the farmer to the *mandi*. Now, through the e-Choupal project, computers with internet access (via phone line or VSAT) are placed in rural farming villages to act as e-commerce hubs for typically 600 farmers in 10 surrounding villages within a radius of 5 kilometres. The farmers negotiate directly with ITC for the sale of their produce. In addition, however, they can get information on *mandi* pricing, place orders for supplies, and learn about good farming practices. The e-Choupals also act as a social meeting point for the exchange of information. The e-Choupal project is both a highly effective and profitable product design system and procurement channel for ITC, as well as being the catalyst for rural transformation by helping to break the isolation that is inherent to rural areas, to create greater transparency for farmers, and to improve their livelihoods. By removing the need for intermediaries, and the margin they command, part of the produce revenue stream can be redirected to fund the ICT infrastructure required by the project without the end-user farmers being explicitly burdened with the cost of that infrastructure. This creates a win-win, sustainable solution for both ITC and the farmers supplying them (see also p. 192).

In addition to commercially oriented knowledge systems, others are emerging that are designed primarily to improve the effectiveness of high-level practitioners such as policy makers and sector experts. The CGIAR's Strategic Analysis Knowledge Support System (SAKSS) is focused on the agricultural sector in sub-Saharan Africa and provides an example of such a knowledge system. SAKSS is a collaborative network 'that compiles, analyses, and disseminates data, information, and tools in order to help design, implement, monitor, and evaluate rural development strategies to achieve economic growth and poverty reduction' (http://www.ifpri. org/themes/SAKSS/sakss.htm). A key aim of SAKSS is to make available and accessible, to both policy makers as well as small farmers, the results of research that is undertaken by the national-level agricultural research institutions as well as by their regional-level counterparts. Currently there is very little engagement with this research by those working at a policy and strategy level. SAKSS is designed to bridge the gap between these practitioners and the researchers on the ground, and it is also aligned with NEPAD's Comprehensive Africa Agriculture Development Programme (CAADP).

Although these knowledge systems represent steps in the right direction, if further efforts are restricted to these approaches alone, any benefits are likely to be limited. Participation must be on the widest possible basis if these knowledge systems are to act as vehicles of transformation. In an agricultural context, for example, a knowledge system should fully include individual smallholder farmers, so that they can engage with all the other players in the system. In addition, while some knowledge systems have been implemented specifically for agriculture, the focus has not been on rural development as a whole. Rural development will be successful only if it is tackled holistically. The full scope of rural development, including on-farm and off-farm, needs to be addressed by a coordinated, interdependent network of such knowledge systems.

### A systemic approach

ICTs are merely tools, and do not offer any inherent benefit in themselves. Thus ICTs may serve to amplify useful and helpful human endeavours, but equally they can serve further to entrench and aggravate destructive or unhelpful actions and activities. ICT development, particularly in rural areas, is more about relationship building within communities than about technology. Much of the innovation that is needed can be more accurately described as social innovation rather than as technical innovation. Even when the technology works, the success of the project is not guaranteed. This highlights the danger for any development initiative of having an over-abundance of expertise in technologies, and insufficient in the social sciences. The technology is the relatively easy part, and dealing with the social situation of the community the more difficult part (Clayton, pers. comm., 2007).

This reinforces the importance of operating within a coherent and viable shared vision for rural development that articulates the desired end state. In order to harness ICTs for rural development, this means that being locally sensitive, locally relevant and locally driven is crucial, but also that any approach must be coherent with a big-picture vision that encompasses all the interrelating aspects that make up a holistic perspective of the rural context and its development needs. In short, a systemic approach is called for, involving a deliberate and methodical approach to development that maximises the involvement of ordinary citizens. A systemic approach sees ICTs as forming one versatile tool in a science and technology toolbox, all of which can be harnessed for rural development.

A development intervention that involves a multi-level systemic approach and includes an ICT-intensive rural component was initiated in 2006 within a framework of cooperation between Finland and South Africa. This consists of a cluster of programmes aimed at applying and adapting the principles of the emerging knowledge society to the reality of South Africa, for the benefit of both countries. One of these programmes, named COFISA (http://www.cofisa.org.za), is designed to investigate and strengthen South Africa's existing and potential innovation systems at the national, provincial and local levels. The rural component is focusing on ICT-enabled innovation in particular, including the Dwesa wireless village project mentioned above. The cluster of programmes constitutes an integrated and coherent intervention, which provides a framework within which a rural innovation can be implemented, monitored and evaluated so as to maximise impact and learning.

## ICT4RD: some future scenarios

The previous sections have highlighted that:

- rural development initiatives are usually not based on a well-thought-out, widely understood and engaging shared vision; and
- within this complex and confused milieu, over the past 15 years the application of ICTs to rural development has been hit and miss.

The disappointing results to date should have been expected, given the lack of a globally shared, coherent and valid vision. This begs the question as to what that vision should be. The rest of this section suggests answers to that question, and gives examples of the roles that ICTs and knowledge management can play in both developing and pursuing that vision.

### Our urban-centric mindsets

In a recent address on the issue of 'asymmetrical development', President Museveni of Uganda compared developed with developing countries in the following way:

- in developed countries (including UK, Canada, Australia, New Zealand and Singapore): 'GDP per capita...is high', and 'people are supported by industries and services rather than agriculture'; 'more people live in urban areas than those that live in the rural areas'; and
- in developing countries (including Uganda, Nigeria, Kenya, Tanzania, Zambia and Ghana): 'GDP per capita...being much lower', and 'more people in these countries still depend on agriculture rather than depending on industry and services'; and 'more people live in the rural areas than in the urban areas' (Museveni, 2007).

Based on these observations, Museveni (2007) observed that:

> [Some] societies have transitioned from pre-industrial societies to industrial societies and that the previous feudal and peasant societies,...have metamorphosed into middle class and skilled working class societies depending on industrial production and services. The others...are still characterised by over-dependence on agriculture and the societies still have a large peasant population with a very small middle-class.
>
> (Museveni, 2007, pp. 3–4)

His major point was that the 'present partial transformation of the [developing] societies is not good enough' (Museveni, 2007, pp. 3–4).

This is a recent articulation of what seems to have become a very broadly accepted (or presumed) mindset for development, in other words that the mechanisms for development are industrialisation and urbanisation, and hence that rural development will be resolved when most of the population has urbanised. In the absence of a clear vision, and alternate mechanisms from the international development community, and given the widespread evidence that this process seems to be unfolding 'naturally' across the developing world, albeit at different rates, the dominance of this urbanisation and industrialisation mindset should not surprise us. Linked to this is an equally widespread presumption that rural activities and communities are peripheral and subservient to the needs of the metropolitan areas where the major political, economic and cultural activities tend to be concentrated (see also Lipton, 1977; Harriss, 1983).

There are many issues related to the uncontrolled urbanisation that is a major feature throughout the developing world. However, by considering who is migrating to the cities, it becomes evident that far from being a solution to rural poverty, urbanisation is amplifying both rural and urban poverty through a negative feedback loop. In many developing countries good disaggregated data are sparse, but in South Africa the statistics on urban migration are clear. It is the young, potentially most productive people who are leaving the most rural areas (particularly those areas with high numbers of smallholder farming units, as in the Eastern Cape) for the main cities (such as Gauteng and Cape Town) (StatsSA, 2006a, 2006b). This may be a successful win–win strategy for a fortunate few, who not only secure reliable urban employment, but also provide valuable support (financial and social) for their rural families (and indirectly their broader rural communities). However, it is a lose–lose strategy for others, arguably the significant majority. For these individuals the promise of the cities is not realised, and they fail to find anything but the most menial, poorly paid and irregular employment, with no clear growth path. They are sucked into the downward spiral of urban poverty in the periphery of the cities (and society), unable adequately to support themselves, let alone send support to their rural families. Even worse, many in these circumstances create a second family (partner and children), and/or turn to alcohol or drugs, and many eventually resort to crime as the only option for them being able to support themselves. In this latter, majority case, the rural areas lose many of their potentially most productive young people who, in urban areas poorly resourced to deal with the influx, find little opportunity to fulfil their potential, but instead deepen the many problems associated with urban poverty and crime.

The perception seems to be that whether or not urbanisation is a good thing, it is at least inevitable. But is it? Even in the developed world, the most remote rural areas are particularly threatened by a similar vicious cycle of negative development trends: young people are moving out, services are declining, there are not enough new jobs to compensate for the disappearance of the traditional ones, and the number of old people is growing (OECD, 2006). Awareness is growing that there is an urgent need to replace the current rural strategies, which are often sectoral and applied uniformly across a country, with integrated strategies that take into account the different development trajectories of rural regions, many of which are based on exploiting local, place-specific resources (although see Ruttan, 1975, 1984).

The Finnish example is particularly instructive in this context (see Finnish Rural Policy Committee, 2004; Halhead, 2004), but other European countries are also seeking to develop similar integrated rural strategies characterised by two main principles:

- a focus on *places* instead of sectors; and
- a focus on *investments* instead of subsidies.

Although these integrated rural strategies point the way to achieving more balanced urban–rural population distributions, they do not in themselves provide a shared vision that is powerful enough to address global rural poverty. Such a global vision is required to promote rural development to the top of the agenda. The recent global acceptance of human-induced global climate change (GCC) as an issue of major international importance (IPCC, 2007) has provided an excellent opportunity to bring rural development in from the cold.

### Impact of global climate change on rural areas

The scientific evidence is now overwhelming that greenhouse gases (GHGs) play a significant role in influencing climate change and represent an immediate global crisis. Currently the combination of GHGs in the atmosphere is equivalent to about 430 parts per million (ppm) $CO_2$, up from 280 ppm before the Industrial Revolution. With annual emissions accelerating due to growing demand for energy and transport, especially in such fast-growing economies as China and India, the $CO_2$ equivalent ($CO_2e$) levels of GHGs may reach the level of 550 ppm $CO_2e$ as early as 2035 (Stern, 2006), and will continue to rise. A business-as-usual approach risks major social and economic disruption, especially after 2050. Moreover, the alarming impacts of GCC as set out recently by the IPCC (2007) may well be significantly underestimated (Weart, 2007). Around the world, GCC threatens the basic elements of people's lives, including access to water, food production, health, and use of land and the environment. What is particularly salient for this chapter is that its impact is likely to be greatest in the rural areas of some of the poorest countries of the world. Thus declining crop yields, especially in Africa, could leave hundreds of millions without the ability to produce or purchase sufficient food. Agricultural output in developing countries is projected to decline by 20 per cent by 2020 (Cline, 2007), while GCC may cause agricultural prices to increase by up to 40 per cent (Easterling *et al.*, 2007). The poorest developing countries, and particularly their rural communities, will be hit earliest and hardest by GCC. Ironically, they will have contributed little to causing the problem.

### Responses to global climate change

GCC is global in both its causes and its consequences. Effective, efficient and equitable large-scale solutions will require innovative approaches to adaptation and mitigation. The goal of such strategies in both developed and developing countries should be to 'decarbonise' their economies sufficiently to stabilise the climate while maintaining economic growth. Stabilisation occurs when annual emissions are reduced to levels that balance the Earth's natural capacity to remove GHGs from the atmosphere. If mediation begins today, estimates put the annual costs of stabilisation at 500–550 ppm $CO_2e$ to be around 1 per cent of global GDP by 2050 (Stern, 2006).

A shared global perspective on the urgency of shifting to a low-carbon economy, and an international approach based on multilateral frameworks and coordinated action, are essential. It is generally recognised that a low-carbon trajectory cannot be achieved without including the following two mechanisms:

- action on non-energy emissions, such as avoiding deforestation; and
- the development and deployment of a wide range of lower-carbon technologies for power, heat and transport.

Both of these are multi-faceted and highly complex, and each must be implemented primarily in rural areas.

### Rural components of global climate change mitigation

Four of the most important mechanisms essential to mitigating GCC are discussed here, namely biofuels, water management, urbanisation and land-use management. ICTs have an important role to play in contributing to the management of all of these issues, and in creating and sharing knowledge about them.

#### Bio-based energy production

Some argue that an innovative, systemic approach to the future of agriculture based on the emerging opportunity of bio-based energy production could have many benefits, including reducing poverty and addressing GCC (Turner, 2006). While unlikely fully to replace fossil fuels, ethanol and biodiesel can be blended with their traditional counterpart or used 'neat' to power cars, trucks and other forms of transport, helping to reduce dependence and increase energy security. Biofuels offer farmers in both developed and developing countries almost unlimited market opportunities driven by the insatiable global demand for transportation fuels (Peskett et al., 2007). The poorest countries could benefit the most because they suffer disproportionately from the high price of oil. If biofuels can be produced in an environmentally sustainable way, they could dramatically cut GHG emissions, and thereby play a significant role in GCC mitigation. However, the adoption of biofuels is not without serious concerns, particularly regarding their impact on the poorest communities, and the amount of land that they require at the expense of basic food production (Stilwell and Rose, 2006; von Braun, 2007). A considered and coherent global approach is needed to elevate biofuels beyond the merely commercial aspects, and include the longer-term systemic issues of energy security, socio-economic development and environmental sustainability.

## Water management

'When it comes to clean water, the pattern in many countries is that the poor get less, pay more and bear the brunt of the human development costs associated with scarcity' (UNDP, 2006, p. 3). For several decades, water deprivation has become a worsening crisis pushing many people all over the world into lives of poverty, vulnerability and insecurity. The overwhelming weight of evidence concerning the likely impact of GCC is that:

- many of the world's most water-stressed areas will get less water; and
- water flows will become less predictable and more subject to extreme events.

The challenge of developing effective adaptation strategies is greatest in rain-fed agriculture, where the livelihoods of millions of the world's poorest people will become more precarious. Despite variations in competition patterns across countries, two broad trends are emerging that threaten agriculture in general and poor rural households in particular:

- the growing urban and industrial demand for water is increasingly at the expense of agriculture; and
- competition for water is intensifying within agriculture.

There is more than enough water in the world both for life and for livelihoods. The problem is that poor people, particularly the rural poor, are systematically excluded from access by their poverty, by their limited legal rights or by public policies that limit access to the infrastructures that provide water. A coherent global strategy for water management is urgently needed since the business-as-usual alternative not only consigns many to lives that are ethically offensive and economically wasteful, but it also limits the effective mitigation of GCC.

## Urbanisation

Cities continue to grow inexorably, and are now home to over 50 per cent of the global population. Although they cover little more than 1.5 per cent of the Earth's surface, there is no doubt that cities are major contributors to global and regional environmental and social problems. But simplistically blaming cities can obscure the primary causes of these problems. 'It fails to point to those responsible for resource overuse and environmental degradation, and fails to perceive the great advantages (or potential advantages) that cities offer for greatly reducing resource use and wastes' (UNEP, 1996, p. 418). The ecological impact of cities can vary dramatically, especially between those in developed and developing economies. For example, the 4 million inhabitants of Atlanta, Georgia, have almost the same global environmental impact as the 200 million Chinese who have moved into cities in the past ten years (Newman, 2006). In developing countries, although large sections of the urban population live in squalid settlements often with serious environmental health problems, their impact on the global environment is relatively low (Hardoy *et al.*, 2001). Hence there is a real danger that if urban poverty is alleviated in a business-as-usual mode, the impact will be to accelerate GCC (see also Elkin *et al.*, 1991; Fischer, 1996; Newman and Kenworthy, 1999). Two mechanisms that are helping to establish this understanding of the global, regional and local environmental impact of cities are ecological footprint analysis (Rees, 1992) and sustainability assessment (Pope *et al.*, 2004). However, for effective mitigation of GCC to be achieved, something similar to sustainability assessment, but that takes into account all aspects of rural dependencies and encroachment, is needed for every major urban area on the planet, whether rich or poor.

*Land-use management*
Although burning of fossil fuels releases two-thirds of the problematic additional GHGs, much of the rest are associated with modern land-use and agricultural practices, which provides opportunities for some major mitigation initiatives (Stern, 2006). Emissions from deforestation are estimated at more than 15 per cent of global emissions, which is greater than the emissions of the global transport sector, making it a major factor in GCC. The well-recognised agricultural contributions to GCC include methane from feed lots, nitrous oxide from fertilisers, and the tilling of soil serving to accelerate decomposition. But there are some additional, lesser-known, more general effects (Calvin, 2007):

- water vapour accounts for two-thirds of the greenhouse effect – humidity increases with GCC because more water evaporates from warmer water bodies, particularly the oceans, and to date these effects have been poorly estimated;

- unlike the light-coloured surfaces they replace, greenery and moist soil produced by agriculture are dark, resulting in less reflection of sunlight back into space, with resultant warming; and

- air-borne soot from agricultural fires used annually to clear fields in preparation for planting absorbs heat from the sunlight and then warms the air around it, raising the dew point, and often reducing rainfall downwind.

A global strategy is needed both to eradicate bad land-use practices, and to preserve the remaining areas of natural forest. This should receive significant support from the international community, which would benefit from each developing country's actions to better manage their land-use.

## ICTs, knowledge management and a new shared vision for rural development
The four mitigation mechanisms above all call for unprecedented investments in the planet's rural areas that will necessarily result in major

development and change therein. This represents an opportunity to utilise ICTs in the crafting of a shared global vision for rural development that both guides and combines investments in GCC mitigation with investments in holistic development for rural populations. It is likely that the inclusion of integrated rural development strategies will enhance both the short- and long-term mitigation mechanisms that will need to be designed and implemented in most of the planet's rural areas. Hence, with little extra investment, but with a great deal more collaborative effort, a globally shared vision could be developed successfully to address the twin problems of GCC mitigation and rural development. The full range of stakeholders (including rural and agricultural specialists, government officials, NGOs, farming communities and industries, as well as the poorest rural householders) must co-own the development and pursuance of such a shared global vision, as well as the design and implementation of the related strategies.

An important step towards the development of such a globally shared vision is the International Assessment of Agricultural Knowledge, Science and Technology for Development (IAASTD, 2008), a major global initiative, developed out of a four-year collaborative effort (2005–2008). It was launched as a multi-thematic, multi-spatial, multi-temporal intergovernmental process, with a multi-stakeholder Bureau, similar to the Intergovernmental Panel on Climate Change (IPCC). Its goal is to reduce hunger and poverty, improve rural livelihoods and facilitate equitable, environmentally, socially and economically sustainable development through the generation of, access to and use of agricultural knowledge, science and technology. Some 400 of the world's experts, working in their own capacity, contributed to the IAASTD reports (comprising a global and five sub-global assessments), which were subjected to two rounds of peer review by governments, organisations and individuals. The Synthesis Report focuses on eight Bureau-approved topics: bioenergy; biotechnology; climate change; human health; natural resource management; traditional knowledge and community-based innovation; trade and markets; and women in agriculture. However, the IAASTD has not as yet provided a global vision, limiting itself to a range of options for action that meet development and sustainability goals, and the IAASTD's focus is primarily agricultural rather than rural.

Given the complexity of the development and pursuance of a shared global vision for rural development in the context of GCC, ICTs and knowledge management could and should play a core support role in its creation and dissemination. The co-creation of this vision by a wide range of stakeholders should be facilitated by a global network of closely linked knowledge systems, dealing with not only the four mitigation mechanisms described in the previous section, but also many other relevant issues.

One of the best examples of a major global knowledge system currently being developed as a public good, and in line with the knowledge economy approach, is the Global Earth Observation System of Systems (GEOSS).

More than 70 nations are cooperating to build GEOSS over a ten-year period (http://www.earthobservations.org/documents/10-Year%20Implement ation%20Plan.pdf). When complete, this network of systems is intended to provide integrated global earth observations to support policy, decision making, economic growth and sustainable development. It will be based on significant national and international collaboration to make existing and new hardware and software compatible in order to supply data and information at no cost to the user. GEOSS will disseminate information and analyses directly to users through GEOPortal, an internet gateway to the comprehensive and near-real-time data produced by GEOSS. For users without good access to high-speed internet, GEONETCast will be established as a system of four communications satellites that transmit data to low-cost receiving stations maintained by the users (http://www.earthobservations. org/documents/GEO%20information%20kit%201107.pdf).

The emergence of these interdependent knowledge systems needs to be understood in the context of the current global transformation from the industrial economy (and its subset, the industrial information economy) to the knowledge economy. Since the early 1990s, modern complex democracies have been seeing radical change in the organisation of information production and dissemination, compared with the previous 150 years of dependence on an industrial information economy. The changes resulting from the emerging networked knowledge society, according to Benkler (2006), are 'deep, structural, and go to the very foundations of how liberal markets and liberal democracies have co-evolved for almost two centuries'.

He emphasises the importance of the increasing role of non-market and non-proprietary production, both by individuals and by a range of cooperative efforts. This marks the emergence of a knowledge economy in which individuals have three dimensions of freedom to take more active roles than is possible in the industrial information economy. Such individuals have improved their capacity to do more:

- for and by themselves;
- in loose commonality with others, without being constrained to organise their relationship through a price system or in traditional hierarchical structures; and
- in formal organisations that operate outside the market sphere.

These three new freedoms hold great practical promise for the shared global vision on rural development, but raise two major issues:

- non-market production of information is likely to be obstructed by those with power and influence in the established industrial information economy, who perceive their vested interests to be threatened; and
- the three dimensions of freedom underlie innovation and growth in the new economy based on an open, networked approach as the major stimulant – hence, emphasis on the industrial economy approach

in knowledge systems aimed at development is counter-productive, constraining both the freedoms and innovation, and limiting the very growth they are intended to promote.

The past several decades have demonstrated the inability of industrial economy models to deliver on rural development. The emerging knowledge economy appears to represent a new way forward. To become viable components of the proposed network of knowledge systems needed for the shared vision for rural development in the context of GCC, open knowledge systems such as GEOSS and SAKSS are required that are able to function as integral components of the emerging knowledge economy.

In conclusion, we contend that, in the absence of an integrated rural development strategy, any ICT4RD projects are at best likely to have only local and usually short-term impact, and will have little influence on the broader dynamics of rural poverty. Hence, the establishment of integrated rural development strategies in all developing countries and regions, within the context of a new shared global vision, and enabled through open, integrative knowledge systems, is essential. Although many challenges will need to be addressed (Ruttan, 1984), the recognition of the global threat of climate change, along with the availability of ICTs that facilitate knowledge systems, provides an excellent reason and opportunity for a wide range of stakeholders and leaders to now focus on integrated rural strategies that will both eradicate rural poverty and also successfully mitigate climate change. In such a context of substantial, coordinated and coherent investments in rural development, the amplifying effects of carefully deployed knowledge systems and ICTs for implementation will come into their own.

## Key readings

Batchelor, S., Evangelista, S., Hearn, S., Peirce, M., Sugden, S. and Webb, M. (2003) *Contributing to the Millennium Development Goals: lessons learned from seventeen infoDev projects.* Washington, DC: World Bank

Burch, S. (2007) *Knowledge Sharing for Rural Development: challenges, experiences and methods.* Quito: ALAI

IICD (2006) *ICTs for Agricultural Livelihoods: impact and lessons learned from IICD supported activities.* The Hague: International Institute for Communication and Development

Mansell, R. and Wehn, U. (1998) *Knowledge Societies: information technology for sustainable development.* Oxford: Oxford University Press

OECD (2006) *The New Rural Paradigm: policies and governance.* Paris: OECD

Torero, M. and von Braun, J. (eds) (2006) *Information and Communication Technologies for Development and Poverty Reduction: the potential of telecommunications.* Baltimore, MD: Johns Hopkins University Press and IFPRI

# References

Action Aid (2005) *Real Aid: an agenda for making aid work*. London: Action Aid International (http://www.actionaid.org.uk/doc_lib/69_1_real_aid.pdf, accessed 17 November 2007)

Ashley, C. and Maxwell, S. (2001) Rethinking rural development. *Development Policy Review*, 19 (4), pp. 395–425

Barrett, C., Reardon, T. and Patrick, W. (2001) Non-farm income diversification and household livelihood strategies in rural Africa: concepts, dynamics and policy implications. *Food Policy*, 26 (4), p. 329

Batchelor, S., Evangelista, S., Hearn, S., Peirce, M., Sugden, S. and Webb, M. (2003) *Contributing to the Millennium Development Goals: lessons learned from seventeen infoDev projects*. Washington, DC: World Bank (http://www.infodev.org/en/ Document.19.aspx, accessed 7 December 2007)

Benkler, Y. (2006) *The Wealth of Networks: how social production transforms markets and freedom*. New Haven, CT: Yale

Bhatnagar, S., Dewan, A., Torres, M.M. and Kanungo, P. (no date) *E-Choupal: ITC's rural networking project* (http://siteresources.worldbank.org/INTEMPOWER MENT/Resources/14647_E-choupal-web.pdf, accessed 12 November 2007)

Booth, D. (2005) *Missing Links in the Politics of Development: learning from the PRSP experiment*. London: ODI (http://www.odi.org.uk/publications/working_papers/ wp256.pdf, accessed 6 June 2007)

bridges.org (2001) *Spanning the Digital Divide: understanding and tackling the issues* (http://www.bridges.org/publications/65, accessed 14 December 2007)

Buckingham, D. (2006) Is there a digital generation? In *Digital Generations*, ed. D. Buckingham and R. Willett. London: Lawrence Erlbaum Associates, pp. 1–18

Burall, S., Maxwell, S. and Menocal, A.R. (2006) *Reforming the International Aid Architecture: options and ways forward*. London: ODI

Burch, S. (2007) *Knowledge Sharing for Rural Development: challenges, experiences and methods*. Quito: ALAI (http://www.alainet.org/publica/knowledge)

Calvin, W. (2007) The great use-it-or-lose-it intelligence test. Crawford Memorial Lecture, CGIAR, Beijing (http://www.Global-Fever.org)

Canagarajah, S., Newman, C. and Bhattamishra, R. (2001) Non-farm income, gender, and inequality: evidence from rural Ghana and Uganda. *Food Policy*, 26 (4), pp. 405–20

Castells, M. and Himanen, P. (2002) *The Information Society and the Welfare State: the Finnish model*. New York: Oxford University Press

Chapman, R., Slaymaker, T. and Young, J. (no date) *Livelihoods Approaches to Information and Communication in Support of Rural Poverty Elimination and Food Security*. London: ODI (http://www.odi.org.uk/rapid/publications/Documents/ SPISSL_WP_Complete.pdf)

Cline, W.R. (2007) *Global Warming and Agriculture: impact estimates by country*. Washington, DC: Center for Global Development

Conway, G. (1997) *The Doubly Green Revolution*. Harmondsworth: Penguin

Cour, J.-M. and Snrech, S. (1998) *Preparing for the Future: a vision of West Africa in the year 2020*. Paris: OECD (http://www.oecd.org/dataoecd/50/17/38512525.pdf)

Dalvit, L., Muyingi, H., Terzoli, A. and Thinyane, M. (2007) The deployment of an ecommerce platform and related projects in a rural area in South Africa. *International Journal of Computational Intelligence Research*, 1 (1), pp. 9–17

Day, R.S. (2003) *3D Interactive Visual Simulations (VR) as an Aid to Learning in Africa: the global approach to teaching and learning*. Pretoria: Naledi 3D Factory

(http://www.naledi3d.co.za/Articles/Evaluation%20of%20Virtual%20Reality%20in%20Africa.pdf, accessed 14 December 2007)

Desfilhes, J. and Dufour, F. (2005) Semences paysannes en danger. In *Pouvoir savoir,* ed. V. Peugeot. Caen: C&F éditions, pp. 83–94

Duch Guillot, G. (2006) *Nueva asignatura para el desarrollo* (http://www.alainet.org/active/12545.html)

Easterling, W., Aggarwal, P., Batima, P., Brander, K., Erda, L., Howden, M., Kirilenko, A., Morton, J., Soussana, J.-F., Schmidhuber, S. and Tubiello, F. (2007) Food, fibre and forest products. In IPCC (2007), pp. 273–313

Elkin, T., McLaren, D. and Hillman, M. (1991) *Reviving the City: towards sustainable urban development.* London: Friends of the Earth

Ellis, F. and Biggs, S. (2001) Evolving themes in rural development 1950s–2000s. *Development Policy Review,* 19 (4), pp. 437–48

Farrell, G., Isaacs, S. and Trucano, M. (2007) *The NEPAD e-Schools Demonstration Project: a work in progress.* Washington, DC: *infoDev* (http://www.infodev.org/en/Document.355.aspx)

Financial Times (2008) PC-makers mull their margins as the low-cost laptop arrives. *Financial Times,* 31 January 2008, p. 11

Finnish Rural Policy Committee (2004) *Viable Countryside – Our Joint Responsibility: rural policy programme 2005–08 summary.* Helsinki: Rural Policy Committee (http://www.ruralpolicy.fi/files/212/kokonaisohjelman_tiivistelma_englanti.pd)

Fischer, C.S. (1996) *The Urban Experience.* New York: Harcourt Brace Jovanovich

Gruber, T. (2008) Collective knowledge systems: where the social web meets the semantic web. *Journal of Web Semantics,* 6 (1), pp. 4–13 (http://tomgruber.org/writing/CollectiveKnowledgeSystems.pdf)

Halhead, V. (2004) *The Village Action Association of Finland* (http://www.ruralgateway.org.uk/cgi-bin/library.cgi?action=detail&id=407&dir_publisher_varid=1)

Hardoy, J., Mitlin, D. and Satterthwaite, D. (2001) *Environmental Problems in an Urbanizing World.* London: Earthscan

Harriss, J. (ed.) (1983) *Rural Development: theories of peasant economy and agrarian change.* London: HarperCollins

IAASTD (2008) *International Assessment of Agricultural Knowledge, Science and Technology for Development (IAASTD): global summary for decision makers* (http://www.agassessment.org/index.cfm?Page=About_IAASTD&ItemID=2)

IFAD (2001) *Rural Poverty Report 2001: the challenge of ending rural poverty.* Oxford: Oxford University Press

IFC (2007) *Selling Solar.* Washington, DC: International Finance Corporation (http://www.ifc.org/ifcext/enviro.nsf/AttachmentsByTitle/p_SellingSolar/$FILE/SellingSolar.pdf)

IICD (2006) *ICTs for Agricultural Livelihoods: impact and lessons learned from IICD supported activities.* The Hague: International Institute for Communication and Development (http://www.ftpiicd.org/files/publications/IICD-agri-impact-2006.pdf)

Ilboudo, J.-P. (2003) After 50 years: the role and use of rural radio in Africa. In *The One to Watch: radio, new ICTs and interactivity,* ed. B. Girard. Rome: FAO (ftp://ftp.fao.org/docrep/fao/006/y4721e/y4721e00.pdf), pp. 199–210

IPCC (2007) *Climate Change 2007: impacts, adaptation and vulnerability.* Contribution of Working Group II to the Fourth Assessment Report of the Intergovernmental Panel on Climate Change, ed. M.L. Parry, O.F. Canziani, J.P. Palutikof, P.J. van der Linden and C.E. Hanson. Cambridge: Cambridge University Press

Jensen, M. and Esterhuysen, A. (2001) *The Telecentre Cookbook for Africa: recipes for self-sustainability*. Paris: UNESCO

Kaul, I. and Conceicão, P. (2006) *The New Public Finance: responding to global challenges*. New York: Oxford University Press

Killick, T. (2001) Globalisation and the rural poor. *Development Policy Review*, 19 (2), pp. 155–80

Kydd, J. and Dorward, A. (2001) The Washington Consensus on poor country agriculture: analysis, prescription and institutional gaps. *Development Policy Review*, 19 (4), pp. 467–78

Lipton, M. (1977) *Why Poor People Stay Poor: a study of urban bias in world development*. London: Temple Smith

Maassen, P. (2005) Human rights and ICTs: rights need rules. *Information for Development*, 3 (7), pp. 6–7 (http://www.i4donline.net/july05/humanrights.pdf)

Mansell, R. and Wehn, U. (1998) *Knowledge Societies: information technology for sustainable development*. Oxford: Oxford University Press

Martens, B. (2005) Why do aid agencies exist? *Development Policy Review*, 23 (6), pp. 643–63

Maxwell, S. and Heber-Percy, R. (2001) New trends in development thinking and implications for agriculture. In *Food, Agriculture and Rural Development: current and emerging issues for economic analysis and policy research*, ed. K. G. Stamoulis. Rome: FAO, pp. 47–86

MCT (2006) *Mozambique Science, Technology and Innovation Strategy*. Maputo: Ministério da Ciência e Tecnologia

Mitra, S. (2003) Minimally invasive education: a progress report on the 'hole-in-the-wall' experiments. *The British Journal of Educational Technology*, 34 (3), pp. 367–71

Mitra, S., Dangwal, R., Chatterjee, S., Jha, S., Bisht, R.S. and Kapur, P. (2005) Acquisition of computer literacy on shared public computers: children and the 'hole in the wall'. *Australasian Journal of Educational Technology*, 21 (3), pp. 407–26 (http://www.ascilite.org.au/ajet/ajet21/mitra.html, accessed 5 February 2007)

Museveni, Y.K. (2007) Social transformation of the Commonwealth societies, Opening Address, Commonwealth Heads of State and Government Meeting, Uganda (http://www.yocomm.com/CHOGM2007/Documents/HE%20Museveni%20Opening%20Speech%2023-11-07.doc)

Newman, P. (2006) The environmental impact of cities. *Environment and Urbanization*, 18 (2), pp. 275–95

Newman, P. and Jennings, I. (2006) *Cities as Sustainable Ecosystems*. Kobe, Japan: UNEP–IETC

Newman, P. and Kenworthy, J. (1999) *Sustainability and Cities: overcoming automobile dependence*. Washington, DC: Island Press

NITF (1998) *Multi-Purpose Community Centre Research Report*. Johannesburg: NITF

OECD (2006) *The New Rural Paradigm: policies and governance*. Paris: OECD (http://siteresources.worldbank.org/EXTGDLREGIONECA/Resources/OECD_The_New_Rural_Paradigm.pdf)

Peskett, L., Slater, R., Stevens, C. and Dufey, A. (2007) *Biofuels, Agriculture and Poverty Reduction*. London: ODI (http://www.odi.org.uk/NRP/NRP107.pdf)

Pope, J., Annandale, D. and Morrison-Saunders, A. (2004) Conceptualizing sustainability assessment. *Environmental Impact Assessment Review*, 24, pp. 595–616

Potter, R.B. and Unwin, T. (eds) (1989) *The Geography of Urban–Rural Interaction in Developing Countries: essays for Alan B. Mountjoy*. London: Routledge

Proenza, F. (2001) Telecenter sustainability – myths and opportunities. In *Bridging the Rural Knowledge Gap: information systems for improved livelihoods*, ed. Dixon and Wattenbach (http://www.fao.org/Waicent/FAOINFO/AGRICULT/ags/Agsp/pdf/ProenzaTelecenter.pdf)

Pyati, A.K. (2005) WSIS: whose vision of an information society? *First Monday*, 10 (5) (http://firstmonday.org/issues/issue10_5/pyati/index.html)

Rahman, A. and Westley, J. (2001) The challenge of ending rural poverty. *Development Policy Review*, 19 (4), pp. 553–62

Ramos, J.M. and Díez, A. (2003) Blending old and new technologies: Mexico's indigenous radio service messages. In *The One to Watch: radio, new ICTs and interactivity*, ed. B. Girard. Rome: FAO, pp. 172–9 (ftp://ftp.fao.org/docrep/fao/006/y4721e/y4721e00.pdf)

Rees, W. (1992) Ecological footprints and appropriated carrying capacity. *Environment and Urbanization*, 4 (2), pp. 121–30

Rosset, P., Collins, J. and Moore Lappé, F. (2000) Lessons from the Green Revolution. *Tikkun Magazine*, 15 (2), pp. 52–6 (http://www.biotech-info.net/lessons.html)

Ruttan, V.W. (1975) Integrated rural development programs: a sceptical perspective. *International Development Review*, 17 (4), pp. 9–16

Ruttan, V.W. (1984) Integrated rural development programmes: a historical perspective. *World Development*, 12 (4), pp. 393–401

SAIDE (2003) *Report on Research into the Use of Computers in 21 South African Schools*. Johannesburg: SAIDE

Schultz, T.W. (1964) *Transforming Traditional Agriculture*. New Haven, CT: Yale University Press

Scott, N., Batchelor, S., Ridley, J. and Jorgensen, B. (2004) *The Impact of Mobile Phones in Africa*. London: Commission for Africa (http://www.commissionforafrica.org/english/report/background/scott_et_al_background.pdf)

Slay, H., Wentworth, P. and Locke, J. (2006) BingBee, an information kiosk for social enablement in marginalized communities (http://portal.acm.org/ft_gateway.cfm?id=1216274&type=pdf&coll=GUIDE&dl=GUIDE&CFID=11694652&CFTOKEN=54062040, accessed 3 January 2008)

Start, D. (2001) The rise and fall of the rural non-farm economy: poverty impacts and policy options. *Development Policy Review*, 19 (4), pp. 491–505

StatsSA (2006a) *Provincial Profile 2004: Eastern Cape*. Pretoria: Statistics South Africa (http://www.statssa.gov.za/publications/Report-00-91-02/Report-00-91-022004.pdf)

StatsSA (2006b) *Provincial Profile 2004: Gauteng*. Pretoria: Statistics South Africa (http://www.statssa.gov.za/publications/Report-00-91-07/Report-00-91-072004.pdf)

Stern, N. (2006) *Stern Review: the economics of climate change*. Pre-publication edition (http://www.hm-treasury.gov.uk/independent_reviews/stern_review_economics_climate_change/stern_review_report.cfm)

Stevens, C. (2001) *Agricultural Trade*. IDS Trade & Investment Background Briefing No. 3. Brighton: Institute of Development Studies, University of Sussex

Stilwell, M. and Rose, E. (2006) Biofuels and trade: peril and promise for policy-makers. In *Linking Trade, Climate Change and Energy*. ICTSD Trade and Sustainable Energy Series, Geneva: International Centre for Trade and Sustainable Development, pp. 17–18

Talyarkhan, S. (2004) *Connecting the First Mile: a framework for best practice in ICT projects for knowledge sharing in development* (http://www.itdg.org/docs/icts/ict_best_practice_framework.pdf)

Thinyane, M., Slay, H., Terzoli, A. and Clayton, P. (2006) A preliminary investigation into the implementation of ICTs in marginalised communities. Unpublished paper given at the Southern African Telecommunication Networks and Applications Conference, Stellenbosch, September 2006

Torero, M. and von Braun, J. (eds) (2006) *Information and Communication Technologies for Development and Poverty Reduction: the potential of telecommunications*. Baltimore, MD: Johns Hopkins University Press and IFPRI

Tripp, R. (2001) Agricultural technology policies for rural development. *Development Policy Review*, 19 (4), pp. 479–89

Turner, T. (2006) Biofuels, agriculture, and the developing world. In *Linking Trade, Climate Change and Energy*. ICTSD Trade and Sustainable Energy Series, Geneva: International Centre for Trade and Sustainable Development, p. 16 (http://www.trade-environment.org/output/ictsd/resource/Energy_issuebriefs.pdf)

UNDP (2006) *Beyond Scarcity: power, poverty and the global water crisis*. Human Development Report 2006. New York: UNDP (http://hdr.undp.org/en/media/hdr06-complete.pdf)

UNDP (2007) *Telecentres 2.0: Beyond piloting telecentres*. APDIP e-Note 14 (http://www.apdip.net/apdipenote/14.pdf)

UNEP (1996) *An Urbanizing World: global report on human settlements 1996*. UNEP/Habitat, Oxford: Oxford University Press

UNICEF (2005) *The State of the World's Children 2006: excluded and invisible*. New York: UNICEF (http://www.unicef.org/sowc06/pdfs/sowc06_fullreport.pdf)

von Braun, J. (2007) The World Food Situation: new driving forces and required actions. Unpublished paper given at the CGIAR AGM, Beijing, December 2007

Wagner, D.A. and Kozma, R. (2003) *New Technologies for Literacy and Adult Education: a global perspective* (http://www.literacyonline.org/products/wagner_kozma.pdf)

Weart, S. (2007) Facing climate change: reasons to be cheerful. *New Scientist*, 2599, 14 April 2007, p. 20

Weingart, J. and Giovannucci, D. (no date) *Rural Energy: a practical primer for productive applications* (http://ssrn.com/abstract = 996766)

Wiggins, S. and Proctor, S. (2001) How special are rural areas? The economic implications of location for rural development. *Development Policy Review*, 19 (4), pp. 427–37

Winrock International (2003) *Future Directions in Agriculture and Information and Communication Technologies (ICTs) at USAID* (http://www.dot-com-alliance.org/documents/AG_ICT_USAID.pdf)

Wong, K. and Sayo, P. (2004) *FOSS: general introduction*. Kuala Lumpur: UNDP-APDIP (http://www.iosn.net/foss/foss-general-primer/foss_primer_print_covers.pdf)

World Bank (2007) *World Development Report 2008: agriculture for development*. Washington, DC: World Bank

World Bank Institute (2007) *Building Knowledge Economies: advanced strategies for development*. Washington, DC: World Bank Institute

# 11 | Conclusions
## Tim Unwin

The previous five chapters have provided practitioners' insights into key sectors in which ICTs have been used to contribute to development practices. Although focusing on very different areas, they share many recurrent themes. Above all, they emphasise that, although ICTs do indeed have enormous potential to contribute to making the world a better place, the enthusiasm and hype associated with ICT4D has often been exaggerated and misplaced. This chapter draws together these diverse threads, and provides an overview of some of the most important principles that can help to ensure that ICT4D practices are indeed effective, sustainable and appropriate. It begins, though, by returning to the conceptual framework outlined at the start of the book, and re-examining aspects of this in the context of the evidence from Part 2 concerning the practical relationships between ICTs and 'development'.

## ICTs and development practices
How we define ICT4D depends entirely on the development perspective that we adopt. The ICT sector can indeed contribute significantly to economic growth. ICTs also have the potential to make a fundamental difference to the lives of some of the world's poorest and most marginalised people. What remains unclear is whether or not these two agendas are compatible. For those who believe that it is possible to eliminate absolute poverty through economic growth (see for example Sachs, 2005), the answer would appear to be a resounding 'yes'. However, the evidence that this is actually so remains inconclusive, especially when one focuses on relative definitions of poverty.

There are strong arguments to suggest that ICTs contribute positively to development when it is defined exclusively as economic growth. This is particularly well expressed in the *Information Economy Report 2007–2008* published by UNCTAD (2007) and subtitled *Science and Technology for Development: the new paradigm of ICT*, which begins:

> It is now well established that technological progress and innovation are the
> long-term drivers of economic growth. In the context of a global knowledge

economy fuelled by the fast pace of technological innovation, it is important for developing countries to lay good foundation for building their capacity to acquire and create knowledge and technology, in order to take advantage of the opportunities offered by globalization and, at the same time, to address emerging global challenges.

(UNCTAD, 2007, p. xxiii)

The report goes on to highlight six aspects of what it defines as a new paradigm for economic activities:

- the externalities and spillovers from ICT development could be more important than the direct contribution to GDP as a production sector;
- ICTs provide a new mode of organisation of production and consumption, facilitating the creation of networks and an increase in information flows;
- the rapid pace of innovation in the ICT sector has reduced costs of access to ICTs, and thus enhanced their democratisation;
- new services such as e-commerce, e-finance and e-government have been created;
- new skills, training and education are all necessary for people to benefit from the knowledge economy; and
- new open-access models of knowledge sharing have emerged that bypass traditional intellectual property rights (IPRs).

Such arguments are convincing, but should not remain uncontested. For example, costs of access to ICTs have gone down in many places, but this does not mean that everyone has access to them. Knowledge networks have always existed; it is merely their scale and ease of communication that have changed. New services such as e-government, e-banking and e-learning may well have been introduced, but the basic practices and requirements of government, banking or education remain largely the same. As Chapter 9 highlighted so clearly, no amount of new technology is necessarily going to improve government unless there is already a desire within government for change. Moreover, returning to the central premise upon which these arguments are based, globalisation is not an external independent force, but is rather the convergence of many distinct processes, most of which are driven by the needs of capital for increased markets and reduced input costs. This system fundamentally depends on the existence of inequalities for its continued growth.

By defining development purely as economic growth designed to reduce absolute poverty, such arguments have two problematic implications: first, they mean that the introduction of new ICTs will often enhance inequalities; and second, they will detract attention away from the potential use of ICTs dramatically to change the lives of some of the most marginalised peoples, such as those with disabilities or young people living on the streets. The partial and selective introduction of computers into African schools, for example, has led to increased differences in skills acquisition and knowledge attainment between children in those schools that have access to such technologies and those that do not. Often this exacerbates existing differences between educational opportunities for those living in urban areas, and those in isolated rural areas without access to electricity, let alone broadband connectivity. Moreover, if we are truly to grasp the life-changing potential of ICTs, we need to pay attention to their wider social, political and ideological dimensions, and not only to their economic significance. The impact of someone using their mobile phone to contact and reunite family members who had become separated as they fled the violence in Eldoret, following the Kenyan elections in December 2007, is thus not something that can simply be measured in economic terms.

If we are to use ICTs effectively to make the world a better place, we therefore also need to utilise their potential to address relative poverty. We must pay as much, if not more, attention to the needs and interests of the poorest people and most marginalised communities as we do to the contribution of ICTs to the productive economy. As Habermas (1974, 1978) has argued, new technologies are created and used by those in power to reinforce their positions of economic and political control. There is a strong argument that market forces will drive the delivery of ICTs for the provision of services and information to those with the means to pay for them, wherever they are to be found in the world. The exciting and innovative dimension of new ICTs, though, is that they also have the potential, perhaps for the first time, to enable dramatically new types of communication and information sharing to take place, providing that means can be found to resource them. ICTs can, for example, transform the lives of people with disabilities, enabling the blind to 'read' digital books by listening to the text being read, and the deaf to 'hear' telephone calls by seeing them written on a screen. However, demand for such technologies is relatively low, and prices consequently remain high. More resources therefore need to be given to initiatives that seek to make ICTs accessible to the most marginalised, and strict regulatory environments also need to be in place to compel producers of new ICTs to build accessibility considerations into all of their products, as with the Universal Access features of Apple's operating system (http://www.apple.com/accessibility). If we are going to create the kind of knowledge society that many aspire to (see for example Weigel and Waldburger, 2004; UNESCO, 2005) then bilateral donors, international agencies, private foundations, civil society organisations and the governments of poor countries need to work together far more effectively to devise innovative ways in which the potential benefits of ICTs can truly be made accessible to everyone (see for example the Shuttleworth Foundation, http://www.shuttleworthfoundation.org/about-us/history).

ICTs are not a panacea that will somehow solve the problems of development all by themselves. The one-off gift of laptop computers to schools or providing nurses with free mobile phones will never contribute significantly to a long-term sustainable reduction in poverty, especially when defined in relative terms. The critical task for those engaged in effective ICT4D is therefore to focus on precisely how different technologies can be used to deliver specific development objectives; the '4' in ICT4D is all important. This is well illustrated by contrasting examples from the Philippines. On the one hand, business process outsourcing (BPO) has indeed contributed significantly to economic growth, as with the emergence of numerous call centres and other ICT support services in Cebu City (see for example http://www.peoplesupport.com). On the other, civil society organisations have supported deaf programmers to develop digital non-formal curriculum content, thereby enabling the government-led eSkwela initiative to provide out-of-school youth with access to digital learning opportunities (http://eskwela-apc-nstp.wikispaces.com). The purposes and ultimate beneficiaries of these contrasting interventions are very different, but both are examples of the ways in which ICTs can indeed be used *for* development.

## Principles for effective ICT4D implementation

Whatever the choice of development objective, the previous chapters have highlighted the significance of eight interrelated principles that need to be taken into consideration if ICT4D initiatives are to be successful. This section summarises some of the most important aspects of these principles.

### A *focus on needs*

One of the main reasons why many ICT4D initiatives have failed is that they have been excessively top-down, externally driven and supply led, with insufficient attention being paid to real development needs, however these are defined. Many ICT4D programmes and strategies are initiated by the private sector, civil society organisations or bilateral donors, full of enthusiasm to use ICTs to deliver practical solutions, without enough thought being paid to the local contexts within which they are being implemented or to the actual information and communication needs of the intended beneficiaries. Once external funding dries up, or a project is 'completed', such initiatives all too frequently collapse. In other instances, enthusiastic managers become tied into an ever more difficult search for new resources to maintain the operation of projects that are inherently unsustainable. Not only is this damaging for everyone involved, but it is also wasteful of all of the previous investments made in such initiatives.

Approaches that are purely demand driven are also often doomed to failure, because their local advocates have incomplete knowledge about the optimal ICT-based solutions that could support their needs. In delivering any ICT4D programme it is therefore important to bring together those who know about the potential benefits of different kinds of ICTs and the intended users, so that they can jointly shape effective and appropriate programmes.

This can often be done most effectively in a series of carefully moderated workshops held at the start of any intervention and designed explicitly to encourage mutual learning and sharing of information.

### Designing appropriate technological solutions

Once the information and communication needs have been defined, it is then crucial to focus on the optimal technologies that are available for their effective implementation. Many different technological solutions exist, and emphasis should be placed on the most appropriate ones for the particular circumstances under consideration. A one-size-fits-all approach is only very rarely appropriate. Hence, a focus on 'best practices' is inherently problematic, and we need instead to concentrate on identifying 'good practices' upon which users can build as they seek to deliver contextually sensitive initiatives. Furthermore, one of the real challenges in doing this is to develop processes that are sufficiently flexible to cope with the implications of technological change. ICTs are being developed much more rapidly than many other technologies, and it is therefore essential that all such initiatives incorporate mechanisms to minimise the adverse effects of technology redundancy.

With the above reservations in mind, three key observations seem appropriate with respect to technological solutions. First, the processes of convergence outlined in Chapter 4 suggest that small but powerful digital devices are likely to become increasingly dominant over the next decade. The combination of small, high-resolution screens, adequate processing power, and a multiplicity of connectivity modes, as are combined in the latest generation of mobile phones, offers great potential for the implementation of a wide range of ICT4D initiatives. We nevertheless need to explore in much more detail how such technologies can best be used to enable the poorest people and most marginalised communities to benefit from them. Second, the growth in importance of Web-based technologies, exemplified particularly in the development of tools such as Google Apps (http://www.google.com/a), suggests that people are increasingly likely to use these to access information and content in the future. Those interested in the development potential of such information need to take advantage of the new possibilities that such technologies offer for the provision of timely, relevant, appropriately priced and personalised content that can benefit the poor and marginalised. Third, digital networking is becoming vastly more prevalent, and this offers interesting opportunities for the creation of new types of knowledge network that can help empower virtual communities in innovative ways. While much exciting work is already being supported in this area of communication, considerable challenges remain to be resolved before such communities can truly be seen to be supporting fundamental enhancements in the life opportunities of the world's poorest people. One of the most interesting aspects of new ICTs is that they offer opportunities on the one hand for exciting, novel and anarchic information sharing and communication, while on the other hand they also permit much greater control and surveillance of such interactions by those in power. Ensuring an appropriate balance between these two extremes in the relationship between the state and the individual is one of the many challenges facing those implementing ICT4D programmes.

### *Sustainability*

The high failure rate of many ICT4D initiatives has led to considerable attention now being paid to the identification of means whereby their sustainability can be assured. However, if initiatives are truly focused on delivering people's needs in a cost-effective and appropriate way, they will automatically be sustainable because people will be willing to pay for them. The very rapid increases in mobile telephony in Africa, for example, clearly indicate that people's needs for communication are being met in an appropriate and effective way. Issues to do with sustainability thus occur primarily in externally initiated ICT4D programmes, and in part reflect a desire by those who create them to guarantee their continued success after the initial period of investment is over. To date, far too little explicit attention has been paid to ways in which such ICT4D initiatives can indeed become self-supporting. Typically, for example, initiatives designed to introduce computers into schools fail to consider how sufficient income will be generated to cover the costs of internet connectivity, electricity, ink and paper, let alone the need to purchase new computers as the original ones break down or become obsolete. Although it seems logical for schools to try to generate income by using their computers to provide training sessions outside normal school hours for people who might be able to afford to pay something for the benefit thereof, very few such initiatives have as yet proven to be successful. All externally introduced ICT4D programmes should thus include as one of their essential components a rigorously thought-through framework for ensuring their continued viability beyond the initial period of funding, so that they do not become a drain on the communities that they were initially intended to benefit. In support of such objectives, much more detailed and realistic total-cost-of-implementation models need to be developed, so that those who are considering implementing such programmes can be better informed of their likely long-term financial implications. Sustainability does not only apply to financial and technological considerations, but is also of considerable environmental importance. As highlighted in Chapter 4, the energy needs and disposal costs of modern ICTs must be taken fully into consideration in the introduction of any ICT4D programmes. We are as yet only beginning to model such issues in sufficient detail to enable communities to make well-informed decisions about their appropriateness, and there is therefore a pressing need for much more rigorous research to be addressed on these issues.

### Vision and commitment

Successful ICT4D initiatives at all scales from national policies to local community telecentres require visionary champions who are able to generate the necessary commitment to drive them forward. ICT4D programmes frequently involve substantial changes in working practices and therefore they need to be led by people who have the vision to comprehend what it is actually possible to achieve. Such programmes are multifaceted and their leaders must understand how best to manage this complexity within the contexts in which they are working. Their leaders also need to be charismatic and persuasive so that they can effectively bring together the required inputs from many different organisations and partners. The role that such people play is well illustrated by the way in which many apparently successful projects collapse once their champions have moved on to other roles. It is critically important for the continued success of these programmes that their leaders therefore take time to embed their expertise, vision and understanding throughout the organisation so that the key elements of success remain in place once their champions have departed.

### Infrastructure

Appropriate infrastructures, particularly electricity and a fair regulatory environment, need to be in place if ICTs are to be used effectively for development purposes. All new ICTs are powered by electricity, and it is therefore absolutely essential that affordable and accessible electricity supplies are made more widely available if ICT4D initiatives are to be implemented effectively. Moreover, innovations are still required to minimise the energy demands of ICTs, not only for poor people and marginalised communities, but also more generally to reduce the global environmental impact of these technologies. Likewise, a wide range of regulatory controls needs to be in place to ensure that appropriate tariff structures exist, and that the private sector does indeed deliver universal access requirements, so that everyone can benefit from the new means of communication and information sharing provided by digital technologies. As yet, one of the largest challenges still remaining in this context is to develop mechanisms to provide affordable solutions in rural areas where usage rates are low and therefore service provision unprofitable. While electricity and the regulatory environment are the two most important dimensions of infrastructure, it is also important for there to be connectivity, be it through fibre optic cables, satellite or radio, so that people can indeed communicate effectively and access the information that they need. As applications become ever more demanding of bandwidth, a prime requirement of such connectivity solutions is that they should be scalable and readily upgradable so that the returns on the original costs of their provision can be maximised.

## Effective partnerships

The complexity and diversity of ICT4D initiatives mean that they often require intricate partnerships to be brought together to deliver successful outcomes. Partnerships, though, do not just happen, and there remains much research to be done in identifying the key success criteria for multi-stakeholder ICT4D partnerships in different contexts. Likewise, more attention needs to be paid to the development of capacity within organisations to enable them to implement such partnerships effectively. Nevertheless, the experiences shared in this book seem to suggest that six main principles need to be in place if such partnerships are to be effective: *transparency* about the expectations and contributions expected from each partner; the need to involve all stakeholders, and particularly the ultimate intended *beneficiaries*, within partnerships from their inception; a focus first on information and communication *needs*, and only then on the means whereby ICTs can be used to deliver them; the fostering of *trust* within an ethical framework that encourages openness and shared responsibility; careful *management*, that is able to bring together the different contributions from partners to respond to the identified needs; and a clear focus on explicit development *outcomes*, while also recognising the potential benefits that can be gained from unintended consequences.

## Monitoring and evaluation

All ICT4D programmes need to have in place clear and effective monitoring and evaluation strategies, both to ensure individual and institutional learning, and also so that information about success and failure can be shared more widely. In this context, it is crucial to distinguish clearly between the two interrelated terms 'monitoring' and 'evaluation'. 'Monitoring' is best used to refer to the ongoing process through which self-reflective individuals and organisations regularly check their progress against intended outcomes, so that they can improve the quality of their performance. It is an essential part of the ethos of all successful organisations. In contrast the term 'evaluation' is more appropriately used to refer to mid- or end-point assessment of a programme against its original objectives, and should normally involve external evaluators (World Bank, 2004). While monitoring and evaluation are thus closely related, the former is essentially formative, while the latter is more usually regarded as being summative. Moreover, effective monitoring should automatically form part of any evaluation process.

To date, there has been insufficient rigorous monitoring and evaluation of ICT4D initiatives, and we are therefore not yet in a position to know with certainty how best to implement initiatives that will indeed benefit poor people and marginalised communities. Moreover, we also need to share the results of such evaluations much more widely and openly. Only then will we be able to prevent the wasteful duplication of effort that continues to beset so many ICT4D initiatives. The box on page 368 therefore highlights

# Guidance for effective ICT4D monitoring and evaluation

## *Monitoring*

1 Ensure that monitoring is involved at all stages of the design and implementation process.
2 Involve all stakeholders in monitoring activities, and ensure that there are incentives in place for them to engage therein.
3 Create an environment in which monitoring is seen as being beneficial both to individual performance and to organisational capacity.
4 Use a diversity of methods, including both qualitative and quantitative indicators.
5 Ensure that monitoring processes address the information, communication, technological and the development aspects of ICT4D.
6 Provide opportunities for participants to be trained in effective monitoring techniques.
7 Build in enough time within the programme for participants to engage in effective self-reflection.
8 Ensure that good practices and lessons learnt are shared among all stakeholders.
9 Involve stakeholders in ongoing revision of the programme in the light of insights gained from monitoring.
10 Continue with monitoring, even when the going gets tough.

## *Evaluation*

1 Ensure that all stakeholders are involved in setting clear targets at the start of any initiative and that delivery against these targets is used as the main framework for evaluation.
2 Incorporate a clear framework (such as a Log Frame and Gantt Chart) in the design of the initiative so that this can provide the basis for subsequent evaluation.
3 Make provision for the costs of evaluation in the original budget.
4 Involve knowledgeable external evaluators, but ensure that they understand the local context of the programme being evaluated.
5 Ensure that all stakeholders, and particularly the intended beneficiaries, are consulted in the evaluation, and that its results are used effectively to enhance the initiative.
6 Ensure that the evaluation addresses the information, communication, technological and the development aspects of ICT4D.
7 Pilot test the intended evaluation procedures, and revise them accordingly, ensuring that the evaluation process remains flexible and adaptable.
8 Identify and report on important non-intended consequences.
9 Use a diversity of methods, including both qualitative and quantitative indicators.
10 Ensure that insights from the evaluation are disseminated externally so that others can learn from them.

(*Source:* developed from Unwin and Day (2005); thanks also to David Hollow for additional advice.)

ten of the most important principles each for effective monitoring and for evaluation of ICT4D programmes, with the intention of encouraging their wider adoption in future initiatives.

## Accessibility

The final principle for the implementation of effective ICT4D initiatives is that they should address issues of accessibility at all stages from inception to completion. Modern ICTs can have an even more dramatic role in transforming the lives of people with serious 'disabilities' than they do in facilitating information sharing and communication among those with lesser disabilities. Accessibility principles therefore need to be built into all dimensions of ICT4D, from the design of hardware, to the provision of content and the social networking processes that contribute to the achievement of shared development objectives. Given the transformational and empowering impact of new ICTs, we should all be doing much more to help ensure that they are used to increase accessibility to information and communication rather than putting yet another barrier in the way of those who are already marginalised.

## Towards a more effective global ICT4D agenda

The diversity of ICT4D initiatives, organisations and conceptual frameworks is an indication of the vitality of the field. Nevertheless, it has also involved considerable duplication of effort, and a failure to learn enough from previous successes and failures. This would not matter so much if the failures were something that the world's poorest and most marginalised people could afford. There is therefore a strong argument for much greater sharing of information and collaboration among those involved in conceptualising and implementing ICT4D agendas and initiatives. Good sources of information are now available, as for example through the work of *info*Dev (http://www.infodev.org), the Development Gateway's ICT4D community (http://topics.developmentgateway.org/ict), the Communication Initiative Network (http://www.comminit.com) and Eldis (http://www.eldis.org/ict), but, despite these, many initiatives continue to repeat the mistakes of their predecessors. At least four main reasons can be adduced for this: that the interests underlying such initiatives are not primarily concerned with making an impact on poverty; that competition between organisations in bidding to deliver ICT4D programmes reduces their willingness to share ideas and practices; that implementing ICT4D initiatives effectively is very much more complex than people imagine; and that the mechanisms for identifying appropriate information from the plethora of sources now available are insufficiently user-friendly. If these hurdles can be overcome, then some progress might be made in delivering more effective and sustainable ICT4D activities in the future.

In particular, not only do we need structures in place through which international high-level advocacy and policy making can be achieved effectively, but we also need to encourage the development of innovative and anarchic movements that can truly empower poor people and marginalised communities through the use of ICTs. One of the most interesting dimensions of this is the difficulty there has been in fostering continuity of institutional structures concerned with ICT4D at a global level. As Chapter 5 highlighted, there have been numerous global initiatives, such as the UN ICT Task Force, WSIS, and now GAID, but none of them has as yet effectively managed to bring together the diversity of interests involved in a way that has led to fundamental changes in the use of ICTs to reduce inequalities and enhance the life opportunities of the poor. In part this may reflect insufficient understanding of the niche expertises that different types of organisation can bring to multi-stakeholder partnerships, but it also indicates the enormous difficulties associated with managing and delivering such initiatives. Moreover, different types of stakeholder have contrasting roles to play, and interests in so doing, depending on the context and the type of intervention.

In trying to resolve such complexities, it is helpful to distinguish between the two broad types of approach to ICT4D (Table 11.1). On the one hand, there are market-driven initiatives mainly resulting from the profit-seeking motives of the private sector. In such instances, the 'development' impacts are generated primarily through the creation of employment opportunities and economic growth. The role of the state is to create an environment where maximum profits can be generated by the private sector. In these circumstances, the state may also seek to ensure that the potential benefits are spread as widely as possible, through the use of regulatory mechanisms, tax-based incentives, and subsidies targeted to the poorest users. Research institutes tend to focus on high-end technical innovation, helping to ensure competitive advantage, and thus maximum profits, both for companies and for states.

However, most such initiatives are unlikely to have a direct short-term beneficial impact on the least advantaged people, because they do not provide a sufficient demand base to generate the necessary profit for the private sector. Thus, many market-led initiatives actually lead to greater, rather than less inequality. It is here that civil society and state-promoted interventions can indeed have a beneficial impact, especially when they are also able to engage the participation of the corporate social responsibility elements of private-sector companies. In such socially led initiatives, the state, civil society and sometimes bilateral donors tend to be the main initiators of interventions specifically designed to use ICTs to benefit the poor. These may also be supported by those in research institutes whose interests are more closely aligned with those of the poor. The case study on pages 372–3 provides one example of such a small-scale initiative led by The Freedom Theatre (http://www.thefreedomtheatre.org) that uses ICTs to empower children and youth in the Occupied Palestinian Territories.

(*continued on page 374*)

**Table 11.1** *Indicative differences between stakeholder involvement in market-led and socially initiated ICT4D initiatives*

| | Market-led ICT4D agenda with an emphasis on economic growth | Socially led ICT4D agenda focusing on equality of access |
|---|---|---|
| **The state/ government** | *Actions:* regulatory environment; taxation; subsidies for least advantaged; overall ICT policies<br>*Interests:* ensuring economic growth and stability; reducing adverse impacts of growth | *Actions:* initiating ICT4D projects to help the poor; overall ICT policies<br>*Interests:* maintaining political stability; reducing inequality |
| **Private sector** | *Actions:* investing in ICT activities; production; business outsourcing<br>*Interests:* maximising profits; expanding markets; reducing input costs notably labour | *Actions:* support for ICT programmes; roll-out of old low-end technologies<br>*Interests:* delivering corporate social responsibility function; expanding markets |
| **Civil society** | *Actions:* monitoring impact; advocacy; shaping networks<br>*Interests:* delivering on agendas of supporters (unions, NGOs, community groups) | *Actions:* initiating and implementing programmes for specific marginalised groups; advocacy; shaping networks<br>*Interests:* social equity; retaining funding |
| **Bilateral and multilateral donors** | *Actions:* shaping global development agendas; enhancing economic growth and good governance<br>*Interests:* maintaining contemporary global system | *Actions:* targeted interventions for the poor; shaping global development agendas for poverty reduction<br>*Interests:* maintaining contemporary global system; reducing poverty |
| **Research institutes/ universities** | *Actions:* high-end technical research and development; content production<br>*Interests:* propagation of knowledge; retaining funding from governments and private sector | *Actions:* research on appropriateness of technologies for needs of disadvantaged; content production<br>*Interests:* social justice; fulfilment of ethical priorities |
| **Users/ beneficiaries** | *Actions:* purchasing products; labour<br>*Interests:* expectation of benefits, usually primarily economic, but also social, cultural and political | *Actions:* mainly as recipients of initiatives, but should also be involved in programme design<br>*Interests:* survival; empowerment |
| **Sustainability** | High | Low – usually requiring continued external support |

# Case study: Empowering youth in Jenin

Jonatan Stanczak

*Operations Manager, The Freedom Theatre Foundation, and Institute for Maternal and Child Health Care (IMCH), Uppsala University, Sweden*

Ziad El-Khatib

*PhD student, Division of International Health (IHCAR), Karolinska Institutet, Sweden, and Jenin ICT Advisor*

Mohammad Moawia

*Media program manager, The Freedom Theatre Foundation*

Jenin Refugee Camp lies in the northern part of the Occupied Palestinian Territories. It is a low intensive conflict area under daily incursion from Israeli military forces. There is little travel outside the camp, thus making the community an isolated enclave. Young people lack self-esteem, are at risk of developing trauma, and have few ways of expressing what it is like to grow up there. This case study reports on an intervention by The Freedom Theatre that was designed to use ICTs to empower these children so that they may be better able to take control of their futures. The aim of the initiative was to teach children and young people how to be critical and become opinion leaders using ICTs.

*When creativity and technology meet (source: The Freedom Theatre).*

The Freedom Theatre is a community cultural centre with a focus on teaching theatre and ICT skills in Jenin. Beginning in 2006, and working in four separate groups divided by gender and age, forty students were trained in Web design and development, photography, film, creative writing and text editing skills. This not only provided them with expertise in basic computer packages, such as Microsoft Office, Adobe Photoshop and Dreamweaver, but was also specifically designed to give them leadership skills. Specific objectives of the programme thus included the development of self-awareness through online publishing, becoming a stakeholder in community information production, and becoming

ICT pioneers in the camp. In the first phase of the programme in July 2007, the young people travelled out of Jenin on a two-day trip to see occupied Palestine and discover their roots. Two buses brought them out of the camp, past the Israeli army checkpoints and through the separation wall into areas they had only previously heard of. They visited Jerusalem and its holy places, Yaffa where they saw the sea for the first time, Haifa, and the villages in the north from which their parents or grandparents were evicted. In one of the villages, completely in ruins apart from a few trees which were still left standing, a child used a mobile phone to speak with his grandfather. The grandfather directed him to a specific tree and the child saw where his grandfather had carved his signature as the last thing he did before he abandoned his village, never to see it again.

When the children returned, they set about telling their stories. They constructed a website (http://www.voices.ps) in both Arabic and English to document their story electronically for the cyber-world. In an international online forum, they discussed their experiences with others working on similar projects. During a photo exhibition and digital video projection they also shared their stories and experiences with their community. Through using ICTs, the young people have been able to articulate their experiences, they are learning to express their feelings, and they can relate them to the outside world. This provides them with concrete and positive ways to deal with their fear and despair, and enables them to overcome their sense of helplessness, inadequacy and victimisation. All this offers hope for a better future.

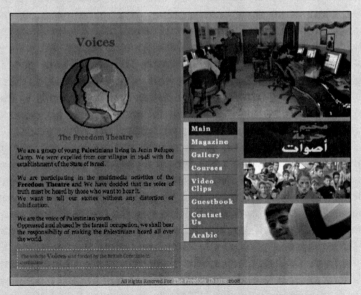

*Snapshot of English version of http://www.*
*voices.ps (source:* The Freedom Theatre).

The two contrasting models summarised in Table 11.1 represent extreme positions, and in reality most ICT4D activities are aligned somewhere between the two, as indicated by the arrows. The table also stresses that there are important issues of sustainability that need to be taken into consideration in developing and implementing such interventions. Where socially led initiatives are begun by governments or civil society organisations, it is important to recognise that these may well need to be funded on an ongoing basis through the public purse or private donations, unless specific additional revenue-generating streams can be created (see also 'Sustainability' above). There is, though, usually an aspiration that such programmes should move from the right to the left. Unfortunately, there have been rather few examples of where this transition has yet been achieved effectively. Instead, private-sector support for such interventions has frequently been targeted to follow the funding streams made available by donors and civil society, in a coalition intended primarily to enhance their market share and profitability. Such initiatives are not sustainable in the long term, unless people can see real benefits from them for which they are willing to pay.

Bringing together the many different interests involved in ICT4D is by no means an easy challenge, and requires visionary leadership and practical action at a range of scales. Globally, there need to be fora where different interest groups can be represented, and where dialogue can take place. However, there is currently considerable overlap between the work of bodies such as the Internet Governance Forum (http://www.intgovfo rum. org), the ITU's Telecommunication Development Sector (http://www.itu. int/net/ITU-D) and GAID (http://www.un-gaid.org). There needs to be much greater integration between the work of these entities, so that wasteful duplication can be avoided. GAID claims that it 'responds to the need and demand for an inclusive global forum and platform for cross-sectoral policy dialogue on the use of ICT for enhancing the achievement of internationally agreed development goals, notably reduction of poverty' (http:// www.un-gaid.org), but as yet it has done little beyond providing a forum for continued discussion on themes of interest to its partners and members.

At the national scale, it is important for governments to develop coherent ICT policies and strategies that will deliver on the hopes of their people not only for economic growth but also for equality of access to the potential that ICTs offer to empower poor people and marginalised communities. This too remains a huge challenge, especially in poor countries where governments have difficult choices to make over the allocation of limited resources. If we are truly to implement effective ICT4D programmes, though, it is essential for governments to take the responsibility for ensuring that any such initiatives reduce rather than increase the inequalities prevalent within them.

Finally, effective partnerships need to be created that draw on global understandings and work within the context of national strategies to deliver sustainable ICT4D initiatives on the ground. As the chapters of this book on health, education, rural development and enterprise have indicated, it is possible to use ICTs to support and empower people to become better educated, to live healthier lives, and to gain fairer incomes. The question that remains is whether we have the collective will to work together to deliver such initiatives so that ICTs can truly be used *for* development, thus permitting the least advantaged to share in the benefits that so many people in the world now take for granted.

## References

Habermas, J. (1974) *Theory and Practice*, tr. J. Viertal. London: Heinemann

Habermas, J. (1978) *Knowledge and Human Interests*, 2nd edn, tr. J. Shapiro. London: Heinemann

Sachs, J. (2005) *The End of Poverty: how we can make it happen in our lifetime.* London: Penguin Books

UNCTAD (2007) *Information Economy Report 2007–2008. Science and Technology for Development: the new paradigm of ICT.* New York and Geneva: UN

UNESCO (2005) *Towards Knowledge Societies.* Paris: UNESCO

Unwin, T. and Day, B. (2005) Dos and don'ts in monitoring and evaluation. In *The Impact of ICTs in Education for Development: a monitoring and evaluation handbook*, ed. D.A. Wagner, B. Day, T. James, R.B. Kozma, J. Miller and T. Unwin. Washington, DC: *infoDev*, pp. 111–22 (http://www.infodev.org/en/Document.285.aspx)

Weigel, G. and Waldburger, D. (eds) (2004) *ICT4D – Connecting People for a Better World.* Berne and Kuala Lumpur: Swiss Agency for Development and Cooperation and Global Knowledge Partnership

World Bank (2004) *Monitoring and Evaluation: some tools, methods and approaches.* Washington, DC: World Bank Operations Evaluation Department (http://www.worldbank.org/ieg/ecd/me_tools_cover.jpg)

# Index

publishers 81, 117–19
publishing 254
pull strategies 63
push strategies 63, 276

R4D 59
radio 57, 77–8, 81, 90, 92, 95–6, 99, 102–5,
    109, 111–14, 119, 156, 178, 180, 185,
    225, 237, 252–3, 328, 339, 366
radio-frequency identification (RFID) 88
Rajasthan 167
rationality 8
readiness 301
reading 65, 210
recycling 101
refurbished computers 101
regulation 113, 159, 164, 196–8, 287, 288,
    311, 370
regulators 117, 128
regulatory agencies 153
regulatory environment 77, 93, 97, 159,
    164–6, 182, 186, 286, 293, 297, 298,
    306, 310, 362, 366
religion 8, 194
research institutes 370
resources 311–13, 363
rights 8
risk management 302
Rostow, Walt 10–11
routers 91
royalties 184
RSS feeds 335
rural areas 12, 81, 93, 98–9, 106, 113, 128,
    178, 187, 192–4, 214, 249, 293, 297,
    315, 321–54, 362, 366
rural development 41, 321–54
rural non-farm economy 327
rural–urban issues 323, 326, 348
Rwanda 112, 191–3, 226, 228–9

SARS (Severe Acute Respiratory
    Syndrome) 254
satellite 77, 81, 93, 97–9, 230, 249, 276, 366
scalability 220
school administrators 226
school principals 222, 225–7
SchoolNet Africa 104
schools 159, 169, 217, 219, 220, 223, 225,
    232–5, 237, 240, 361; primary 235;
    secondary 235, 237, 241
science 20, 30–4, 210, 263
security 138, 153, 221, 259, 276, 300, 321
self-reflection 34, 224

Senegal 190
senses 64
servers 90
service-oriented architecture (SOA) 290
services 283, 287, 307
shamanism 9
Sierra Leone 62, 182, 217
Silicon Valley 197
Simputer 337
Singapore 153, 220, 346
skills, 21st-century 222, 240
Skype 104, 186
Slovenia 270
small and medium enterprises (SMEs)
    180, 189, 194–6, 198, 309, 314–15, 343
smallholders 326–7, 344
SMS (text messaging) 66, 190
social change 30–4
social entrepreneurship 266
social justice 159
social networks 57, 106
social sciences 345
social structure 54
software 28, 77, 114–17, 157, 181, 284, 290,
    291, 297, 314, 338–9, 342, 353
software industry 184
software programming 302
solar power 99, 156
Solomon Islands 156
sonar 95
Sony 184
Soul City 113
sound 332
South Africa 48, 106, 113–14, 128, 136,
    158, 185–7, 191, 196, 219, 232, 237,
    255, 270, 330, 338, 345, 347
South America 215
South Korea 153, 197
Southern African NGO Network
    (SANGONeT) 159
Soviet Union 14
space 17–19
Spanish 258
special educational needs (SEN) 238, 241
Sri Lanka 57, 153
stakeholders 243, 310, 313, 316, 323–7,
    334, 352, 354, 367
standards 97, 105, 117, 260, 277, 283–4,
    289–90, 292, 328, 339, 342
state (see also government, public sector)
    153, 160, 283–320, 365, 370
strategic plans 256
strategies 150–9, 258, 301, 316, 352, 374